BEHIND THE YOI

BEHIND

THE YOI

The Life of Myron Cope, Legendary Pittsburgh Steelers Broadcaster

DAN JOSEPH WITH ELIZABETH COPE

University of Nebraska Press | Lincoln

Manufactured in the United States of America

The University of Nebraska Press is part of a land-grant institution with campuses and programs on the past, present, and future homelands of the Pawnee, Ponca, Otoe-Missouria, Omaha, Dakota, Lakota, Kaw, Cheyenne, and Arapaho Peoples, as well as those of the relocated Ho-Chunk, Sac and Fox, and Iowa Peoples.

♾

Library of Congress Cataloging-in-Publication Data
Names: Joseph, Dan, author. | Cope, Elizabeth (Broadcaster's daughter) author.
Title: Behind the yoi: the life of Myron Cope, legendary Pittsburgh Steelers broadcaster / Dan Joseph with Elizabeth Cope.
Description: Lincoln: University of Nebraska Press, 2024. | Includes index.
Identifiers: LCCN 2024002532
ISBN 9781496237637 (hardback)
ISBN 9781496241443 (epub)
ISBN 9781496241450 (pdf)
Subjects: LCSH: Cope, Myron. | Sportscasters—United States—Biography. | Pittsburgh Steelers (Football team) | BISAC: BIOGRAPHY & AUTOBIOGRAPHY / Entertainment & Performing Arts | BIOGRAPHY & AUTOBIOGRAPHY / Sports
Classification: LCC GV742.42.C66 J67 2024 | DDC 070.4/49796092 [B]—dc23/eng/20240124
LC record available at https://lccn.loc.gov/2024002532

Set in Adobe Text Pro by A. Shahan.

Contents

Illustrations

Following page 178

Preface

When my coauthor, Dan Joseph, first approached me about writing a book about my father, I was excited. He asked me if I wanted to write some chapters as well, which elated me. My dad had started as a writer, and I was eager to try to follow in his footsteps—as if anyone ever could.

Dan would cover my dad's career, and I would focus on personal memories of him, things most people aren't aware of. This is why we came up with the title *Behind the Yoi*. I wanted people to get to know the man behind the public persona, behind *Myron Cope on Sports*, and behind the Terrible Towel. I wanted them to know that he was much more than that.

The Towel and his radio/television career were only part of who my father was. I sometimes tell people the story of how when I was in kindergarten, we had to go around the room and say what our dads did for a living. I remember that when it got to be my turn, I thought about it and replied, "My dad gets dressed up in a suit every day and leaves the house and then comes home later to tuck me into bed and kiss me goodnight." To five-year-old me, that was what he did for a living.

Often I would run home from the bus stop crying because other kids would taunt and tease me, chanting, "This is Myron Cope . . . on sports!" and they would imitate his voice. I didn't get it. He was just my dad.

When I wrote the chapter about how my father and I were estranged for a time, everyone discouraged me from putting that in the book. I mean, everyone; even Dan, my coauthor, didn't like it. They all thought it made my dad look bad. I disagreed. I think it makes him look human. I also clearly explain in the chapter why he acted the way he did. He was gravely ill during that time of his life.

I, too, was no angel many times in my life, and I wanted to give the reader the meat of the story. I wanted to dig beneath the surface and try to reveal the many layers of the father I knew and loved. Beneath his name and dates, his tombstone reads, "Devoted Dad and Husband. Loyal and True." No mention of the Steelers or the Terrible Towel. Sure, people often drape Terrible Towels on his grave, and this makes me smile. But he was *not* the Terrible Towel, or that signature word of his, "Yoi!"

I want people to know that he was a real person. He didn't talk at home the way he did on broadcasts. He knew that if he talked like that at home, my mother and I would surely kill him. There was no "yoi" or "double yoi." He was a kind and soft-spoken man. People were often surprised by this side of him when they met him.

My dad didn't like change. When computers first came out, I tried to convince him to try one instead of typing on his old and ancient typewriter. Two days later he threw his hands up in the air and returned what he called "that damn thing." My dad just liked to do things his own way. And he was good at it. That's why everyone knew Myron Cope.

I hope the reader can begin to get to know the man I love with all my heart.

ELIZABETH COPE

A Few Words of Thanks

The first thank you in this book has to go its subject. Myron Cope passed away in 2008, but he saved so many artifacts of his career and left them all in such good order that one suspects he *wanted* another writer to dig through it all and pen a fresh biography. Regardless of his intentions, researching Myron's life and career was like stepping into a secret vault. Creak open the door, flip on the light, and it's all there—scrapbooks, photo albums, cassettes and VHS tapes, file boxes stuffed with contracts and correspondence, plus assorted containers that hold every plaque, memento, and tchotchke that Myron felt was worth preserving.

Call me a Steelers nerd, but unpacking the boxes, I felt like a prospector striking gold. Sift through the folders in one box, and you'd find 1979 sales reports for the Terrible Towel. Open another and there'd be a reel-to-reel tape of the radio broadcast from Super Bowl IX. There were early fan letters, early not-a-fan letters, and some truly singular items, like a 1964 check made out to Myron by Steelers defensive tackle Ernie Stautner for "One Million Thanks." The famously tough and hard-hitting Stautner attached a note: "Just a little token of appreciation for being nice to me during my playing career."

It was this treasure chest of all things Myron that provided the bedrock for this biography, especially in the pre-Steelers portion of his career. But the book wouldn't have turned out as nicely as it did without the help of many other individuals who devoted time to helping Elizabeth and me tell Myron's full story.

Thank you to all who gave me time for interviews: Kevin Cherilla, John Conomikes, Chuck Finder, Rob Fleder, Joe Gordon, Marcia Grodsky, Randy Grossman, Bill Hillgrove, Michael Lisicky, John Poister, the late Stan Savran, Bob Smizik, Sally Wiggin, Craig Wolfley, Sam Zacharias, and, of course, Elizabeth Cope. Thank you to Milton Wolf, my beloved uncle, who in addition to sharing a few personal memories of Myron gave me use of his VCR and DVD player to review some of Myron's old speeches and TV appearances. Milton enjoyed watching Myron tell the story of recruiting Frank Sinatra into Franco's Italian Army as much as I did.

Thank you to the staff of the Heinz History Center in Pittsburgh for facilitating my research in their archives. Thank you to Mariam Meislik at the University of Pittsburgh Archives & Special Collections, who located and shared some clips of Myron's early TV commentaries—particularly the 1972 dress-off in the Steelers' locker room. It was won, as always, by Frenchy Fuqua.

Thank you to Cynthia Gorney for allowing the liberal use of her 1979 *Inside Sports* article "You're on the Air" for the chapter on Myron's talk show.

Thank you to the companies, schools, and individuals that have put so much old Pittsburgh media online. Twenty years ago, this book would have taken twenty years to research. Now, old issues of the *Press*, *Sun-Telegraph*, and *Post-Gazette* are mere keystrokes away, as are issues of the *Pitt News* and the *Jewish Criterion*, as are many an old Steelers broadcast featuring Myron with Jack Fleming or Bill Hillgrove. Special regards go to McMillen and Wife, the unquestioned *numero uno* site for original Steelers telecasts and radio broadcasts on the web. Tim McMillen was kind enough to post a couple of games featuring Myron on his site after I pestered him.

Thank you to everyone at University of Nebraska Press who brought this book to print. That includes acquisitions editor Rob Taylor, who gave me the green light; his former assistant Courtney Ochsner and his current one, Taylor Martin; project editor Sara Springsteen; and copyeditor Richard Feit.

On a more personal note, thank you to my parents, Bill and Nancy Joseph, who in addition to raising me—no easy task, I tell you—took me to my first Super Bowl parties during that golden Steelers dynasty of the '70s. Thank you to my son Elani, a budding researcher who spent an afternoon helping me dig through boxes of Myron's papers. Thank you to my son Sammy, a true Steelers fan who loves watching T. J. Watt as much as I used to love watching Jack Lambert.

Thank you most of all to my wife, Yona, who made the connections that led to the writing of this book. In all honesty, she is not a fan of Myron Cope's voice. But she understood that this was something I needed to write. Honey, I love you with all my heart.

DAN JOSEPH

BEHIND THE YOI

Prologue

ORIGINAL PASSION

The teenaged boy looks down at his wristwatch. It's almost 9 a.m. Time is running short. He bounces and fidgets in his seat. Can't this dang trolley go any faster? But the driver pays no heed. The streetcar clatters down Fifth Avenue at its usual fortyish miles per hour, stopping every few blocks for a red light or to pick up more passengers, each one dropping coins in the fare box with a metallic *clink*.

The trolley finally reaches the corner of Fifth and Bouquet—the Forbes Field stop. The boy hops down the stairs. A quick glance for traffic, and he's gone, zipping across the avenue, half-walking, half-skipping down the slope of Bouquet Street until he reaches the ballpark. He slips through a narrow doorway into the vendors' room—the dungeon, he calls it—a low-lit area furnished with a few benches and two battered picnic tables. Maybe a dozen other teens are already in there, hoping they'll get picked to work that afternoon's Steelers game selling beer, popcorn, hot dogs, and the like. If a good crowd shows up, a hardworking youngster might earn the grand sum of $10 for his labors. Mind you, a good crowd for the

Steelers in this era is twenty thousand people. Most Sundays, they get closer to ten thousand, or five.

No one questions the presence of the skinny, frizzy-haired kid who has yet to reach 5 feet tall. He's a familiar face, having vendored plenty of Pirates games that summer during baseball season. He's not planning to work today, though. He positions himself near an iron gate that separates the vendors' room from a ramp leading into the ballpark. Sooner or later, he knows, one of the supervisors going in and out will leave the gate unlocked. When that happens—*whoosh*, the boy is gone again, running as fast as his short legs will carry him, up the ramp, through the empty concourse, up a staircase, down a second concourse, his steps echoing off the concrete walls. Finally, he reaches his destination: a men's room, the single most remote men's room in the entire stadium. He dashes inside and locks himself inside a toilet stall, his feet on the lid, his rear end planted atop the tank.

Here the boy will sit for the next two and a half hours. The hiding place is tough on the nose, tougher on the behind. But he sticks it out, with only the rosters ripped from the Sunday newspaper to keep him entertained, until a rising swell of crowd noise signals that it's safe to venture out and find a spot to watch the football game.

This is a cash-strapped but diehard Steelers fan, circa 1943. This is a kid willing to break the law and test the limits of his derriere to see his team.

This is Myron Kopelman, one day to be better known as Myron Cope.

Myron may have been the most devoted Steelers fan of all time, though he does have competition. Richard Peterson, a resident of Pittsburgh's South Side, wrote that during the 1950s, he and some pals gate-crashed Steelers games by scaling the Forbes Field walls several hours before kickoff and hiding in a tomb-like slot under the right-field stands. The space was dark, cramped, grimy, and home to rats, but when the gates opened, they knocked the filth off their clothes and melted into the crowd admission-free.

In 2005 the family of another fan, James Henry Smith, arranged for a Steelers-themed viewing of his body after he died from prostate cancer. The funeral home placed Smith's body on his favorite recliner, with a remote control in his hands, a Steelers blanket across his legs, and a loop of Steelers highlights playing on the TV. Smith's sister saw the layout and couldn't stop crying. "It was just like he was at home," she said.

But Myron wins the "most devoted" title by virtue of his thirty-five years in the Steelers' radio booth, his creation of the Terrible Towel, and his still-standing record for elapsed time spent on toilets prior to a football game. "I loved the Steelers so much," he told Pittsburgh sports historian Jim O'Brien early in the new millennium, trying to explain actions that to modern-day fans must sound cuckoo. Anyone who concludes that *cuckoo* was an apt descriptor here should remember two things. First, Pittsburgh had no TV in the mid-1940s; one had to attend a game to see it. Second, Myron was fine with a little cuckoo.

His passion for the Steelers would never dim, even as the franchise limped through decades of losing before striking gold with four Super Bowl wins in the 1970s. By then Myron was employed to deliver his one-of-a-kind commentary during the games ("He eluded the pass rush and went through like a sandwich, like mayonnaise dripping out of a sandwich!"). To Myron, it was just child's play.

"Doing the color on Steelers broadcasts is the only job I've ever known that sooner or later did not become work," he said after the first of those Super Bowl seasons. Being a sportswriter, a commentator, a talk show host—those were things that left him drained at day's end. "But to broadcast the games of a football team you've been involved with since you were ten years old, sneaking into the ballpark for free? Well, that's just showing up for an afternoon of fun and getting to mouth off about it in the process."

Showing up, mouthing off, and having fun—that was Myron's general mode of operation, whether he was in front of a microphone, a camera, or just a roomful of pals. The approach served him well, from the first time he laid eyes on a Steelers game to the last.

1

Sports Nut in Squirrel Hill

If any boy was born to be a Pittsburgh Steelers broadcaster and icon, well, that boy was not Myron Cope. The Pittsburgh part, yes. He arrived at Magee Women's Hospital on January 23, 1929, a chilly Wednesday when snow fell on the city, Cal Coolidge was still president, and the stock market was doing just fine. It was a quintessential 'Burgh day for the era, judging from a headline in the *Post-Gazette*: "Smog Pays Return Visit with No End in Sight." Pittsburgh was still the Smoky City then, a place where enormous furnaces in steel mills and littler ones in people's homes burned cheap, dirty, bituminous coal and pumped out black clouds that left even sunny afternoons tinted gray. The day before Myron's birth, the air was so inky-dark that three incoming planes could not find the runways at Allegheny County Airport. Radar hadn't been invented yet, so rescue planes had to go up and guide them down.

It's doubtful that Ellis and Elizabeth Kopelman noticed the tumult in the sky. They were just excited to have a baby boy, their first after three girls. They named him Myron Sidney Kopelman—their reasons for those names lost to time—and brought him home to the three-bedroom house they owned in Squirrel Hill, then the fastest-growing residential section in

Pittsburgh. Myron was born near the end of America's prosperous Roaring Twenties, and the decade had roared very much to the Kopelmans' liking. Ellis and Elizabeth got married just as the good times began, in July 1920—she a native Pittsburgher, he from the nearby manufacturing town of New Kensington. Both were of Lithuanian Jewish descent, and both were twenty-five years young, as Myron might say. Just nine months later, they had a family, after Elizabeth gave birth to twins Marie and Violet. A few years afterward, Ellis opened a successful wholesale clothing store on the edge of downtown Pittsburgh, and in 1927 the family expanded again with the arrival of sister Shirley.

That was the year the Kopelmans bought their house on the back of Ellis's success. Ellis wasn't making big money, but he was doing well. The family had a phone and a radio, luxuries not enjoyed by the majority of Americans in the 1920s. They employed a part-time housekeeper to keep things in order. Each autumn, they were among the families who took out a five-line notice in the local Jewish newspaper, the *Criterion*, wishing friends and relatives a happy and prosperous new year. The arrival of a baby boy? Icing on the cake of life.

The Kopelmans' newest member had his father's brown eyes, a slightly cleft chin, a head that soon erupted with blondish waves of hair, and cheeks with just enough baby fat to be pinchably cute. Both Ellis and Elizabeth were enraptured, and within a short time, the boy had established himself as the center of the Kopelman universe. "He was definitely the spoiled favorite," says Elizabeth Cope, Myron's daughter. "Oh my gosh, my aunts used to complain that the house revolved around my father."

Myron's niece Marcia Grodsky confirms: "My grandmother would wait on him hand and foot. And my grandfather [Ellis] would come home from work and go out and play ball with him. My grandfather was definitely closer to him than he was to the girls. They said he didn't talk to them much unless he was giving them orders."

Ellis, as that comment implies, was the authority in the Kopelman household—the breadwinner, the doer, the decision-maker. Also, the talker, a quality he passed on to his son. "I wouldn't say either of my grandparents had electric personalities, but Myron was more like my grandfather," says Grodsky. "My grandmother was very quiet and ladylike; everyone adored her. My grandfather was a raconteur. When he worked at Metropolitan Life [Insurance], he was always the toastmaster or the emcee for all their parties. So Myron took after him in that regard."

Was Ellis funny? "He could be," Grodsky says. "He wasn't the same kind of funny as Myron. He liked to tell jokes. He was known for repeating the same jokes all the time. Everyone would say, 'Not again!'"

The Kopelmans' decision to settle in Squirrel Hill was no accident. The area, five miles due east of downtown Pittsburgh, was factory free and bordered by two city parks, Frick and Schenley, which boasted acres and acres of trees and rolling hills. Smog in the neighborhood wasn't so damn eye-wateringly thick. Equally important were the area's demographics. Most of the new arrivals, like Ellis and Elizabeth, were Jews, and by the time Myron came along, Squirrel Hill was turning into a majority Jewish neighborhood, rare in any part of the United States outside New York. The Koplemans were not especially religious, although they belonged to big Beth Shalom synagogue, a relatively short uphill walk from their house. More than anything, Squirrel Hill was comfortable; they were among their own kind. There, Elizabeth had no trouble finding fresh bagels, brisket, or the other Jewish foods her son liked to eat. There, no one asked why Elizabeth lit the candles every Friday night or maintained a kosher home, never mixing dairy foods with those containing meat. There, they didn't have to worry about being redlined out of a neighborhood or being barred from a social club because of their religion—though Myron and his sisters did recall hearing their schoolteachers, of all people, make antisemitic remarks.

The setting also assured that Myron would grow up hearing a swirl of Yiddish, Hebrew, and German mixed into everyday English, courtesy of the thousands of European Jewish immigrants and their children, first- and second-generation Americans, who made up the backbone of the new Jewish community. Myron never learned to speak anything but English. But certain words from those other tongues lodged in his brain, such as *mazel tov*, Hebrew for congratulations; *dummkopf*, a German word meaning blockhead; *feh*, a Yiddish expression of disgust; and *oy*, a Yiddish exclamation of dismay. Years later, they'd all spill out into microphones when he began broadcasting Steelers games.

Myron would spend his first twenty-seven years or so living in Squirrel Hill, putting down roots among family and friends that helped anchor him to Pittsburgh throughout his life. As a boy, he did many of the things that kids still do in Squirrel Hill today: sled on the hills of Frick Park, snack in the delis and bakeries along Murray Avenue, watch movies in the dark of the Manor Theater, get bar mitzvahed at Beth Shalom, and walk the long, long steps up the hill to Taylor Allderdice High School. When not on his home turf, he was usually on a trolley to the Oakland neighborhood—home to Forbes Field and other sports venues like Pitt Stadium—or to the Hill District, home to the Irene Kaufmann Settlement, a sort of proto-Jewish community center that provided English and "Americanization" classes for immigrants and that hosted art, music, and sports activities for kids.

In fact, if one pores over his writings and scrapbooks, one gets the sense that the young Myron almost never left the Pittsburgh area. The scrapbooks contain no photos of Kopelman family vacations; his autobiography and the hundreds of articles he wrote make no reference to him visiting other cities until he was in his twenties, when sportswriting duties began to take him off his home turf.

Maybe it was the sheer volume of time spent in the city or the exposure he got to its people during Pirates and Steelers games. But from an early age, Myron developed a severe case of what came to be known as the Pittsburgh accent. The accent—distinguished by an array of flattened-out vowels, rushed and crushed-together syllables, and scattered extraneous *r*'s—dated from the late nineteenth century, when the booming steel mills, hungry for manual labor, welcomed immigrants from all corners of Europe.

Author Elana Passarello, who devoted an entire chapter to Myron in *Let Me Clear My Throat*, her 2013 book on voices, said Pittsburgh's compact geography, defined by steep hills and the city's famous three rivers, encouraged the birth of a distinct accent as the newcomers, living in close quarters, all learned a new language at the same time. "Scots-Irish verb forms and Yiddish vocabulary and Slavic vowel changes were reined in by neighborhoods and mutated in riverfront markets," Passarello wrote. "Once their sound had evolved into the least likely of speech patterns, Pittsburghers united to fight the flattening of regional sound that ran rampant through the East in the nineteenth and twentieth centuries. Together, they forced Pittsburghese to clot."

In time, the sounds coming out of Myron's mouth would be held up as the epitome of this local dialect. He generally didn't use stereotypical Pittsburgh words like *yinzer* and *gumband*. It was more the way he spoke when he read a commercial for the favorite local beer—*Ahrn* City—or told listeners about a function he attended *dahn-tahn*. The Pittsburghiness was heightened by the rough, raucous quality of Myron's voice, a good fit for a city built around heavy industry.

In Myron's larynx, Passarello said, Pittsburghers heard the noise of their industrial and social heritage. "Piped through his lungs, throat, teeth, cheeks, lips were horns, factory exhaust, incline bars, bar gibber, even occasional birdsong. . . . His stubborn speech eventually became music to millions of people. No longer jarring or unconventional, his voice became *the* voice" (emphasis added). And that was the voice, Pittsburghers decided, that they wanted to narrate their Sunday afternoons as they opened a can of Iron City, plopped onto their easy chairs, and watched the games of their favorite team.

So from day one, Myron was a Pittsburgher to his core. But football? That wasn't part of the boy's genes or environment. Ellis Kopelman had been born in 1895 in Vashilishok, a mostly Jewish town in western Russia, a *shtetl*, and sailed to the United States at age five with his mother and younger brother. Ellis liked sports plenty, but like a lot of early 1900s Jewish immigrants trying to adapt to American society, his sport of choice was the national pastime, baseball. "From the time I was little, every Pirates game was on the radio or later the TV. He never would miss a baseball game," remembers Grodsky.

Even had he loved football, Ellis wasn't built to play it. He was a relatively small man at 5 feet 7, 160 pounds and had lost the sight in his right eye as a youngster, either from an auto accident or an improperly treated childhood cataract, depending on who was telling the story.

Meanwhile, Elizabeth Kopelman and Myron's three older sisters weren't geared toward sports in the slightest. Elizabeth had a weakened heart due to a childhood bout of rheumatic fever. The girls were healthy, but their energies went into more artistic pursuits. "They were all into painting, drawing, crocheting, designing clothes," says Elizabeth Cope. "They would wear pearls, beautiful clothes, dressed to the nines wherever they went." Even if the girls had been sports minded—and girls weren't encouraged to be that way back then—they weren't necessarily built for the task. Marie and Shirley both stood 4 feet 10, about the same height as their mother. Violet, at 5 feet even, was the tall one.

Myron wasn't constructed for athletic glory either. He had a skinny, wiry build, low in fat but short on muscle, and his height would top out at a self-reported 5 feet 4¾ inches, leaving him staring up at most of the athletes he interviewed during his career. When he suggested the nickname of Killer to Pirates pitcher Bruce Kison, Kison shot back, "How'd you like it if I called you Shorty?" A close friend, 6-foot-2 Steelers linebacker Andy Russell, liked to joke that he carried around a life-sized photo of Myron in his wallet.

Myron didn't let his surroundings or stature hold him back. From an early age he emerged as a full-blown, half-crazed sports fanatic. Squirrel Hill was a good place to be such a creature, having plenty of fields and courts to play on and an abundance of boys to play on them. As a teen, he partook in neighborhood baseball and softball during the summers, pickup football in the autumn, indoor basketball in the winter, and even some boxing at the Irene Kaufmann Settlement. There, in November 1943, he won his lone documented bout in the ring, defeating a fellow hundred-pounder, a boy named Sol Kantor, during what was billed as a "midget boxing tournament."

"I loved the fight game," Myron said more than once, and he considered entering other amateur bouts until he was invited to train at a gym in the Hill District. There, as Myron told the story, the boxing coach suggested he work out with a light heavyweight, Sailor Jack Kelly. Kelly outweighed him by fifty pounds. Kelly also had just bloodied another fighter at the gym who outweighed *him* by fifty pounds. As the topper, Kelly was missing part of his right arm but fought effectively with a boxing glove strapped to the stump.

Myron gulped and asked the coach, "Could I take a little more time to get into shape?" The coach said sure and Myron hightailed it home, depriving the world of a plucky flyweight, Kid Kopelman.

Myron continued playing other sports, but even on the ballfields, his true nature was already coming through. John Conomikes grew up in Squirrel Hill, three classes behind Myron. Decades later, as an executive at WTAE television and at Hearst Broadcasting, the station's owner, he'd enthusiastically boost Myron's career. But he first got to know the future broadcaster when his older brother Peter played on a softball team with Myron in the mid-1940s. "If I remember correctly, they called themselves the Squirrel Hill International Tigers. That's S-H-I-T. They had a lot of fun with that," Conomikes says, with a laugh.

Conomikes's main impression of the young Myron was that of a kid who simply would not stop talking. "Myron was always a yakker," he says, and playing third base for the softball team, Myron was constantly jawing with the umpires, annoying Peter Conomikes to no end. One day, says John, "my brother came in from center field and said, 'Myron, if you don't shut the hell up, if you keep arguing with the umpires, I'm gonna come in and throw your ass in the bushes.' The bushes were along the third base line. Two innings later, Myron started on the umpires again about a play at third base. He started yakking, my brother went in, picked him up and dumped him in the bushes behind the third base bag. Myron said, 'Why'd you do that?' My brother says, 'Myron, I warned you.'"

At a roast in 1999 Conomikes joked that Myron made a sound when his rear end hit the bush: "Yoi!" But those who knew him in his pre-broadcasting years say that as a youngster, Myron had yet to create his signature word or any of the phrases—like "Mmm-hah," "Okel dokel," and "How do?"—for which he later became renowned. "That was strictly radio and TV stuff," says Grodsky.

Like all athletic wannabes, Myron had moments of glory that he held onto for years. As a teen, he recalled, he got to spend ten days out in the countryside in a nonprofit summer camp for city kids. "The first day, playing center field in a softball game, I made a running catch, whereupon a kid from Oakland yelled, 'Hey, Lloyd Waner!' Waner was the Pirate center-fielder headed for the Hall of Fame. Throughout the stay, the Oakland contingent called me Lloyd Waner. It was heaven."

Playing touch football for his college newspaper team in 1948, Myron even got a writeup that made him sound like Slingin' Sammy Baugh:

"Little Myron Kopelman sparked the News aggregation. He collaborated with Bob Van Atta on a field-length pass play for one TD, pegged a flat pass to Stan Shapiro for another, and scored the third himself on a jaunt around left end." One caveat: the article had no byline, raising the possibility that it was penned by the paper's chief sportswriter, also named Myron Kopelman.

But the young Myron's efforts to advance beyond recreational sports all came to naught. He thought he saw an opening with the Pirates. "My God, I went to bed when I was fifteen years old every night dreaming that I could play second base in the big leagues. Clem Koshorek, Frankie Zak—they played shortstop at different times for the Pirates and they weren't no taller than me," he remembered. Each summer, the Pirates held an open tryout at Forbes Field. Myron would don baseball shoes and report with dozens of other hopefuls. A coach would crack a few grounders to him at second base, which he'd field cleanly. Then he'd step into the batter's box. Three pitches—strike one, strike two, and strike three, all swinging. Go home, Myron.

In basketball, Myron claimed to have made the roster of the Allderdice JV team but never even sniffed the varsity ("I had not yet reached my full height," he deadpanned). One year, he tried out for the Allderdice football team—or more accurately, tried to try out. However, head coach Bob Irvin took one look at his tiny frame and refused to issue him a helmet. In his autobiography, Myron recalled Irvin's parting words: "Son, I just can't take responsibility for you."

Irvin's wisdom was borne out when the teenage Myron attempted to play sandlot football wearing a cheap cardboard helmet and shoulder pads. During one game, by his own account, Myron fielded a kickoff and charged up the right sideline behind a wall of blockers. When he ran into a traffic jam, he cut to the middle of the field, hoping to find running room. Instead, he found an acquaintance and a fellow sports lover named Jerold Finn. Finn was three years younger than Myron but about twelve inches taller and outweighed him by at least 120 pounds. "He did not even bother to lower his shoulder," Myron recalled. "He simply ran over me and kept running, pausing only to pick up the football I had fumbled." Five minutes passed before Myron could think clearly again.

Upon regaining his senses, he decided to walk away from football while he could still walk.

In a late-career interview, Myron gave a retrospective scouting report on himself. "I was a frustrated athlete," he said. "I had good coordination. I could play ball. But I was too small and I had no speed. So that settled that."

Fortunately, unfulfilled athletes like Myron had an outlet for their energies in Pittsburgh's sports teams. At the top of the heap were the Pirates, one of the better teams in baseball during Myron's youth, though the World Series kept eluding their grasp. The city also had a popular Minor League hockey squad, the Hornets, and three respected college football programs at Duquesne, Carnegie Tech, and the University of Pittsburgh, the last universally referred to as Pitt.

Pitt Panthers football was the real show in town. Starting in the year of Myron's birth, Pitt lost only eleven games over a ten-year period, getting invited to four Rose Bowls in the era before that game became a matchup between the champions of the Big Ten and Pac Ten conferences. Myron's later description of the team for *Sports Illustrated* was as good as any: "Jock Sutherland, a tall, grim man with a Scottish burr, coached Pitt at the time, presiding over a sort of thresher-type single-wing offense that ground opponents to ribbons, all the while abjuring the forward pass as a frill for sissies." When a national power like Notre Dame or Ohio State came to town, Pitt Stadium filled up with crowds of more than seventy thousand. In the late thirties Pitt even had a Jewish star, running back Marshall Goldberg, who finished third in the Heisman Trophy voting in 1937 as Pitt went undefeated and won a national championship.

Yet somehow, the Panthers never caught the young Myron's fancy. His eye wandered over to the professional football team in town, then known as the Pirates but soon to be rebranded as the Steelers.

The Steelers were even younger than Myron. The team was launched in 1933, when a well-known "sportsman" from Pittsburgh's North Side, Art Rooney, paid $2,500 for a franchise in the National Football League. Rooney, a stocky, muscular man with a fat cigar usually stuck in his mouth, had enjoyed a wide-ranging athletic career to that point. He started out as a boxer, qualifying for the 1920 U.S. Olympic team as a welterweight, though he decided not to go to Belgium for the games. Five years later, he took a fling at baseball, batting .369 for a class-C Minor League team in Wheeling, West Virginia. Rooney eventually settled on football, operating and sometimes quarterbacking a local semipro club that ran through multiple names before becoming the J. P. Rooneys to promote Art's brother when he ran for (and won) a seat in the Pennsylvania state legislature.

The NFL had wanted into football-mad Pittsburgh for years but was blocked until the state of Pennsylvania relaxed the "blue laws" that had banned professional sporting events on Sundays. The league was small potatoes at the time—ten teams playing a slightly haphazard schedule, sometimes for crowds that numbered in the hundreds, not thousands. Clubs routinely came and went; of the twelve teams in the league the year of Myron's birth, two-thirds had moved or shut down a mere four years later.

The Steelers stayed alive but remained below .500 and drew poorly at the gate in the early years, in part because Rooney's focus on his team could also be haphazard. His real love was betting on the horses. In August 1937 Rooney enjoyed an extraordinary winning streak at New York's Empire City and Saratoga racetracks, raking in a reported $360,000, a sum equal to nearly $8 million today. When he came home, Rooney told his wife she'd never have to worry about money again.

The football team couldn't manage a comparable winning streak, but not long past first grade, Myron Kopelman had formed an attachment to Art Rooney's franchise. "I became aware of the Steelers from the time I was able to read a sports page or listen to the radio. Even when they had losing teams, I was still a fan," he said.

At this stage Myron didn't get to Steelers games often, being too young to fake-volunteer his services as a vendor. His main conduit to the team was the radio. Radio was America's number-one electronic medium in these years, and Myron listened to all the voices piping through the family's wooden box-style receiver. The comedian Jack Benny was a favorite, later earning periodic mentions on the adult Myron's radio show. He paid closer attention to the sports guys, later singling out the gravelly speed-talker Clem McCarthy, a horse racing specialist, as one he admired. "I never heard anybody who made it [horse racing] as exciting," he said.

Two men in particular made an impact on the young Cope-to-be. One was Pirates' play-by-play man Rosey Rowswell. At a time when most baseball announcers delivered a straight account of the action, Rowswell added whimsical touches, calling an extra-base hit a "doozie maroonie," referring to a sharp breaking pitch as the "ol' dipsy doodle." When a batter smashed a home run, Rowswell would call out to a mythical woman who lived outside the Forbes Field walls, shouting, "Raise the window, Aunt Minnie! Here it comes!" Listeners would then hear a sound effect of shattering glass, akin to a window breaking. After a pause, Rowswell would intone, "She never made it."

"So far as I know, he was the first guy to introduce humor to baseball broadcasts," Myron said. Myron wouldn't hold back on the funny either when he entered the Steelers' radio booth.

Myron especially liked the Steelers' radio announcer, Joe Tucker. A round-faced man with rounded tones, Tucker enjoyed a thirty-two-year run broadcasting Steelers games that began in 1936, when Myron was seven years old. Tucker had a nickname, the Screamer, the origin of which was never quite clear. Some observers thought he earned it by being loudly emotional when the Steelers scored or made a big play. Some thought he had to scream to be heard over weak microphones. In Myron's recollection, the name was "for screaming at the officials when their calls went against the Steelers."

Other than the shouting and a tendency to openly root for the home team, Tucker was a straight-ahead, professional announcer, not terribly colorful. But Myron retained a fondness for Tucker's work. "I consider him to be as big as [Bob] Prince was with the Pirates," he once said. When an illness forced Jack Fleming to miss a Steelers game in 1981, Myron arranged for Tucker to come out of retirement and call a Steelers offensive series in the third quarter. He got audibly excited when Tucker described a running play as "Franco on a full head of steam," employing one of his go-to phrases from the old days. "I'm transported back to my youth, Joe," Myron exclaimed, "back to my youth!"

MYRON'S FOCUS AS A youngster was not *exclusively* on sports, mind you. The big-band era was at its height in the early 1940s, and Myron learned to play the clarinet, then a popular instrument for teens who wanted to emulate famous bandleaders like Benny Goodman. Myron's total inability to sing and his knack for bruising eardrums across a three-state area when he did would become a running joke during his radio career. So it may surprise some that he had a good sense of rhythm and was proficient enough on the "licorice stick"—a clarinet in 1940s slang—to make the Pittsburgh all-city band in high school.

"I think he actually thought about becoming a musician," remembers Grodsky. "He loved jazz, he and [his wife] Mildred loved to dance, they were wonderful dancers. He actually considered at one point going into music instead of being a journalist. He must have been good enough that he considered it as a career—whether that was just in his mind or not, I can't tell you."

Regarding dancing, Myron learned from the best, Gene Kelly—yes, the movie star Gene Kelly, best remembered for *Singin' in the Rain* and a raft of other classic Hollywood musicals. Kelly, a native of Squirrel Hill's neighbor East Liberty, attended the University of Pittsburgh in the early 1930s and taught classes at his family's dance school. When his dad lost his job, Kelly accepted an offer from the Kopelmans' synagogue, Beth Shalom, to teach dance to children on Sunday afternoons and produce a show starring the kids for the Kirmess, an annual outdoor festival. Kelly wasn't Jewish but quickly developed a fan base among the congregation, especially after the 1932 Kirmess raised over $1,000 for Beth Shalom's building fund.

Even as he built his showbiz career, Kelly gave dance lessons and staged shows at the synagogue for the next several years. "He had this incredible magnetism," recalled a leader of the Beth Shalom sisterhood, "and he could somehow get children to do anything he wanted them to do. . . . Children who didn't really have much talent would shine under his guidance."

Elizabeth Kopelman could not resist the temptation to put her boy under the budding star's tutelage. When Myron was nine years old, she signed him up for tap dancing classes at twenty-five cents per session. Myron howled in protest ("I wanna play ball!"), but his cries fell on deaf ears. He endured several weeks of lessons from Gene Kelly and his brother Fred. The ordeal culminated with Myron being part of a dancing chorus line in the Kirmess show, decked out in little top hat and formal tailcoat and brandishing a miniature walking stick.

It was not the start of something big. His dance partner, one Phyllis Manheim, got paralyzed by stage fright, and he had to drag her through the routine. Afterward, he refused to dance another step under a teacher's training, though he came to greatly enjoy social dancing, calling himself "king of the jitterbuggers."

Myron did not look back in awe at his brush with a Hollywood star. "I was just one of the little punks in the class, and I'm sure he looked at all of us like little amateurs," he said.

IN HIS AUTOBIOGRAPHY, Myron referred to himself as a Depression kid. He didn't mean a kid who got depressed. He meant a kid who grew up during the *Great* Depression, the worst economic disaster the United States has ever endured. The stock market, which hit a record high on the day of his birth and rose even higher later that year, sunk like the *Titanic* in October 1929, pulling down thousands of investors, banks, and businesses in its wake. Unemployment jumped to 10, 20, then 25 percent. Things were especially bad in Pittsburgh, where shriveled demand for cars and construction left the city's steel mills running at a fraction of their full capacity. The Strip District, usually the city's prime market area, came to host a shantytown where hundreds of homeless men set up shacks built out of scavenged wood, brick, and tin.

Ellis Kopelman was neither a stockbroker nor a steelworker. But the Depression would have profound effects on him and the Kopelman family.

Ellis was a bright man, renowned for his ability to do complex equations in his head. "Ask him to multiply, say, 2,063 times 3,120, and he would spit out the correct number from his head in seconds. Surely he could have been a physicist," Myron wrote. But being the oldest of six children, Ellis had sacrificed a college education to support the family, in part so his sisters could get teaching degrees and his younger brother Nathan could study to be a cardiologist.

His main chance for success seemed to arrive in June 1924, when he and a partner, Oscar Robbins, opened a wholesale clothing business on Fifth Avenue, on the edge of downtown Pittsburgh. An ad in the city's Jewish newspaper, the *Criterion*, said the new store offered "a complete line of ladies and gents' furnishings." The pair must have done well, because another ad published a year later said they were moving up the street to a bigger store.

Two years after that, Ellis and Elizabeth purchased their newly-built house at 6309 Crombie Street in Squirrel Hill. The price was $10,600, a nice chunk of change for a home in that era. The red-brick, three-bedroom house had a basement and a small backyard and was within walking distance of Frick Park, Colfax Elementary, and Allderdice High School—perfect for a growing family, and a sign of Ellis's success.

In May 1928 Robbins & Kopelman moved yet again, "because of a need for larger quarters and the desire for a more central location," reported the *Criterion*. This was one expansion too many. Once the Depression hit in late 1929, people suddenly weren't so keen on buying new clothes, wholesale or otherwise. Pittsburgh phone books from the early 1930s show the business moving to other, presumably smaller, locations. After 1932 it vanished from the Yellow Pages entirely. Like hundreds of thousands of other businesses across the nation, Robbins & Kopelman had gone bust.

With it went the family's rising middle-class lifestyle. Previously, Ellis had employed a maid several days each week to help Elizabeth with the kids and the housework. Now the family lost not only the housemaid but the house itself, which was sold off at a sheriff's sale.

Give him credit, though. Ellis Kopelman worked hard to stay on his feet. Myron explained in his autobiography, "To make ends meet, he bought a truck and made the rounds of failing clothing stores, buying their inventories for resale to still-existing businesses." The returns on this venture were limited, in part because Ellis, with only one working eye, had to pay a driver to haul the clothes. So Ellis switched fields and found work with the Metropolitan Life Insurance Company. Technically, he was a salesman peddling life insurance policies, but his main duty was walking a "debit," a route for collecting payments from policyholders. According to Myron, the route took Ellis through the declining Hill District, where he climbed tenement stairwells to knock on doors and collect pennies from Black folks, most of them poor, who'd taken out small policies so they could pay for their own funerals. "Through snow and rain and sweltering summer weather, dad plodded along with his debit," Myron wrote.

Ellis wasn't above making some less hard-earned dollars on the side. In his book, Myron relates a tale of his father sitting among gamblers at a Pirates game one afternoon when the home team was down 10–0. "One hundred to one the Pirates lose," cried out a voice from a nearby seat. Ellis took the bet for a buck. "The Pirates roared back, and we ate steak that night," Myron said. Myron may have gotten the score wrong—there's no record of the Pirates *ever* coming back to win from a 10–0 deficit—but the rest of the story is plausible.

However, steak nights during Myron's childhood were apparently rare. "Times were really hard, his family had no money," says Elizabeth Cope. "He could remember being hungry, that's how poor they were." Ellis somehow kept his brood in the familiar environs of Squirrel Hill, but everyone made sacrifices. After losing the house on Crombie, the Kopelmans moved to a rented duplex on nearby Tilbury Avenue. The residence had only two bedrooms, and Myron was odd boy out, sleeping in what he called a cubbyhole while his parents took one room and his three sisters got the other. When money got especially tight, Myron became an only child for a time as his sisters were sent to live with relatives.

A few years later, in the mid-1940s, the family was able to buy a house at 6346 Alderson Street. The residence was bigger than the one on Tilbury but came with a drawback—one had to walk up twenty-seven outdoor steps, pitched at a forty-five-degree angle, just to reach the front door. It was a chore to haul up groceries at any time of year and a real hazard when ice or snow was coming down. The Kopelmans put up with it; inconvenience equaled a lower mortgage.

The general tough times prevented Myron's oldest sisters, Violet and Marie, from getting a post–high school education. "My mother [Violet] and her twin sister, they won scholarships to an art school, but it was the Depression, and they had to go to work to help support the family," says Marcia Grodsky. "Myron was still young, and my grandfather had lost his business, and so they weren't able to take the scholarships." There was an element of sexism at work, too, she says: "At that time, in Jewish families, it was important that the boy go to college, not so much for the girls."

Myron later said Ellis's business struggles made him short-tempered and caused tension in the house. "My dad remembered a lot of fighting [between his parents] about money, and he felt sorry for his mother," says Elizabeth Cope. "It ingrained in my dad the belief that he'd better make some money. He always said if we wanted a successful marriage, one of the ingredients was to make money. Of course, it's love too, but he grew up with parents who fought about money, and he knew that was going to be important to avoid."

That's probably why at the tender age of eleven, in 1940, Myron got his first job. It was his inaugural step into the world of sports, sort of—he was a pinsetter in a bowling alley. In the days before mechanized pinsetters, boys were positioned behind the lanes to set up pins after every frame and roll the ball back to the bowler. Glamorous work it was not. A boy might earn one or two dollars per night and had to be on constant high alert to avoid getting whacked by incoming balls and flying pins. Myron said the job left him with a sore back and a lifelong aversion to bowling. But it did contribute to the family finances.

The young Kopelman's next job, starting at age thirteen, was also in the sports field, working as a vendor at Pirates games. He likened the job to being a dockworker. Before home games, he and maybe twenty other boys would gather at Forbes Field in the aforementioned "dungeon." There they'd wait for concessions chief Meyer O'Brisky—"a stumpy, open-collared man with a magnificent head of glistening skin," in Myron's words—to decide how many vendors the team would hire that day.

"We would report to his domain under the first base stands four or five hours before game time and anxiously await the shape-up," Myron remembered, somewhat dramatically, in a 1960 *Pittsburgh Post-Gazette* article:

> Then we would line up before one of Mr. O's lieutenants, hoping to be chosen for a day's work. We would stand as tall as possible and beseech the hairy straw boss with starvation eyes, praying that he would look our way and grumble, "Awwright, you—get a uniform." After dressing in a faded blue suit starched like a bedboard, we would fall into line again, this time to get our assignments from Mr. O'Brisky himself. Gradually, the line would move forward until we came face to face with him, all one hundred six pounds of us. "Hot dogs," he would snap. And we would strap on that monster of a hot dog oven and reel forth on buckling legs.

This passage, incidentally, is an example of Myron's only bad writing habit: replacing *I* with *we* to make his experience or opinion seem more universal. The practice would pop up in his articles and commentaries for decades.

Once loaded up with his tray, Myron would walk the aisles, barking "Hot dogs! Get your red hots!" Vocally, the young teenager was well equipped for the job; physically, not so much. But he made himself carry the hot, heavy tray because he got a token for each complete load he sold, convertible to cash at the end of the game.

The job had a secondary benefit; it gave him an intimate knowledge of Forbes Field. When he began sneaking into Steelers games, he knew precisely which bathroom to run to, which one gave him the greatest chance of staying undiscovered until game time—as long as he kept his keister planted atop that commode.

BY HIS LATE TEENS, it had dawned on Myron that if he was to make sports his life, his hands would have to work a typewriter instead of a bat or a ball. As a child, he had spent hours poring over the work of famous sportswriters. "I was a voracious reader," he recalled. "A. J. Liebling [in] *The New Yorker*. And Ring Lardner. I used to stay up as a kid 'til three a.m., reading Ring Lardner, laughing out loud and waking up my family." Liebling was a Big Apple–based journalist renowned for his essays on boxing and horse racing as well as politics and food. Lardner was an early twentieth-century writer best remembered for his humorous 1916 novel, *You Know Me, Al,* written in the form of letters sent by a fictional Minor League baseball player to a hometown friend. Early in his writing career, in fact, an admirer suggested that Myron was "another Ring Lardner"—though Myron as an adult seemed to disavow a Lardner influence: "Not too many years ago, I picked him up again and I thought, 'Why did I enjoy this guy?' Tastes change, I guess."

In his midteens, Myron began writing a sports column for the Allderdice High School newspaper, the *Forward*. Elizabeth Cope says her father considered the column the worst writing he ever did, and Myron's extensive scrapbooks contain not a single example of it. But it must have been halfway decent, as in April 1946, Myron, along with dozens of other budding writers, won a merit award in a high school writing contest sponsored by the *Pittsburgh Press*. The most notable aspect of the column, in retrospect, was its title. For the first time, Myron shortened his last name for the general reading public. Conomikes recalls the title as being "Kope's Corner." A more contemporary and presumably more accurate account comes from the Allderdice 1947 yearbook. In the blurb next to his senior picture, the yearbook staff wrote, "Everyone will remember Kope and his 'Komments.'"

Had he graduated a few years earlier, during the war, Allderdice might have been the end of the line for Myron's education. He would have been drafted, or family finances would have blocked his advancement. But now an unexpected opportunity arose. A relative on his dad's side of the family, Bob Davis, a state health inspector, used political connections to get him a scholarship to attend the University of Pittsburgh. Myron was qualified; he had made the honor roll in his senior year. And his sisters were grown up and either married or working. There was no immediate reason to quit school and find a job.

He'd have to live at home and take the number 68 trolley back and forth to classes at Pitt, but that was a minor inconvenience. He was going to be a college man, and from the start, he had his sights set on Pitt's writing department. They had journalism courses, English courses, even courses in radio. His mind was set on being a newspaper reporter, and a good one at that. There's gonna come a day, he thought, when people will sit up and take notice when they see my name in the paper—Myron Kopelman.

2

"An Industrious Young Journalistic Prospect"

"I always wanted to be a newspaper man," Myron once said, referring to his teenage self, and within a few months of starting classes at Pitt in January 1947, he was. The university had a highly respected student newspaper, the *Pitt News*, and soon after enrollment, he made a beeline for the sports department. By that April he was writing bylined articles; by September, an eager and no doubt brash Myron had gotten himself assigned to football coverage.

His talent came quickly to the fore. Led by rookie coach Mike Milligan, Pitt had a ghastly squad that year, winning only one game out of nine, losing one contest to Indiana by five touchdowns, dropping another to Michigan by ten. Not ten points, mind you—ten *touchdowns*. When Ohio State arrived for a visit in mid-October, fans expected more of the same. Somehow, the Panthers rallied that day and upset the Buckeyes 12–0. As the final seconds ticked down, thousands of ecstatic rooters stormed the field at Pitt Stadium. The freshman reporter stayed out of the throng, however, and instead made his way to the locker room. There he saw an emotional scene that he fashioned into his lead:

> Chancellor Rufus H. Fitzgerald rushed into the Pitt dressing room, pitched his arms around Mike Milligan in a very unchancellor-like fashion and cried, "Bless your soul, Mike, bless your soul."

That intro helped Myron land his first front-page byline and was also notably more attention grabbing than any produced by the sportswriters at Pittsburgh's daily newspapers. In fact, his prose during that miserable season was often professional-level creative. Motivating fullback Paul Rickards, he wrote, was as difficult "as waking up the statue that fronts Carnegie Library." After one horrific loss, players were "less talkative than Harpo Marx in a muzzle." As for the Pitt defense, it wasn't just bad, it was "non-resistant."

In time, Myron began writing columns that further showcased his already sharp sense of humor. In a November 1949 piece he said his heart goes out to the cross-country team running cold-weather races in their underwear. "However," he added, "the heart is all that goes out to them, for the rest of the body prefers the comfort of the indoors."

By his senior year, Myron, now the *Pitt News* sports editor, was traveling with the football team on road trips and mining laughs from the tension between school officials trying to keep the players focused and guys just wanting to have a good time. During one trip to the University of Illinois, he noted, the school didn't give the players a chance to visit Chicago. "Obviously," he wrote, "this is disappointing to the curious young men, who wanted desperately to take in the Museum of Natural History, the Civic Opera and other cultural centers that tempt youthful football players."

It wasn't long before the full-time sportswriters in town took notice of their collegiate counterpart. Roy McHugh of the *Pittsburgh Press* said he arranged to meet the young Myron because of the writing. "It was so much better than anything you'd expect to read in a college paper," said McHugh, who became one of Myron's lifelong friends and informal editor of his magazine and book projects. Other sportswriters began using him as a source for stories on the Pitt football program. When the Panthers announced a switch in 1950 from the single-wing offense to the modern T formation, Myron came down on the side of tradition. "I personally like the single wing," he told the *Post-Gazette*. "I think that, with imagination, a lot can be done with it."

When not newspapering, Myron took all manner of writing and journalism courses at the school. His work was accomplished enough that he was one of several students honored at Pitt's Western Pennsylvania Conference for Writers in May 1949. He was also active on the Jewish social and athletic scene—jitterbugging at dances, playing softball and basketball on weekends, picking up a few bucks as a summer camp counselor. He earned a few more taking care of his young niece, too, though that didn't always work out so well. "He was sometimes my babysitter when I was little," says Marcia Grodsky. "I know the story that my parents came home one night and found him sound asleep. They found me crawling on top of the piano."

An acquaintance from Allderdice and Pitt, Milton Wolf, recalled that Myron also refereed recreation-league basketball games around this time. Myron gave it up, according to Wolf, after a tight game between two deaf teams devolved into a melee, with players from both sides pushing and shoving while using their hands to furiously sign insults at each other. "Myron was trying to get ahold of things, and he kept blowing the whistle," Wolf remembers, with a laugh.

The newsroom was young Kopelman's real home away from home. Several photos in Pitt yearbooks show him there, a twentyish young man with a ruddy complexion and dark wavy hair, invariably looking down at some papers or a typewriter. One shot in particular could be captioned "Study of the Baby Sportswriter." In it, Myron sits at an L-shaped desk surrounded by that day's newspapers, a copy of *Life* magazine, and another publication titled "Basketball 1950." Behind him, a piece of paper tacked to the wall shows league standings of some kind. Loose wires stick out from the same wall, pleading for attention. But Myron pays them no mind; he is in the zone, the writing zone, his gaze fixed on the black manual typewriter before him, his fingers resting on the keys, his brain trying to pump out a story before the deadline arrives and the paper is "put to bed," or closed to new stories for the night.

Myron proceeded through Pitt in four years with little difficulty save for a medical issue that cost him a small chunk of his junior year. "He had a cold, and he went to a football game, a night game," says Elizabeth Cope. "He didn't wear a hat, and it was freezing. He woke up the next morning with a really bad ear infection." Bad, as in lasting for several weeks. Bad, as in requiring hospitalization. In time, penicillin shots brought the infection under control, but not before it partially deformed Myron's left ear, leaving the top half looking bent over and shriveled, like it had been bitten by a dog.

He had already lost some hearing in that ear due to otosclerosis, a form of abnormal bone growth around the eardrum. This was a potential complication for a man planning a career as a reporter. But it did carry an upside of sorts. When the Korean War erupted in June 1950 and Uncle Sam began drafting young men, Myron was rejected due to his hearing loss. The development left him with mixed feelings—he didn't mind sidestepping the horrors of war, but Elizabeth says he wanted to do an army hitch like many young men did at the time. "He always felt bad about that," says Elizabeth. "He wished he could have served."

With his other ear intact, Myron began haunting the offices of Pittsburgh's newspapers as graduation approached, trying to line up a job. The newspaper industry was a robust creature in 1950; an estimated fifty-two million Americans subscribed to or purchased papers each day. Pittsburgh had three dailies—the *Post-Gazette* in the morning, the *Press* and the *Sun-Telegraph* in the afternoon. All three boasted circulation of more than two hundred thousand, though the *Sun-Telegraph* was losing ground to the other two. The papers at this point faced almost no competition from television, as Pittsburgh had only one station, WDTV, which programmed little news.

That said, it wasn't the best time for an aspiring reporter to be looking for work in Pittsburgh; a strike by delivery drivers and mailroom workers had forced all three papers to shut down for seven weeks that fall, costing each one tens of thousands of dollars in advertising revenue. The losses put the kibosh on any new hires. All Myron found on his job search were signs that read "No Vacancy."

Myron fought back with his strongest weapon, his creativity. A few weeks before graduation, he wrote, laid out, and printed up a highly unique job résumé—a one-page mock newspaper he titled *Editor's Opportunity*.

At the top, the paper boasted a double-deck headline that declared in bold, black letters: "Myron Kopelman Still Available for Hiring." Below, a five-hundred-word article alerted newspaper hiring managers to what they were missing:

> After six weeks of street-pounding, Myron Kopelman, an industrious young journalistic prospect, is still waiting for some alert editor to give him an opportunity.
>
> . . . Caught in the aftermath of the Pittsburgh newspaper strike, the diligent but undaunted job-hunter has been met thus far with little encouragement from local editors. He is hoping they—or any other editors—will soon come to the realization that above-average ability pays for itself.
>
> From his temporary headquarters in the State Unemployment Bureau, Kopelman this week issued the following statement:
>
> "Undoubtedly the budgetary concerns of editors present real problems. But let me stress the financial wisdom of investing in an unusual prospect even when no additional personnel is ordinarily deemed necessary. Some day that prospect may become a featured columnist or an editor of notable talent, so is it not wise to attach him to your organization while the attaching is good?"
>
> "I have no intention of being a liability. I am no ordinary job-seeker. I am industrious and resourceful. Samples of my past works will speak for my writing ability, which, by the way, is bound to improve still more."
>
> "I revel in writing. I glory in the opportunity to run down a story. In short, I am bound to contribute substantially to the future prosperity of that newspaper which gives me a break. Would hiring me constitute poor fiscal policy? Would it be foolish budgetary practice?"

Myron added that he would not enter the contest for Mr. Modesty of 1950. The all-Kopelman enterprise also included a cartoon, a sidebar, a masthead, even a short weather report: "Cloudy today. Fair tomorrow, contingent on response of editors." He wouldn't have used the term, but Myron was building a personal brand, an identity of who he was as an individual and a journalist. The Kopelman model for 1950: bold, smart, inventive, funny. Already, at age twenty-one, an ace self-promoter. There was no hint yet of wanting radio or television work. But even in print, he was clearly original and stood out from the pack.

Toward year's end, Myron got a bite from *Post-Gazette* city editor Joseph Shuman, who hired him as a stringer, a reporter who provided the paper with short stories or bits of information. Dropping off his work, Myron got his first look at the PG newsroom, also known as the city room, and was enthralled. The newsroom looked the same as any across the country: a small sea of wooden desks bearing manual typewriters, rotary phones, glass ashtrays, and piles of paper. There was no attempt at interior décor, unless one wanted to count the fluorescent lights humming overhead or the radiators along the walls. But the room sprung to life around 4 p.m. each day, when the reporters, mostly men with short-cropped hair wearing suits and ties over white button-down shirts, began drifting in to compose their stories for the next morning's edition, "charging the air with their clattering typewriters," in Myron's words.

Actually, the typing was just one instrument in the cacophony of newsroom sound, along with ringing phones, chattering teletype machines, and people shouting to be heard over the din. Reporters had to tune out the noise and get words on the paper in a minimum of time with a minimum of mistakes. One too many flubs or cross-outs and they'd unroll the paper from the typewriter, toss it in the trash, and start again. Once a story was written, editors penciled in their changes and gave it back to the reporter to type up a clean copy. Upon finishing, a reporter would shout, "Boy!" and a so-called copyboy—usually a guy in his late teens or early twenties "scrounging for a living," in Myron's description—would fetch the paper, stuff it inside a cylinder-shaped container, and send it via pneumatic tubes down to the composing room, where workers at linotype machines laid it into hot metal type for printing.

Myron's zeal for newspapering would eventually fade. But in 1951 he said, "I hungered to be part of that city room action."

His hunger would be satisfied, after two brief detours.

Ellis had pressured Myron to find work immediately after graduation, so when the local papers didn't bite, the would-be journalist scanned the want ads and took a job as a door-to-door salesman. The gig entailed convincing people to let a photographer visit their home and take a portrait of their baby or family. Myron began his new career on a weekday in January, walking the steep hills and snow-covered sidewalks of Uniontown, Pennsylvania, in ten-degree weather. Almost immediately, he said, he realized that he had no talent for salesmanship. The man who would one day record scores of radio commercials and be renowned for the impact of his voice in those thirty- and sixty-second ads was reduced to stammering and sweating and walking away empty-handed whenever he tried to make a face-to-face sale.

"At the end of the first day, I had earned three dollars in commissions," Myron wrote. As he drove back to Pittsburgh with three fellow salesmen that night, Myron remembered, he said a silent prayer that a newspaper editor would call and rescue him from a forlorn future of selling baby-photo shoots.

The newspaper gods were listening. When he got back to the family's home on Alderson Street, Ellis informed him that a man named Gene Cuneo had called. Cuneo was sports editor for the *Erie Times*.

Myron barely had time to eat dinner. That night, he caught a Greyhound bus going north.

The seven subsequent months he spent in Erie constituted the only time in his seventy-nine-year life that Myron lived outside the greater Pittsburgh area. It was an interesting if not exactly rewarding experience. Myron earned the grand sum of $38.50 per week, lived at the YMCA, and survived on baloney sandwiches until he got his first paycheck.

He was initially assigned to sports, mostly answering the phones each night and collecting scores from the area's numerous bowling leagues. After a few weeks he requested a switch to the city desk, only to land on the paper's graveyard shift, staying in the office until three in the morning doing little except checking police reports and working Erie's small-time crime and public disturbances into stories for the *Times*. "A loud domestic argument could land the noisy couple two paragraphs in the newspaper," he remembered.

When he got the chance to leave the newsroom, though, he turned out some funny work. He had a blast when an old Squirrel Hill neighbor joined the local Minor League baseball team, the Erie Sailors. He didn't want to ruin the morale of anybody on the team, he wrote, "but I cannot resist the temptation to divulge that pitcher Jack Flynn is known in his Pittsburgh camping grounds as 'Itchy.' His fellow players are requested to show consideration and not plant this tag on the guy, as he doubtless spent considerable effort in trying to lose it."

When a woman with a traveling exhibit on atomic bombs rolled through town, Myron was right on it: "The huge trailer truck unit was set up for three days this week in peaceful Perry Square. A loudspeaker blared phonograph records of 'Dancing in the Dark' and 'Chattanoogie Shoe Shine Boy' as a voice invited the people to come in and see the weapon which one day might blow them into many assorted pieces."

His best piece for the *Times* came after a June day when he checked out the beach at Presque Isle, on the shores of Lake Erie. He boarded a bus for the isle, planning to enjoy an afternoon of gentlemanly ease, he wrote. However, at "three humans per square foot," the bus was a mite crowded, so he got off early. "Disembarking at Cemetery Road, I found to my dismay that I was still quite a ways from the beach, so I thumbed a ride. This did not turn out to be quite so bad, as there is nothing more down-to-earth than a ride in a 1926 grocery truck."

Upon reaching his destination, he reported:

> I got into my bathing trunks, a fine figure of a man at 128 pounds, five feet four inches, and sashayed on down to the beach where I was fortunate to find a pleasant spot decorated by only a dozen or so rocks.
>
> Having long been an addict of yoga, I lay there with a contentment unmatched by Charles Laughton in "The Beachcomber" [a 1938 movie about a beach bum].
>
> This was really living.
>
> But inasmuch as all good things must end, I reluctantly prepared, about 15 minutes later, to return home.

Myron spent only seven months in Erie, but the paper would claim him as one of its own for at least forty years thereafter as his fame expanded.

His tenure there ended in August, when he received a telegram from Joe Shuman at the *Post-Gazette* saying that the paper had an opening for a general assignment reporter. Myron finished up his last shift in Erie at 2 a.m. and caught the 3 a.m. Greyhound heading south. He'd be a Pittsburgher forevermore.

THE WAY MYRON told the story, on his first day at the *Post-Gazette*, Joe Shuman led him to an open cubicle and announced, "First thing we've got to do is find a byline for you."

Taken aback, Myron said, "Pardon me?"

Shuman explained that the paper already had several Jewish reporters and several others whose names could be perceived as Jewish, pointing at a city desk reporter named Jack Weisgerber. It wouldn't do to have too many Jewish-sounding bylines in the paper, he explained.

Shuman picked up a thick phone book and said, "Kopelman, huh? Let's see if we can find something resembling that."

He flipped the book open to the *c*'s and ran his finger down the page, landing on Cope.

"That's it—that's your byline, Myron Cope," he said, making no attempt to solicit Myron's opinion on the issue. Myron surmised that Shuman went to the *c*'s rather than the *k*'s because the former was more likely to turn up names of Anglo-Saxon origin.

"Today, of course, no editor would dare suggest to an employee that he change his byline for purposes of disguising his or her religion, race or ethnicity; litigation would follow," Myron wrote in his autobiography. But in 1951, being the new guy on the job, being grateful just to *have* a real newspaper job, Myron went along with his boss's edict.

Later in life Myron made noise that he resented the name change. "I greatly disliked the surprise Joe Shuman had sprung," he wrote. But the fact is Myron's buddies had called him Kope or Kopey since high school. His column at Allderdice was titled Kope's Komments. The *Pitt News* even referred to him as Kope in a headline when he won the annual "yogi" contest for being the most accurate prognosticator of college football games. And it took no genius to see that Myron Cope was a shorter, punchier byline than Myron Kopelman.

Less than four years after Shuman imposed the change on him, Myron moved to formalize it in May 1955, filing a petition with the Court of

Common Pleas of Allegheny County. The court approved the petition the following month. Legally, he was now Myron Sidney Cope.

In his early years at the *Post-Gazette*, Myron toiled on the city desk, writing obituaries, helping with layouts and headlines, and doing anything else that needed doing. About three months in, the paper's managing editor asked him—told him—to swap places with another recent hire, a sports-desk writer whom the paper wanted to try out as a copy editor. Myron, who as noted liked the action of the city room, was initially disgruntled by the move. He loved sports and loved the idea of covering big-city, Major League teams after dealing with bowling-mad Erie. The problem was the *Post-Gazette* sportswriters. The way Myron saw it, the city room was a beehive, the sports department a den of sloths.

He didn't hold back his views in his autobiography. "Almost the entire sports staff, I judged, had been working there at least twenty years, showing no remote grasp of grammar, let alone any flair for writing. They were likeable fellows who in one way or another had obtained a job there," he wrote. One could not blame them for hanging onto a steady job, he added—but that didn't mean they earned their keep.

In Myron's view, the problems began at the top, with PG sports editor and chief sports columnist Al Abrams. Abrams, a jowly, thick-eyebrowed fellow who slicked back his hair and dressed in sharp-looking suits, was known as sociable man-about-town and a fixture at sports banquets. He is credited with originating the Dapper Dan charity campaign that has raised millions for Pittsburgh-area nonprofits over the decades. But in Myron's opinion, Abrams had no talent for writing. Most of the time his column consisted of one- and two-sentence gossipy sports notes, tied together by ellipses. "When Al attempted a full-length essay on a newsworthy issue," Myron said, "he usually lapsed into intolerable dullness, and he surely knew it."

To sidestep his weakness, according to Myron, Abrams would sometimes wander into the city room, rummage through out-of-town newspapers, find a sports column he liked, make a handful of changes, and run it as his own—a serious allegation, but one that nobody came forth to challenge when Myron raised it in the early 2000s, years after Abrams's death.

Facing no pressure to produce great work, certain reporters—Myron singled out PG veterans Fred P. Alger and Jack Sell in particular—were content to stay at their desks and collect news passively by phone. Longtime Steelers publicist Joe Gordon confirms Myron's observations about Sell, a friend of Art Rooney's who covered the team for decades. "Sell was a throwback to the old-time reporters, did no enterprise," he says. "When I came to work for the Steelers [in 1969], I would call Jack Sell at the end of practice, tell him what happened. He came to practice only one day a week. He was a nice guy and all that, but he was from the old school where reporters very seldom left the newspaper."

Alger, in Myron's view, was distinguished mainly by his habit of spitting his chewing tobacco at the spittoon parked next to Myron's desk. Sometimes, Myron recalled, Alger's aim was off, and he'd hit the cuffs of Myron's trousers. Requests to spit elsewhere were ignored until Myron purchased chewing tobacco of his own and fired back, scoring several hits on Alger's pants. The encounter had the unintended effect of turning Myron into a consumer of Mail Pouch tobacco, adding to a heavy smoking habit that he'd picked up as a teenager. By his midtwenties at the latest, Myron was a full-blown nicotine addict—not an unusual thing to be in mid-1950s America, when one could scarcely turn on a radio or TV without hearing ads touting the wonders of various cigarette brands, but an unhealthy habit just the same, one that would persist to the end of his days.

Despite the disdain for his colleagues' work habits, Myron would stay in the *Post-Gazette* sports department for eight-plus years, until the dawn of the next decade. In many ways, he enjoyed his work. He got to attend all the sporting events and press conferences he desired. His superiors recognized his writing talent and gave it space to flourish. And after growing up in Ellis Kopelman's household, he, like his colleagues, valued having a steady job.

"My dream of the ultimate in those days was to be a sports columnist and make ten thousand dollars a year," he later said.

As it had on the *Pitt News*, Myron's talent quickly shone through. He earned his first byline in November 1951 and was soon writing short features that showed off his funny bone. One of the earliest was on the prison football team at the Allegheny County Workhouse. “The team owns the distinction of having four tackles on its starting [offensive] line,” he wrote. “No squad member would vilify a teammate by calling him a guard.”

Ahead of the Pitt-WVU football game, Myron mentioned Billy Reynolds, a Pitt player who hailed from St. Marys, West Virginia. “Folks down that way wailed when he chose Pitt,” he wrote. “They cried that Pitt gave him a Cadillac. Strangely enough, Billy is still having his shoes resoled as often as the next pedestrian.”

Regarding a local boxer, Billy Wagner, Myron wrote, “The young lightweight has an angelic face that makes him look like a choir boy more than most choir boys and a pair of fists which rap out a tune bearing none of the gentleness of Ave Maria.”

By early ’52 Myron was gaining notoriety as the hot new sportswriter in town. Duquesne University’s journalism association named him the “outstanding young reporter of 1951” and honored him at a banquet at the Parkway Hotel where he received a scroll and a $50 prize. In a more casual manner, he was honored by the same people again just a couple of months later and met one of his long-term friends in the bargain.

Frank Haller was an editor of the Duquesne newspaper, the *Duke*, and was set to graduate that spring. He and some buddies, “a group of twelve bums,” in Haller’s words, wanted to mark the occasion. “One guy said, ‘What we need to do is have a graduation dinner for ourselves but get one of the TV stars and honor them,’” Haller recalled to sportswriter Chuck Finder. “[Someone said,] ‘No . . . they’re never going to come to that.’ Somebody said, ‘Let’s get somebody who’s the best new face in town.’ Another guy said, ‘Hey, Myron Cope.’ We had it at a bar. I forget where. Drinks and burgers. We took up a collection among ourselves. We got twenty-one dollars and fifty-five cents. And Myron was great.”

Years later Haller would be a neighbor of Myron’s in Scott Township, south of the city, and would call in to Myron’s talk show as a character, a spoiled ex-athlete named “Lance Boyle.” He’d also help Myron launch an annual golf tournament to benefit the Autism Society of Pittsburgh. By the time Haller died in 2013, the tournament had raised over $1.5 million for the charity.

Around the same time, Myron met another longtime friend, one with a considerably higher public profile. Joining the *Post-Gazette* sports staff had only encouraged Myron's fixation with the Steelers. Before going to work around 4 p.m., he'd sometimes hang out at the team's offices in the Union Trust Building, a ten-story edifice in downtown Pittsburgh with an ornate mansard roof. During one of those visits, he was introduced to Art Rooney.

The greeting, in all likelihood, was engineered by the Steelers' owner himself. "Chief was terrific," Myron told Jim O'Brien, using Rooney's nickname. "He always befriended young newspaper guys. He'd stop in the pressroom, and he'd see a new face, and he'd go over and introduce himself. He'd say, 'Hi, I'm Art Rooney. What's your name? You're new around here, aren't you?' The new kid would be overwhelmed that the owner was talking to him. And then Art would ask all kinds of questions about where the kid came from, who his folks were, what nationality he was, what church he went to. He always had a soft spot for newspaper guys."

In future years Myron would interview Rooney at length several times—for a *Saturday Evening Post* article, for his book *The Game That Was*, and for his WTAE radio show less than three weeks before Rooney died. But Myron rejected any suggestion that the Steelers' owner was ingratiating himself to win good media coverage or publicity. "He was just doing what came natural. He was just a terrific guy," Myron said. As evidence, he pointed to a time early in his *PG* tenure when he booked a winter vacation in Miami and happened to mention his plans while loafing around the Steelers' offices. Rooney overheard the conversation and asked for Myron's contact info in Florida. A few weeks later, to Myron's surprise, Rooney actually called him in Miami, drove by, and picked him up for an afternoon at the Hialeah Racetrack.

Rooney's famous horse sense wasn't working that day, and he bet on several losers. Finally, before the eighth race, he followed a recommendation from Myron to place money on a gray horse racing at twenty-to-one odds. The horse came in first, and a happy Rooney scooped up his winnings.

"I was an inside man, a desk guy at the *Post-Gazette* then. I was nothing," Myron said. "Who'd expect the owner of the pro football team in town to come by and pick me up and take me out for a day at the races? He was just amazing that way. I'll never forget his generosity."

IF ONLY HIS SUPERIORS at the *Post-Gazette* had been so generous. As the months and years passed by, Myron made himself a key part of the staff, writing eighty to one hundred bylined articles per year. Within four months of his arrival, editors allowed him to write a weekly entry for the Roamin' Around column, rotated among all the sports reporters. However, he faced resistance inside the building. When the paper's managing editor voiced approval of Myron's features, a jealous colleague wrote an anonymous postcard to the editor suggesting that Myron be fired (fortunately, the editor laughed). When the sports department's second-in-command Gil Remley told Myron to write two columns per week, Abrams overruled him and cut the youngster back to one, in what Myron saw as a pure act of turf protection.

Meanwhile, the PG sportswriters were so entrenched in their positions that Myron could never land a "beat"—a team or sport that he covered regularly. "They used me as a swing man on other people's days off," he explained to Roy McHugh in 1984. "If the college writer was off, I'd write the college story. If the pro writer was off, I'd write the pro story, and so on. And they threw a few feature stories at me. The system was you had to wait for a beat until somebody died."

Between the "system" and the general futility of Pittsburgh's sports teams in that era, morale in the PG sports department hovered between low and underwater. Jack Sell had become "professionally numb" after years of covering hopeless Steelers teams, according to Steelers public relations director Ed Kiely. "He felt no emotional involvement with the team," wrote Art Rooney Jr. in a biography of his father. "Going to the games was a job, nothing more."

Equally dispirited was one of Myron's best friends on the staff, Dan McGibbeny. A dozen years older than Myron, "McGib" had joined the *Post-Gazette* shortly after World War II and would stay until 1980. But one night in the late '50s, McGibbeny told his younger colleague that he was merely going through the motions of his job. Myron, always a hard worker who insisted on high standards, urged McGibbeny—probably over drinks, probably with some yelling—to overhaul his attitude. Shortly thereafter, McGibbeny sent an undated letter that Myron kept for the rest of his life.

> Cope:
> Without any horse manure, fan fare, etc., etc., I want you to know that I sincerely appreciate what I accepted as your friendly advice the other night. I'm not too old yet to develop the attitude that I can't learn anything from a younger man or as you described it with unbecoming modesty, a "junior partner." Your advice prompted me to re-evaluate my attitude which has gone sour over the last seven or eight years. However, this isn't intended now as an excuse, although I had talked myself into plenty of alibis until you prompted me to start thinking of the every-day blessings that I believe all of us have a tendency to overlook.
>
> In the past—back before the past seven or eight years—I became a workhorse and when it became evident to the higher echelon that I could handle the load with at least moderate ability I was looked upon with favor. . . . However, because of a series of broken promises, etc. etc., etc., (you've gone through some of the disappointments which the etc., etc., etc. represent) I started to fluff off, if you follow me.
>
> Well, in taking stock last night, after your suggestions, I realized that sensitivity has no place in this business. The pay is good, the hours aren't exactly appetizing, but it is the best newspaper to work for in this city . . .
>
> We haven't always seen things in the same light, as you no doubt will readily agree. But this is one of those times you hit the ball smack on the beam. And although we disagree in theory on some things, I believe now that we have a mutual friendship.

Years later, Myron would give ample attention on his radio show to the Triangles, Pittsburgh's entry in the World Team Tennis league, which happened to be managed by McGibbeny's son, Dan Jr.

Facing professional barriers at the *PG*, Myron began to seek other outlets for his writing. He had taken a stab at fiction while in Erie, composing a tale about a professional wrestler and a woman he convinces to join him in his act. He mailed the story off to *Sir!*, a New York–based magazine aimed at the same horny-male audience that *Playboy* would soon exploit to grand success. To his surprise, it was published. To his dismay, he wasn't paid. Multiple letters demanding the $50 that *Sir!* had promised him went unanswered.

Finally, the poor but infuriated Myron decided to hitchhike—"a perfectly safe way to get from here to there in that era," he recalled—the 430 miles from Erie to Manhattan. Upon arriving, he stormed into the offices of *Sir!* and demanded his compensation. The publisher, impressed by Myron's gumption, paid him on the spot. Myron cashed the check and hitchhiked back to Erie but swore off fiction and small, sleazy magazines.

The following year, 1952, he branched out again, writing an article for *Pittsburgh Spectator*, a would-be regional magazine that lasted only two issues. A bigger breakthrough came in 1954, when he connected with *The Sporting News*, a venerable weekly newspaper that billed itself as "The Bible of Baseball" but had recently expanded coverage to other sports. The paper employed a vast network of stringers around the country, and Myron became one of its men in Pittsburgh, writing stories about Pitt football, Duquesne basketball, and the Steelers. *The Sporting News* paid about $75 per article, a nice supplement to his PG salary—though it's worth noting that for the majority of the '50s, Myron continued to live with his parents at their home on Alderson Street in Squirrel Hill, with its steep, twenty-seven-step climb up to the front door. The Depression had taught him to be cautious before splurging on a home or apartment of his own.

The next logical step for Myron was to go after the real money pot—magazine writing. Far more than newspapers, magazines in the 1950s were the place that non-fiction writers could make their name and fortunes. About three dozen U.S. magazines boasted circulations of a million readers or more, with the biggest, such as *Life*, *Look*, and the *Saturday Evening Post*, boasting circulations of north of three million. Advertisers showered money on the publications, which, in an era of black-and-white TV and newspapers, were the only way to showcase cars, clothes, edibles, and other products in color to a mass audience. Faced with reams of pages to fill, editors turned to freelance writers to supply content. And some of those stories, inevitably, originated in the world of sports. That's where Myron saw his opening.

In 1955 Myron made his first approach to one of the major publications, *True*, a so-called man's magazine focused on stories about adventure, combat, and athletics. One night while enjoying a beer, he had made the acquaintance of an ex-boxer, Fritzie Zivic. For ten months at the start of the 1940s, Zivic owned the welterweight champion belt after knocking out Henry Armstrong at Madison Square Garden. Fifteen years later he had been reduced to working as a bartender with a busted-flat nose in a saloon across the street from the *Post-Gazette*. But Zivic had another talent: entertaining barflies with stories about how he used illegal tactics like headbutting and below-the-belt punches to win his bouts. A fascinated Myron suggested that he compile the stories for a magazine article and split the proceeds with Zivic.

Zivic agreed, and Myron mailed a draft of the article to *True*. The magazine's sports editor, Donald McKinney, sent back a letter of encouragement, not a yes but not a no. The September 1, 1955, letter sheds light on where Myron's abilities stood as a fledgling twenty-six-year-old writer, while exposing something of the magazine's priorities:

> Dear Mr. Cope,
> We think you have an interesting and provocative theme—that you can't get anywhere in boxing without fighting dirty—but we think you should expand on that theme even more. The background material on Zivic's life is interesting and should be kept in, but we would like to see more anecdotes about how dirty fighting enabled him to win bouts. And more about contemporary fighters who don't stick to the Marquis of Queensbury rules—Sandy Saddler, Willie Pep, even [Rocky] Marciano . . . What Zivic should be doing is explaining one of the facts of life about boxing—it's a rough sport, and the roughest guys get to be champ.
>
> This should be the kind of article that will cause the same kind of stir the Preacher Roe spitball piece caused. We don't want you to soup this up beyond recognition—rather, we want you to build upon what you've already written. Keep what's here, but make the point

> stronger and keep making it throughout the article. . . . You might think of this as a kind of application of the [Leo] Durocher maxim to boxing—"Dirty Fighters Finish on Top"—or something like that.

Earlier that year, former Brooklyn Dodgers pitcher Preacher Roe had caused a minor scandal by admitting in the pages of *True* to use of the illegal spitball pitch. The magazine obviously hoped to generate a similar splash with Zivic's admissions. Myron made the requested changes, though the revisions apparently took a while, as *True* didn't publish the story until June 1958.

In the meantime, Myron, still working for the *Post-Gazette*, attempted another feature on a Pittsburgh athlete, Pirates pitcher Bob Friend. Friend was an above-average starter on many a losing Pirates team but hardly a topic for a national magazine on that alone. Myron found another angle: Friend the financial advisor, recommending stocks and bonds and investments to teammates and others in their orbit. The *Saturday Evening Post* liked it enough to publish it in June 1956, paying Myron a thousand bucks. The story gave Myron official entry into the world of "the slicks," a term for the magazines printed on high-quality, glossy paper.

Over the next few years Myron became a semi-regular for the big national mags, writing mostly about athletes with a Pittsburgh connection, like Pitt-turned-Detroit-Lions linebacker Joe Schmidt, or Lions-turned-Steelers quarterback Bobby Layne, or baseball's 1958 manager of the year, Pirates skipper Danny Murtaugh. The stories, while undoubtedly polished by New York editors, featured Myron's already distinctive voice and flashes of his trademark humor. His best story was probably his *Saturday Evening Post* profile of Pitt basketball superstar Don Hennon, a scoring terror despite being only five feet eight inches tall. Myron found the perfect image to open the piece: "When the Pitt players jogged single file onto the court," he wrote, "they resembled a comb with a broken tooth, for there amid the lean and tall boys trotted one who was broad and short."

The piece was filled with little gems like that. Describing Hennon's personality, Myron wrote, "When interviewed, he blushes so furiously he embarrasses the newspapermen." Regarding Hennon's practice habits, he wrote, "Last summer, Don went to the dirt square [at his house] each night and shot a hundred free throws. His goal was to make every shot, but the best he could do was a paltry eighty-six in a row."

The Hennon piece brought Myron his first real wave of notice and praise. One fan letter came from a competitor, Pat Livingston of the *Pittsburgh Press*: "I just finished reading your story on Hennon. . . . I enjoyed it very much and thought it was excellently and tastefully done. As a matter of fact, I would have to regard it as one of the finest stories of its kind I have ever read."

Penn State sports publicity director James H. Coogan jotted a note to Myron: "Your *Post* article on Hennon is a first-rate job. . . . You should do more and more of this kind writing. Your style is meant for it." Even his boss, Al Abrams, told readers, "Myron Cope's piece on Don Hennon makes for good writing and reading. Don't miss it."

The more four-figure checks he collected (*True* paid him $1,200 for the Zivic piece, though he had to split it with Fritzie), the more Myron began to think about leaving his regular job. August of 1959 marked his eighth anniversary at the *Post-Gazette,* but he still didn't have a regular beat. Some evenings, he was assigned to the paper's latest bright idea—covering Little League baseball action. As he explained to Roy McHugh, the paper

> ran Little League scores in those days, inning by inning and the pitchers and who hit the home runs, and I bore the brunt of it myself, jumping from one phone to another. Then, to go with the scores, a story would have to be written about the highlight game, in which always seemed the same kid, an overgrown twelve-year-old six-footer, had pitched a no-hitter for the seventeenth time that year, hitting three home runs in the bargain.
>
> One night I said to myself, "What am I doing this for?" I had started writing magazine articles . . . sometimes getting paid over one thousand dollars a story. When I went to New York or Philadelphia, where the *Saturday Evening Post* headquarters were, I'd be given a very nice reception by the sports editor and the managing editor. They'd take me to lunch and say, "Let's talk about your next assignment." Then I'd come back to Pittsburgh and scramble around taking Little League scores.

Toward the end of '59, Myron hit a freelance roll, landing one feature in *True* and two in the *Saturday Evening Post*, the big strike being a feature on college basketball star and future NBA Hall of Famer Jerry West—one of Myron's first stories that did not have a Pittsburgh angle. He had finally moved out of his parents' home by then, a late twentysomething getting his first bachelor apartment in Shadyside, an area north of Squirrel Hill with Victorian mansions and an artsy Greenwich Village–style vibe. Between the checks and the newfound freedom, he decided it was time to leave his professional home, too, and become a full-time freelance writer.

He received an encouraging letter from the sports editor of the *Post*, Harry Paxton, who wrote, "Not many people succeed in making a good living this way, but I think you have the ability to be one of the exceptions. And I trust the *Post* will prove to be one of your best markets."

Shortly after New Year's Day 1960, Myron gave notice to the *Post-Gazette* of his impending departure. Al Abrams was not encouraging. For the rest of his life, Myron relished telling the story of how Abrams told him, "Kid, you'll starve. You'll be back in six months."

What Myron always left out was that he *was* back at the newspaper within six months—and that he came back in triumph.

While Myron was establishing himself as a full-time freelancer in 1960, the Pittsburgh Pirates rose up and won the National League pennant for the first time in thirty-three years. Local interest in the team ran red-hot, and Abrams called in Myron to help meet the demand. Myron wrote profiles of Pirates announcer Bob Prince, his old vendor boss Meyer O'Brisky, and several key players, including shortstop Dick Groat and pitcher Wilmer "Vinegar Bend" Mizell (the nickname came from Mizell's hometown in Alabama). When the Pirates clinched the league title in late September, the paper contracted with him to help cover the World Series. Myron would be handling "humor and drama," the *PG* told readers. Behind the scenes, he'd also ghostwrite a daily "player's column" supposedly written by third baseman Don Hoak.

That's how Myron came to be sitting in Forbes Field's rooftop press box the afternoon of October 13, 1960, covering the final game of the Series between the underdog Pirates and baseball's perennial champion, the Mickey Mantle and Yogi Berra–led New York Yankees. The Yankees had outscored the Pirates 46–17 over the first six games, but the Pirates had won all the close ones, forcing a game seven. The Bucs jumped out to an early 4–0 lead, the key blow being a two-run homer from first baseman Rocky Nelson. The Yankees crept back—a home run from Bill Skowron in the fifth, a three-run blast from Berra in the sixth, assorted other hits and RBI, until the Bronx Bombers led 7–4 going into the bottom of the eighth inning.

Trying to rally, the Pirates got a pinch-hit single from Gino Cimoli. Bill Virdon was up next and hit a sharp grounder right at Yankee shortstop Tony Kubek—a tailor-made double-play ball. But Forbes Field itself came to the Pirates rescue. The ball hit something in the infield—a pebble by some accounts, a spike cut in the dirt insisted others—and took the wickedest of hops. Myron's description of the moment: "The ball hopped higher than Kubek had gauged it and struck him full in the Adam's apple. His mouth flew open as if he were trying to scream. He clutched his throat with his hands and sagged backward, like a fighter smashed onto queer street by a right hand."

After a delay, Kubek was replaced by Joe DeMastri, and the rally continued. Dick Groat knocked in Cimoli with a single. A pair of outs advanced Groat to second, Virdon to third. Roberto Clemente hit an infield bouncer that could have been out number three, but he dashed down to first before the Yankees could get off a throw, scoring Virdon. The next batter, catcher Hal Smith, worked a count of two balls, two strikes. Yankees pitcher Jim Coates, going for the strikeout, threw a fastball low—right where Smith liked it, as Myron reported: "Over the left-center wall at the 406-foot mark sailed the ball. It cleared the wall by the height of a tall tree and landed perhaps thirty feet behind the wall in Schenley Park. Smith raced around the bases in long, merry strides. Children leapt into the air. Men and women embraced. Unobjective sportswriters cheered. The Pirates were leading 9–7."

The Pirates were only three outs from winning the Series. But as Myron put it, the Yankees came to bat unready to surrender and scored twice in the top of the ninth to tie the score. The key play came with one out. With Mantle on first and Gil McDougald on third, Berra hit a one-hop scorcher down the first base line. Rocky Nelson speared it and stepped on first to retire Berra. He looked toward second, expecting to see Mantle headed that way. But Mantle had hit the brakes two steps off the first base bag. "Suddenly Mantle darted and dove and then wriggled. Nelson reached for him but had been faked out as though by a halfback," Myron wrote. "Mantle was back at first safely. McDougald, meanwhile, had scored from third and the game was tied, 9–9."

The first Pirates batter in the ninth was Bill Mazeroski. Any self-respecting Pittsburgher knows what happened next.

Final score: Pirates 10, Yankees 9.

When the game was over and the *Post-Gazette* sportswriters quickly divvied up assignments, Myron was given the task of summarizing the twists and turns of the game. Settling down at his typewriter, knowing he had just a few hours to write, Myron began punching out the finest deadline story of his career. The best part was his description of Mazeroski's game-winning home run:

> Mazeroski, blank-faced with a baseball-sized chaw in his jaw, cocked his bat and Terry pumped. A fast ball sizzled past Mazeroski, shoulder high, for a ball.
>
> Terry took his sign from catcher John Blanchard and pumped again. In came the fast ball again. It was high but a touch lower than the last one.
>
> Mazeroski stepped forward, whipped his bat against the ball, and the crowd was on its feet. Berra was chugging to the wall in left center. Mantle was gliding, swiftly but effortlessly, to meet Berra.
>
> Terry stood on the mound watching, his arms limp at his sides. Mazeroski was running hard for first, but watching over his shoulder—watching and hoping. Clearly the ball did not have the power behind it, the unquestionable power, that Hal Smith's drive had.
>
> It was dropping now, close to the left-center field wall. Berra was at the wall, facing it, but looking up, gauging the fall of the baseball. The crowd waited, hushed, for the leap by Berra or the running leap by Mantle, who was drawing near.
>
> But Berra did not leap. Mantle did not leap. The crowd's roar exploded like a bomb. Mazeroski was rounding first, whirling his arms in the air, roaring like a madman to the world, waving his cap over his head.

> He was rounding second and fans were climbing over the railings. He rounded third and the crowd poured down on him like a mob attacking a public enemy. Mazeroski disappeared from sight, smothered by the crowd that swept over him and ran with him and on him as he made his way home.
>
> It was all over.
>
> Ralph Terry walked slowly off the field, head down. There would be no champagne for Ralph Terry. The New York Yankees were dead, buried by a high fast ball.

Terry later said it was a slider but cut Myron some slack—there were no TV monitors in the press box at the time and no instant replay. Myron wrote his piece based on his own observations.

Two days later the paper published a letter from an impressed reader: "Permit me to emphasize Myron Cope's brilliant play-by-play in Friday's issue. It and the entire Friday's *Post-Gazette* has been filed away among my most precious possessions for future posterity."

The same day, Myron got a letter from a local advertising executive for Ketchum Communications, R. J. McCully. "This is a hymn of praise, pure and unadulterated. I think some of the finest writing that has come out of Pittsburgh in the last few years has come from the typewriter of Myron Cope," McCully wrote. "You have a wonderful light touch in your writing. Don't lose it. Congratulations again on what you have done and what you will do."

Myron would never again write regularly for the *Post-Gazette* or any other daily newspaper. He wouldn't need to.

3

The Nut Specialist

It's a chilly fall day, November 1960. Myron Cope drives north through winding, autumn-colored Pennsylvania backroads to the village of Roulette, home to eleven hundred hardy souls living among farms, mountains, bobcats, and bears. Sportswriters don't usually venture up this way, but Myron has an appointment with the town's most noteworthy resident, Don "Tiger" Hoak, third baseman for the Pittsburgh Pirates. A month earlier, the Pirates pulled off their jaw-dropping, against-all-reason upset of the Yankees in the World Series, and magazines are clamoring for stories about the team's stars, of which Hoak is one. Myron motors into town and finds Roulette's lone hotel. It's a simple country establishment—"not exactly the Hilton," in the guest's opinion—but it's the only option, and it'll do for the night.

The next morning Myron gets up and dresses as he would for an interview at, say, a Midtown Manhattan restaurant, in a three-piece herringbone suit. He's getting ready to head out when he hears a loud banging at the door to his room. It's Hoak. Dressed in hunting clothes.

"Come on," he says, "we're going turkey hunting."

Myron knows nothing about turkeys except how they taste. He's a stranger to hunting, to mountains, to any place where creatures that go gobble-gobble spend their time. But he's here, and he's driven 170 miles to do a profile on Hoak, soooo . . .

"All day long we're out there traipsing through the mountains, and they were big mountains I'll tell you, and I'm there in my three-piece suit," Myron remembered. "We spent the whole damn day in the mountains with him going, *Ahnt, Ahnt, Ahnt,* issuing these turkey calls, and no turkeys were saying hello."

The failure to bag a turkey upsets the intense Hoak, who at day's end declares that they will deal with the frustration by drinking. Myron, still suited up for the Manhattan bistro, goes along for that ride, too. "Boy, that was an adventure," he recalled. "The next morning, I wished I never had the adventure."

A bad hotel, a hangover, a presumably ruined herringbone suit—on the surface, it sounds like a dud of a trip. But in the end Myron got what he wanted, an interview with the Pirates third baseman and a story that he could write for a national magazine. "The Toughest Pirate Since Captain Kidd" appeared in the May 1961 issue of *True, the Man's Magazine* and won praise from the small but growing band of Cope fans in the sportswriting world. "If you're a baseball fan in general, a Pirates fan in particular, or just plain appreciate good writing, buy, borrow or beg a copy of the current *True* magazine and relax in an easy chair one of these rainy evenings with Myron Cope's outstanding profile of Don Hoak," wrote one reviewer.

If he saw it, Myron no doubt loved the praise, but he couldn't take the time to curl up in an easy chair. He no longer enjoyed a weekly paycheck from the *Post-Gazette,* and the paper stopped hiring him for short-term projects once the magical 1960 Pirates turned into pumpkins who played sub-.500 ball. He was a full-time freelance writer now, and that meant hustling. His days were filled with gathering information for articles, writing articles, mailing off finished articles, and pitching ideas for even more articles to editors in New York. Some proposals got a yes, some a no, some a counterproposal. He accepted the offers that stoked his interest, that felt doable, and enabled him to pay his bills.

The trolley no longer took him everywhere he needed to go. Now he flew off to California, to Florida, to Puerto Rico, or made drives up to middle-of-nowhere villages like Roulette. Phone talks weren't going to cut it in this line of work. He needed to go places in person, to gather sights, smells, sounds, stories—details that would enable him to draw a captivating, three-dimensional portrait of the person or persons he was being tasked to describe, preferably enlivened with few splashes of humor.

Getting those details meant jotting down notes and committing key moments to memory, for he had no smartphone or even a tape recorder to chronicle what he saw. His notes and perhaps a few newspaper clippings would be the only documents he could reference when he sat down at his Hermes manual typewriter aiming to compose a story long enough to fill several magazine pages (amid the ads) and captivating enough to keep the reader glued to the text. If Myron hit a wall at the typewriter, he'd try writing out an article on paper, longhand. Faster writing implements were not for him. He never warmed up to the electric typewriter and came to regard computers as alien objects.

While Myron could certainly punch out articles on deadline, like his World Series piece, most of the time he wrote slowly. "Writing, for me, was hard work," he explained in a 2003 interview. "I could write well for no more than four hours a day, and then I'd have to knock it off and do paperwork or something. It seemed to me that every sentence had to be crafted, that the writing had to have a rhythm to it, to hold the reader's attention to the end of the piece. And I could spend an entire morning on the first paragraph of my magazine article. I'm not exaggerating. For me, it was like working in a steel mill, except that I could quit after four hours."

In going solo, Myron was attempting a leap that countless writers had tried, most of them falling short. In a 1955 article, *Time* magazine sketched the world of the freelance writer. Such writers provided more than half the stories that appeared in the most popular U.S. mags, the article said. One editor called them "the backbone of the industry." But competition for spots in the top publications was fierce. In a single week, the *Saturday Evening Post* might get three hundred unsolicited manuscripts.

If a writer broke through, the rewards were significant. *Collier's* magazine paid an average of $1,500 per article. *Reader's Digest* paid $2,000. The *Post* might go as high as $3,000, which was enough, before taxes, to purchase a nice new Ford Thunderbird or Chevy Bel Air.

The vast majority of writers never saw checks that big. Of the multitudes who had tried freelancing magazine articles, "only about seventy or eighty in the U.S. earn upwards of ten thousand dollars a year," the unbylined *Time* article said. "The successful full-time free-lancer who depends only on the articles he sells to magazines is a rare breed."

But by 1961 Myron had joined the breed. He wrote two pieces for the *Post* that year, three for *True,* three for *Sport* magazine, and one for *Parade,* a weekly supplement stuffed into the thick Sunday newspapers. Late the previous year he had landed his first article in one of the newer mags, *Sports Illustrated,* a publication giving the increasingly sports-crazy American public a weekly dose of superb writing on their favorite games and athletes, accompanied by striking photography.

Myron's first article for *SI* was a signpost for his writing career. The subject was neither an athlete nor photogenic. Carroll "Beano" Cook did have a colorful personality, however—a quality that by now, Myron knew was more essential to a good article than simple athletic skill. Cook, later an ESPN college football commentator, was deemed magazine worthy because of his work as publicist for the University of Pittsburgh sports department. He approached his job like an old-time boxing manager, Myron explained in the November 7, 1960, article, and didn't mind publicly insulting Pitt's opponents if he thought that would grab newspaper space and sell tickets.

> Beano has berated West Point brass, labeled Penn State Coach Rip Engle a crybaby and denounced West Virginia University fans as incompetent drivers who create Saturday afternoon traffic jams. Police ejected him from the press table during a basketball game at Duke University when he directed a blunderbuss charge of insults at the referee, and the Penn State publicist threatened to have him censured for having flooded State territory with literature ridiculing, of all things, State's wrestling team.
>
> "In short," adds [Pitt athletic director] Frank Carver, whose placid charm is the antithesis of Beano's unruly enthusiasm, "he is the best press agent in the business."

SI editors liked the piece enough to put it on page 6, the lead article in that week's edition. It was the start of a fruitful relationship between Myron and *Sports Illustrated* that would encompass some forty articles over twenty years.

A few months later, writing for *True*, Myron turned out another gem, a piece on Villanova University basketball coach Al Severance. Severance was known for being absentminded, long-winded, lacking in technical know-how, hopelessly behind the times strategy-wise, yet turning out winning teams year after year. Myron stuffed the story with tales of Severance's eccentricities, like the time he told his team to play a 2-1-3 zone defense—that's six players—or the night he brought his wife and children to a game at the Villanova Field House then forgot about them after the game. When he drove back to the house and let himself in, he called out, "Anybody home?"

The best part was Myron's description of Severance himself: "Alexander Girard Severance is an erect man of fifty-three with bushy white hair, a face that is in shape and color not unlike a kerosene construction lantern, a splattered nose that supports horn-rimmed glasses, a stentorian voice, and a repertory of oratorical platitudes that spill one upon the other in a purple flood. Altogether, he looks and acts like a caricature of a U.S. Senator who has been punched in the mush by an angry constituent."

Mush was Myron's personal slang for one's face, especially the most punchable part—the mouth.

As the years rolled on, Myron would also write plenty of stories on the superstars of the sports world—Elgin Baylor and Red Auerbach in basketball, Arnold Palmer and Lee Trevino in golf, Rocky Marciano in boxing, Frank Robinson in baseball. A 1962 piece for *Sport* on Jim Brown, then at his peak as the NFL's dominant running back, led to Myron's first book, *Off My Chest*, a revealing biography in which Brown aired his grievances over racism in college football, the NFL, and the world in general—though in retrospect, the voice of Jim Brown channeled through the pen of Myron Cope comes across as less than authentic.

But Myron found writing about superstars less than satisfying. Too many were keen on hiding their personalities or just didn't seem to have them outside of uniform. The guys who were honestly, loudly, proudly their quirky selves—those were the ones he wanted to profile. In time, he carved out a niche. A *True* editor dubbed Myron "our nut specialist," a designation that he warmly embraced.

"I have been a biographer of a species that ballplayers call 'flakes,'" Myron wrote in his 1968 compendium of "nut stories," titled *Broken Cigars*. Flakes, he explained, often leave their colleagues uneasy, wondering what kind of disturbance they'll cause next. "Such men are seldom palatable to the fan who places sports on a pedestal alongside his religion, for they create disorder wherever they go," he wrote. "In one way or another, they are men of excesses. But they are as much the lure of sports as Mickey Mantle's home run totals and Bart Starr's touchdown passes."

Over time Myron acquired a stable of his favorite flakes that he'd return to in multiple articles and later as guests on his radio show. Prominent among them: Bo Belinsky, hard-throwing LA Angels pitcher who won his first five starts in the Major Leagues, including a no-hitter, but whose real talent was chasing and catching beautiful babes; Belinsky's teammate Dean Chance, a superior and almost absurdly uber-confident pitcher who was nevertheless glad to play Robin to Belinsky's Batman; Greg "Fido" Murphy, a Chicago Bears scout who was convinced that he was the most brilliant mind professional football had ever seen and liked to share his belief with whoever was standing nearby; and Mossie Murphy (no relation to Fido), a short, fat, loud Duquesne University fan who appointed himself the basketball team's chief recruiter and cheerleader, despite the school's unease with his even showing up at games.

From the Mossie Murphy piece:

> When Mossie teams up with coach [Red] Manning on recruiting trips . . . the two men match as beautifully as ham and milk of magnesia. Manning is a pale, austere, tight-lipped man of thirty-four who has been linked in appearance and vivaciousness to [Soviet diplomat] Andrei Gromyko. He dines on whole-wheat toast and skim milk, admonishes wives of his friends to cook wheat-germ into their meat loaves, and when asked by his wife to pick up cigarettes on the way home, purposely forgets. Manning also regards Mossie's girth with revulsion. "Red absolutely tortured me to go to a doctor for a checkup," says Mossie. "So I finally

went and the doctor found I have a heart condition. Red was delighted! He's rooting for me to die."

The two Murphy pieces were published by *Sports Illustrated.* When Myron visited the *SI* offices in New York, an editor told him, "We refuse to believe in the existence of whatever Murphy that you intend to sell us next."

On occasion, Myron's love for nuts and the top magazines' love for superstars converged, and Myron got to train his talents on men who were becoming legends—usually in their own mind as well as the public's. His first encounter with such a figure came in 1962, when *True* sent him to Miami to talk to a rising young heavyweight who was rattling the boxing world with fast hands and footwork and an even faster mouth. People remember him today as Muhammad Ali, but at the time, he didn't mind shouting out his birth name, Cassius Clay.

Myron needed just a few sentences to capture the twenty-year-old Clay and his belief that he would soon be champion:

> Cassius is, as a matter of fact, so certain of his destiny that he speaks of it at least twenty times a day, in case anyone has not heard him. The very thought of winning the title lights up his cherubic, walnut-colored face; his great brown eyes twinkle and he flashes a boyish smile that would warm the heart of a mortgage banker. Restlessly impatient for the great day, he shadow boxes as he walks the streets, pummeling the air with short rights and lefts. He punches away furiously while sitting in taxis and riding trains. "Floyd Patterson must fall!" he cries.

Clay found Myron entertaining as well, nicknaming him Mickey Rooney after the famous but very short actor. Cope and Clay shared a twenty-eight-hour train ride together to Louisville, Kentucky, Clay's hometown and the site of his next bout. "It was an experience I'll tell you. That kid never shut up," Myron remembered in 2005. "We'd go back to the dining car, go through a series of coach cars to get there, and he'd be behind me, shadow boxing . . . 'Watch my form, Mickey Rooney!' And when we went to bed, we had sleeping berths on the opposite sides of the aisle, he'd open the curtain, reach over and open my curtain, and say 'I just wrote a poem,

Mickey Rooney!' And he'd read me some darn poem and I couldn't sleep. It was terrible—but it was fun, and it was great material for a writer."

A great writer given great material knows how to produce a great article. That's what Myron did—did so well that because of the Clay profile, Myron won the prestigious E. P. Dutton Prize for the best magazine sports writing of 1962. The prize carried an award of $250.

A few years later *Sports Illustrated* sent Myron to Puerto Rico to interview the Pirates' star right fielder, Roberto Clemente. Clemente, then thirty-one years old, was known for his multiple batting titles, his unmatched throwing arm, and his immense pride in his abilities. Myron, however, focused on a more intriguing angle: Clemente's tendency to sound like the testy, battered survivor of an eight-car pileup on the Pennsylvania turnpike. Sitting in the vast living room of Clemente's resplendent San Juan home, he heard the future Hall of Famer complain about a wandering disc in his lower back, a wayward disk in his upper back, chronic brain-pounding headaches, the pain in his left heel caused by an ailing Achilles tendon, and intractable, sleeping-pill-resistant insomnia. "By all odds," he wrote, "Roberto's most exotic infirmity struck him after the 1964 season, when he fell desperately ill in Puerto Rico. [His physician] Dr. Buso is not certain to this day whether Roberto contracted autumnal malaria barnstorming in Santo Domingo or had picked up a systemic paratyphoid infection from the hogs on a small farm he owns, but Roberto himself knows what he had. 'Both,' he says."

Myron reported that Clemente endured periods of delirium and stupor and lost twenty-three pounds. But "alas, none of the Pirates had been in Puerto Rico and been an eyewitness. When Robert reported to spring camp and began cracking line drives, all hands agreed that if he had had malaria, they wanted some."

Rob Fleder served as executive editor at *Sports Illustrated* for a good chunk of the 1990s and 2000s. In that capacity he began rereading stories from the magazine's early years for a series of books celebrating *SI*'s history. Naturally, he ran across some of Myron's pieces and came away highly impressed. "He had a great eye for the telling detail, of course, and his language was elegant and precise, but without the slightest hint of pretension or self-consciousness," Fleder says. "He could paint a true picture that might not be flattering to say the least, but without any hint of meanness or hostility. He could be scathingly funny—jocular and incisive at the same time."

Myron's most celebrated piece for *SI* was probably the March 1967 profile he did of sportscaster Howard Cosell. Within a few years, Cosell's staccato cadence, verbose commentary and credo of "telling it like it is" would become familiar to tens of millions via *Monday Night Football*, the NFL's first weekly showcase on primetime television. In '67 he was a well-known but not yet truly famous sports commentator and ABC boxing announcer, notable for being one of the few in his profession who referred to the former Cassius Clay by his new name, Muhammad Ali, and who also defended Ali when the champ refused to be inducted into the U.S. military during the Vietnam War. Many found Cosell insightful and entertaining. Many others found him aggravating as hell. All kept listening. He was impossible to ignore.

SI editors asked Myron to profile Cosell in his natural habitat, New York City. Myron spent about a week there, hanging out with his subject at his house, office, studios, and favorite bar. Myron recalled that when he returned home to write the piece, he got repeated calls from Cosell asking how the story was coming along and adding such comments as, "You have never had a better subject, have you? Tell me the truth now, you have never had a more colorful personality to write about, have you?"

Myron, playing along, told Cosell that the piece was coming along beautifully and added, "You are indeed an interesting and electrifying man."

The ego stroking almost overloaded Ma Bell's phone lines, but Cosell might have had a point. When *SI* celebrated its first half century in 2004, it named Myron's profile one of the best in the magazine's history.

Myron opened the piece with Cosell sitting at the bar fondling a martini, wondering how a man of towering intellect and integrity such as himself managed to survive in an industry peopled by pretty-faced ex-jocks and fence-straddling play-by-play men who lived in fear of offending sponsors. Myron quoted him: "There's one thing about this business. There is no place in it for talent. That's why I don't belong. I lack sufficient mediocrity."

Cosell's belief—not unfounded, by any means—was that he brought the ethics of journalism to sportscasting. Myron described him as a truth teller, an opinionated lone wolf, at a time when most on-air talent shied away from direct criticism of teams, coaches, and athletes. Still, Cosell's self-importance was something to behold, and Myron illustrated that throughout the story: "Cosell himself points out that when he walks into the Yankee clubhouse, for example, manager Ralph Houk at once turns his way, ignoring the newspapermen around him. 'I'm sensitive to this situation and embarrassed by it,' Cosell says. Somehow, his words translate to mean he's delighted by it."

Myron closed the piece with Cosell going through a minor professional crisis. That morning, a radio station in an American Football League city had informed ABC that it was dropping Cosell's radio show because it didn't like one of his commentaries about AFL football. An outraged Cosell wondered, aloud, what the world was coming to. "Are people so juvenile that you can't tell the truth in sports?" he shouted. This wasn't politics, this was sports—the toy department, Cosell called it. "I don't take myself that seriously," he added.

But in the next breath, he began expounding on his own significance, in the third person:

> "ABC has been the only network to permit a Howard Cosell, and that's why Howard Cosell is important. That's why Howard Cosell is a story. If ever there was a trailblazer, if ever a broadcaster sought to bring sports out of the juvenile, out of the banal—this you see, is my mission. I have been an electronic first," Cosell declared, "and I don't mean that egotistically."
>
> The electronic first gazed at the ceiling, as if the trails that he blazed were etched in the beams for him to see.
>
> "Yes," he at last declared, "When you get right down to it, I am a hero."

The story is Rob Fleder's favorite Cope piece for *SI*. "The Howard Cosell profile remains a classic, because it was a character writing about a character," he says. Myron, he explains, excelled at writing mini-portraits of his subjects that were "authoritative, but also stylish. It was the combination of the substance and his voice that came through in the writing."

Fleder said he particularly likes a line in the story where Myron said Cosell's long nose and pointed ears "loom over his gin in the fashion of a dive bomber swooping in with fighter escort."

"There's stuff like that everywhere, running like lodes of gold through Myron's *SI* stories," he says. "Beautiful, hilarious prose. As Peter King put it in his introduction to [the *SI* anthology] *Great Football Writing*, 'Cope went on to national fame as the Steelers' radio color guy, but boy, could he write.'"

NOT AS FLAKY BUT equally prominent in Myron's writing were several members of the early 1960s Steelers. Myron didn't hang around the Steelers' players much after dark during his *Post-Gazette* days; he was working a lot of evening shifts and still living with his parents. Now, with the freedom to set his own schedule and return to a Shadyside bachelor pad, he embraced the local nightlife, as defined by the Steelers players and their unquestioned leader on and off the field, Bobby Layne.

Layne had arrived in Pittsburgh in 1958 as something of a savior. The team had not enjoyed a winning season in nine years when coach Buddy Parker acquired the thirty-one-year-old quarterback from the Lions in an early-season trade. In Detroit, Layne had led the Lions to two NFL championships and helped them win a third as a part-timer. Now he rallied the Steelers to a 7-4-1 record, the second-best in the team's choppy history. But when practices and games were done, Layne needed to unwind, as Myron noted in a 1959 article for *Sport*: "Bobby cannot sit in a hotel room and look at the walls. Driven by a restless sociability, he mixes well in all company. He is a frequent dinner companion of the Right Reverend Austin Purdue, Episcopal bishop of Pittsburgh. Unlike some players, he likes to talk football. He also digs good jazz, and when so doing, naturally does not ask the waiter to bring him a glass of milk. In any case, he circulates without regard to the hour when small children and large athletes are supposed to be tucked in."

Eschewing milk had its consequences. Layne once crashed his car into one of Pittsburgh's trolleys. Trolleys, for the uninitiated, run on rails embedded in the street. But when police arrived at the crash scene, Layne insisted it was the trolley that had jumped its lane.

The most frequent hangout for Layne and fellow Steelers was Dante's, a bar and restaurant in Brentwood, six miles south of downtown, near the Steelers' practice site at county-run South Park. When Parker declared an end to the day's drills and film sessions, many players would drive over to the lounge to get a few drinks, meet women, and hang out with pals. The establishment was helmed by one Dante Sartorio, described by Myron as having "an ear-to-ear smile and large doe eyes that spread good cheer throughout the joint." Aesthetically, Dante's was nothing special—a darkened room with a dining area in back and a long bar in front manned by a red-jacketed bartender. But for Myron, for a while, it was almost a home away from home.

"It was the 'Cheers' of Pittsburgh," Myron told sports historian Jim O'Brien. "Everybody knew your name. There were so many regulars, and it was the football hangout. Dante was a very congenial guy, a swell guy. . . . He could get along with athletes and he knew how to look after them and how to talk around them." That meant, among other things, using code names when talking about Layne to protect his privacy; shooing out hookers, bookies, and other types who could land players in hot water; and discouraging the presence of "yonkos," a term used to describe a yappy bar patron who bothers everybody around him, especially if that person is a celebrity.

When it came to Layne, Myron himself was a little starstruck and would put up with tongue lashings he wouldn't tolerate from anyone else. He recalled the encounters in *The Game That Was*, a book of interviews with early NFL players that grew out of a highly acclaimed article he wrote for *Sports Illustrated*.

> Surrounded by teammates and cronies, [Layne] enjoyed telling a story or hearing one, but there was one surefire way to plunge him into an ugly mood. One needed only to mention the press. The blood would rush to his face, and he would launch into a tirade that rambled on and on. . . . Although he had a scattering of close friends among the sportswriting fraternity, he saw the press as one great mass of gossip-mongers waiting to feed on his traffic tickets and nightclub celebrations.

His argument was that the press had no consideration for the feelings of his wife and two sons. On one occasion, while the two of us sat in a parked car outside his apartment at 3 a.m., he stated his argument plaintively, keeping a grip on his temper. But at the table in Dante's, he sometimes would turn on me, remembering that I was a member of the press, and denounce me in the strongest possible terms. I would leave the table and go to the bar. The next night he would beckon me to his table, and when I refused, he would insist. Finally, I would approach the table. He would utter the beginnings of an apology, but then his pride would stop him and again he would explode with a denunciation of me. I would return to the bar.

Even at those times, I always liked him. One does not expect even temperament from genius, whether it be in the field of painting, letters or quarterbacking.

Fortunately, Myron had several other, safer drinking buddies on the early '60s Steelers. It so happened that Myron, now in his early thirties, was about the same age as many of the players. Buddy Parker preferred veterans to young, untested talent, and he traded most of the Steelers' top-round draft picks to get players he felt he could count on. The policy brought mixed results on the field; the Steelers were barely over .500 during the eight years Parker led the team. But his method allowed Myron to fit right in with the Steelers regulars at Dante's, and during his first full year as a freelancer, he became an accepted member of the Aggregation, as the Steelers gang at Dante's was dubbed by another bar patron.

Myron used the access to score articles as well as make friends, and over the next few years, he would write profiles of defensive tackle Ernie Stautner, running back John Henry Johnson, and offensive tackle Charlie Bradshaw, a Pro Bowler whom Steelers fans inexplicably booed and blamed for the team's mid-1960s miseries. But his masterpiece in this vein was a story he penned for *True* called "Pro Football's Gashouse Gang." (Trying to recall the story, Bill Hillgrove gave it a more appropriate title: "The Drinking Man's Choice in the NFL.")

The article concerned the 1963 Steelers, who won only half of their fourteen games but found themselves in the running to win the NFL's

Eastern Division due to an unprecedented three ties, which kept their winning percentage artificially high. The way Myron told the story, Parker made little attempt to enforce a curfew or a general sense of restraint among his players, especially after a midseason loss to the defending champion Packers.

> "These guys choked," growled Buddy Parker. "Maybe they'll play up to their capacity if they're loose and relaxed from here in."
>
> Parker thereupon decided that the Steelers would practice little more than was necessary to remain acquainted with the shape of a football. He ordered his men to concentrate on relaxing. Did the Aggregation dissent? Does a horse object to being led to water?
>
> Following orders faithfully, the Aggregation poured into Dante's and relaxed with all their might. The next Sunday they throttled Cleveland's Jimmy Brown and beat the first-place, milk-drinking Browns.

The season came down to a final game against the Giants in New York. A win would give the Steelers their first-ever division title. Most of the players prepared for the game under coach Dante, with one major exception. Quarterback Ed Brown, who had taken over the position when Layne retired at the end of the '62 season, decided to abstain for the week. For most quarterbacks, clearing the brain of alcohol is a good thing. In Myron's view, the move spelled doom for the Steelers: "His body well rested, his insides dry as a temperance union president's, his head disgustingly clear, he totally lost his timing and sangfroid. Time and again he overthrew receivers who had no one between them and the goal line. In short, Brownie had trained himself into the most miserable performance of his career."

Video footage available on YouTube suggests that the loss wasn't entirely Brown's fault. In the first quarter he completed an on-target pass to Gary Ballman, who ran it down to the 3-yard line, only to get hit and fumble the ball a step outside the end zone. On the other hand, Brown's final stats—only thirteen completed passes in thirty-three attempts, along with three interceptions—are those of a man whose aim had deserted him.

True published the story in September 1964 to general praise. The only people not happy, Myron remembered, were the Steelers' players.

"I wrote what I perceived to be a very humorous story but the players reacted badly to it," he said. "I walked into Dante's and they started calling me names you wouldn't believe. After they get done calling me all these rotten names, names you couldn't print in a newspaper, I walk up to Brownie and I said 'What about you, Brownie? If anybody's got a beef, you do.'"

According to Myron, Brown said his mother had verified the description of her son.

"She said she read the article and was very angry," Myron recalled. "Then she poured a martini, read it a second time and said, 'That's my Brownie.'"

WHEN IT CAME TO predicting outcomes of football games, Myron wasn't half-bad. But when he got it wrong, boy . . . no, *oy* did he get it wrong.

In the mid-1960s, Pittsburgh journalist Jim O'Brien put out a small newspaper called *Pittsburgh Weekly Sports*. Myron wrote quickie articles for it to make some extra shekels. By this time, the big mags regularly gave him two or three thousand dollars per article; O'Brien gave him a hundred bucks. That was night-on-the-town money for a guy like Myron. But Myron had plenty of nights on the town, so he took the money.

In late December 1963, *PWS* published Myron's preview of the coming Cotton Bowl matchup between the number-one ranked team in the country, the Texas Longhorns, and the formidable squad from Navy led by Heisman Trophy–winner Roger Staubach. Myron was familiar with Navy, who had defeated Pitt in October, the only dent in the Panthers' 9-1 record that season. He apparently hadn't seen Texas play until he sat down to watch their game against rival Texas A&M. He came away rather unimpressed—and went big in expressing his disdain.

> Texas is the biggest fraud ever perpetrated on the football public. If you missed Texas' performance against Texas A&M on Thanksgiving Day, your first reaction when you see this team in the Cotton Bowl will be one of incredulity. You will say, "No, this can't be the number one team in the country. This can't even be a big-time college team. The Texas players must have come down with flu and been replaced by a high school team."

> By the second quarter, the shock will have worn off and given way to unrestrained mirth. You will roll on the floor laughing, if you are the type that rolls on the floor laughing. I am, and I did on Thanksgiving Day. I watched the game at the home of a man who is in the banking business, and he too rolled on the floor laughing.

Myron went on to deride the Longhorns' offensive strategy ("on third down, Texas punts"), their starting quarterback ("executes a handoff like a construction foreman handing a plank to a carpenter"), and the backup QB, who "throws a pass that flutters, wobbles and finally limps to its destination." The only reason the quarterback completes some passes, he said, was because "Southwest defenses are still waiting for the mailman to arrive with their paperback copies of 'Elements of Pass Defense.'"

"Take a look at the Texas linemen," he added. "They do not look like linemen. They have skinny legs, like centipedes or girls, and high rear ends. Maybe it was the TV set, but that's how I saw them."

Why would Myron write such an outlandish column? Two possibilities come to mind. One, he wrote it with tongue pressed firmly against his cheek. Two, people's legs look smaller when refracted through a hot toddy.

Myron finished off the column with a prediction that Navy would expose Texas as "the biggest hoax in modern football history." And, he added, "Pitt would beat Texas by three touchdowns."

PWS published it, and there the story might have ended except that a few days before the game, copies of the paper found their way into the hands of Texas coach Darrell Royal and assorted Texas newspaper men (a Philadelphia columnist voiced suspicion that Myron himself mailed the copies). A long-distance laceration of Myron's vision and soundness of mind began in the *Dallas Morning News* and swelled to the size of a small avalanche as Texas crushed Navy on New Year's Day, 28–6, to claim the national championship. A Richmond columnist wrote, "When Cope is over his acute attack of indigestion, he should have his TV set worked on."

Some folks even took the time to write to Myron personally. One said, "After reading your December item about the inept Texas team that would play in the Cotton Bowl, I have tried desperately to think about you in a charitable way. It helped when I remembered that ever since Chaucer some people have made a living writing nothing but fiction."

Another fellow was more succinct: "I once knew a fellow from Pittsburgh. He was a screwball nut too."

Myron took the criticism in stride; if nothing else, he had gained some valuable publicity. He told the *Fort Worth Star Telegram* that after the game, he received many calls. "Most of the calls were friendly," he said. "Of course, I couldn't open my mouth. My foot was in it."

MINOR EMBARRASSMENTS ASIDE, Myron's stock as a sportswriter continued to rise. He remained a freelancer, but the *Saturday Evening Post* signed him to a contract in 1964 that gave him a guaranteed sum in return for the right of first refusal on his stories. As a result, the *Post* published six of his pieces that year alone. He squeezed in other stories for *SI*, *Sport*, and *True* and broke into a new market that October when his book with Jim Brown was released and excerpts appeared in back-to-back issues of *Look*, then the country's second-biggest magazine, with a circulation of 7.5 million.

After this run of success, Myron ended '64 with one more story, one that took up just a few inches in a couple of newspapers. He got married.

It was not a nutty thing to do. Myron had known Mildred Lindberg for the past seven years, ever since they were set up on a blind date. "I came up here to visit [*Post-Gazette* writer] Si Pickering and his wife, they were having a big dance that night, and they fixed me up with Myron," Mildred explained in a rare early 1990s interview. The two hit it off, but nothing happened right away; Mildred lived in Indianapolis, where she worked as a medical technician at a hospital. They stayed in touch, stayed friends, until the relationship deepened. In December of '64, two days after Christmas, they took the plunge, tying the knot in Mildred's hometown of Charleston, West Virginia. Myron was thirty-five, Mildred thirty-three.

Mildred later joked, "He says it was love at first sight, even though it took us seven years to get married."

The sportswriter and his new wife were not what one would call an obvious match. Mildred spoke with a slight country drawl, was a half inch or so taller than Myron, and had only a minor interest in the athletes and games that made up Myron's world. Her father, Gus "Lefty" Lindberg, had been a class-B Minor League baseball player in the 1920s. But Mildred developed a dislike for his sport. "My father used to own a franchise in baseball, in Williamson, West Virginia," she explained, "and we had to go all the time. I went, you know, to every game. And I think that's maybe why I don't like it now—I was made to go."

The biggest mismatch was in a more sensitive area, religion. Myron classified himself as agnostic at the time of the marriage but took considerable pride in his Jewish heritage and culture. Mildred was a churchgoing Catholic who would in time transition to being Presbyterian. Intermarriage was not yet a common thing in the mid-1960s, and Myron worried about how his parents would react when he introduced them to his bride-to-be. "I expected Ellis and Elizabeth to be shocked when I broke the news, and I suppose they were, but if so, they hid their shock well," he recalled in his autobiography. Addressing Mildred directly in the text, he added, "They liked you at once, as did every member of my family—my sister Violet loved you as she would a sister."

Myron's niece Marcia Grodsky more or less confirms Myron's account. "It was a shock to my grandparents. They accepted it, but it was a shock to them—well, to all of the family it was somewhat of a shock," she says. "But my mother [Violet] was the one who took Mildred in right away. I think there was more reserve between the rest of them."

Mildred knew from the start that she'd have to share Myron with the world. Even before his broadcasting career, he was gone a good chunk of the time, gathering material for his articles. The first half of 1965 alone saw him travel to Cleveland, Philadelphia, New York, Chicago, the spring training spot of Clearwater, Florida, and the little town of Lewiston, Maine, the unlikely site for Muhammad Ali's rematch with Sonny Liston. In 1966 *Sports Illustrated* would send him to Puerto Rico and Mexico, while the *Saturday Evening Post* dispatched him to Texas for a long piece on college football rivalries.

The former Miss Lindberg was generally able to deal with the situation. "I'm very self-reliant. That's how I've managed to cope with his schedule," she explained. It helped that Myron, in all his travels, showed no inclination to seek out other female company—and that Mildred had no desire to share the spotlight. “She’s from the old school, I think you’ll agree, where they taught girls that you get your name in the paper three times: when you’re born, when you’re married and when you die,” Myron told an interviewer, as Mildred laughed in seeming agreement.

Still, as in all marriages, the couple had to weather some tough times. Grodsky says Mildred desperately wanted to be a mother but had health issues that made pregnancy difficult. She endured multiple miscarriages before giving birth to a daughter prematurely in January 1967. Doctors couldn’t do much for preemies back then, and the girl, Martha Anne Cope, lived only four days—“easily long enough to love her and clearly remember the face I saw through a hospital nursery window when I visit her grave, marked by a small, flat, heart-shaped stone,” Myron wrote.

The couple was undeterred, and Mildred was pregnant again within weeks. She gave birth again in January 1968, this time after a full-term pregnancy, to a boy. The elated parents named the child Daniel Lawrence Cope.

Myron was a family man now, with a wife and a child and a new home, a split-level, three-bedroom house that he and Mildred had purchased in Scott Township, a twenty-minute drive south of downtown. He was at the top of his field and just about on top of the world.

What better time for a phone call that would change the course of his life and career?

4

A Trend toward Obnoxious Voices

Irony of ironies, the radio station that called Myron Cope in January 1968 was best known for broadcasting soft, sweet, melodious sounds. Until about six months earlier, WTAE-AM played the format known as "beautiful music"—symphonies, string quartets, instrumental versions of classic and classy pop songs, maybe a little Nat King Cole for variety. No rock music, no Top 40 hits, absolutely nothing that would jar the nervous systems of the station's mostly adult, well-to-do listeners. For most of the decade at WTAE, the Four Seasons meant Vivaldi, not Frankie Valli. Cutting edge meant Frank Sinatra.

In 1967 the station's owners hired a new general manager, Don Shafer, who sensed that between the growth of high-fidelity FM radio and the rock-leaning tastes of young listeners, the days of pretty music on the AM dial were winding down. That year, Shafer pushed WTAE closer to a middle-of-the-road format, with a mix of pop, jazz, and classical music, call-in contests, newscasts, and timely public affairs shows. "WTAE plays good good music with boss radio hits," read one review of the overhauled station. Audience share grew significantly, enough to cut into the eternal ratings lead held by KDKA, the fifty-thousand-watt Goliath of Pittsburgh radio. KDKA quickly turned more middle-of-the-road itself, retooling its playlist around artists like the Fifth Dimension and adding a popular new morning man in Jack Bogut. The changes paid off, and Goliath regained its dominance. Still, WTAE executives had gotten a glimpse of real success and wanted more.

The next step was to dip a toe into sports programming. Not a horribly expensive toe; WTAE paid just $90,000 to air the inaugural season of the expansion Pittsburgh Penguins in 1967–68. But it was a portent of things to come.

One day shortly after New Year's 1968, Shafer called a staff meeting. Among those who crowded into Shafer's office was an amiable, reddish-haired booth announcer for WTAE's sister TV station, Channel 4. Twenty-seven-year-old Bill Hillgrove was bored in his job, which required little more than reading station identification notices and taglines for commercials. Later that year he'd accept a pay cut to join WTAE's radio operation, spinning records on the afternoon shift. In 1969 he'd find his true calling as a sportscaster, doing play-by-play for University of Pittsburgh football and basketball games—a job he'd keep for more than half a century. In time, he'd also join the Steelers' radio booth and spend over a quarter-century there, eleven of those years with Myron.

On that cold January morning, all that lay in the future, and Hillgrove was just another staff member listening closely as Shafer explained his reason for the gathering.

"The program director called us all in, and he said, 'We need to jazz up the morning, we need sports commentary,'" Hillgrove recalls. "He said, 'Any suggestions?' I said, 'You probably have to get a good sportswriter, and probably the best sportswriter in town is Roy McHugh.' And I no sooner got that out of my mouth than our newsman, Ron Rininger, said, 'Well, I loaf at a place called Dante's, and you know, the Steelers all loaf in there as well, and there's a guy there, a freelance writer named Myron Cope. He's off the wall, and I think he'd be perfect.'"

Cope. If Shafer had read a magazine in the past ten years, he knew the name. It's possible that he even knew the voice. Hillgrove says his future colleague had zero broadcasting experience at this point, but in fact, Myron was not a total stranger to the Pittsburgh airwaves. As far back as 1955, he had popped up on local radio, starting with panel shows hosted by Ed King, host of KDKA's *Party Line*. In 1961 he made his first TV appearance, answering questions on Channel 11's *Beat the Experts*, a sports-themed game show. In 1965 he was a semi-regular on a short-lived TV talk show hosted by funnyman Sterling Yates. As recently as the previous January, he had been on KDKA again, offering his prediction on who would win the very first Super Bowl.

However, none of these gigs had generated offers for Myron to take a deeper dive into broadcasting. No mystery as to the reason why.

"How best to describe my voice? Harsh? Abrasive?" Myron wrote in his autobiography. Noooooo Myron, his critics might say—those adjectives just touch the surface. How about irritating? Or grating? Or shrill? Even Myron's fans had to acknowledge that his voice was scratchy and nasal, and just plain . . . odd. It sounded like the poor thing had been in an accident. One writer compared it to silverware being pureed in a blender. Another likened it to the squeal of pigs inside a slaughterhouse. Still another suggested that his larynx had survived torture, like being dragged across chopped-up blocks of cement. Myron himself provided one of the best descriptions: "I suppose my voice falls upon the public's ears like china crashing from shelves in an earthquake."

Some of those descriptions came in later years, after decades of scotches and cigarettes and high-pitched yelling had done undeniable damage to Myron's vocal cords. But at no point in his life did Myron possess the clear, rounded tones that one usually associates with pleasant broadcasting. Former WTAE executive John Conomikes knew Myron during his teenage years. Even then, he says, Myron had a voice that "was not very good." Was it raspy and scratchy? "Oh yes, absolutely," Conomikes says. "When you just sat and talked with him, it was maybe *close* to normal, but yeah, you could tell it was different."

Different, however, can be a big plus in the broadcasting world. Any broad-minded program director could hear that Myron's voice, despite its flaws, leaped out from radio speakers and all but drilled into the listener's ear. It was loud. It had a certain piercing quality. And there was seemingly no other voice on earth like it. "Anybody can have a rotten voice," Myron once said. "But how many can have a rotten voice that's distinctive?"

Even more important, Rininger and others at WTAE believed that once listeners got used to the sound of the voice, they would like what Myron had to say. "People don't realize, he was a really smart guy," says Conomikes. "When you'd look at him and hear his voice, you'd say, 'What the hell is this guy?' But he was very bright, an excellent writer, great at expressing himself."

"Some people would react in that manner, you know, 'What's he doing on the radio?'" says Hillgrove. "But they failed to listen to what he had to say. Most true sports fans could hear what Myron had to say—and he had a lot to say—and that he knew his sports and knew Pittsburgh."

To this point in his career, Myron had never thought of exploiting his unique vocal qualities, so he was genuinely surprised when he picked up his home office phone that morning in 1968 and heard Shafer introduce himself on the other end. The ensuing conversation was one Myron liked to recount, so let's let him tell the story:

> He said to me, "Hey, we're trying to develop a sports image out here and you're known around town a little bit as a writer for *Sports Illustrated*. Would you be interested in doing a morning sports show? We'll put equipment in your home, a microphone and all, and you can do it from right there, and when you're out on the road and traveling around for your writing assignments, you can do it by telephone from your hotel room. . . . Before you go on the air, we'll fill you in on yesterday's ball scores and any interesting stories we have from the AP wire. Rattle 'em off and then give us a two-minute commentary—an opinion, an anecdote, anything you choose relating to any sports topic under the sun. You've been recommended highly by a couple of our people who drink with you."
>
> And I said, "Don't kid me, I've heard my voice on tape and it sure as heck is not a broadcasting voice." And the guy said, "Well, we like to think we're a forward-looking station and we think we see a trend in this business toward obnoxious voices."

At this point in the story, Myron usually either shrugged or injected an emphatic "Mmm-hah!"

> So, I said, "Well, let me think it over, I'll call you back." So, I hung up the phone and I told my wife about this conversation and she said, "Don't do it, you'll embarrass me." Well, I got very angry, so I called the guy back and said, "You've got a sportscaster."

Mildred, for the record, always denied making such a comment. Myron insisted otherwise: "It happened, believe me! The story is true." Elizabeth Cope has her own theory: "She probably said it as a joke."

Whether or not he was trying to spite his wife, Myron did not see the call from WTAE as the opening of a golden door. His writing career was at its height. *Sports Illustrated* alone had published three of his stories in the last quarter of 1967 and would print another four in the first half of 1968. Publishing company Prentice-Hall was prepping the book of his magazine pieces, *Broken Cigars*, and that would go on sale in June. There was no dire need for him to take on extra work; Danny's birth that month had gone smoothly, and Myron could easily afford the mortgage on the house.

But when Shafer called, the child of the Depression inside Myron spoke up. The man wanted to hire him; why not earn some extra bucks? A few minutes on the radio wouldn't steal time from his writing. And the show, such as it was, would probably disappear unnoticed in a short time anyway. "I thought it would last two or three weeks as a lark, a sideline I'd been invited to do," he said, many years later.

He admitted in one interview that he hoped it wouldn't be a lark. "When the invitation to go on radio came up," he told his friend Roy McHugh, "I was about forty years old. I told myself that maybe it was the age when a change of occupation is good for you." Was that a hint that Myron was getting burned out on magazine writing? That he was experiencing a midlife crisis? It's hard to say, as he didn't elaborate.

But he did express concern that he had reached the top of the freelance field and was bumping up against a hard ceiling. Around this time, he said, he asked his *Sports Illustrated* boss, Pat Ryan, to improve his contract. She gave him a flat no. "She said, 'My God, Myron, you are now paid as much as any of our contract writers.' And that included George Plimpton and a few other people," he remembered. Plimpton was a New York bon vivant and the author of several books, most notably *Paper Lion*, which recounted his experience as an amateur athlete trying to train and play with the NFL's Detroit Lions. Plimpton's book had been a bestseller and was being turned into a movie starring Alan Alda. Myron's book with Jim Brown, meanwhile, had slipped into un-filmed obscurity. There was no way *SI* was going to make him its top-paid writer.

A few days after Shafer's call, Myron made his first visit to WTAE's headquarters, a brown-brick, three-story building at 400 Ardmore Boulevard in the Wilkinsburg area, a few miles east of downtown. His writer's eye probably noticed that the building was distinctly modern in style—"midcentury modern," it's called today—with clean, straight architectural lines, plenty of floor-to-ceiling windows, and a near-total lack of exterior decoration save for a pebble garden and a few trees. The structure could be mistaken for an ordinary office building if not for the hundred-foot-high weather radar tower adorned with the station call letters and topped by a giant "4." Station owner Hearst Broadcasting had built the complex ten years earlier, at a cost of $2.2 million, to house its combined radio-TV operations in the city. Studios and offices for WTAE-AM and its sister FM outlet took up the ground floor, facilities for Channel 4 television occupied the middle, and the executive suites, naturally, sat on top.

Myron entered and had his first face-to-face meeting with Shafer, a ten-year veteran of the radio biz who had made stops in Oklahoma City, Cincinnati, and St. Louis before coming to Pittsburgh. The two men chatted a little more about the parameters of the show—it would be three minutes long, including the intro and the commercial. Shafer emphasized that he could comment about almost anything, even something he read in *SI*. Then they went into a studio so Myron could do a dry run. Overseeing the exercise was the staffer who had suggested Roy McHugh for the gig. "A young disc jockey named Bill Hillgrove, lovely fellow, he put me through the paces," Myron remembered. "You know, you talk into the microphone like this, say blah blah blah blah." It was the start of a work association and a friendship that would last forty years.

When the run-through was finished, Shafer asked Myron what he wanted to call the show. He thought for a minute and said, "Why not 'Myron Cope on Sports.' What could be simpler?" Soon after, WTAE technicians installed a microphone and control box in Myron's wood-paneled basement office, putting them on his desk next to the rotary phone and the ashtray. The station sent notices to the newspapers: *Sports Illustrated* writer Myron Cope would offer a commentary on sports each weekday at 7:35 a.m. He'd appear during the morning show hosted by disc jockey Perry Marshall.

Marshall (real name, Sheldon Lewis) was a popular, grade-A radio professional who'd been on the air for about ten years at different Pittsburgh stations. In later years, he'd enjoy success hosting an overnight talk show on KDKA, *The Marshall's Office*. His baritone voice was ideal for late night or early morning time slots—warm and engaging but rich and mellow, almost the aural equivalent of velvet. Myron's voice was more like a scouring pad. The contrast was bound to make listeners sit up and take notice.

LIVE FROM HIS BASEMENT, Myron made his WTAE premiere on a chilly, rainy Monday, January 29, 1968. No one preserved a tape or a script of that broadcast, so it's unknown what he said. We do know that in Myron's recollection of that day, the station was besieged with protests after his debut—not on the scale of a medieval army charging the locked castle doors with a battering ram, but close.

"I went on the air," he recalled, "and people called the switchboard and the poor girl was flooded with calls, and they said, 'Get that man off the air, I can't hear that in the morning when I've just gotten out of bed.'" On another occasion, he said he received "nasty notes" from irate listeners during his early months on the air and claimed that female listeners in particular "hated my guts."

The problem, as Myron described it, was that in the beginning, he was a complete broadcasting *Dummkopf*. "I was doing things all wrong," he recalled. "The station set up a microphone on my desk and I did my commentaries from home. I was living in Scott Township at the time. I found it hard to believe that I could sit in my office talking and people could hear me on the Parkway. . . . So, I started shouting to be on the safe side, shouting every sentence."

Judging from the few early Cope commentaries that survive on tape, Myron wasn't shouting per se, not in the way he'd later yell at the top of his lungs when Hines Ward or Lynn Swann made a leaping catch for a touchdown. However, he was talking VERY LOUDLY, at a much higher volume than the urbane Marshall, the folksy Jack Bogut, or anyone else outside Top 40 radio in Pittsburgh at the time. At the early hour, it took some getting used to.

But as for the alleged flood of angry callers, Myron seems to have made that up. "I do not recall that level of negative response," says Hillgrove. The Pittsburgh newspapers didn't say anything about a listener uprising, either. Strong evidence that Myron exaggerated: within a month, WTAE had him doing a second commentary each morning, this one at 8:35. If there were nasty notes coming through the mailroom, they were outnumbered by the fan letters.

Cooking up two original, engaging commentaries per day took some effort. However, Myron had plenty of material to work with, between the Pirates, Steelers, Penguins, Pitt's football and basketball teams, the strong Duquesne basketball program, and the Pipers, the city's American Basketball Association entry, who won the ABA championship in May 1968 and then left town because of cricket sounds in the seats. The rookie commentator turned his gaze on all these teams, their players, and their front offices. "He spread around his sports," says Hillgrove.

But, foreshadowing the future, he seemed to generate more heat and attention when he focused on football. When the 1-6 Steelers played the 0-7 Philadelphia Eagles that October, he dubbed the contest "The Futility Bowl." If the Steelers somehow played 1-9 Pitt, he said, both teams would find a way to lose. He also predicted that both teams would soon have a coaching vacancy, and he openly lobbied Pitt to hire Chuck Klausing, a small-college coach who would eventually win six conference championships at Carnegie Mellon University. Instead, Pitt went with a former assistant coach, Carl DePasqua, who racked up a 13-29 record in four years.

When the Steelers agreed in May 1969 to move to the American Football League (soon renamed the American Football Conference) as part of pro football's realignment, many old-time Steelers fans were dismayed. Not Myron. "It's kind of exciting," he proclaimed. "The AFL has demonstrated they are playing football on par with the NFL and it's not a step backwards. By 1970 the two leagues will be equal in caliber and the league you're in won't make any difference." Time would prove him right—in fact, more than right, as the AFC dominated both interconference play and the Super Bowl throughout the '70s and early '80s.

Unlike a later generation of "shock jocks" and radio flamethrowers, Myron didn't go out of his way to be controversial. But he didn't shy away from strong opinions, either. When he learned about a local creek where fishermen pounced on the trout mere seconds after the game commission dumped them in the water, he denounced the fishermen as unsportsmanlike. When the first generation of women sportswriters pushed for access to press boxes and locker rooms, Myron proclaimed those areas to be all-male preserves—an undeniably sexist stance, but a commonly held view at the time. When an Associated Press poll named Arnold Palmer the "Athlete of the Decade," Myron was incredulous, arguing that golfers weren't real athletes. (Palmer said nothing publicly at the time and two years later graciously agreed to play a round with his belittler. As soon as Myron stepped to the first tee, Palmer said, "Now we'll see what a *real* athlete looks like.")

Longtime Pittsburgh sportswriter and columnist Bob Smizik was an early fan of the Cope commentaries. "I listened whenever I could, and they were outstanding right from the get-go." he says. In his early months on the air, Smizik recalls, Myron tended to fall back on stories from his writing career: "He was very big on the national stage, and he wasn't immersed in the Pittsburgh bubble yet, 'cause he had just started that, so you got a lot of Cassius Clay/Muhammad Ali stories, things like that. Then, once he got immersed in the Pittsburgh sports culture, he fell into doing commentaries of a local nature, and they were also very good."

Despite his remark that women hated his guts, Myron was also picking up a sizeable number of female listeners. Many liked his tendency to forgo numbers and strategy in favor of personalities. A *Press* writer talked to some women who had sent in fan letters, noting that they were all people Myron didn't know. "I listen to him because he turns sports into a gossip column," said Margaret Egan of Mt. Lebanon. "I like to hear what the coaches and players are saying about each other, and especially what he has to say about them." Joan Pupik of Edgewood said, "I like him because he tells a little bit of the story behind the games. Scores don't mean as much [to me] as what's behind them. George [my husband] starts talking about sports, and I have to know what's going on." Another letter writer said she listened to Myron precisely to improve her connection with her husband and sons. "I just use your commentaries as my own and they are actually interested in what I have to say for a change," she said.

Myron didn't object to the word *gossip* to describe what he did. "I've never been strong on statistics. I try to give a little background and follow it like a story," he said. "What she [the female listener] is getting is the human side of athletes, their foibles. The athletes, she finds, turn out to be something like her old man."

Self-deprecating comments aside, Myron was actually doing more things right than wrong. Besides focusing on personalities, he made the smart choice to mostly script his commentaries in advance, both to sharpen the text and to reduce the chance of verbal flubs. He also adapted his writing style, realizing that what worked in magazines didn't always fly on the air. "There's a difference between the spoken word and the written word," he said more than once—though his explanation of that difference could be hard to follow. "When you're writing for the printed page," he told Roy McHugh in 1984, "you're writing for the eye, and the eye is the ear. You're writing music as the eye would hear it. When you're writing for radio . . . it's conversational writing, and conversational writing is poor writing when transferred to paper. The trick is to write badly, well. And having been a writer, I think I can write badly well better than the next guy. Is that clear?" McHugh's response was not recorded.

Myron, wisely, also built the commentaries around his own reporting rather than simply reacting to events. "I was not a barroom commentator," he said in a late-career interview. "[That's when] a guy comes into a bar and says, when you're talking about something, 'I think that's wrong,' or 'I think that's right!' I would tell people *why* I thought it was right or wrong, with facts that they weren't, as average fans, privy to knowing."

Smizik, who spent twenty-three years at the *Press* and another twenty-three at the *Post-Gazette*, often saw Cope in fact-gathering mode. "I once wrote that he was the hardest working guy in Pittsburgh, beyond doubt," Smizik says. "I believe he had a policy of coming to one Pirates home game in every series. He went to a lot of hockey games too. He came to all the luncheons, the Pitt football luncheon, the basketball writers' luncheon, whatever it was, he was there." On a typical night in the early to mid-1970s, he recalls, Myron would arrive at a Pirates game about halfway through, take a seat in the press box, and watch the action until the final out. Then he'd zip down to the clubhouse and spend a half hour chatting with the manager and players. "And the players were always so glad to see him," says Smizik. "After, he'd come back up to the press box, get a toddy, sit down at one of his tables, and type his commentary for the next day. When he was finished, he'd go up to the bar and have another drink."

A well-written script was only half the battle, though. There was also the matter of the delivery. Popular broadcasters often develop a distinctive speaking style to go along with a naturally engaging voice; think of Chris Berman barking out nicknames and catchphrases on ESPN, Lester Holt's crisp, perfect diction on the *NBC Nightly News*, or the distinguished lilt Alex Trebek used to host *Jeopardy!* Myron certainly found his own style, and it's tempting to picture him laboring over his new craft just as he did with the old, experimenting with pace and pronunciation, fine-tuning his delivery so he could connect more deeply with the great, unseen radio audience.

But dear lord, no. By every account, including his own, from day one Myron just faced the microphone with his script and let 'er rip. While he was careful to enunciate, his way of speaking from the start made trained announcers cringe. He made no effort to sand down his Pittsburgh accent, pronouncing words like *Washington* as *Warsh*-ington. He came down extra hard on consonants like *b* and *t*, popped every *p*, and hissed many an *s*. Sometimes, he just sounded too close to the mike, undoubtedly because he was.

Myron described his delivery as "singsongy," but that word connotes a steady, monotonous rising and falling of pitch. Myron's pitch could shoot up and settle down unpredictably three or four times in the same sentence, and he would unpredictably inject a shout, a sudden aside, or a stage whisper into his performance, wiping out any chance of monotony. He also tended to speak in long sentences broken up into numerous clauses, and he didn't mind tossing in four- or five-syllable words that were more at home on the SAT or National Public Radio.

That latter habit and his nasally tone made some listeners compare him to the king of loud, verbose sports commentary, Howard Cosell. But in fact, the two sounded nothing alike. In fact, *nobody* spoke like Myron on the air—or in daily life. So listeners could be excused for thinking they were hearing a true one-of-a-kind.

However, Myron did have something of a predecessor.

"People used to accuse him of sounding like Pete Smith," says Hillgrove. Smith, a tall, thin man with an oblong head and protruding chin, was a producer of short comedy films for MGM in Hollywood from the early 1930s to the mid-1950s. The *Pete Smith Specialties* were eight- to ten-minute documentaries of a sort, dealing with just about anything that Smith found funny, like hair loss, memory problems, insects, dancing lessons, or bowling. Not astoundingly creative or well acted, the films would have little to recommend if not for the narrator, who happened to be Smith himself. Smith spoke in a nasally tenorish voice, had his own rhythm, possessed a knack for multisyllabic, even tongue-twisting, dialogue, and used his own brand of slang for comic effect.

Watching *Sure Cures*, a 1946 film about faulty home remedies, one line in particular jumps out: "And the belief that raw beefsteak is a sure cure for a black eye is pure bunk-ola." That last word, and the way Smith says it, seems like a template for Myron's dismissive phrase "that's a lot of gorgonzola." The narration, if played at a faster speed and slightly higher pitch, would sound more than a little like Myron Cope—who, as the teenaged Myron Kopelman, may well have seen Pete Smith's films while waiting for the main feature at a Squirrel Hill theater.

Myron never cited Smith or anyone else as an influence on his broadcasting work. Truth be told, the influence of Smith or anybody else was buried and incidental. Myron was a unique voice, both aurally and creatively, and he seems to have realized early on that his untrained amateur's approach to speaking on air was the way to go. "I've seen so many people who were well trained in broadcasting, had good voices, and knew how to do everything in a very professional manner still get shown the door," he said. All he wanted from WTAE, he liked to proclaim, was to be told when to start talking and when to shut up.

WTAE WAS NOT TELLING him to shut up. Far from it. The higher-ups had noticed the positive feedback Myron was getting, and six months after his radio debut, they put him on television. Starting the third week of July 1968, he appeared the station's 11 p.m. newscast every Sunday, offering more of what the *Press* called his "incisive commentary."

John Conomikes, then the station's general sales manager, takes credit for putting Cope on camera. Initially, he says, his push for more Myron had less than unanimous support. "People said, 'Are you crazy? Why would you do that? He's one ugly guy, his one ear is chewed off, he's got a high-pitched terrible voice—you know, what are you doing?'" Conomikes recalls, with a laugh. "I said, 'He's a real character, he writes for *Sports Illustrated*, and he's really, really a smart guy.' He really was. I said, 'He's just different. The main thing he'll be doing is commentaries.' He wouldn't do a whole sports report, reading the report, with his voice, you know. So, we did the commentaries, and he was a big success."

Actually, Myron did read the nightly sports report on occasion, but only in a pinch. He never got entirely comfortable on TV sets, and in delivering his commentaries—often dressed in a snazzy three-piece suit—he was noticeably quieter and less animated than he was on radio. He also tended to ignore the camera in favor of his script or fellow sportscasters when talking, a habit that drove TV directors batty. ("He's got to look up," one director muttered in the presence of a magazine writer.) But his comments were just as insightful and well received as they were on radio, and within a few months, WTAE was promoting him in print ads along with lead sports anchor Ed Conway. "How Do Conway and Cope Grab Ya, Sports Fans?" read the headline, above a picture that showed Conway in the background and Myron up front, wearing a plaid suit and clutching a baseball bat.

Myron's transition from writer to broadcaster was underway. He was now delivering a total of eleven commentaries on radio and television per week, a significant workload by anyone's measure. Even with WTAE allowing him to tape segments in advance, something had to give, and the natural casualty was Myron's magazine writing. In 1968 he composed at least nine full-length articles for major magazines; in 1969 he would produce just five, and two of those were essentially oral history transcripts he gathered for his book *The Game That Was*.

It was just as well, because the presses were gradually coming to a halt for the big general-interest magazines where Myron made his name. For decades, the mass weeklies and monthlies had raked in vast sums of advertising money because they, unlike newspapers and television stations, could show products in full color. Once TV broadcasts also blossomed into color, in the mid-1960s, companies that had relied on magazines to show the real-life appearance of their products migrated to the tube. The magazines, while still popular, began to hemorrhage money, and over the next several years, several of Myron's customers—most notably *Life*, *Look*, *True*, and the *Saturday Evening Post*—either shrunk into irrelevance or flatlined into history. *Sports Illustrated* continued to thrive, but that was because it focused on a specialty market, one that was growing explosively. In fact, when Myron wrote magazine articles after 1969, it was almost exclusively for *SI* and only when he could squeeze in the time.

The loss of writing work probably cost Myron around $10,000 per year—a heavy hit for the average American worker in 1969. Fortunately, his income from broadcasting was already on the rise.

That July the big dog of Pittsburgh media came calling. KDKA was a radio-and-television operation just like WTAE but far bigger. The radio side, as mentioned, broadcast at fifty thousand watts, ten times the power of little WTAE, and could be heard across half of North America at night. The station's TV side was affiliated with the first-place CBS network, while WTAE aired the programs of third-place ABC. Myron was no fool and knew that switching stations would put him in front of many more eyes and ears. He agreed to a business lunch with the right-hand man of KDKA's general manager of radio, Bill Hartman.

The way Myron told the story, the aide met him for a hush-hush meal at a restaurant near Pittsburgh International Airport, at a table behind a curtain. The aide offered him a fat raise plus pension and health-care benefits, things he hadn't received to that point at Ardmore Boulevard. Myron, who had been working for WTAE without a formal contract, immediately said yes and made plans to sign with KDKA the following night at the Pittsburgh Press Club, a plush, mahogany-lined restaurant that catered to journalists and residents of the city's executive suites.

The next afternoon he verbally gave his resignation notice at WTAE and drove to the Press Club to sign the new contract. Only one problem—Hartman, pulling a bait and switch, cut KDKA's offer nearly in half, suggesting that Myron should be happy to take less money for the chance to work at Pittsburgh's number-one station.

An insulted Myron walked out. "Now," he recalled, "I had no new job with KDKA and had resigned at WTAE. Whoops."

Fortunately, wheels had been turning during his brief absence from WTAE. The next afternoon, he got a call from Conomikes, who offered a full-time contract that gave Myron a hefty raise and, crucially, benefits. A relieved Myron accepted and even agreed to take on more work. Beginning that August, he would crank out three radio commentaries per day and appear three times weekly on the TV side—a total of eighteen commentaries each week. Conomikes says he doesn't remember the dollar figure Myron signed for except that it was less than the $40,000 per year received by popular weatherman Joe DeNardo.

Talking to the *Press*, Myron made no mention of the last-minute rug-pulling by KDKA, saying simply, "It was a good offer but WTAE started me out in this business and I decided to stay with them."

That was a quarter-truth at best, but no one raised a dissenting word in print. Myron was happy. WTAE had sewed up their man. And as it turned out, both sides had made the right move. Staying with the smaller station, Myron was about to turn into a broadcasting giant.

5

Into the Steelers' Booth

As Myron's fortunes climbed in the second half of the 1960s, the Steelers were sinking like a leaky barge adrift on the Monongahela. The hard-drinking '63 team Myron wrote about so memorably came within a game of reaching the NFL championship. The rest of the decade was one long hangover, as the Steelers won only nineteen games against sixty-two losses and three ties. Even the reporter pals Art Rooney had cultivated stopped sticking up for the team. "Steelers Lose—So What's New?" read one headline in the *Press* after a 1967 loss to the Redskins that dropped the team's record at home that season to 1-6. The fans adopted a similar why-bother attitude. The Steelers had moved their home games to Pitt Stadium in 1964 in part to take advantage of its greater capacity. Instead, the team played to acres of empty seats, especially in frigid late-season contests where the official attendance might be only twenty-four thousand and half the crowd departed by the fourth quarter.

There seemed no way to pull out of the tailspin. Buddy Parker's policy of trading draft picks for veteran talent had starved the team of new blood. In 1963 the Steelers didn't have a single pick until the eighth round. In 1965 they used a rare round-two selection to draft a top-notch receiver,

Roy Jefferson, but lacking picks in rounds one, three, four, five, and six, it was hard to give him a supporting cast. Front-office fumbles worsened the problem. In the '66 draft, the Steelers made a smart choice in round seven, selecting future Pro Bowl running back Emerson Boozer. However, when the team offered him a less-than-dazzling contract, Boozer signed with the New York Jets of the rival American Football League. "It's the same old story for the last-place Steelers this week," moaned the *Post-Gazette.*

On the occasions when the Steelers did have a top-round pick, they often flushed it down the toilet. Prime example: in '66, the Steelers used their first-round pick to sign a big fullback, Dick Leftridge of West Virginia. The idea was that Leftridge would replace the retiring John Henry Johnson in the backfield. The problem: Leftridge was motivated more by food than football. On the rookie's first post-draft visit to the team offices, the scale groaned under his 268 pounds, about forty more than coaches were expecting. Leftridge trimmed down to a degree but played all of four regular-season games before getting cut.

The Steelers' myriad problems ultimately traced back to Art Rooney—much beloved as a master at the racetrack, a boxing promoter, a giver of charity, a guy to share a beer with, but in the end, a second-rate owner and operator among the lions of the NFL. For decades Rooney hired (and sometimes rehired) old friends to be the Steelers' head coach and let them run the team with only casual oversight. When the team needed a new top dog after the '65 season, he went the other direction and hired a man he had just met, Green Bay Packers assistant coach Bill Austin, turning away his son Dan's pleas to be more thorough and to look at other candidates. Austin became best known for putting the players through rough, injury-causing practices and his tendency to subject the team to Vince Lombardi's speeches word for word, minus the Lombardi charisma. The Steelers canned him after a 2-11-1 season in 1968.

Myron, as noted, had a good relationship with Art Rooney and interviewed him at length several times over the years. But he was almost forced to chide him in print to maintain his reputation as a credible sportswriter. In a 1969 *Sports Illustrated* article, he referred to the Steelers' owner as "pro football's champion loser," noting that the team had yet to win so much as a division title in thirty-six years under the Rooney helm. There and in other articles, he also mentioned the Steelers' disastrous decision to cut the young Johnny Unitas in 1955. The problem, as Myron saw it, was that The Chief was more interested in horse racing than football. Dan Rooney thought it was baseball that dominated his dad's brain. A six-part series published by the *Post-Gazette* in 2012 showed that into the late 1940s, at least, Art Rooney owned or part-owned then-illegal gambling operations like slot machines and private horse-betting rooms, using his political connections to ward off publicity and arrest. That must have taken up a chunk of his time as well. In any case, the Steelers didn't get proper attention from their owner, allowing the Lombardis and Paul Browns and George Halases of the NFL to walk away with all the wins.

Rooney defended himself in *The Game That Was*, telling Cope, "I am positively sure that had I run my ball club like some of the other owners ran theirs, we would have won championship after championship. I was able. I was competent. I knew football, knew football material." Regardless, in the late 1960s, Rooney gradually and wisely transferred authority to his sons, with Art Jr. taking over the scouting department and Dan assuming control of general football operations. The sons made a series of sea-change decisions, starting with their hire of *Pittsburgh Courier* sportswriter Bill Nunn to connect the team with what are now called HBCUs (historically Black colleges and universities), a traditionally under-tapped source of football talent. The team began to hoard draft choices instead of trading them away. In January 1969 the Steelers finally made a first-round pick with impact, signing Joe Greene, a highly motivated and nearly unstoppable defensive lineman out of the University of North Texas.

The same week, Dan Rooney engineered the key move in Steelers history, hiring Chuck Noll, a sharp, serious-minded defensive assistant from the Colts, to be the Steelers' new head coach. It would take a few years, but the Steelers had found the path out of the desert toward the promised land.

As a commentator, Myron followed the team's moves from a close vantage, not part of the organization but still a frequent presence at Steelers games, practices, and hangouts. Some of the faces were changing. Myron's favorites from the early '60s teams—John Henry Johnson, Bobby Layne, Ernie Stautner—had retired and moved on. His pal Joe Tucker, who had called Steelers games on radio since Myron was seven years old, was forced out by behind-the-scenes politics after the '67 season. But Myron, never shy, made pals among the new personnel.

One of the first was a young, highly capable linebacker from Missouri, Andy Russell. Russell had joined the Steelers in 1963, a rare draft pick who impressed Buddy Parker enough to stick on the roster. After spending two years in the army to fulfill ROTC requirements, Russell returned and established himself as the team's defensive star. He'd be one of only five men from the pre-Chuck Noll era still on the roster when the Steelers won their first Super Bowl.

Elizabeth Cope thinks Myron was closer to Russell than any other Steelers player. "They had such a good rapport together," she says. "Out of all the football players, he could just call Andy. They were friends. I loved seeing them together." Cope and Russell were more than buddies; they were sparring partners. "I can remember having a lot of fun with Myron, in some bars talking to him about journalism and so forth," Russell recalled in a 2012 video. "One time I told him, 'Myron, it must be really difficult to have so much stress in your life.' He said, 'Whaddaya mean by that, Russell?' I said, 'Well, you make a living talking about something you know nothing about.' Myron, of course, got back at me."

In his book *A Steeler Odyssey*, Russell summed up Myron in two sentences: "Myron has always reminded me of a Jack Russell terrier. He's small, clever, feisty and yaps a lot."

"Andy would always say my dad didn't know anything about football," Elizabeth says. "He'd say, 'You don't even know what a cover-two defense is.' My dad would say, 'I know a slow linebacker when I see one. You don't need to play football to know that!'"

But there was more to the relationship than flying insults. "One time when I was attempting to write my first book," Russell recalled, "I gave Myron a chapter to edit, and he said, 'Well, it'll take me a number of weeks to do this.' I said, 'It's just one chapter.' And he of course came back two weeks later, and I mean, you've never seen so much red ink in your life. You would've thought I'd never written a sentence in my life. It was incredible. But he had helped me. He was all into detail, and I believed in Chuck Noll's theory that success is in the details, and I think

Myron believed in that as well." Russell would write three books about his football career and life.

Myron made an even closer friend in the team's new publicist. Joseph R. Gordon—known to everyone as Joe—had sprung from the same soil as Myron, growing up in Squirrel Hill, graduating from Allderdice, getting a college education at Pitt. Like Cope, Gordon was a sports fanatic from childhood; his 1949 bar mitzvah at Tree of Life Congregation was delayed a month because he broke his arm playing street hockey. And like Cope, he was something of a frustrated jock, good enough to cocaptain the JV basketball team in high school but lacking the talent to play professionally. So after a post-college stint in the army, he entered the sports world by way of the front office, working for the Pittsburgh Rens, a team in the short-lived American Basketball League. After they folded, he began doing publicity for the Hornets, Pittsburgh's pre-Penguins Minor League hockey team. He filled the same role for the Pens when they started play in the fall of 1967.

At first, Gordon had a mainly business relationship with Myron. "Occasionally, I would give him ideas for his commentaries," Gordon says. "At one time, he was doing three commentaries a day, and if you had an idea, he was always receptive because he needed subject material." The relationship turned into a friendship once Gordon joined the Steelers in mid-1969, and the two men began sharing meals and drinks. "We'd have dinner on Saturday nights before a game, and he kind of became my confidant. In a relatively short period of time, we became very close," Gordon says. "I can't pinpoint one particular time [we bonded], like there was a fist fight and one guy protected another. We just had a common background and mutual respect for each other. It's like any friendship that grows—it starts shallow, then develops."

In a distant time to come, Gordon would become Myron's most trusted friend, the one tasked with telling him that his on-air performance had slipped, that it was time to retire. In the more immediate future, he'd help get Myron the job that changed his life.

THE STEELERS CLOSED the 1969 season with thirteen straight losses and opened 1970 with another three. During one especially brutal four-game stretch during the '69 season, the Steelers were outscored 156–34.

Sixteen-game losing streaks usually leave rope marks around a head coach's neck. But in Chuck Noll's case, there was no player revolt, and the Steelers' owners stood by their man. "Noll didn't lose the team," Dan Rooney remembered in his autobiography. "I noticed it, and so did my father."

And so the team's top-to-bottom transformation gained speed. The Steelers had the top pick in the 1970 NFL draft and used it to select a young man from little Louisiana Tech, an athletic, rocket-armed quarterback named Terry Bradshaw. The third round brought the first real bonanza from Bill Nunn's HBCU connections, a fleet, hard-tackling cornerback from Southern University, Mel Blount. Both men would make the Hall of Fame.

Meanwhile, a new home for both the Steelers and Pirates, Three Rivers Stadium, was rising in downtown Pittsburgh, and as soon it was ready in July 1970, the team abandoned its decrepit South Park training facility. In later years, Pittsburghers would come to look down on Three Rivers for its bland design, far-away seating, barren concrete surroundings, and hard artificial surface, known at the outset as "Tartan Turf." But the stadium did wonders for team morale. At South Park, the Steelers' dressing room was in the basement of a hundred-year-old house where ice sometimes formed in the showers and the practice field turned into a mud bath every time it rained. When that happened, players were forced to practice inside a horse barn with a smell reminiscent of, well, a horse barn. "When we came to Three Rivers Stadium, new and sparkling and clean, and walked into this sumptuous locker room, with carpeting on the floor and all this stuff, these guys were just sitting there, they were glowing," Chuck Noll remembered. "There was no question, it was a real factor."

The transformation extended to the team's radio contract. NFL historians tend to focus on the huge impact that television and TV money made on the league, especially in the 1960s and '70s. But on a local level, radio was still the key link between teams and the fans, a result of the NFL's strictly enforced blackout policy, which prohibited teams' home games from being televised in their home markets. For several years, KDKA had served as the Steelers' radio outlet. In theory, that maximized the Steelers' potential audience; the station ruled the local ratings.

But—and this was a huge *but*—KDKA treated the Steelers like a ho-hum side dish to the filet mignon. The Pirates had been Pittsburgh's dominant sports franchise throughout the sixties, and baseball was the station's top priority. If the Pirates and Steelers played at the same time on Sunday, one of two things happened. One, the station would broadcast the Steelers game later on tape delay—after most people had already heard the final score. Or two, the live broadcast would be kicked over to another station, usually WJAS, a five-thousand-watt operation with a shorter range and a much smaller audience.

"My father was fine with his arrangement, but I couldn't stand it," said Dan Rooney. After the 1969 season, Dan got the Steelers off KDKA—"as a matter of self-respect," in Myron's words—and signed a new contract with WTAE. WTAE was also five thousand watts, but at least the Steelers would be with a station that truly wanted them on the air and would promote them accordingly.

Next task was to update the Steelers' radio team. In 1969 the broadcasting chores were handled by two seasoned pros, Jack Fleming and Tom Bender, who switched off each quarter between play-by-play and analysis. No one had thoughts of replacing Fleming; he was regarded both by the public and professionals alike as one of the most engaging play-by-play men in the business. Bender was a different story. Blessed with a deep, almost froggy speaking voice, Bender did a fine job relaying action on the field but offered little in terms of personality or opinion. Several years later, he would be canned from his WTAE evening sports talk show for being too dull.

"He just gave it straight," remembers Joe Gordon. "He was just your typical play-by-play broadcaster in that era or generation." The Steelers hoped to find someone who could better convey the excitement of the games to the radio audience—or at least keep them listening if the Steelers were being squished 38–6.

The Steelers brain trust met in the early months of 1970 and discussed their options. Someone suggested a bright young sportscaster who'd been on the Pittsburgh airwaves only a couple of years but was winning fans with his smart, witty, sometimes hard-hitting commentaries. Joe Gordon was delegated to approach the man with an offer, and he said yes. In June 1970 the Steelers announced Fleming's new partner: Dick Stockton.

Stockton, then twenty-eight years old and the sports director for

KDKA-TV, would go on to a highly successful fifty-year career calling baseball, football, basketball, and the Olympics for several major television networks. But the team of Fleming and Stockton was never to be. Within two months of the Steelers' announcement, Stockton had accepted an offer to host NFL studio shows and do other work for CBS. He also bruised feelings by saying that Pittsburgh sports fans were simpletons compared to those in his native New York City. "I'm not knocking the fans for being 'Gung ho home team,'" he told the *Press* that July. "But where I come from—and I know New York is not like Pittsburgh—the fans have an understanding, shall we say, of reality and the possibilities." He added, with a little too much pride, "I'm not criticizing provincial people, but I'm not provincial myself. I'm not Pittsburgh." Several letter writers to the *Press* agreed that he sure the hell wasn't and suggested Stockton catch the next out-of-town bus, one with plenty of storage space to hold his overstuffed ego.

Back at the drawing board, the Steelers still needed a new partner for Jack Fleming. Joe Gordon and Ed Kiely met with Dan Rooney. Discussions turned to another local sportscaster, this one a proud local. "It was my initiative," Gordon remembers. "I said, 'Why don't we try to get Cope?'"

Dan Rooney had no objection, despite Myron's having called his dad a champion loser. It helped that Myron was already employed by WTAE; Joe Tucker had been forced out, in part because Steelers games were on KDKA and Tucker worked for WWSW. "Dan Rooney said he sounds like a good idea, contact Cope to see if he'd be interested," Gordon recalls.

Kiely was delegated to reach out to Cope. It apparently took only one conversation to reel in his man. Myron remembered: "Kiely called me and said, 'How'd you like to be the color analyst for the team now that we're moving to your station?' And I told him what I told that [WTAE] program director—you've got to be nuts. I said, 'I'm no color analyst, I've never been a color analyst.' He said, 'Don't worry, you know the football team, just go ahead and do it.'"

Myron accepted the job but added a caveat, one designed to protect his reputation as a journalist: "I said, 'Okay I'll try it, but I'll tell you one thing, I'm gonna say whatever I think. If the Steelers are playing great, I'm gonna be ecstatic. If the Steelers are stinking out the joint, I'm gonna say they're stinking out the joint.' . . . Ed said he was surprised, that he thought I knew the Steeler organization too well, that it wasn't even necessary to say such a thing."

The *Press* announced the new radio team in a one-line note on July 24: "Myron Cope will do the color and Jack Fleming the play-by-play on WTAE-Radio's Pittsburgh Steelers coverage in the fall."

New coach, new talent, new stadium, new radio guy; things were changing rapidly across the Rooneys' realm. Even before the first snap of the '70 season, the new decade was shaping up to be very different from the old.

OVERLOOKED IN THE Steelers' choice of analyst was the fact that Myron, despite covering dozens of football games for newspapers and magazines, had never called one on the air. He had done some pre- and postgame commentary here and there. While a student at Pitt, he had served as a "spotter"—the guy in the radio booth who helps announcers quickly identify the ball carrier and the guys who tackled him. But as far as complementing the play-by-play man with instant analysis of the action, background info on the players, funny stories, and whatnot—all of it to be delivered in fifteen or twenty second bursts between plays—Myron was the rawest of rookies, one who'd be learning on the job.

WTAE could take comfort that Myron's new partner knew everything there was to know about calling an athletic contest. A newspaper in his native Morgantown, West Virginia, once estimated that "Jack" Fleming—his real name was Leo—had done the play-by-play for nearly one thousand games at the pro, college, and high school levels. And that guess was made in 1966, not even the halfway point of Fleming's fifty-year radio and TV career. Fleming was well known by then as the Voice of the Mountaineers, a title he earned calling football and basketball games for his alma mater, West Virginia University. He had also earned a good reputation in Pittsburgh for his work calling Steelers games, a job he had done with various partners since 1958. No less an authority than Bob Prince called Fleming "one of the finest I've ever heard."

Fleming was lucky to be broadcasting at all. Eighteen years old when the United States was sucked into World War II, Fleming joined the U.S. Army Air Corps and was sent to England as part of a B-17 bomber crew that conducted air raids on Germany. On his twenty-third mission, in September 1944, his plane was hit by enemy fire, knocking out two of the four engines. With the plane struggling to stay aloft, the crew bailed out over northern France. Fleming parachuted to safety, landing in Château-Thierry, a village that had been liberated by Allied troops only weeks before. Unfortunately, on his way down, he struck a tree and sustained serious injuries to his face, including a cut lip, broken jaw, the loss of his upper front teeth, and various facial abrasions. French villagers rushed to his aid and got him to a field hospital. From there he was flown to England, where he was hospitalized but soon suffered another setback, hepatitis. In early 1945 he was sent back to West Virginia so he could fully recover.

While recuperating at the famed Greenbrier Hotel, which had been converted to a military hospital during the war, Fleming began entertaining the patients as a disc jockey and quiz-show master over the public address system. Patients liked his affable manner and resonant voice, a light bulb went off, and upon his release from the army, Fleming obtained a job with radio station WAJR in Morgantown. By the fall of 1947, at the tender age of twenty-four, he was the lead announcer on WVU football and basketball broadcasts, a job he would hold with a couple of short breaks for a half century.

Fleming's chief hallmarks as a play-by-play man were clarity, an eye for detail, and a natural enthusiasm. Basketball Hall of Famer Jerry West, a WVU alumnus, called Fleming "an artist with words." Few were better at describing a person, a game situation, or a beautiful fall afternoon on a college campus. Fleming also had an almost devilish sense of humor that came to the fore when WVU's chief rivals came to town. Take this scene-setter ahead of an October 1988 WVU-Penn State game. The Nittany Lions, he told listeners, "are led by a crafty little guy with horn-rimmed glasses, the man who promotes himself as the savior of college football. West Virginia is not fooled on this October day. It's Joe Paterno, the Darth Vader from Mount Nittany. He'll do anything to win this football game, to pacify Penn State's newfound horde of hors d'oeuvre-chomping, wine-sipping, Mercedes-driving yuppie followers. My friends, this isn't a football game today, it is a crusade!"

When broadcasting, Fleming explained, "I strive for accuracy but I also strive to entertain, make it as colorful as possible, because you can't lose sight of the fact it is a show." He also didn't mind letting the audience know he was rooting for the home team—openly when he worked for the Steelers, rabidly when he called a Mountaineers game. This latter trait occasionally got him into trouble with opposing fans; after a 1975 basketball game in Morgantown, he was physically threatened by visiting Pitt fans for cheering on WVU with such fervor. Police had to wade in before punches were thrown.

In later years he was photographed several times carrying a sign that simply read "Beat Pitt." No wonder that Fleming, despite his work for the Steelers and his other roles in Pittsburgh radio and TV, never gained any real popularity in the city.

Like the Steelers, Fleming and Cope would have a few exhibition games to work out the kinks. The two made their debut at a Steelers-Dolphins contest on August 8, 1970—also the first preseason game for the Steelers' new QB, Terry Bradshaw. If Myron entertained any notion that Steelers broadcasting was vaulting him to a world of fortune and glamor, this preseason game obliterated it. The teams played on a humid, rain-battered Saturday night in Jacksonville, then a pro football backwater. The crowd at the Gator Bowl was officially announced at a hair over thirteen thousand, a figure one Miami sportswriter termed "imaginative." The Steelers lost 16–10, in part because the team's top receiver, Roy Jefferson, dropped a pass in the end zone.

Given the sad state of Steelers football in 1970, it's doubtful that many were listening back in Pittsburgh. But three days after the game, Cope got his initial review as a Steelers broadcaster. "Myron Cope, whose analysis is fifty times better than his voice, described it perfectly when he said [QB] Kent Nix couldn't seem to move the team but Bradshaw seems to inspire them," wrote Steve Kittey of the *Latrobe Bulletin*. Just one line, but it was a thumbs-up. Kittey weighed in again a few weeks later, after four more exhibition games. "Though Myron Cope's voice isn't the most pleasant over the air, his commentary and color are excellent additions to the broadcasts," he opined.

Both Cope and Bradshaw made their regular season premieres on September 20 at Three Rivers Stadium against Houston. For the highly touted rookie quarterback, it was a rough initiation—he completed just four of sixteen passes, got booed by the home crowd, and was pulled in the third quarter as the Steelers lost 19–7, their fourteenth loss in a row. Myron lasted the entire game and had no reported troubles, except in preparations for the postgame show, when he asked Bradshaw for an interview and was initially turned down. The emotional Bradshaw related in his autobiography, *It's Only a Game*, that he didn't want to discuss his difficulties. "I knew I was a failure. I didn't have a need to broadcast that news," he said. But teammate Preston Pearson convinced Bradshaw that doing postgame shows was part of the job. He talked to Myron, then retreated to his car in the Three Rivers parking lot and cried.

Unlike Bradshaw, who threw a league-topping twenty-four interceptions in 1970, Cope got through his rookie year without any booing or controversy. There were no public calls for his removal. That doesn't mean that everything behind the scenes was copacetic. Fleming was used to working with other seasoned game announcers like Bender and Joe Tucker. Now he was paired with an excitable neophyte, and the transition was jarring. Myron, used to flying solo on his daily commentaries, simply didn't know when to shut up.

In a football radio broadcast, the play-by-play man is supposed to call the action; the commentator provides details and insight. But Myron kept stepping on Fleming's toes, either by speaking too early or speaking too much.

"There was a time, the first year I believe it was, in Philadelphia and Frenchy Fuqua ran like eighty yards for a touchdown," Myron recalled years later. "Fleming is trying to describe the play, and one rule was the audience cannot hear when two people talk at the same time on a mike on radio. The audience can't make out what they're saying. But I don't know that and I'm on my feet yelling, 'Frenchman, quit looking behind you!' He keeps looking for who's going to tackle him, and I'm yelling like that and Fleming, oh my God, was he mad."

Fleming was too much of a professional to boil over on the air, but Myron saw what was happening, on that day and others: "He would turn beet red and at the first commercial break he would leave the booth and go out in the hall or whatever it was to cool off and come back when the play resumed. . . . You just knew he was thinking, 'Why did they give me this amateur?'"

"Early on Jack was frustrated, because Myron was not a pro in broadcasting," confirms Joe Gordon. "Myron would interrupt him and Myron would go off on these tangents that were unrelated to the game. Jack was the ultimate pro and he resented that."

"We thought, this will never work," recalled Dan Rooney. "And it was a struggle. Jack exercised some tremendous patience." Rooney said it was three years before Fleming and Cope could work comfortably together. Myron said it was more like five.

But work together they did, and Steelers broadcasts were better because of it. The contrast in their voices was interesting in itself, Fleming's resonant baritone alternating (or competing) with Cope's scratchy tenor. Neither was an ex-player or coach, a minor problem from a marketing standpoint, but a nonissue for the bulk of listeners, who had little use for technical analysis or inside-football jargon.

The key element in their partnership, though, was chemistry. For all the friction caused by Myron's inexperience, the two men clicked on-air. Both were high-energy broadcasters, though Myron could crank it up a couple notches higher. Both could be witty without overshooting their audience. Both took football seriously but always remembered that it was a game, meant to be fun. And after a while, they evolved into a captivating and—counter to Myron's memory—a professional radio team. When the game was intense, they focused on the action, with Cope delivering concise, enlightening bursts of information between Fleming's description of the plays. If the game slowed down or the Steelers took a comfortable lead, a lively banter began.

COPE: That fumble was awfully propitious for reasons we'll explain just as soon as the first opportunity presents itself.

FLEMING: Then you can tell me what propitious means. That would help.

During the Steelers' first Super Bowl in party-hearty New Orleans, Fleming noted that players were frequently slipping on the Tulane Stadium turf.

> FLEMING: One thing we did not mention was a thunderstorm in the middle of the night last night. That came in the dead of night last night and added to the footing problems here today.
> COPE (after a pause): What would you be doing up in the middle of the night in New Orleans?

The back-and-forth got especially spirited several years later once Cope started promoting the Terrible Towel.

> COPE: Do you think it's strange that John Stallworth made a miraculous touchdown run after a great catch? Do you think it's strange that Lynn Swann found himself so wide open in the end zone that he didn't have a man within ten yards of him? None of that is strange. The Terrible Towel was poised to strike! It has been striking repeatedly today, dishing out one miracle after another!
> FLEMING: We're gonna throw the Towel out there and let IT play.
> COPE: It'll be a massacre then, a massacre!

"Myron appreciated the chemistry that a two-man crew can develop," says Hillgrove. "It's almost like comedy teams, Martin and Lewis, Abbott and Costello, where there had to be a straight man and funny man, but the chemistry that develops between them makes them a success." Fleming and Cope even looked like a comedy team, with the tall-but-portly Fleming towering over his partner, who had to sit atop two taped-together phone books so he was high enough to see the game.

The Cope working the Steelers' broadcasts of the early and mid-1970s is not quite the Cope of Steelers Nation's cherished memory. The voice is certainly there: loud, nasal, buzzsaw like, able to cut through crowd noise and AM-band static with little difficulty. He flaunts his strong Pittsburgh accent ("When Franco's rolling, he's tough to bring *dahn*") and deploys SAT-level words—resolute, salient, consternation—that no other sportscaster except Howard Cosell would even try to use.

But listening to the handful of game broadcasts that survive from this era, one is struck at how restrained Myron is compared to later years. Even with Myron butting in when he shouldn't, Fleming does at least 80 percent of the talking. When he does speak, Myron mostly maintains an even keel, never taking off into high-pitched fits of excitement, never conjuring up metaphors that involve ballet dancers or food.

Also missing: Myron's catchphrases. No "Yoi!" No "Okel dokel." Not even an "Mmm-hah." None of these expressions had entered his vocabulary yet, at least not on the air. The Bengals at this stage are the Bengals, not the Bungles. Chuck Noll is still awaiting promotion to the Emperor Chaz.

But boring the listener is something that Myron simply cannot do. In early Copespeak, runners don't escape tacklers, they "give 'em the zig and the zag" or run a "real zig-zagger." A leaping receiver doesn't use his fingertips—he makes a great finger*nail* catch. A possibly concussed Terry Bradshaw is said to be on "dream street." Steelers who drop easy passes are told to "get some glue on their hands." Describing one hard tackle, Myron barks out, "If Joe Greene hit me the way he just hit Jim Kiick, I wouldn't wake up for a year!"

In a way that might not be accepted today, he also doesn't mind referring to a player's race or religion. In the opening game of the 1974 season, the Steelers' first Black quarterback, Joe Gilliam, completed a pass to the team's first Jewish tight end, Randy Grossman. Myron's analysis: "All I can say is play that soul music and dance that Hava Nagila!"

Nor does Myron ignore his promise to criticize the Steelers when they stink. In the second quarter of a September 1974 game against Denver, with Noll's men trailing 21–7, he opens fire on the receiving corps. "Will those Steelers please start holding Joe Gilliam's passes? This is brutal. They dropped, I would say, four passes this afternoon that were easily catchable," he grouses. Minutes later, rookie John Stallworth lets another ball get away, and Myron suggests that the Steelers replace him with a guy who's on injured reserve. "This is terrible! Stallworth should have had that!" he exclaims. Fleming jokes that maybe the Steelers could trade the rookie to Denver. Luckily, Dan Rooney wasn't listening and hung on to the future Hall of Famer.

From the start, Fleming & Cope were more engaging than anyone the national networks sent in to cover Steelers games, and thousands of Steelers fans developed the habit of putting the game on television, turning down the sound, and cranking up the radio so they could hear their favorite local broadcasters call the action instead. It wasn't a perfect system; the radio call tended to lag a few seconds behind the TV picture, or vice versa. But a big slice of Steelers fandom didn't care.

Bill Hillgrove was among those who picked the Steelers' radio team over TV men like Curt Gowdy and Dick Enberg. "If I watched it on television, I had to have the radio game," he says. "I wouldn't miss Myron's comments. The entertainment value was immense. He could make you laugh, he could get you fired up. He connected with Steeler fans instantly."

Future *Post-Gazette* sportswriter Chuck Finder, growing up a half hour south of Pittsburgh in "Little Washington, PA," came from a family that chose Fleming & Cope to narrate their Sunday afternoons. "The TV announcers didn't know the team as well—the TV networks not having as much talent in those days—while Jack Fleming and Myron were part of your furniture," Finder says. "They told the Steeler stories you wanted to hear. They entertained you good, bad or tie, and most of it was good. [Los Angeles Dodgers announcer] Vin Scully is probably a good approximation of what they were, Scully or Haray Caray, people who were welcomed into your front door or into your cars. They were part of your family."

MYRON BIRTHED OR midwifed many names and concepts in Steelers lore—the Immaculate Reception, the Terrible Towel, Slash, the Bus. But occasionally, his fertile imagination produced a dud.

The Steelers' 1971 defense was nothing spectacular; the team gave up 292 points, only the seventeenth best in the NFL. But the young defensive line was getting rave reviews. Left tackle Joe Greene, now in his third season, was an all-around terror, a constant threat to slice through the opposing linemen and slam the quarterback or ball carrier to the ground. Teams often double covered Greene, leaving openings that were exploited by his linemates, particularly Dwight White and L. C. Greenwood, who racked up nine and eleven sacks that season, respectively. Two veterans, Ben McGee and Lloyd Voss, capably filled the fourth slot.

Seeking to stir up interest in the still mediocre team, WTAE radio sponsored a contest that October: name the Steelers' front four. It wasn't an original concept. The Los Angeles Rams' defensive line had been dubbed the Fearsome Foursome. The Minnesota Vikings had the Purple People Eaters. Surely a sack-happy line anchored by Mean Joe Greene deserved a nickname, too.

Myron announced the contest during one of his morning commentaries. Listening on his family's kitchen radio, Greg Kronz, a sophomore at Montour High School, west of Pittsburgh, thought for about thirty seconds and turned to his mother. "I've got it—the Steel Curtain," he said. The name was a play on the term Iron Curtain, coined by Winston Churchill to describe the Soviet-imposed dividing line between communist and democratic Europe after World War II. At his mom's urging, Kronz mailed his suggestion to WTAE.

A month passed with no word from the station. Then, one day, Kronz's mother ran out of the house, shouting, "You won! You won!" Kronz came inside to find his father on the phone with Myron. It turned out a total of seventeen people had suggested "the Steel Curtain." The station held a drawing, and Kronz was selected as the winner. The prize was a four-night trip to Miami for two, plus tickets to see a Steelers-Dolphins game. Kronz was deemed too young to go, so his parents went in his place, enjoying a second honeymoon on the strength of their son's brainstorm.

And the Steelers' defense was known as the Steel Curtain happily ever after.

Except that it wasn't.

At first, the Steel Curtain tag simply didn't catch on. The Steelers' defense grew soft toward the end of '71 season as the team dropped three of its final four games and let a possible playoff berth slip away. The nickname was all but forgotten until the following year, when the defense suddenly rose to new heights, especially in an October game where they held the visiting Houston Oilers to only seven first downs. Again, the issue arose: What do we call this defense? Myron, who wasn't totally sold on Kronz's idea, came up with his own: the Anvil Chorus.

Classical music lovers know the "Anvil Chorus" as a tune written by Italian composer Giuseppe Verdi for his 1853 opera *Il Trovatore.* The scene featuring the tune depicts Spanish Gypsies striking their anvils with hammers at dawn. Somehow, Myron connected this image to Greene, Greenwood, and White. "They were so tough they reminded me of blacksmiths," he later explained. That part of the idea made sense. The problem was that Verdi's stirring tune, familiar to operagoers, was not on the hit parade of the Steelers' blue-collar fan base.

Steelers receiver Dave Smith didn't even like the sound of the name. "The Anvil Chorus? That name don't have no soul," he told Myron.

Myron pressed ahead. Before the Steelers' mid-October home game against New England, he arranged for the band that played during timeouts and halftime to perform the song each time the Steelers sacked the Patriots' quarterback, Jim Plunkett. Fans at Three Rivers got very familiar with the melody that afternoon, as the Steelers dropped Plunkett a total of seven times. But it generated no enthusiasm from the crowd. "Nobody recognized the Anvil Chorus when it was played," Myron lamented. And Patriots owner Billy Sullivan complained that the band taunted Plunkett with a "funeral dirge" each time he went down.

Myron abandoned his idea thereafter. "With that one," he said, "I guess I was overreaching." By season's end, Steel Curtain had emerged as the popular choice. In time, the name would grow to cover not just the front four but the Steelers' entire smothering defense, which by the mid-1970s was regularly holding opponents to less than ten points per game and sending five or six players to the Pro Bowl each season.

But imagine if Myron's suggestion had caught on. Instead of carrying Terrible Towels into Steelers games, each fan might be lugging an anvil.

MYRON WAS PART OF a much better idea when WTAE decided to provide live coverage of the 1972 NFL draft. In media terms, this was the Stone Age of the draft, years before the proceedings were televised and eons before fans were permitted onsite to cheer their teams' selections and pummel the NFL commissioner with boos. Most fans learned of the picks on the evening news or in the next day's newspapers.

But Myron had always liked the drama of draft day, hanging out at the Steelers' offices as far back as the early '50s to see which players the team chose. Most likely at his urging, WTAE radio decided to get the jump on the '72 draft, held the first of February, and positioned Myron and Tom Bender inside the Steelers' offices to report and analyze the picks starting at 9:30 that morning. Sports talk radio did not exist in that era, and this may have been the first time any media outlet *anywhere* provided day-long coverage of the draft.

The station chose a good year to begin; the Steelers used their number-one pick to select a big, fast running back from Penn State, Franco Harris. Another building block in the coming Steelers dynasty had arrived.

Myron also broke new ground when he got wind of a quasi-contest brewing in the Steelers' dressing room. Several of the team's Black players—most notably running back John "Frenchy" Fuqua, defensive end L. C. Greenwood, and safety Chuck Beatty—had taken to wearing the flamboyant, ghetto-chic clothes popularized in early 1970s "Blaxploitation" movies. Bell-bottom pants, wide-lapelled jackets, and hugely brimmed hats, all of it rendered in the newly available Day-Glo colors and cut tight to show off the athletes' physiques, became common sights in the hallways of Three Rivers Stadium.

Greenwood and Beatty weren't trying to make a point; they just liked how the stuff looked. Fuqua, however, made clear that he viewed style as a contest, of equal if not greater importance to the games on Sundays. "I am the best dressed player in the league," he declared toward the end of the '71 season, his second with the Steelers. "Chuck Beatty used to be best dressed, but he conceded the title to me," he added during preseason the following year.

Advocates of the Brooks Brothers suit-and-tie school no doubt disagreed. If flash was your barometer, however, Frenchy was the undisputed champ. He had arrived in a trade with the New York Giants prior to the 1970 season and decided what the Steelers needed was, in his words, a touch of class. He had a "superstar" outfit, highlighted by blood-red pants and a sport jacket decorated with red stars. He had a Pancho Villa outfit, with a skin-tight black jumpsuit and a huge black sombrero. Then there was the Count Frenchy outfit—a skin-tight, shiny lavender jumpsuit with a huge lavender cape, a Three Musketeer hat, and a cane. Count Frenchy was more or less Fuqua's public persona, a reflection of an outsized personality stuffed into a slightly undersized running back. He was born to European royalty, the Detroit-raised Fuqua would patiently explain, but fell asleep one day while sunning in the French Riviera, and when he woke up, his skin had turned dark.

This was the kind of character that Myron understood and welcomed, especially now that he was doing commentaries for television. In the fall of 1970 Myron called for a "dress-off" among the Steelers' fashion plates, with himself as the announcer and judge, the other Steelers as the hooting and hollering crowd, and a cameraman present to capture it all for the Channel 4 six o'clock news. Myron called the action like a prizefight, Fuqua recalled: "L.C. breaks out with the hot pants, but Frenchy counters with fringed briefs. Beatty slugs back with a sock; [Lee] Calland whips out a shoe."

"It became a happening, with Myron giving the blow by blow. That was right up his alley," recalls Joe Gordon.

Judge Cope declared Frenchy the hands-down winner. Next year, same competition, same result, Fuqua in a landslide.

In '72 teammates convinced an unlikely candidate, center Jim Clack, to take on the champ for the now annual event. ("Clack was a good guy, but I didn't think he'd go in for something like that!" says Gordon, with a laugh.) Clack outfitted himself as gaudily as he could—blue silk underwear, zebra-striped socks, blue velour pants, sweater vest, plaid bow tie—but didn't stand a chance. The original film shows Fuqua came decked out in a three-piece black-and-white plaid suit augmented with a red shirt, a red snap-brim hat, black leather gloves, and a white wool coat monogrammed with his initials, JFF.

He also wore two watches. The dress-off was essentially over when Fuqua pulled out one of the watches, gazed at his opponent, and said, "Your time is running out, Clack," as his teammates howled.

Myron announced the results that night on the news: "A young white hope made a strong challenge. He has a great future ahead of him. But any man who can wear two watches and have Franco Harris as his butler is the winner and still champion, Frenchman Fuqua!"

That's right; Franco Harris, the Steelers' prize number-one draft pick, served as Fuqua's assistant during the contest. At other times that season, Harris was assigned the role of walking behind Fuqua to hold up the showman's cape, like a royal courtier, lest any dust from the floor touch the champion's clothes. It was a task for a rookie, a sign of the pecking order in the Steelers' clubhouse.

The order of things was about to change.

6

Gorillas, Franco, and Frank

It was time for something to happen. For three years, Chuck Noll and the Rooneys had steered the Steelers through sweeping change, clearing out nearly every player from the old regime, switching conferences, moving to a new stadium, and stuffing the team with young talent through the draft. Five guys on the 1971 roster would end up in the Hall of Fame; another ten would play in at least one Pro Bowl.

But the fans were getting impatient. In three seasons, Noll's teams had racked up only twelve wins against thirty defeats. The defense was still too porous, the offense still prone to stalling. In the '71 season finale at Three Rivers, a loss to the Rams, the less-than-sellout crowd of thirty-nine thousand boiled over, booing once when the Steelers left the field at halftime, again when they returned for the third quarter, and, in case the Rooneys missed the point, once more when the stadium PA guy wished everyone a merry Christmas.

Dan Rooney assured the press near season's end that Noll's job was safe. "Sure, I'm disappointed, but we're not going to do anything rash," he said. Rooney said nothing about the club's radio team, which from Myron's perspective was a good thing—it wasn't on his radar. Still, a voice inside

Myron said don't bet the house on this Steelers gig, not yet anyway. In the early months of '72, while continuing his commentaries at WTAE, he picked up extra bucks working the banquet circuit and kept his writing career alive with a long *Sports Illustrated* article about Arnold Palmer, his first magazine story in a year.

SI publisher Rick Munro penned an introduction both lauding and kidding Myron for his radio work ("Cope soon became a household word in Pittsburgh. That word was often unprintable"). But in the last line, Munro made it clear that he desired more content from his wayward writer. "It would be better for our readers not to have to wait so long between *SI* bylines, Myron," he said.

And indeed, Myron did not yet consider his magazine career a thing of the past. "I'm a realist about broadcasting," he told the *Philadelphia Daily News* that year. "I know the day will come when I'll be dumped unceremoniously on my can and I'll have to go back to writing. Meanwhile, I'm taking their money and having a lot of fun."

By this time, Myron had discovered a new way to generate fun *and* money: radio commercials. Pittsburgh-area businesses had gotten wise to the fact that his voice jumped out from the aural clutter of the airwaves and that his reputation for honesty, delivered with humor, might reflect well on their wares. Myron had no qualms about being, well, commercialized. He had entered radio for the bigger bucks, after all. In the best situations, he had a hand in writing the ad as well as voicing it, and the resulting commercial had an unmistakable Copeian stamp. A good example was this 1972 car ad, which Myron delivered in his usual animated style:

> You're looking for an economy car, so you go down the line: Vega, Pinto, Volkswagen, Toyota. Not bad! Might do! But hey, don't buy anything till you've seen Plymouth's economy car, the '73 Duster. . . . In a Duster you get room for five people, not four. You're not driving a telephone booth on wheels. Zounds, you get a trunk you can stuff a Steeler into! You get an engine that doesn't give you heart failure wondering if you're gonna make it on the Parkway before that car a quarter-mile back crawls up your rear window!

In the coming years, Myron would record dozens of similar commercials, promoting convenience stores, mattress stores, ski shops, banks, food brands, amusement parks, gas stations and most any other business willing to pony up for the Cope voice. An executive for Ketchum Communications, Pittsburgh's leading advertising agency, summed up Myron's appeal. "His voice is part of his shtick, if you will," said Dave Austin. "He's a good self-promoter and almost a caricature of himself, but if a spot is written with the right sense of humor, it can be very effective."

However, Elizabeth Cope says her dad was somewhat selective about the commercials he accepted. "He tried to be ethical about it to some degree," she says. "He wanted to make the money, but if there was a product he hated, he wasn't going to endorse it." She says businesses would sometimes give him free goods in exchange for his services, but her dad would draw the line there too. "In fact, they tried to give him a Porsche, a free one, and he turned it down, which I was upset about," she remembers. "He said he wouldn't be caught dead in a Porsche. I said, 'Why?' He said, 'People would look at me, they'd say there goes Myron Cope in a Porsche, he must think he's really something.' And he was older at the time, and he's like, 'They're gonna think I'm going through a midlife crisis, or trying to show off. I'm not going to drive a Porsche!'"

In 1972 no one was giving Myron luxury cars, though he did get use of a Duster. And truth be told, not everyone was on board yet with Cope the broadcaster. That fall the *Pittsburgh Press* received and printed a letter signed by twenty-nine petitioners calling for his removal as the Steelers' analyst. "We are at a loss as to the thinking behind local Steeler radio," wrote the unhappy listeners. "Why WTAE permits live broadcasts to sink to high school level with the irritating, constantly-interrupting voice of Myron Cope completely escapes us. There must be several thousand ex-football players who could enhance Jack Fleming's play by play and not be as repulsive as Cope, who obviously never participated in football and who certainly must have been a broadcasting school dropout."

So disparaging was the letter that *Press* sports editor Pat Livingston was suspicious. "This sounds like something Cope would put you guys up to," he wrote in response. But he went on to chastise the petitioners: "You're vastly outnumbered. Petitions which approve of Cope usually come in with many more signatures. Put up with Cope. How would you like the whining, condescending voice of an ex-player like Al DeRogatis polluting your air every week? Or Cosell?"

If Myron was at all unsettled by the public naysayers, WTAE executives likely gave him plenty of reassurance. The financial ledgers spoke for themselves. Prior to the Steelers' 1970 season, the station had sold only 50 percent of its commercial time for the games. In 1972 all commercials for both regular and preseason games were sold out by July 4, as were pregame and postgame shows hosted by the Steelers' color commentator. No doubt the Steelers' marginal improvement played a role, but so did Myron's popularity.

Tooling around town in his Duster as the '72 season approached, Myron had to wonder if the Steelers were ever going to start clicking like his career. The coming season would be the Pittsburgh's fortieth in the NFL, and as *Sports Illustrated* pointed out, the team had yet to earn so much as a Kewpie doll for the office trophy case. The prognosticators saw reason for hope. "The Pittsburgh Steelers just could win their first title—if. If they can find a pass defense, if the team can win away from home and if quarterback Terry Bradshaw has grown up," said *SI* in its 1972 NFL preview.

Noll expressed stronger faith in his team, as did Art Rooney and some of the players. "This is the money year," said Joe Greene. Frenchy Fuqua, as always, was more colorful in his forecast. "Hey man," he said, "this year is going to be a beautiful thing."

The Sporting News acknowledged that the team's fanbase might be more circumspect. "Steeler fans are among the NFL's most cynical," it said. "This is the fourth decade in which they have heard about rebuilding programs, next year and the future."

The fans' cynicism was about to be slayed. Blown to kingdom come, in fact.

AS THE CALENDAR flipped to October, Pittsburgh was still a baseball town, the Steelers were just another football team, and Myron Cope was still a sportswriter working his jaws to make extra money. No one sensed the tectonic plates of the Pittsburgh sports world were about to undergo a massive, thunderous shift.

Cope and Fleming were at Busch Stadium in St. Louis that October 1, relaying the action to radio listeners as the Steelers pulled out a 25–19 victory over the Cardinals. Bradshaw enjoyed one of his finest games yet as a pro, completing twenty-five of forty passes. His final pass was a beaut, a perfectly thrown loop over the Cards' secondary that Frank Lewis grabbed along the left sideline and ran in for a game-winning, 38-yard touchdown.

But the win was second-string news in Pittsburgh. One day earlier the Pirates' superstar outfielder, Roberto Clemente—easily the best known, most revered sports figure in town—had pounded the three thousandth hit of his career, a line drive double to center field, joining a club that to that point had only fourteen other players in baseball history. Now Clemente rested as the Pirates sold tickets at a rapid clip for their playoff showdown with the Cincinnati Reds. The Bucs had just captured their third straight division crown and were looking to defend their 1971 World Series title. Games one and two of the National League Championship Series would draw crowds of more than fifty thousand to Three Rivers Stadium, a number inconceivable a few years earlier, when the team still played in the confines of ancient Forbes Field.

The first rumble of change was felt a week later. The Bucs led the deciding game of the NLCS in Cincinnati, just three outs from another pennant, when ace reliever Dave Guisti hung a curveball and the Reds' Johnny Bench blasted it over the right field wall to tie the score, 3–3. Minutes later, with a runner on third, Guisti's replacement, Bob Moose, tossed a pitch that bounced freakishly over the head of catcher Manny Sanguillen, letting in the winning run. The Reds jumped and danced on the field while the Pirates trudged into the dugout, their hopes for a dynasty turned to dust. The loss was a double blow to the Bucs; according to general manager Joe L. Brown, it cost the franchise $1 million in World Series revenue—bad news for a club that was enjoying good attendance but was also carrying high salaries and stadium maintenance costs and had quietly started to drip red ink.

A second tremor was detected a few days afterward, when the Steelers hosted the Houston Oilers. Noll's men entered the game with two wins and two losses, good enough for second place in the AFC Central, a game behind Cincinnati. The head coach, however, was dissatisfied with his chief running backs, Frenchy Fuqua and Preston Pearson, and shifted the workload to the team's first-round draft pick, Franco Harris. Harris exploded for 115 yards on nineteen carries and scored the go-ahead touchdown in the 24–7 victory. The defense, meanwhile, was starting to live up to its Steel Curtain nickname, piling up five sacks and limiting the Houston offense to just 108 yards on the day.

The game drew a crowd of forty-two thousand—short of a sellout, but excellent by Same Old Steelers standards. Fans accustomed to seeing their team sink out of playoff contention by Halloween felt stirrings of hope. For the first time, a few enterprising souls hung banners in the stands. Some were of the generic "Go Steelers!" variety, but one in particular caught Myron's eye. It read "Gerela's Gorillas."

"I didn't know who the hell they were," he later said, "but the concept was intriguing."

The Gorillas were the product of eight die-hard Steelers fans from Port Vue, a manufacturing town of a few thousand souls southwest of Pittsburgh. The group had formed in 1971 under the influence of what Myron liked to call adult beverages. As charter member Chuck Witkowski remembered it, "We were sitting around a bar watching a game on television. We all decided to get behind a guy and decided on Roy Gerela." Why Gerela, the team's placekicker? "We had met him and he's been really nice to us," Witkowski explained. Okay, fair enough, but it was an odd choice, nonetheless. On a team packed with budding stars and big personalities, Gerela was human wallpaper: pleasant, in the background, a low-key Canadian quietly doing his job. The last guy to inspire a fan club, under normal circumstances.

But Steelers fans were done with normal. The club's ringleader, a thirty-four-year-old forestry worker named Bob Bubanic, attended each game at Three Rivers in a rented gorilla suit (weekly cost: $50). His fellow club members wore white T-shirts emblazoned with the group logo, a gorilla swinging from a crossbar. The eight men bought front-row seats in the end zone's mezzanine section, in full view of the kickers, and when the Steelers' opponents lined up for a field goal, Bubanic and friends went into full distraction mode, jumping around and making ape noises. The whole thing was just for fun, Bubanic explained late that season. "We've had a good time and the fans get a kick out of us."

Despite the ruckus, the Gorillas might have escaped public notice if not for Myron, who spotted their banner and mentioned it on air during the Houston game. Bubanic and friends decided to return the appreciation. At the next home game, they banged on the press box door at halftime and offered Myron a Gerela's Gorillas T-shirt. He accepted. A connection was made. And an idea took root in Myron's fertile brain. The Steelers were set to host Cincinnati the first Sunday in November. Two weeks earlier, Bengals kicker Horst Muhlmann had missed three short-range field goals in Los Angeles against the Rams. Wouldn't it be interesting, Myron thought, if Muhlmann was given a prominent reminder of those failures when he entered Three Rivers?

Using his WTAE platform, he issued a special message that week to his new comrades: "Attention Gerela's Gorillas—Attention Gorillas—assignment for Sunday—make a sign—embarrass Horst Muhlmann, the Cincinnati kicker—that is all." The Gorillas enthusiastically followed orders, constructing a yellow banner that screamed out in giant block letters: "Horst, Remember L.A.!"

Muhlmann was not a factor in the game, as the Steelers blew out the Bengals 40–17 for their fourth straight victory. But Myron realized he was onto something: an interactive bond between broadcaster and fans that could, conceivably, affect the game on the field. He insisted that he was acting at the behest of the Steelers' head honcho. "Noll is one of those coaches who are always after the press and radio guys to contribute something positive to the team," he explained. "Just for the hell of it, I decided to take him up on it."

The Steelers hosted Kansas City the following week. Again, Myron radioed instructions to the Gorillas: remind KC kicker Jan Stenerud of a critical field goal he missed in the Chiefs' epic double overtime playoff loss to the Dolphins the previous January. The Gorillas responded with a sign that read "Jan, Remember the Miami Playoff!" It also featured a drawing of a goalpost with the ball sailing to the right. Did the sign affect Stenerud, one of the most accurate kickers of his era? Stenerud didn't say it did, but facing the sign in the third quarter, he missed an easy 27-yard field goal. "Wasn't even close," noted the *Press*. Meanwhile, Harris rushed for 134 yards, Gerela kicked a trio of field goals, the defense sacked Len Dawson five times, and the Steelers prevailed 16–7.

The Gorillas were off the following Sunday as the Steelers traveled to Cleveland and lost a nail-biter, 26–24—ironically, on a last-second field goal from Browns kicker Don Cockroft. Next up: a match at home against Fran Tarkenton and the Vikings, who boasted one of the NFL's best placekickers in ten-year veteran Fred Cox. The situation posed a minor moral dilemma for Myron, as Cox was a native of nearby Monongahela, Pennsylvania, had attended the University of Pittsburgh, and was known to be an overall nice guy. In his now weekly message to the Gorillas, Myron suggested adding a friendly element to the sign, like "We love ya Monongahela Freddie, but choke!"

The Gorillas, feeling less charitable, shortened the message to a blunt "Mon City Freddie, Choke!" If Cox didn't feel the pressure, his holder Paul Krause did, fumbling two snaps on field goal attempts ("Even the centers and holders are starting to choke," Myron boasted). Meanwhile, Harris topped 100 yards rushing for the fifth week in a row, and the Steelers rolled to a 23–10 win. With three games to go, the team was 8-3 and tied for first place in the AFC Central.

Pittsburgh found itself gripped by a mounting case of football hysteria. In their tortured forty-year existence, the Steelers had contended for a postseason slot only three other times. The Chief, Art Rooney, hated losing but was inured to it. "I keep waiting for something to happen, something bad," he told *New York Times* columnist Dave Anderson the week of the Vikings game. But with each passing week, the Steelers seemed to get stronger—as did the fans' fervor. Example: Steelers linebacker Jack Ham, a resolute Catholic, went to evening Mass at St. Bernard's church in Dormont a few hours after the Steelers beat Kansas City. The monsignor was discussing routine parish matters when he suddenly switched topics and proclaimed, "How about those Steelers?" The congregation sprung to life and someone pointed out that the team's great young linebacker was in the pews. The worshipers turned toward Ham and gave him a standing ovation. It was "just like we were out at the stadium," Ham said. "I even stayed after Mass and signed autographs."

Inside Three Rivers, the Gorillas had been joined by two other fan clubs. The smaller one rooted for Ham and was distinguished mainly by its creative name: Dobre Shunka—"Good Ham" in Slovak. The big one, growing by the day, was created to celebrate the Steelers' sensational new running back. Franco Harris had dark skin, wore a sizeable Afro, and from a distance looked primarily African American. But his mother, Gina, was a full-blooded Italian; she had met Harris's dad, an army man named Cadillac Harris, while he was stationed in Italy during World War II, and their son had an undeniably Roman face.

Inspired by Harris's string of 100-yard games, a group of Steelers season-ticket holders led by bakery owner Tony Stagno and pizza maker Al Vento equipped themselves with Italian flags and infantry helmets and began to dedicate Sundays to their new hero. Into the stadium they sneaked bottles of Italian wine, concealed in hollowed-out loaves of Italian bread, and toasted Harris as he romped through opposing defenses. The revelers called themselves Franco's Italian Army. They started to get on-air callouts from Myron, too—a situation they helped along by sending him hoagie sandwiches to consume at halftime ("That certainly hit the spot!" a satisfied Myron announced).

Myron would soon report for army duty. First, though, he had to help the Gorillas take care of the incoming Browns and their kicker. Don Cockroft was having a stellar season, leading the NFL in field goal percentage and doing double duty as the Browns' punter. Wracking his brain for an angle, Myron thought back to a year earlier when the Browns' placekicker was locked in a horrific slump. He remembered that the Browns' head coach, Nick Skorich, had said that his kicker's problem was that he tended to think too much. "Now what could the Gorillas do with that?" Myron wondered aloud in one of his morning commentaries.

Acting on Myron's observation, the Gorillas unveiled their most brilliant sign yet that Sunday, a bright yellow banner that read "Hey Cockroft, THINK!"

One out-of-town writer labeled it "expert psychological warfare."

Cockroft said he laughed when he saw the sign. "I thought it was a pretty good idea," he added. He claimed that the sign didn't bother him—but given a chance to make a 37-yard field goal in the first quarter, he kicked the ball wide right. "Gerela's Gorillas have struck again!" Myron exclaimed on the broadcast. That was the Browns' only scoring chance of the day. The Steelers annihilated the visitors 30–0, avenging the loss in Cleveland from two weeks before and seizing the top spot in the division. Harris topped 100 yards for the sixth week in a row, Gerela kicked three field goals without a miss, and the defense held Cleveland quarterback Mike Phipps to just 59 yards passing. "The Steelers' sweetest triumph in forty years," said the *Pittsburgh Press*.

The Browns game marked the greatest display of Steelers frenzy yet. The team had sold all fifty-thousand-plus seats a month in advance, and Three Rivers Stadium was draped with a record number of banners bearing slogans like "Chew 'Em Up, Franco" and "Pgh Wants Phipps Face." One group of fans hung Phipps in effigy from the upper deck. Less menacingly, some thirty members of Franco's Italian Army climbed atop the Pirates' dugout waving their red, white, and green flags and carrying a sign that read "Run Paisano Run." Some Black fans had expressed resentment at the implication Franco wasn't one of theirs, too. Tony Stagno gave assurances that the army was open to all. "Black is beautiful. Italian is beautiful. Franco is beautiful," he said.

Those who couldn't get in followed the action with Fleming and Cope—or drove to locations in central Ohio so they could sidestep the NFL's despised local blackout rules and watch the game on TV. Dozens of raucous Steelers fans took over one motel in Zanesville, Ohio, roaring at every good play, sharing tubs of beer and ignoring the motel manager's pleas for quiet. "This is an insane asylum," said one irritated motel guest. "All the way!" replied two of the Steelers rooters, raising their beer bottles in salute.

In the midst of the mania, a thirty-year-old *Post-Gazette* writer named Mike Kalina decided to put his love for the Steelers on record—literally. Like a growing number of Steelers fans, Kalina could do a decent Myron Cope impression, a little more high-pitched than the real thing but on-target in terms of the speaking style and the rhythm. In early December Kalina and two friends exploited this talent to produce a "cut-in" record, a type of comedy disc where a fake interviewer asks questions and the answers consist of soundbites pulled from current popular songs. On the record, titled *Steelers '72*, Kalina played Myron-Cannot-Cope-With-Sports, a sportscaster supposedly firing queries at Art Rooney, Terry Bradshaw, and other Steelers figures. The record was "aimed at generating more enthusiasm for the Steelers, and hopefully, a few laughs," Kalina explained.

If laughs were the goal, Kalina and pals missed wide right; the only truly funny part of the record is where "Bradshaw" responds to questions in the deep bass voice of Isaac Hayes. Still, the 45 RPM single got played on some local radio stations and earned a place in Steelers history as the first piece of music—the first of many—to be inspired by the fans' zeal for their team. Within a year, a local accordionist named Jimmy Psihoulis would take an old Andrews Sisters tune, "The Pennsylvania Polka," and give it new Steelers-centered lyrics beginning with the stirring words "We're from the town with the great football team / We cheer the Pittsburgh Steelers!"

The Kalina record also reflected the rising popularity of the team's color analyst, a development affirmed that December when Franco's Italian Army welcomed its first Jew. Forty-five minutes before kickoff at the Browns game, Stagno and company held a short ceremony outside the Three Rivers Stadium press box to induct Myron Cope into their ranks, appointing him a one-star general despite his lack of Italian ancestry. If there was still any loose talk about the Steelers getting a new partner for Jack Fleming, this surely put the kibosh on it. The fans didn't just like Myron; they were embracing him, *inviting* him to take part in their fun and excitement, a phenomenon that had never happened with Fleming, Joe Tucker, or any other Steelers announcer.

Strange as it seemed, a 5-foot-4, 140-pound writer, a man who had not played a single down of organized tackle football in his life, a guy whose larynx produced sounds that folks likened to an attack-dog whistle or anthracite tumbling down a coal chute, was becoming the voice of the Steelers.

No one could have predicted it. And no one could see that the events of the previous two months, thrilling as they had been, were merely the beginning.

DECEMBER 13, 1972. The Steelers were some 2,300 miles from Three Rivers Stadium, in the arid climate of southern California, preparing for their season finale against the San Diego Chargers. The team's record now stood at 10-3, assuring them a wild-card slot. They needed a win to clinch the division title. Taking no chances, Noll brought his men out to California six days early to adjust to the weather and time difference. Myron had flown west on the team charter, planning to file commentaries from the Steelers' training site, a Minor League baseball stadium in the resort community of Palm Springs.

But he came with a secret second agenda. Tony Stagno had given his new one-star general a mission: find Frank Sinatra and induct him into Franco's Italian Army. The esteemed Sinatra, then in the midst of a short-lived retirement, lived in Rancho Mirage, about ten miles west of Palm Springs. On the surface, the idea must have sounded ludicrous. Why would one of America's most famous singers, a legendary symbol of artistry, romance, and success, want to join a little band of football fans from Pittsburgh? Why would he even know that Franco Harris existed? But Myron did not question the orders. He and Stagno shared a desire for fun, a flair for winning attention and—critically for this mission—a potent reserve of chutzpah.

The events that transpired became a landmark moment in Myron's career and gave him a go-to story that he never seemed to tire of telling at speaking engagements, during interviews, in his autobiography, to random strangers over lunch. So it seems fitting to let Myron describe the events in his own words. He gave his most extensive account of Sinatra's induction in a 1990s speech to, of all things, the Western Pennsylvania Cemetery Association. More than twenty years had passed, but Myron seemed to recall every detail like the whole thing had happened the week before.

> So, I get out to Palm Springs, and I start putting out lines to people who [say] "He's my gumbah, no problem Myron," all these people who are gonna get me Sinatra. So, the days go by, and it is Wednesday night, and I am having dinner at a fancy restaurant called Lord Fletcher's, in the company of about a dozen media types and Steeler front office types. And I am sitting across the table from a man named Jim Boston,

who was the Steelers traveling secretary, known to his intimates as Buff Boston. He's a large man, balding, with a funny head shaped like a football. So, Buff Boston says to me, "How's your mission coming? Have you gotten Sinatra?" I says, "No, and I'm through with that, because I'm supposed to be having a good time in Palm Springs and I'm tied up with this Sinatra business, the heck with it."

And he says, "Don't give up yet, because here comes your man through the front door." I turn around and there he is, the great Sinatra. He is in the company of Leo Durocher, the controversial baseball manager, and Ken Venturi, the great pro golfer, and a tall, good-looking brunette woman. OK, they are shown to a table on the other side of the restaurant. Everyone at our table is saying, "Here's your chance Cope, here's your chance. Get into action!" I say, "Settle down." I take a cocktail napkin and write, "Dear Mr. Sinatra, we are a party of reporters and front office people traveling with the Pittsburgh Steelers" and I tell him—mind you, Franco's Italian Army has had national publicity, and is well-known by now throughout the country—I tell him we would like him to appear tomorrow at practice to be inducted as a one-star general, and that I hope I'm not interrupting this dinner. And I sign it and I write "P.S., Franco's from Hoboken," which was Sinatra's home town. Well, Franco was from New Jersey but that was a damn lie. He was from Mt. Holly. But what the hell! You do what you gotta do.

I call Lord Fletcher over and I hand him the cocktail napkin and I said, "Would you mind delivering this to Mr. Sinatra? If it's an intrusion, don't do it." He looks at it and he chuckles and says, "No problem." He goes over. These guys at the table, they say, "He's got the note! He's reading the note!" I say, "You're embarrassing me, settle down!" They say, "He's getting up! He's getting up!"

It was much rumored for some years that Frank Sinatra bet a few dollars on football games, like about ten grand a game. Those were the rumors; I didn't know if they were true or not. Also, that week in Palm Springs, Terry Bradshaw, from the last game, was suffering a dislocated pinky on his throwing hand, and it was a source of great anxiety to all Steeler fans as well as bettors across the country. [They wondered] could he throw the football? And early in the week I had spoken to the Emperor Chas Noll about this and he said to me, "Don't worry about a thing, the guy is throwing it better than he's ever thrown it in his career, because now instead of throwing it into a guy's chest and it coming out the back of the receiver, he's taking something off the ball, he has to, and he's throwing a perfect pass."

So, OK, I know that, and Sinatra puts that chair down, and confirming the rumors about his being a wagering man, the first words out of his mouth are, "How's the quarterback's finger?" And I said, "Mr. Sinatra, don't worry about a thing, the guy is never throwing the ball better." He says, "Thank you," and he talks a while with us, and goes back to the table with the two flunkies. Lord Fletcher starts bringing us bottles and bottles of the finest wine from his wine cellar, compliments of Mr. Sinatra.

Buff Boston, the traveling secretary, says you really oughta call Tony Stagno, tell him that Sinatra has agreed to be at practice tomorrow to be inducted, in case Tony and Al Vento wanna be there. I says, "Good idea." I get on the phone, it's one in the morning in Pittsburgh. His wife answers on the bedroom phone, Tony gets on, I tell him what's happening, and he says, "I can't be there, Myron." And this, mind you, was December, and he says, "I'm behind on my Christmas cookies." I says, "What are you talking about?" He says, "I'm a baker, and I'm behind on my Christmas cookies." Well, the fact of the matter, as I was to learn later, Tony had never flown on an airplane in his life and was scared stiff of 'em. But his wife, when he told her what the call was about, she said, "My God!" And all the relatives started coming from all over East Liberty and meeting in the living room and say, "You're going to Palm Springs!" And the next thing you know, Tony and Al Vento were at the airport, buying tickets and the girl was saying, "Coach or first class?" and they were saying, "Always, the Italian Army flies first class!"

The next day, Myron, fighting a hangover (compliments of Mr. Sinatra), stepped out of the hotel to board the team bus to the practice field. Chuck Noll came up to him and said, "What's this I hear about you planning a distraction at my practice today?" Myron replied something to the effect that he didn't want to hear it, that he *knew* Noll was a Sinatra fan, too, and sulked off to find a quiet seat on the bus.

That afternoon, various reporters and photographers gathered at the field alongside Myron, casting eyes nervously in all directions, waiting for Ol' Blue Eyes to appear. The Steelers players, who knew little or nothing about the previous night's events, went about preparing for the Chargers game. About an hour into practice, Sinatra had yet to appear, and a sense of disappointment began to filter through the ranks.

But the assembled journalists had underestimated Myron's powers of persuasion.

> And reporters are coming by, and looking at me, "Where's Sinatra, Cope? Cope, you're a loser again." Now, Buff Boston is on an outdoor telephone, outside the locker room, to the team's publicist Joe Gordon, who's in San Diego. Gordon says, "Did Sinatra show?" Boston says, "No, Sinatra's a no-show. Cope's a loser again." Whereupon he feels a finger tapping him on his shoulder. And a little guy in an orange cardigan and a white porkpie hat tugging his earlobe as he was wont to do, says to him, "When Sinatra says he'll show, he shows." Yeah, he had been up there in the bleachers for an hour just watching practice by himself.
>
> Now, everybody's screaming, "Sinatra's here!" And the cameras are popping and everything. And at the same moment, here come Tony Stagno and Al Vento, racing across the field, carrying baskets of red wine, cheeses, and bruschetta for the ceremony. Yeah, they made the trip! And in the induction of course there's much kissing on either cheek.
>
> And I says, "Hold everything boys, we gotta get Franco." And I race out on the practice field. I find myself in the middle of the practice field and I say, "My God, what am I doing here?" And I says, "Franco's the man's here, get over there!" Franco is a very modest rookie, very humble, he truly was, didn't want to be singled out. He said, "Myron, I'm practicing." I say, "Listen, you're crazy. The man's here, get over there!" He said, "Myron, I'm practicing." I turn to the Emperor Chas and says, "Will you tell him to get over there?" And he says, "Franco, get over there!" So, Franco gets over there.

> We hold the ceremony, everything's wonderful. Tony and Al say to me, "We gotta get the next flight out of here." Tony says, "I got my Christmas cookies. Can we stop at your hotel room and wash up? I gotta call my wife." I say, sure. We stop there, and he calls his wife and he says, "Ooooh, it was marvelous, it was like kissing God!"

Myron's pal at the *Press*, Pat Livingston, characterized the Sinatra-Cope encounter as a meeting between "the best voice and the worst voice in the English-speaking world." A California reporter, Pete Boal, noted that Cope wore an Italian Army helmet during the ceremony, which, he said, "looked as appropriate as Golda Meir's picture would on a box of pizza."

About the only people not put in a jolly and joking mood by the induction were Myron's three sisters. "His sisters were huge, huge Frank Sinatra fans," says Myron's niece Marcia Grodsky. "They were groupies when they were young, and when they were older and they would travel to see him. They gave Myron a hard time. They were jealous that he got to meet Frank Sinatra and they didn't!"

Stagno and Vento flew home to Pittsburgh that night, but pro-Steelers banners, including one that read "Franco's *Polish* Army," were much in evidence when the Steelers took the field at San Diego Stadium that Sunday. The team did just fine without their fan club generals, especially the defense, which forced seven turnovers, four on interceptions. Appropriately, Harris scored the first touchdown, which was all the Steelers would need in the 24–2 victory. At 3:45 p.m. Pacific time, the clock ran out, and an exuberant band of players lifted a beaming Chuck Noll onto their shoulders and carried him off the field. For the first time in their four-decade history, the Steelers were true winners, owners of the AFC Central title.

"Life Begins at 40 as Steelers Try First Crown on for Size," declared the headline in the next day's *Post-Gazette*. No one was happier than Art Rooney, who made the cross-country trip to see the crowning. "I'm not jumping up and down because that's not the way I am," he said as he passed out victory cigars. "But inside, I'm bubbling like a volcano."

Back in Pittsburgh two crowds began to form. Outside Three Rivers Stadium, dozens of hardy fans lined up with blankets and lawn chairs, ready to brave a night of twenty-degree cold so they'd be in line when tickets for the following weekend's playoff game against Oakland went on sale Monday morning. The other, toastier group assembled at Pittsburgh International Airport to greet their conquering heroes. The Steelers' return flight from San Diego landed well after midnight, but an estimated four thousand people were present to clap and whistle and yell their heads off as the players disembarked.

Among them, naturally, were the top generals of Franco's Italian Army. Stagno and Vento had decided something special was in order to commemorate Cope's coup in landing Sinatra. Right there in the terminal, the army brass held an impromptu ceremony promoting Myron to a two-star general. It was late, the crowd was noisy, and in the midst of the speeches and toasting and general hubbub, the army's K-9 corps—a single Great Dane wearing an army helmet—decided to relieve himself right on the new two-star general's shoe.

It was a memorable if not quite fitting end to a remarkable week. Five years later, Myron joked that he still couldn't get the smell out of the shoe.

7

Great Name for a Kosher Play

It's the Big Bang of Steelers Nation, the team's AD moment, the one that separates the dim, dark past from the glorious new era that followed. The fact that so many people remember it as such is due in part to a football announcer who wasn't even on the air when it happened.

Myron Cope liked to joke that when he died, his obituary would be headlined, "Creator of Towel, Dead." But he was selling himself short, for Myron also played a central role in naming the Immaculate Reception, the most celebrated play in NFL history and the one that boasts the most unforgettable name.

Even without the name, the play would be highly memorable, marked as it was by a desperation pass, a massive hit, a deflected ball, and a fleeting sense that the Steelers' remarkable 1972 season was over—only for Franco Harris to come swooping in from stage right to make a shoestring catch and run for the game-winning touchdown. The score sealed the Steelers' first-ever postseason victory, and in retrospect, it's seen as the starting point for the great Steelers dynasty of the 1970s.

At the same time, naysayers argued then and argue now that the catch, for any number of reasons, was illegal. In 2012 NFL Network aired an hour-long program examining the reception's legitimacy and legacy, subjecting videos of the play to a frame-by-frame analysis like JFK obsessives poring over the Zapruder film. Clearly, most people have concluded that the catch was legit, for in 2020, on the occasion of the NFL's centennial, fans picked it as the league's single greatest moment.

Still, it's worth asking if the play would be recalled so vividly if it was known by something more mundane. There are other great Steelers moments, like Lynn Swann's leaping, juggling catch in Super Bowl X, or Ben Roethlisberger's game-saving tackle against the Colts in the 2005 playoffs, or James Harrison's 100-yard touchdown dash in Super Bowl XLIII, or Santonio Holmes's toe-tip game-winning catch in the same contest, that could be considered equally momentous. But they don't have striking nicknames to make them stand out in history.

"I *do* think the name has something to do with the enduring memory," said Myron's old colleague, the late Stan Savran. "It's very clever, very creative."

From a creativity standpoint, the name has the advantage of sidestepping the overused term "miracle" (e.g., Music City Miracle, Miracle of the Meadowlands) as well as the easy one-word "The" format (The Catch, The Drive, The Fumble). There's a higher level of inventiveness and originality at work, which seems appropriate for a play so unique that there's never been another like it in NFL history.

Then there's the religious aspect. Calling it the Immaculate Reception, a pun on the name of a Catholic holy day, implies that the play was not just important, not just incredible, but also perfect, free of sin, maybe even blessed by God—which happens to be the way the founding fathers of Steelers Nation saw it. Talking to a New York reporter an hour after the game, Art Rooney remarked, "It looks like the Lord had his hand on our shoulder, doesn't it?" Dan Rooney chimed in years later, "I don't know if the Lord is worried about every football game that's played, but in this case it sure seemed like an act of divine intervention."

Myron steadfastly, correctly refused to take credit for coining the name. It came from a fan, a young man who was struck by inspiration over some postgame beers. If not for Myron, however, the name might have drifted off with the cigarette smoke in a Pittsburgh tavern, never to be heard except by a few dozen drinking revelers. Like the good showman he was, Myron knew a catchy name when it was brought to his attention and knew the masses would think so too when it was brought to theirs.

"No question naming the play The Immaculate Reception did wonders for establishing its legacy," says Pittsburgh newspaperman Bob Smizik. "I guess a fan coined it, but Myron made it famous."

Myron himself thought the name was key to ensuring the play's immortality. "If it didn't have such a great name," he once asked, "do you think people would still remember it as the greatest play of all time?"

THE DAY AFTER the Steelers returned from their division-clinching win in San Diego, Art Rooney convened a meeting of the Steelers brain trust at his house on the North Side of Pittsburgh. The main order of business? Prayer. Rooney hosted a Mass of thanksgiving in a chapel adjoining his home, thanking God for his family's and his team's good fortune. Chuck Noll served as the reader, Dan Rooney and Steelers PR director Ed Kiely as the altar boys. The service was led by Father John Duggan, a priest from Kilkenny, Ireland, who was studying at Boston College and had befriended Art Rooney's middle son, Tim, a few years before. The service said a lot about the Rooneys—they were devout Catholics, attached to their ancestral Ireland, and profoundly grateful to finally have a winning football team.

The choice of Duggan to lead was significant in itself. The Rooneys considered him a good-luck charm; of twelve games he had attended, Kiely told reporters, the team had lost only one. The team made sure he'd be there for the December 23 playoff game.

Myron, not a Catholic, no doubt glad to see his family after a week in California, didn't attend the Mass. He had his own pressing business to tend to, namely what instructions to give Gerela's Gorillas in preparation for the showdown with the Raiders. Oakland's kicker, George Blanda, had been in pro football for over two decades, spending a full decade with George Halas in Chicago, quarterbacking the Houston Oilers to a pair of AFL championships, then finding a late-career home in Oakland as a backup QB and full-time kicker for the Raiders. At age forty-five, he was by far the oldest player in the NFL, but he still had an accurate toe, converting 100 percent of his point-after attempts in '72 and about two-thirds of his field goal attempts, a solid percentage in the days before kickers began swinging their feet soccer-style. Blanda was also known for fueling late-game comebacks as a substitute quarterback and had tossed a touchdown pass against the Steelers during a seesaw battle with the Raiders earlier that year.

Myron decided that it was best not to poke the bear, and he advised the Gorillas via his morning commentary to go easy. "He said Blanda gets a little better when he's riled up so he decided to lay off him," explained charter Gorilla Chuck Witkowski. "We figured he's such an old guy anyway we wanted to give him a break." The Gorillas did produce a wide, black-on-gold sign, but the message was innocuous: "Blanda, Welcome to Gorilla Country!"

At least the eight-man Gorilla squad, as season-ticket holders, would get to *see* the Saturday afternoon game. The vast majority of Pittsburghers would not, as the NFL refused to lift its despised television "blackout" rule for the day. Mayor Pete Flaherty had written to NFL commissioner Pete Rozelle several weeks earlier and asked him to suspend the rule. President Richard Nixon, a huge football fan, had done the same. But Rozelle refused, insisting that televising home games in a team's home market would harm attendance—ignoring the fact that all fifty thousand seats for the playoff game at Three Rivers Stadium were sold out five days in advance.

A lawsuit filed by Washington Redskins fans who were blocked from seeing their own team's first-round playoff game went nowhere. So hundreds of Steelers fans booked reservations at motels and restaurants in northeastern Ohio or central Pennsylvania, places outside the seventy-five-mile-radius blackout zone. If they had to travel to watch a home game, so be it.

The higher-ups at WTAE radio sat notably quiet on the whole issue; they knew that for every fan who'd make the drive to Akron or Altoona to avoid the blackout, another twenty were staying at home and would have no choice but to turn on 1250 AM to follow the action. Myron and Jack Fleming were about to broadcast to the biggest audience of their careers.

FOR MOST OF THAT Saturday afternoon, the Steelers radio team broadcast the sound of suffocating defense. In the first fifty-eight and a half minutes, neither team found the end zone. Actually, neither team managed a play worth even 25 yards. The Steel Curtain was especially impenetrable, holding quarterback Daryl Lamonica, who was battling the flu, to just six completions for less than 50 yards total. After Lamonica tossed his second interception late in the third quarter, Raiders head coach John Madden yanked him from the game. Forgoing Blanda, Madden replaced him with young Kenny Stabler, a.k.a. the Snake. Stabler was scarcely better at first, getting sacked three times and losing a fumble in his first couple of series.

The Steelers' offense was pretty much shut down as well and could manage only a pair of second-half field goals, courtesy of Gerela. That made the Gorillas happy, but they, like everyone watching (or listening), were on the edge of their seats as the Raiders took the ball on their own 20-yard line with less than four minutes to go and the Steelers holding that slim 6–0 lead. With the defense protecting against the long bomb, Stabler finally got the Oakland offense untracked, completing a quartet of first-down passes and driving the Raiders to the Steelers' 30. One minute twenty-two seconds remained on the clock.

Then, for the first time all afternoon, a hole opened in the Steel Curtain. Fleming, a touch of dismay in his voice, relayed the action: "Stabler back again, stumbles . . . Runs out of the pocket. Stabler's running with the football! Down to the 20, the 10. Stabler's going for an open touchdown! He's into the end zone. Stabler rolling out to the left, kept the football!"

The Snake had slithered 30 yards down the left sideline without being touched. Blanda jogged in to kick the extra point. Raiders 7, Steelers 6.

Steelers fans didn't give up hope. There was still a minute-thirteen to play. A field goal would win the game. Watching the game in Mt. Holly, New Jersey, the mother of Franco Harris put on a recording of "Ave Maria." Listening to the game in so-called Little Washington, Pennsylvania, half an hour south of Pittsburgh, future *Post-Gazette* writer Chuck Finder appealed to higher powers through a different method. "I called Dial-a-Prayer, which a Jewish boy really shouldn't do," he says with a chuckle.

But at Three Rivers, Art Rooney was preparing himself for defeat and left his seat in the third-level press box after the Raiders kicked off, heading downstairs to console his players and congratulate them on what had been, even with the looming loss, a great season. The announcer for the national radio broadcast told listeners, "Art Rooney, the owner of the Pittsburgh Steelers, has just left the booth behind us, extremely disappointed and upset."

While Rooney walked toward the elevators, chatting with a few people along the way, two Bradshaw passes—one to Harris, one to Fuqua—took the Steelers out to their 40. Bradshaw launched his next three passes down the middle. All were broken up, one by safety George Atkinson, the other two by Jack Tatum, the Raiders' all-pro linebacker known for delivering and relishing bone-jarring hits. The Steelers now faced fourth down and were still at least 30 yards out of Gerela's field goal range.

By this time Jack Fleming was flying solo on the WTAE broadcast. Myron was in the practice of leaving the booth late in the fourth quarter so he could walk down to the clubhouse and get ready for postgame interviews. Even now, with the Steelers making a last-ditch drive to save the game and their season, he stuck to procedure. On some radio teams, this might leave listeners with the sound of one hand clapping. Not so with Fleming, who had no trouble being descriptive or loquacious and didn't mind operating without a partner.

"Fleming could very easily do a whole game without a color analyst. It wouldn't bother him at all," says Joe Gordon. If anything, says Gordon, the Steelers' listening audience at that moment was in the finest possible hands: "Jack was the best play-by-play football and basketball announcer I ever heard. He could be a little bit creative, but his real strength was calling the plays. He called the plays with such clarity."

The full picture: fourth and 10, Steelers on their own 40-yard line, twenty-two seconds left on the clock. In the huddle, Bradshaw announced the play, 66 Circle Option, a pass to rookie receiver Barry Pearson. The players went to the line, and Bradshaw took his spot behind Jim Clack at center. Frenchy Fuqua set up 3 yards behind the quarterback, a step to the left. Franco Harris stood 3 yards behind Bradshaw and a step to the right.

Clack snapped the ball, and Bradshaw swung into action, as did Fleming:

> And Bradshaw's back and looking again. Bradshaw running out of the pocket . . . looking for somebody to throw to . . . fires it downfield. And there's a collision . . .

There were actually two collisions, maybe a tenth of a second apart. In one, Tatum rammed a hard right shoulder into Fuqua, who was reaching for Bradshaw's desperation pass at the Oakland 35. In the other, the ball hit . . . somebody, either Tatum or Fuqua. With the speed of the crash, it was hard to tell. In any case, the ball flew backward, spinning end over end, a distance of more than 8 yards, about 25 feet in the air. Blacked-out Pittsburghers couldn't see it, but the ball briefly exited the live TV picture, and NBC announcer Curt Gowdy informed viewers that the pass had been broken up.

Fleming didn't make the same mistake.

> And that's . . . AND IT'S CAUGHT OUT OF THE AIR! The ball is pulled in by Franco Harris! Harris is going for a touchdown for Pittsburgh! Harris is scoring! . . . Five seconds left on the clock. Franco Harris pulled in the football. I don't even know where he came from!

Harris had come out of the Steelers' backfield, abandoning his blocking assignment to run downfield and give Bradshaw another target. He was charging toward Fuqua when the ball suddenly came floating in his direction. Never breaking stride, the alert rookie grabbed it no more than an inch above the turf and rumbled down the left side of the field, chased by a string of stunned and flailing Oakland defenders. The last of them, cornerback Jimmy Warren, was able to lay a hand on Harris at the 11-yard line but was shoved back by a stiff right arm.

Five steps later, Harris crossed the goal line. Field judge Adrian Burk, who'd had an unimpeded view of the entire play from the left sideline, raised his hands straight in the air—touchdown.

Three Rivers Stadium erupted like a geyser of jubilation, as every last one of the fifty thousand people in attendance seemed to jump and clap and shriek and go bananas at their seats, except for several dozen who leaped out of the stands and into the endzone, hugging and pounding the backs of both Harris and Bradshaw, who had run downfield trying to figure out how Franco scored. One well-wisher dressed as Santa Claus tried to follow Harris back to the sideline before being pushed off by security. Another applied an enthusiastic bear hug to 210-pound safety Mike Wagner and lifted him clear off the ground.

Meanwhile, the stadium's electronic scoreboard flashed depictions of fireworks and a giant "6."

No one, at first, seemed to notice that the referees were conferring near the goal line, discussing whether the play was legal. The question was whom did the ball hit—Tatum or Fuqua? Under NFL rules of the time, a catch was incomplete if it touched two members of the offense consecutively. If the ball had ricocheted off Tatum—which was the call on the field—then it was six points for the Steelers. If the ball bounced off Fuqua, Franco's touchdown didn't count, and the Steelers would lose the ball on downs. They'd lose the game, too.

Today, with the NFL using instant replay, the play would be clarified within sixty seconds; officials would see that the ball clearly bounced off Tatum. In 1972 that wasn't an option, and several Raiders, including Tatum, argued vehemently with the officials, insisting that the ball hit Frenchy. The reporters in the press box could see the replays, but the televisions were small and hung above the seats, making it hard to get a good read on the path of the ball. Bob Smizik, who was covering the game for the *Press*, says his colleague Phil Musick climbed up on a chair to get a closer look. "He looked at the replay and dictated to me what happened and I put it in the early editions," Smizik remembers. "I'm sure there were many other writers in the press box who borrowed Musick's dictation."

The long discussion, and the fact that chief referee Fred Swearingen made an impromptu phone call up to the press box to check with Art McNally, NFL director of officiating, gave fuel to skeptics who argued that the ball had hit Fuqua or that Harris had trapped it against the turf—or that the refs were just plain scared that the fans would lynch them if they nullified the TD. In some retellings of the story, the officiating crew conferred for fifteen minutes before making a final ruling. Game tape posted to YouTube suggests that it was less than five. The controversy would simmer for decades, but in the end, Burk's signal stood. Touchdown.

After the extra point and one failed play by the Raiders, the game ended as a Steelers 13–7 victory.

For the rest of his life, Fleming was rightly proud of his call and the fact that NFL Films, for many years, used his voice exclusively over footage of the play in any segment about Franco's catch.

"If you listen to the broadcast of that play, you'll see how quickly Jack picked up what happened on the field," Joe Gordon says. "The ricochet off Tatum, Franco scooping the ball inches off the ground. Jack had unbelievable vision and understanding of the plays."

Myron concurred. "Fleming was right on that play," he said, referring to how quickly his partner relayed the action to listeners. "It happened so fast, it would have thrown nine of 10 guys for a loop." Gowdy was one such guy. Raiders radio announcer Bill King was another. When Franco caught the deflection, King shouted, "*Caught out of the air by Fuqua! Fuqua at the 40! Fuqua at . . . no, it's Franco Harris!*"

Ironically, the one person who didn't see the Steelers seize their first-ever postseason victory was the man who'd been awaiting that moment for forty years. Art Rooney had reached the third-floor elevator just seconds before Bradshaw snapped the ball; Pirates announcer Bob Prince held open the door so he could get in. The elevator was descending to ground level when the men heard a tremendous, stadium-vibrating roar. When the doors opened, Rooney burst out and asked what had happened. A stadium attendant rushed up to him with the news: "You won it! You won it!"

Myron might have missed the play, too, if not for a fateful decision. Instead of taking his planned route to the clubhouse, he had wandered onto the field and found an inconspicuous spot on the Steelers' sideline, next to one of the field crew, to watch the end of the game. He was standing at the 2-yard line when Franco caught the deflected pass and steamed downfield. As a result, Myron can actually be seen in films of the Immaculate Reception, a guy in black trousers and beige trench coat, bald spot faintly visible atop his head, watching from the sideline as Franco slips by the last Oakland defender. When Harris crosses the goal line, Myron jumps back like he's just been dealt an electric shock.

More than a few Steelers fans would hand over a month's salary if they could have been standing in that spot, at that moment, at *the* great turning point in Steelers history. Not Myron. He would have preferred to be upstairs, on the radio broadcast.

"It wasn't worth missing out on being part of the call," he said a quarter-century later. "It's played more than any call in history. I think I might have gotten a few words in edgewise."

"Fleming did a great job with the call—that's the one you hear in all the replays," he said on another occasion. "But I would have liked to have been in that booth."

Myron was denied that particular wish. But before the day was through, he'd get to make his mark on Steelers lore and NFL history.

IN 1972 THERE WAS no such thing as social media, texting, or email. If one wanted to quickly send a written message to somebody across the country, the most reliable option was still the old-fashioned paper telegram. For the cost of $3.75, the Western Union company would transmit a fifteen-word message. In-person delivery cost another $1.50.

Approximately an hour after the game ended, two telegrams arrived in the Steelers' clubhouse. One came from Hollywood composer Henry Mancini, a Pittsburgh-area native and the writer of 1960s hits such as "Moon River" and the "Pink Panther Theme." The telegram read, "Where do I go to join Franco's Italian Army?" That pleased Tony Stagno, who upon learning of Mancini's message said, "Maybe he'll write us a theme song."

The other came from another Hollywood figure, one a bit more familiar to the Steelers, and was delivered to Harris. It read, "The following is an order: Attack. Attack. Attack. Attack!" It was signed, "Colonel Francis Sinatra." Nine days after his induction into Franco's Italian Army, Sinatra had evidently watched Harris score the winning touchdown, and very likely scored a few grand betting on the Steelers, too. No matter that he forgot that Stagno had made him a general, not a colonel.

Myron read the telegram over Franco's shoulder and got excited. Having been the one who recruited Ol' Blue Eyes into the army, he wanted to relay news of the telegram to WTAE radio listeners as soon as possible. Glancing at the clock on the clubhouse wall, he saw that it was just about 5 p.m.

He recounted what happened next in a 1982 commentary, on the tenth anniversary of Franco's catch:

> I knew that WTAE radio had a five o'clock newscast just underway, so I grabbed the locker room telephone and dialed the newsroom and said, "Put me into the newscast live." And the guy in the newsroom said, "OK, stand by." So, I stood by, waiting for the newscaster to say, "Here's Myron Cope from Three Rivers Stadium." But I heard nothin'! I'm looking at my watch and I saw that the five-minute newscast was just about over. I'm totally frustrated. So, I uttered a terrible, awful expletive—and wouldn't you know it, I was on the air! Outside, the roads, they were jammed, and I'm told my terrible words, my expletive, caused at least half-a-dozen fender benders.

WTAE executive John Conomikes was among those out on the roads, listening to the news on his car radio. He says he was almost home, just about to pull into his driveway, when Myron's voice came over the air. "He said the word f—k," Conomikes recalls. "He didn't know that they had him live, he was frustrated, and he said, 'Why don't you answer the f—ing phone?' I almost wrecked my car. I said, 'Ah shit. This is going to be a real pain in the ass. We're going to be in trouble with the FCC now.'"

The FCC—the Federal Communications Commission—oversees the use of the nation's radio and television airwaves and is authorized to enforce section 1464 of the U.S. Criminal Code, which states, "Whoever utters any obscene, indecent, or profane language by means of radio communication shall be fined under this title or imprisoned not more than two years, or both." Due to First Amendment concerns, the FCC to that point had rarely tried to implement the law, though it fined a Philadelphia radio station $100 in 1970, when it aired an interview with musician Jerry Garcia that was littered with four-letter words. Still, broadcasters dreaded the prospect of trouble with the FCC, which in theory could lead to loss of their licenses. In an era of more straitlaced public norms, the stations also feared an outcry against foul language invading people's homes.

The way Conomikes tells it, the matter of Myron's slip-up was discussed by WTAE executives but quickly dropped. "Nothing came of it, because it was inadvertent," he says. "Myron was just upset that the call wasn't getting through. I think that's the only time he used the F-word on the air."

Myron characteristically remembered the aftermath of the incident with a bit more drama and humor.

> On Monday morning I was summoned to meet with two radio executives. They informed me that the big boss, the man in charge of the whole radio and television operation combined, was going up the wall. They also informed me that under FCC regulations, the possible penalties for what I'd done, were a fine of up to ten thousand dollars and a jail term of up to two years. To which I said, "Who does the two years, me or the big boss?" And the answer was, "The big boss." So, I said, "Good, I'll send him a fruitcake." Well, as matters turned out, nobody got fined or jailed, and ten years later, I'm still working here—or at least I think I am. Big boss, if you're listening, you do appreciate my willingness to send you a fruitcake, dontcha?

ONE OF THE STRIKING things about Franco's play was how *instantly* some observers, along with the Rooneys, saw it as possibly engineered by a higher power. Thirty seconds after Franco crossed the goal line, Curt Gowdy's NBC broadcast partner Al DeRogatis said, "Curt, Mr. Rooney is a very religious man, and I think it all paid off." Watching the instant replay, Gowdy concurred. "You talk about Christmas miracles? Well, here's the miracle of all miracles."

A minute later, Gowdy made the first stab at naming the play. "What was the movie, *The Miracle of 34th Street*? This is the Miracle of Three Rivers Stadium," he said. The name was just like Gowdy's announcing: accurate, unpretentious, and devoid of any real pizzazz. A few newspaper writers around the country subsequently used it, but it never took off.

Several headline writers, in Pittsburgh and elsewhere, simply dubbed the play "the Miracle Touchdown," another correct yet unimaginative tag. In New York, the *Daily News* called it the "Impossible TD." Better, but still a touch generic.

A more memorable name was brewing in the mind of one Michael Ord, the owner of a leather shop in Pittsburgh's Shadyside neighborhood. Ord, a season ticket-holder, had attended the game that afternoon with his girlfriend Sharon Levosky, his father Barney, and several friends. The group had seats in the lower rim of Three Rivers Stadium's upper deck, right at the 50-yard line, and they were in perfect position to see Franco make his running shoestring catch—all except for Barney Ord, who had buried his face in his hands when the ball bounced off Tatum. Startled by the eruption of cheers a second later, the elder Ord looked up and began badgering his son, "What happened? What happened?"

After the game the group repaired to the Interlude Lounge, a downtown restaurant and tavern. The mood inside the second-floor barroom was festive, buoyed by the approach of Christmas and the sudden arrival of good fortune for the Steelers. After a beer or two, Ord, who had attended Catholic schools, was struck by an inspiration. "I climbed up on the table like you do at an old firehall wedding, you know, you get a spoon and you bang on the glass," he remembered, "and I said, 'I would like to suggest that from this day on, we refer to this day as the Feast of the Immaculate Reception!' And the place went *bonkers*."

Ord's idea was a takeoff on the Immaculate Conception, a doctrine of the Catholic Church that says the Virgin Mary was free of original sin from the moment she was conceived. Her life is celebrated every December 8 with a holiday feast.

The bar crowd lustily cheered Ord's announcement, then went back to gabbing and drinking. The earth below downtown Pittsburgh did not shake. But Ord and Levosky felt his brainwave deserved greater attention. Today they could launch it on Twitter or Instagram or some other avenue of social media. In 1972 they had to turn to a broadcaster. They considered only one person. "I remember thinking, 'We really should tell Myron,'" Levosky recalled.

A few hours later, sitting in the Highland Park home of Levosky's parents, the two decided to call him. It was shortly before the 11 p.m. Channel 4 news. Ord insisted that Levosky make the call; he thought himself too inebriated to pitch his idea. A game Levosky dialed the rotary phone, got the station's switchboard operator on the line, and asked to speak with Myron. To her surprise, she was put right through.

Myron was at his desk, writing his Steelers commentary for the upcoming newscast. Levosky got right to the point and offered her boyfriend's name for Franco's play. "I couldn't believe it. When I told him 'The Immaculate Reception,' he was laughing," she recalled.

Still, Myron hesitated.

"He said, 'I can't say that on TV,'" Levosky recalled.

"I said, 'Sure you can.'"

"He said, 'I'll have to think about it.'"

Myron didn't think about it for long. "I said, 'That's fantastic. Let me give it some thought,'" he recalled. "I thought it may be in poor taste. Catholics might object. I thought it over for three minutes and said the heck with it, I'm going with it."

Minutes later, Myron was on the air, giving his two cents about Franco's catch and declaring that yes, it should be called the Immaculate Reception. The tape of the broadcast appears to be lost, but Ord and Levosky remembered that he also mentioned Sharon's name and reported Sharon to be a good Christian girl—probably to head off cries that calling a mere football play immaculate was an act of sacrilege. In reality, according to Levosky, Myron didn't ask what religion she was. "He didn't know if I was Jewish or what," she said. She was actually Presbyterian.

Ord remarked that the name was an "instant success." That wasn't quite the case. Neither of the Pittsburgh newspapers mentioned the name in their coverage leading up to the AFC Championship Game the following week. Neither Fleming nor Cope used the term during the AFC championship broadcast. At least one important person said he *did* think the name was sacrilegious. That person was Dan Rooney, the Steelers' de facto top executive who, like his father, was a devout Catholic. If anyone had the power to quash the name, it was him. But at the time, Rooney said nothing, and Myron's minions began to forcibly move the needle. When the Steelers hosted Miami, fans hung a sign in the stands that read "Dec. 23, Feast of the Immaculate Reception." Myron's buddies at *Sports Illustrated* then used the name in a cover story. By the time of the Super Bowl in January, the name was in wide circulation via the newspapers. By the time the Steelers reached their first Super Bowl two years later, it was set in concrete.

Unlike with the Terrible Towel. Myron was never proprietary about the name. In 1997 Harris claimed a trademark on the phrase "Franco's

Immaculate Reception" so an image of him scooping up Tatum's deflection could appear on beer cans. A Pittsburgh newspaper columnist asked Myron what he thought about that. Myron gave a thumbs-up. "I have no claim on it for sure," he said.

But he did have a certain attachment to Franco's catch, proclaiming himself to be the world's leading authority on the play. In late '97 Myron wrote his first major article in years, a piece for the *New York Times*, where he insisted that the most controversial, most debated play in the history of American sports was, without question, 100 percent legal. Two days after the playoff game, he explained, he had borrowed WTAE's 16 mm film of the play and analyzed it through a viewer, cranking the handle very slowly so he could study the film closely, zeroing in on the moment when Tatum, Fuqua, and the football all converged.

If one did that, he said—which one can now essentially do by slowing down the video of the play online—the reality became clear.

"[The ball] bounced off Tatum's shoulder pad, a hard material, which is why it shot off," he said. "If it hadn't struck his shoulder pad, there's no way that ball is going eight yards back to Franco. I issued a commentary that night, and I said, 'I looked at the film, and the play was perfectly kosher.'"

Kosher, as in valid. One can argue whether Franco's grab was immaculate, but in Myron's view—the correct view, in this author's opinion—it was indisputably a reception.

ONCE THE POSTGAME celebrations were over and the hangovers cleared, Pittsburghers woke up to the fact the Steelers would host the AFC Championship Game the following week, playing the perfect 15-0 Miami Dolphins. A game plan was needed to psyche out the Dolphins' kicker. Myron promised fresh instructions to the Gorillas the day after Christmas. By now, said New York columnist Jerry Izenberg, Myron's men awaited each message like the World War II French resistance listening for code words on the BBC. "In McKeesport and Aliquippa," he wrote, "in Coraopolis by the airport and in the golden triangle, the men of Pittsburgh adjusted their transistor radio settings to Radio Free Steeler, 1250 on the dial, and waited."

The instructions burst over the airwaves on December 26 at 7:35 a.m.: "Attention all Gorillas," Myron shouted. "Garo Yepremian, a native-born

Cypriot who makes neckties in the off-season, will be the Miami placekicker Sunday. You are hereby ordered to do the following: Call all public libraries and local colleges at once and find the Greek word for 'choke.' Make an enormous sign of that word. Make another sign with the following message: Hey Garo, your necktie is getting tighter!"

The Gorillas produced a sign that read "Hey Garo, Pnigo!" and hung it in the end zone before the AFC championship. Myron issued fresh directions a few minutes before kickoff to make sure their work was not in vain. "I'm worried about that sign because there are so many banners hanging around it," he mused over the air. "I wish they'd get some of the banners around the Pnigo sign down. How about it, Gorillas?" He knew fans listening on their portable transistor radios would hear him. By game time, Yepremian had an unimpeded view of the sign.

Unfortunately, the Gorillas misspelled the word—the correct translation was *bnegho*—and Yepremian was unfazed, kicking three extra points without a miss. It may not have mattered, anyhow. The Dolphins' No Name defense knocked out Bradshaw, stifled Harris, then intercepted Bradshaw twice when he returned. For all their momentum, the Steelers could not overcome a team of destiny. The Dolphins won 21–17, then went on to beat the Redskins in the Super Bowl and become the first and still only NFL team to complete a perfect season.

Strangely enough, the Steelers' loss would not be the major sports story in the Pittsburgh newspapers the next day. That night Roberto Clemente boarded a plane in his hometown of San Juan, Puerto Rico. Over the previous week, Clemente had collected goods to help earthquake victims in Nicaragua, a county where he had played winter ball and had many friends. There were reports that humanitarian aid was failing to reach the intended recipients, so the great Pirate right fielder hired a plane on his own, a DC-7 being leased by a one-man air cargo operator. Clemente's heart was in the right place, but he didn't take time to learn about the operator's previous safety violations or the plane's troubled mechanical history. Nor did he supervise the loading of the plane, which left it overstuffed and poorly balanced. Just after 9 p.m., the plane took off from San Juan but flew no more than a few miles before crashing into shark-infested waters. Everyone on board, including Clemente, was killed.

It wasn't necessarily noticed at the time, but the crash marked the final step of a drastic, permanent sea change in the Pittsburgh sports world. The Pirates had suffered a tragedy. The Steelers had been blessed by a miracle. The Pirates had lost their superstar. The Steelers had several on the rise. The Pirates had loyal fans. The Steelers suddenly had hordes of fanatics, people who seemingly overnight had forged a powerful, personal connection to the team.

Pittsburgh was now and forever more a football town, a Steelers town. The change would soon show up in the bottom line. The Steelers would sell out every one of their home games for decades to come. The Pirates, despite continued success through the '70s, would struggle with chronically subpar attendance and at times flirt with insolvency.

The core of the Steelers' appeal, of course, was their newly winning ways, which would soon result in a string of Super Bowls. "The Steelers were simply an avalanche that nothing could contain," says Bob Smizik. But, he adds, the team's popularity also got a big boost from their color commentator.

"Part of it was Cope," he says. "He had a lot to do with bringing the fans on board. I'm sure the Steelers would have dominated Pittsburgh, but perhaps not as quickly or as fully without Cope."

8

Growing Up Cope

Amid the Steelers' newfound success and his own rising popularity, there was only one dark cloud troubling Myron Cope's horizon. His son could not speak.

Danny Cope had been born seemingly healthy in January 1968. He was a handsome child, with a huge smile, his mother's blue eyes, and soft, light, straight brown hair that draped down over his forehead. There's a picture from that year of Myron, dressed in a light-blue polo shirt, holding and gazing at his baby son, every inch the proud and happy dad, while a nine-month-old Danny laughs and emits that heart-warming smile. It looks like the start of a tight lifelong bond between father and son.

But while Danny was still a baby, Mildred Cope sensed that something was wrong. He was slow to crawl and reach other basic milestones. Routine noises seemed to irritate him. When she took him outside, the sound of the neighbor's dog barking caused him to fearfully wail. As he moved into nursery school age, the odd behavior grew worse. Sometimes he'd bang his head against a wall. When the family went out to dinner, he'd unleash long, piercing screams. When Mildred took him to the supermarket, he'd throw tantrums and kick the shins of complete strangers. There were moments he could have fun—this author remembers him splashing around in the kiddie pool at the Bower Hill Swim Club, next to the (curiously rough-surfaced and rock-hard) white whale with the waterspout. But even then he'd sometimes cry or scream, and never did he utter an understandable word.

When Myron was home, the Copes took Danny to multiple doctors, looking for a cause for his problems and a solution. This was before MRI brain scans were available, and even the specialists could make only an educated guess. Initially he was diagnosed, in the terminology of the era, as being severely retarded. Then a psychologist deemed him to have a serious case of autism. "Doctors believe some autistic children like Danny have extremely sensitive touch, smell, hearing vision or taste," said a *Pittsburgh Press* article on autism in July 1976, when Myron and Mildred went public with their son's struggles. "A soft touch feels like hot pokers piercing their skin. They cringe and pull away at their mother's cuddling embrace."

The psychologist recommended that Danny, at age five, be placed in an institution that could treat autistic kids. None existed in Pittsburgh. The Copes visited about a half dozen up and down the East Coast and decided that the only one acceptable was the Devereux school in Chester County, Pennsylvania, outside Philadelphia ("The other places," Myron said, "you wouldn't put a dog in them"). Danny would live at Devereux for the next seven years, with Myron or Mildred driving him cross-state for a home visit one weekend each month. The monthly bill for his care came to about $6,000, quickly burning through Myron's earnings and savings. He might have gone broke if not for a recent innovation, major medical health insurance, which he obtained through the American Federation of Television and Radio Artists. Initially, the insurance carrier balked at paying for Danny's care, arguing that his problems were mental, not physical. The carrier backed down only in the face of pressure from the union and its local president, Bill Cardille—"Chilly Billy" on Channel 11's horror-movie showcase, Chiller Theater.

Danny's condition brought sadness to both Mildred and Myron—how could it not? Myron sometimes lamented that he and Danny couldn't play a simple game of catch. "Every father ought to be able to play catch with his son," he said. "We tried it once, but it didn't work. That thought crosses my mind more than anything."

But Myron was never one to sit on the couch and feel sorry for himself. With his friend Dan Torisky, who had an autistic son several years older than Danny, he helped launch the Autism Society of Pittsburgh to encourage awareness and study of the disorder. In later years, he'd create and organize two annual fundraising efforts for kids with autism and other disabilities—the Pittsburgh Vintage Grand Prix, an annual auto race in Schenley Park, and the Myron Cope/Foge Fazio Golf Tournament for Autistic Children, named after Myron and the mid-1980s Pitt football coach. Both events benefited the Allegheny Valley School, a facility west of Pittsburgh for people with severe mental and developmental disabilities, where Danny was transferred in the early 1980s and lives to this day.

Over time doctors recognized that Danny's problems went deeper than autism and diagnosed him as brain-damaged with autistic tendencies. Myron grew philosophical about Danny's condition, realized it wasn't going to change, and decided it would not define his life or hold back his career. "I would often wonder to myself when he was younger if he was puzzled by seeing me on TV when I was sitting there next to him," he said in 1986. "I wondered what he thought of that, if he had anyway of understanding it. But I came to understand that there was no way of knowing. I've accepted this as something that happened and went on. . . . You think about the guy a lot, you have to, but you can't bring it to work with you. There's no other way you can do it."

The Copes' sadness over Danny was balanced out by Myron's unstoppable zest for life, the excitement surrounding the Steelers, and the arrival of the couple's third child, Elizabeth, born healthy two and a half years after Danny. With her, the Copes could peacefully go out to dinner, to social gatherings, and to family events and be part of the community in Upper St. Clair, the upscale suburb in Pittsburgh's South Hills where they bought an orange-brick, four-bedroom house in 1972.

Elizabeth grew up highly aware that she had an unusual brother and an unusually prominent father. Some nights her dad would conduct his talk show from the house, and the Copes might share a pre-show dinner with a four-time Super Bowl champion quarterback or a budding National Hockey League superstar. During football season, the family got a weekly visit from Chuck Noll, coming over to tape his pregame coach's show with Myron. Noll doubled as the Cope family's repair man. Myron was helpless on technical matters—"He couldn't even work the VCR," Elizabeth laughs—while Noll knew his way around the inner workings of a stereo or a dishwasher. Some weeks, taping of the show was delayed so the head coach of the Pittsburgh Steelers could get the TV working or change a burned-out light bulb.

Both her brother and her father had a profound effect on Elizabeth's life, as she writes:

I always knew I was lucky. The word blessed *was a word that popped into my head often as a child. My dad had just begun broadcasting for the Steelers the year I was born. There seemed to be a feeling of magic and specialness in the air surrounding us and our home. Most people, I suppose, only realize this feeling in retrospect, but I specifically recall feeling it as I was growing up.*

I was way too young to appreciate the significance of having Terry Bradshaw over to the house with his two little miniature dachshunds he brought with him everywhere, or Chuck Noll coming over once a week to fix things around our home. I knew him as our handyman. I had no idea he was a big-time coach for the Pittsburgh Steelers, nor would I have cared.

Mario Lemieux ate dinner at our house more than once, but I was still too young to get it. I remember once coming down to the dinner table wearing a green pore-refining mask and my dad yelling, "Go wash that dumb thing off! Can't you see we have company?" Mario laughed, I remember. I remember him being very shy. I think he was like nineteen years old at the time and had just started playing with the Penguins, but he was already a star.

This was all part of my "normal" life. I knew no different. What I did seem to sense, though, was that I was in some kind of charmed station in life. I knew I had two loving parents who showered attention on me and a "special" brother I loved, although for some reason, he could not talk. I was also aware that everywhere we went, my dad was fawned over, with people saying, "There's Myron Cope." I would overhear people whisper and not too discreetly point at him. People approached our family constantly while we were at a restaurant eating dinner, or on vacation, or anywhere, to ask for my dad's autograph. They would always ask him, "How do you think the Steelers are going to do this year?" My dad was almost always gracious about these intrusions. He knew it went with the territory, as he liked to put it.

I am somewhat ashamed to admit I felt "special." I often prayed for things to always be this way for me, even though a part of me knew, even as a little girl, that nothing lasts forever.

As a young child, I would sometimes sneak into my parents' room and stare at them while they slept to make sure they were still breathing. I was terrified of losing them. I knew that my parents were older than all my friends' parents, as they had me when they were around age forty. Many times my mother would suddenly awaken to me leaning over her face. She would startle and reprimand me to go back to my own room and stop hovering. Other nights, my brother, Danny, and I would climb into bed with my parents, as would the cat and dog. My dad would scowl and say, "I don't know why I work so hard to provide us with a nice home with four bedrooms when we all crowd into one bed every night!" But I loved falling asleep with my mother's arms around me and waking up that way. I felt so safe and loved. Whenever my mom and I hugged, I always felt her love. It was so strong as to be almost a physical sensation.

I can honestly say that when I recall my childhood, I have only the happiest of memories. Trips to the beach, Disney World, cruises, and a loving home often filled with my friends. I truly believe my friends even felt the magic and essence in the air of our home because my house was the one everyone wanted to go to. My parents also loved to entertain, and people were always in and out of the home. It was a social hub, especially during football season, of course.

In retrospect, though, I realize now that it probably wasn't all as perfect as I like to remember it. My brother, Danny, being mentally handicapped and autistic, threw daily fits during which he screamed bloody murder and overturned chairs and hit and kicked all of us. My mother would often have to drive hunched over the steering wheel because my brother would be trying to reach her from the back seat so he could hit her. (This was before kids were belted into safety seats.) Once, when I was a baby, he apparently tried to suffocate me with a pillow. My parents caught him doing this and ran to save my life just in the nick of time! Apparently, Danny was jealous of me when I was brought home from the hospital and he sensed he was no longer an only child.

There are pictures of me with black eyes as a young child because my brother had thrown a toy at my face. My mother always put a description and a date on the back of every photograph in our family photo albums. There's one that reads, "Elizabeth, age 1, first black eye." I laugh when I see it. I am smiling in the picture, with my left eye a swollen black mess. First black eye, my mom wrote, as if I were bound to have many more in my lifetime.

When I got a few years older, I utterly hated it when my brother threw a tantrum in public, screaming at the top of his lungs, throwing himself on the ground. I felt like everywhere we went, we were a spectacle. In fact, I got angry. I used to tell strangers, "Don't you know its impolite to stare?" That was something my mother told me, that it's not polite to stare. I'd go up to people and say, "Why are you staring at us?" My mom would say, "Oh, Elizabeth!"

Sometimes, I was the one who tested my parents' patience. Both my mother and father were deaf in one ear—my mom from having scarlet fever when she was twelve, my dad from an ear infection in college. Everyone screamed in our house, and the TV was always turned up really loud. But once, when I was in high school, I threw a party at the house while my parents were sleeping upstairs. Because they were both sleeping on their good ears, they couldn't hear the music or the noise.

We were drinking beer, things got out of control, and the police were called to the house. The officers could hardly rouse my parents out of bed. Once they got them up, they said, "Are you aware there's a huge party in your basement?" My dad was furious, because he did broadcasts from the basement, and some of the guys at the party were messing around with the microphones and other equipment. I was grounded for weeks.

But overall, the happy memories outnumber the sad. Many of my happiest involved our beloved dachshunds, Pretzel and Holly. We had dachshunds because my mother fell in love with Terry Bradshaw's dachshunds when they would come over (with Terry, of course!). Other traditions I shared with my dad were our annual kite flying at the beach and sitting together on a blanket and watching fireworks on the Fourth of July.

Christmas time was always a special and festive extravaganza at our home. My mom always went overboard with gifts and they would be spread out all over the place under the tree. My dad would shake his head and complain that I was "being spoiled rotten." My mom would promise to cut back the next year, but the same thing would inevitably happen.

Our Christmas Eve dinners were always fancy and warm times. My mother would cook a huge feast and bring out the fancy china in our formal dining room. Roy McHugh, who worked with my dad on his books, always joined us for Christmas Eve dinner, as he was a lifelong bachelor and had no family nearby. My mother would put Christmas music on in the background as we ate, and the house would be decorated beautifully for the holidays. I really think my dad loved Christmas, even though he was Jewish and never celebrated it until he married my mother.

Throughout my childhood, teen years, and early adulthood, I always felt secure and somewhat untouchable as long as I had my dad. He seemed to know everyone and to be able to fix any problem or dilemma I found myself facing. When something went wrong, I would call my dad, and he would tell me what to do, or he would call someone and they would know what to do. I am embarrassed to admit that I even got out of many speeding tickets because of my dad. Charges would mysteriously be dropped after a few phone calls.

Today I'm just like anybody else. Back then, there was this feeling that anything was possible. My dad seemed larger than life. It was a feeling of an extra cushion, a safety net. Yes, we got stared at a lot in public. But I felt that nothing could go wrong as long as my parents were around.

9

The Lines Are Open

The hands on the studio clock glide toward 7 p.m. as a man with a loosened necktie, puffing on an eighteen-cent cigar, flips through a stack of wire stories. He quickly scans each piece of paper, checking for ball scores or major trades, scrawling notes with a pen if necessary. Then his producer gives him a signal, and the papers are set down and the stogie goes in the ashtray, because it's the top of the hour and the microphone is now live. It's time for *Myron Cope on Sports.*

> Golly gee, as Terry Bradshaw would say, "Gol-lee-gee." It's like old times in football today. Yeah, did you see Jim O'Brien's story in this afternoon's *Pittsburgh Press*, about Jack Splat Lambert getting in the hayrub in the wee hours of last Thursday morning?

The date is May 8, 1979, near the start of what will become a very special baseball season for the city of Pittsburgh. The night before, in Atlanta, the Pirates triumphed 4–2, with long, lean submarine hurler Kent Tekulve coming in to nail down the final two outs. There will be more than a hundred such victories this season, resulting in a World

Series title for the Pirates, the club's first in eight years and their last in several decades since.

But the man with the cigar and the papers knows his listeners. For them, baseball is page 2 news. Steelers football is what stirs their blood, even on a Tuesday evening in May, and with the help of the local evening paper, he's got a juicy story.

> Piecing the story together, both from O'Brien's, uh, material, and from material that I have been able to get, uh, while having my ear pressed to a dozen telephones today, uh, it sorta happened like this. Uh, these three guys, you see, there were a few minor words—I'm told minor—passed between them and Splat early on in the evening down there. This is how I get it, see?

Somewhere, a broadcasting teacher is writhing in agony. The uhs, the you-sees, the bad grammar, the stop-and-go sentences—they violate every rule in the radio announcers' textbook. But this is the way Myron Cope addresses the audience five nights a week on his WTAE 1250 AM talk show. A handful of Pittsburghers shudder upon hearing him speak. A few might turn off their radio. However, a vastly greater number turn up the sound and listen as Myron imparts what he's learned about the fracas involving Lambert, the Steelers' star linebacker, whom Myron nicknamed Splat for the noise generated when he flattens an opposing ball-carrier.

> But then, much later on, which is like past two a.m. in the morning, the Splat, the bartender was preceding Splat out of the men's room—they've both gone to the men's room, and . . . and . . . here comes Splat. All of the sudden, bam, he catches it with, with a glass upside the head.

The listeners can't see it, but Myron is getting a minor workout as he speaks. Cynthia Gorney, a writer for the magazine *Inside Sports*, happens to be in the control room this night gathering material for a story on the fledgling trend of sports talk radio. When her story comes out, she will capture the full scope of Myron's performance, visual as well as auditory: "He will shout only a little at first, and then he will shout a lot, bouncing up and down, waving his arms and pointing into the distance, grabbing the seat of his chair and lifting his whole body into the air. He will shout in a frenzied, grating, Pittsburgh-pitched voice, swallowing his l's and crying 'uh-uh' in the middle of his sentences."

As Myron finishes talking about Lambert (who needed stitches after his skirmish but was fine), dozens of listeners are calling WTAE, ready to wait forty minutes for a chance to talk with Myron for three or four. These are not run-of-the-mill callers, Gorney notes. The Munhall Flash is a steelworker who likes to expound on how close to saintly perfection the Steelers really are and will toot ballpark charges on his trumpet to emphasize his point. The Vile Canard speaks in a cultured baritone and glides into debates with soothing pats of reason—now, now, he might say, anyone can see that Terry Bradshaw is *not* a God-forsaken mush-brain. The Hanging Judge tends to inflict punishment on athletes who have sinned in some fashion, like the Duquesne basketball player who refused to play against West Virginia just because WVU fans hung him in effigy before the game. Naked City Normy is a youngster who tends to dump so hard on Penn State football and head coach Joe Paterno that Myron temporarily banned him from the show, until Normy wrote letters begging to return. Myron said okay, on the condition that Normy stopped slandering the Nittany Lions and the guy whom Myron calls Dark Glasses Joe.

Myron remains in demand after sign-off. During an hour-long dinner at a suburban restaurant, Gorney notes, he is interrupted seven times by fans offering compliments or seeking autographs. One young woman tells him, "When you sang, I swear to God my whole family was pissing in their pants." The woman is referring to Myron's performance of "Deck the Broncos, They're Just Yonkos," a ditty set to the tune of "Deck the Halls" that Myron composed and belted out before a 1977 Pittsburgh vs. Denver playoff game. Myron, of course, cannot sing, not in the usual carry-a-tune sense. What he lacks in pitch and tone, though, he makes up for with volume and enthusiasm—thus the entertainment value of the song, the laughter in the woman's family, and ultimately, the piss. The Cope "Christmas Carol" will become an annual tradition.

"What is it about this man, lighting his Optimo cigar five evenings a week in a cluttered little Pittsburgh studio?" Gorney asks rhetorically. She doesn't have a definitive answer, but there's no doubt that Myron is in possession of "it." According to the early 1979 Arbitron ratings, between thirty and thirty-five thousand people across the greater Pittsburgh area are listening to Myron at any one moment as he gabs with his guests. That makes *Myron Cope on Sports* the number-two offering in its 7–8 p.m. time slot. Eternal ratings leader KDKA and talk-show host Roy Fox have a hold on number one with eight thousand more listeners, but that's with a broadcasting signal ten times as strong.

"If memory serves," writes *Post-Gazette* media reporter Win Fanning, Myron's show comes "as close as anyone has come to the fifty-thousand watter in the four-county metro area—ever." Myron also commands the largest share of male listeners over the age of eighteen, a slice of the audience highly desired by advertisers.

Maybe that's why in interviews around this time, WTAE radio general manager Ted Atkins makes a point of praising Myron and his drawing power. "He has improved the ratings dramatically—not just significantly—dramatically," Atkins says in one. "Pittsburgh, as you know, is one of America's great sports cities and Myron is a Pittsburgh phenomenon," he says in another.

What Atkins neglects to mention is that six years earlier, he nearly snuffed out his phenomenon's broadcasting career. Had he listened to his gut, the Cope talk show and an entire subculture it spawned would never have taken the air.

TED ATKINS ENTERED Myron's world in the spring of 1973, when the Hearst Corporation, owner of WTAE radio and TV, hired him to be the radio side's new GM. For his first assignment, Atkins's new boss, Franklin Snyder, told him to come to Pittsburgh, listen the station for two days, and start thinking about what he wanted to do. Atkins checked in to a downtown Pittsburgh hotel room and turned on the radio. One of Myron's daily commentaries came on the air. Atkins listened closely for a minute, picked up his legal pad, and jotted down a note: "Fire Myron Cope."

"My initial reaction was that his was one of the worst voices I had ever heard," Atkins later said.

Such reaction to the Cope voice was nothing new, but Atkins's take was going to be one that mattered. Snyder had hired Atkins to rejuvenate WTAE's ratings, which after a flurry of good showings in the late '60s had fallen back like a runner with a bum leg. In the fall of 1972, then general manager Bernie Armstrong replaced nearly the entire lineup of deejays in an effort to turn things around. It didn't help, mainly because the music the station played, reasonably in step with local tastes circa 1968, had slipped toward the most vanilla form of easy listening, shrinking and aging the station's audience. According to one article, WTAE's policy in the early '70s was to never play a hit record by the original artist. Atkins said the first song he heard on the station was "Tie a Yellow Ribbon 'Round the Old Oak Tree." Not a hip song, but that was okay; Tony Orlando's recording had hit number one in *Billboard* that spring. Problem was, WTAE played an electric organ version by Muzak specialist Lenny Dee.

Armstrong departed in the spring of '73, replaced by Atkins, a big, mustachioed bear of a man who had spent fifteen years in the radio industry and was coming off major success programming two major California stations, KFRC in San Francisco and KHJ in Los Angeles. Looking to move up in the business, Atkins heard from a friend that WTAE was seeking a new general manager. "I interviewed three times for the job," Atkins later said. "[Going] from LA to Pittsburgh was a lifestyle trauma, from leather and feathers to Brooks Brothers suits, if you will, but the situation was absolutely right." WTAE's ratings and revenues had shrunk, he acknowledged, but he believed that the other Pittsburgh stations were complacent and that WTAE had the tools for a rebound, including its sister FM station and its ownership of rights to Steelers and Pitt Panthers games. "The overall attitude of the man that hired me [Snyder] was: 'You've got two years to fix it. If you do it, you've got a great future with us and if you don't, we'll get someone else,'" Atkins said. "I appreciated the frankness."

Myron knew nothing of Atkins's firing plans when the new GM installed himself at 400 Ardmore Boulevard that June. At the time, Myron was promoting a charity tennis match against Franco Harris, charitably dubbed the Iron City Tennis Classic. Myron went into Joe Namath mode ahead of the July 1 event, guaranteeing a victory. "I've been taking one tennis lesson per week and I'm going to whip Franco from here to Wimbledon," he boasted. It didn't work out that way, but the crowd of 3,500 got an entertaining show, with Frenchy Fuqua serving as ball boy, Bob Prince winning the other celebrity match, and Myron more or less hanging in there against Franco, amid a few clown stunts like serving a bagel instead of ball.

"Cope said he didn't rely enough on his muscle, which, when flexed, was as thick as the racquet handle," joked the *Press* in a postmortem. The reporter also noted that while the kids flocked around Harris, there was a surprising amount of vocal support for Cope. "I noticed that," Myron said. "That has never happened before. It worries me."

But maybe Atkins noticed the cheering too, or perhaps he just listened to more of Myron's commentaries and started to like what he heard. For whatever reason, Myron hung onto his job. "Once you get over the initial shock of his voice, you come to realize how respected he is in this town. He has innate ability as a showman," Atkins later said, adding that Myron was knowledgeable, honest, and a "real character," the latter quality being a positive. Atkins added, "His voice is a very big plus in making him such a character."

Instead of firing Myron, Atkins turned to the real problems on his schedule, which included the sports talk show hosted by former Steelers announcer Tom Bender. Bender's nightly one-hour program, launched in March 1971, was groundbreaking in a way; never before had Pittsburgh heard a talk show focused strictly on sports. For the first time, fans could vent over the air in real time when something concerned or disappointed them or just pissed them off. In March 1972 the Bender show was in the newspapers three days in a row after his listeners came down hard on Pirates pitcher Nellie Briles, who had allegedly told a St. Louis radio station that Pittsburgh fans were unsophisticated, had a mill-worker mentality, and wouldn't back a team that lost, referring to the Penguins. (Briles, it turned out, was somewhat misquoted.) The show made news again that October when an anonymous caller to Bender said a Steelers player had punched out someone in the hallway of a Buffalo hotel. The report turned out to be true, the guilty party being defensive tackle Craig Hanneman. ("Yeah, I did it," Hanneman said. "Three guys drunker than hell were keeping me awake all night.")

Bender, unfortunately, couldn't add sizzle when presented with the steak. Pat Livingston of the *Press* described him as mild mannered, "a moderator with the soul of peacemaker"—pretty much the opposite of what sports fans, even then, wanted from their talk show hosts. Bender knew that the show wasn't popular, and he worried about it. "Worst thing about ulcers," he told buddy Al Abrams, "is that you can get them without being a success!" Atkins dropped the axe the first week of August '73. To the papers, at least, Bender sounded more resigned than angry, saying simply "That's the business; it happens."

Atkins's next move must have surprised even himself. Two months after planning to fire Myron Cope, he offered Myron five extra hours of airtime per week, hosting what had been Bender's talk show.

Myron initially said no. He didn't want to shove aside Bender, a longtime friend. A talk show would also virtually eliminate his time for writing. Myron was still under contract with *Sports Illustrated* in 1973; he had written a nice profile of Boston Red Sox pitcher Luis Tiant that spring, and the magazine was about to publish his recap of the Steelers' wondrous '72 season, appropriately titled "The Immaculate Reception and Other Miracles."

Atkins appealed to Myron's professional loyalty. "I'm trying to turn this station around, and you can help me," he said.

Myron still said no.

Atkins turned up the pressure. Myron described it like this: "He said, 'Let's put it another way. I *want* you to take a shot at it.' He was about six-foot-three and figuratively put his foot on my chest."

Myron finally gave Atkins a yes. They agreed to a four-month trial. If Myron didn't enjoy the show after then, he'd quit—and of course Atkins could terminate the show at any time. WTAE set the premiere date for Monday, September 3, about two weeks before the Steelers' season opener. Letter writers to the Pittsburgh newspapers were split on the prospect of hearing Myron every night. One rejoiced, saying, "At last Pittsburgh radio will have a little excitement and controversy!" Another could not believe WTAE put Cope on the air at all and wondered aloud if he secretly worked for free. "How else could someone of his caliber keep his position?" the writer asked.

Myron, meanwhile, was trying to decide on the correct tone for his new show. He didn't want to take Bender's meek-and-mild route, nor did he want to go the other direction and argue with a bunch of cranks and kooks for an hour, the format of many a radio talk show before and since. "In the beginning, you know, I thought this thing through, how am I gonna do this show, what am I looking for here?" he recalled in 2000. "And I decided that I want to do it just as if I were a kid again, with the other kids, standing on the corner in front of the neighborhood drug store, arguing about sports."

The neighborhood drug store, in Myron's case, had been Sol's Pharmacy, an establishment at the corner of Phillips and Murray Avenues in Squirrel Hill, across the street from Ross's poolroom.

"We debated the sports issues of the day past nightfall, or until a familiar red-faced cop arrived in a patrol car and ordered us to disperse," he recalled in his autobiography. "'There's your talk show, Cope,' I thought. Go back to the street corner. Nothing pompous. Make it fun, because that's what sports is supposed to be."

However, Myron didn't foresee the street corner coming back to *him*. The week of his premiere, he took a call from a guy with a booming, rough-hewn voice and a Slavic-sounding name. "He announced himself as Zivko Kovulcheck," Myron recalled, "but I immediately knew who it was. I went along with the gag."

"Zivko" was actually Jerold Finn—the same 270-pound Jerold Finn whom Myron knew growing up in Squirrel Hill, the same guy who left Myron in a flattened heap at midfield during his final attempt to play sandlot football. While Myron was building his writing and broadcasting careers, Finn had lived in relative obscurity, working as a salesman for a Pittsburgh restaurant-supply company. When Myron premiered, however, Finn decided to create an alter ego to banter with, argue with, and sometimes razz his old buddy.

"The first time I called Myron, I felt sorry for him," Finn, in persona as Zivko, told the *Press*. "I mean, here's this fellow who's six inches shorter than the insurance company charts. He has this raspy voice and a Brillo pad for hair. Hey, where's he gonna go? I mean, this was his second show and they were ready to call back Tom Bender. I felt sorry for the guy, so I thought I better give him a call."

As one might infer, Finn was not your standard-issue talk show caller.

"Jerry was a character, really a nice guy," says Milton Wolf, an acquaintance of Myron's, a friend of Finn's, and like them, an alumnus of Allderdice and Pitt. "They called him Jelly Finn, because he was heavyset, and he looked like a blob of jelly. But he was a real sports enthusiast." During their college days, Wolf says, he and Finn would sneak into Forbes Field during the afternoon and watch the Pirates take batting practice. Myron said in his autobiography that Finn had a scholarship to play college football, but that memory is at odds with Wolf's, who says Finn "had probably played football, but he was not a performing athlete [as an adult]. He was just engrossed in sports."

More important, Finn had a great sense of humor and an imagination that equaled if not surpassed Myron's. Establishing himself as a weekly presence on Myron's show, usually by phone but occasionally in person, Finn-as-Zivko styled himself as the unofficial mayor of Pittsburgh's South Side and a representative of the city's Polish American community. Myron played along with every twist and turn, such as when Zivko said he was organizing a cross-country bus tour to Super Bowl XIV ("the Popular Polish People's Package to Pasadena") or talked about the hundreds who flocked to the Spaghetti & Beer breakfasts sponsored each weekend by his South Side Moose lodge ("The spaghetti with tart cucumber sauce is our big mover," he boasted).

One time when Zivko was live in the studio, a caller known as the Pigeon King got suspicious about his true heritage and asked him how to say pigeon in Polish. Zivko didn't miss a beat: "I'm sorry, we're not allowed to give out that information unless you have security clearance."

The idea of callers with wacky on-air handles predated Zivko. A friend and neighbor of Myron's in Scott Township, advertising writer Frank Haller, had appeared in his commentaries now and then as a spoiled ex-athlete named Lance Boyle. But Finn took the idea to new heights, so high that he eventually began making personal appearances and doing his own radio commercials as Zivko. Inspired by Finn or by the sheer fun of talking to Myron, other people created their own personas and began calling his show each night, hoping to get on the air. The Munhall Flash, the Hanging Judge, and the Vile Canard were some of the early ones. Later on, they were joined by, among others, the Sarcastic Sword, Ralph the Plumber, Mr. Monday Night, Kid Genius, the Prodigal Son, Titleman, the Lady from Monroeville, Greenfield Ray, Fanfare Frank, the Ghost of Tradition, and the Caterer. The Caterer, a particularly big fan, would sometimes drop off cheesecake for Myron to nosh on during or after a show.

"What was neat about it, it was like a club, a giant club," said Stan Savran, whose own popular sports talk show followed Myron's on WTAE for over a decade, and who heard from many of the same callers. "If you had popular callers, especially ones that could make you laugh, they'd become celebrities in their own right. Listeners would say, 'Oh, we couldn't wait for so and so to call in!' We'd only let them call in once a week, because otherwise the same people would dominate all the time."

Handling the flow of calls was Myron's producer, Eartha Jackson. Jackson, a graduate of Slippery Rock College who had majored in communications, had started at WTAE as a receptionist but quickly moved into the producer's chair. She'd be the public's main conduit to *Myron Cope on Sports* for nearly all the show's twenty-two-year run. Her job, as described in a 1983 article, was "to try to evaluate the callers, eliminating those who might be irascible, irrelevant or downright disasters." She also punched up the commercials, signaled Myron when to hurry up with a call, and cut the sound if a caller used foul or abusive language, a rare occurrence on the usually lighthearted show.

Occasionally, Myron would switch things up and hold "Fight with Cope Night," a chance to let more argumentative folks have their say. "No agreeable callers, you hear?" he'd shout. Then listeners would hear the sound of a boxing ring bell, and Myron would announce, "You're in the ring with Cope!" But even those evenings tended to stay on the lighter side. "I will argue with people on a point, but I don't get rude with them," Myron said. "It ends up as a friendly fight in most cases."

If the whole notion of talk show *culture* seems odd, consider the era. The internet, smartphones, and social media didn't exist in the 1970s. Radio stations that focused full-time on sports were still years in the future. Pittsburgh's TV stations had (surprisingly) few regular shows focused on sports. If one wanted to hear the latest news, analysis, rumors, gut reactions, and funny takes on all things Steelers-related, Myron's show was the place to be. It was filling a need in the market—a fun, communal outlet for discussion of sports, especially football.

"Back in those days, people actually sat around the kitchen table, with an AM radio and a rotary dial phone, calling sports talk shows, or just listening to it," remembered Savran. The people were mainly men, he acknowledged. "I can't tell you how many times I heard good-natured complaints from women who said, 'He won't eat dinner until the show's over! I want to watch TV but he has to listen to your show! He's ruining our dinner hour!' And they were serious."

One of Myron's regulars, the Munhall Flash, confirmed Savran's observation. "Every evening, *every* evening, Myron was on when we were eating," he told talk show host Lynn Cullen on the day Myron died. "My wife, she didn't like his voice. There was a lot of fights about that stuff, you know? But Mrs. Flash came around; she said, 'You know what? You're right, Don.' She loved him after that." Incidentally, Arbitron research confirmed that Myron's audience contained a significant number of women, not all of whom were captive listeners. A smattering of kids tuned in, too, listening with their dads or waiting for the funny moments.

One group that *wasn't* tuning in, ironically, were the players. While Myron often had Steelers (and Pirates and Penguins and Panthers) on his show as guests and frequently pumped members of the team and the staff for information about injuries, strategy, contracts, and the like, the Steelers' players didn't consider the show required listening, says Randy Grossman, a veteran of all four '70s Super Bowl teams. "I don't think it was something that the guys were tremendously concerned about," he says. "Everybody knew what was going on within the team. They didn't need a sportscaster to tell them about it."

He notes that Myron, unlike some later sports talk show hosts in Pittsburgh and elsewhere, generally didn't try to sensationalize stories or drag down anyone's reputation. "To Myron's credit, and I think to all the sports folks back then, there wasn't this gotcha mindset, this investigative journalism mindset to dig up dirt and then to publicize it," Grossman says. "It was really about the game and people's personalities on the positive side. There was a mindset of, you know, what happens in Vegas stays in

Vegas. . . . It sounds like an old guy, but I am an old guy. It's a lot healthier circumstance."

In the case of the Lambert fracas, Myron did make some calls—but only after Jim O'Brien made the story public via the *Press*, a decision that O'Brien later said he regretted. In most cases, says Elizabeth Cope, her father respected people's privacy and didn't report it if a player was dealing with, say, a drinking problem or an encounter with the law. "He was very privy to things but very trustworthy," she says. "He knew everyone's secrets and he never told them. I don't think he'd even tell me and my mom, cause he'd say, 'People aren't going to tell me things if I'm a blabbermouth.'"

That said, Myron wasn't above passing on some old-fashioned hearsay. In the mid-1970s Myron's close friend and de facto agent Sam Zacharias was in the habit of meeting Andy Russell and some other Steelers pals at a restaurant on McMonagle Avenue in Dormont. "Just about every day, guys would stop off, have a beer. . . . I would go there to meet Andy and other friends, and while I was there, I would hear things, like so-and-so hurt his foot, he's probably not going to play on Sunday, but the coaches aren't going to tell anybody. So what would I do when I heard these so-called secret things? I'd call Myron up and tell him."

Myron put the information to good use on his talk show. Naturally, he didn't report it without some showmanship. Listeners would hear the sound of a little birdie chirping—*cheep cheep cheep*—and Myron would begin a conversation. "He'd go, 'Yeah?' and act like he's listening to the birdie," Zacharias says. "He would go, 'Really? No kidding? He's not gonna play?'" Listeners got the inside scoop on the Steelers' injuries—and any players or coaches who tuned in were left highly confused, as they couldn't understand where Myron was getting his info.

This went on for a period of weeks until, Zacharias says, "the players finally figured it out. But they don't tell me they do. One day I'm there, and they make up an injury; it was not true. And I think it's another thing, and I call Myron before seven o'clock and say so-and-so has a sore leg, or whatever. Myron used it, and of course it was false. The next time I went in, I said, 'You guys got me, didn't you?'"

When Myron called a few days later, Zacharias told him, "Myron, I think we're done with the birdies."

THE CALLERS WERE the backbone of the show, but not the only attraction. Myron often began the show talking to a guest, usually a local sports figure of prominence, such as Terry Bradshaw or Lynn Swann, or an athlete with Pittsburgh roots, like Tony Dorsett. Some notable people resisted; Chuck Noll refused to come on the show for the entirety of his twenty-three-year run as Steelers coach, relenting only after retirement for a May 1992 appearance. ("I think you know my feeling on talk—talk is cheap," Noll quipped when he finally made his debut.) On occasion, Myron reached back to his writing days to pull in one of the "nuts" he had interviewed, like playboy Los Angeles Angels pitcher Bo Belinsky or football scout Fido Murphy, or he chatted with a prominent out-of-town guest, like flamboyant boxing promoter Don King or boastful Hall of Fame slugger Reggie Jackson.

After ten or twenty minutes of talk, Myron would open up the phone lines. The ensuing conversations were sprinkled with Myron's own lingo, some of it sounding vaguely Yiddish, some of it just distinctively Myron. Before going to the phones, he'd announce, "Anything you want to talk about pertaining to sports, that's *okel dokel* with me." When welcoming a caller, he'd say, "What's on your noodle?" or, "What's on your cranium?" When pausing to collect his thoughts, he might utter his placeholder word, "mmm-hah." If flustered, he'd produce a sound like a tape being run backward at high speed, *bdllipp bdllipp bdllipp bdllipp*. And when the call was through, listeners would often be dispatched with a friendly but final, "Bye now!"

If a guest or caller made an especially good point, Myron might see fit to bestow the highest honor in his kingdom: the Copeanut award. He had created the award ahead of the show's premiere in 1973 as a fun way to encourage insightful and entertaining conversation. "I asked one of our radio engineers to put together a sound effect of a coconut falling from a tree," Myron explained in *Double Yoi*. When a caller earned the award, Myron would shout, "Let's see if we can get one . . . brace yourself!" and the caller would hear a rustling sound akin to a tree being shaken, followed by a whistling noise as the coconut came down. Then—boom! The coconut would figuratively bonk the caller square on the noggin with a cartoon-like explosion.

"Do you feel okay? DO YA?" Myron would yell. Invariably, the caller did. Good things happen to those made a Copeanut, Myron liked to say—things like good grades or a job promotion. And the listener knew he or she had been admitted into a special club, as Myron did not give out Copeanut awards indiscriminately.

Given the general jocularity of the show, inevitably there were some pranks played, perpetrated by Cope or *on* Cope by various parties. In May 1975 Myron brought Bradshaw and his backup Terry Hanratty on the show for an evening of football talk. Every time Myron tried to ask a question, though, the two Terrys responded with "I dunno" or "no comment" or talked about the baloney sandwiches they were eating. The quarterbacks giggled like schoolkids as an increasingly agitated Myron accused them of plotting to ruin his show. "Your public will think that you are the two biggest idiots that ever walked a football field!" he snapped. "So what's new?" Bradshaw replied. It got a hearty laugh out of the host.

A few years later Howard Cosell played a similar trick on a Monday night broadcast, refusing to discuss the upcoming Steelers-Raiders game, choosing instead to fire mock insults at Myron. When Myron joked that his *Sports Illustrated* profile of Howard made his career, Cosell responded, "Well, it gave you a start. Unfortunately, it never worked out," adding a trademark heh-heh-heh guffaw. More than once, an exasperated Myron said, "Can we talk some football?" Cosell wouldn't let up. "By the way, I love that jacket," he said. "I never thought I'd see it again. They buried Capone in that jacket." A small crowd watching the exchange burst into laughter. Myron, not so much.

In 1980 a local impressionist, Butch Luick, called in to the show and tried to fool the host with his ace Muhammad Ali imitation. Myron picked up the call and heard a familiar sounding raspy-whispery voice saying, "Myron Cope, Myron Cope." Myron sputtered, "Yeah? Yeah? Who is this?" Luick insisted he was Ali. Myron went along with the call for a minute, not sure what to believe. Finally, he said, "Yeah, it sounds like him, but if you're really Ali, you'll know the nickname you gave me after spending twenty-eight hours beside me on a train." Luick was stumped. "Musty," he guessed. The correct answer was Mickey Rooney, and the ruse was blown.

But Myron could play the impersonation card, too. In the run-up to Super Bowl XIV in Pasadena, Myron was preparing to broadcast his talk show from the locker room of the Steelers' practice facility when Bradshaw walked in. Myron could tell he was hyped up. Earlier that day, Los Angeles Rams quarterback Vince Ferragamo, who was a medical student in the offseason, predicted that his team would beat the defending Super Bowl champion Steelers. Upon learning of the remark, Bradshaw became livid. Now, entering the locker room, he saw Cope at the microphone and sat down. With no advance preparation, the two began to improvise:

> COPE: An amazing thing has just occurred in the Steeler locker room. Vince Ferragamo, the opposing quarterback training some ten miles down the road, finished practice, showered, dressed and strolled over and has actually appeared in the Steeler locker room. Now Vince, back in 1969, the New York Jets were a substantial underdog to the Baltimore Colts, just as the Rams are an underdog to the Steelers today, and Joe Namath came out and flatly predicted a victory for the Jets. He said, "I guarantee it." Now Vince, here you are a young quarterback only in your first season as a starter, you've only started seven games . . .
>
> BRADSHAW-AS-FERRAGAMO: I'm going to medical school, Mr. Cope. . . . Surgery is my specialty. I'm going to do surgery on the Pittsburgh Steelers' secondary.
>
> COPE: My goodness, that's a brash statement from a young quarterback, about twenty-five years young.
>
> BRADSHAW-AS-FERRAGAMO: Namath only wishes that he had half of my talent and ability.

They went on for about eight minutes this way. Myron asked his guest if, as a medical student, he was better qualified to defeat the Steelers than Fran Tarkenton, a highly successful businessman off the field, or Roger Staubach, who had been an officer in the navy.

COPE: What I'm saying to you, Dr. Ferragamo, is a doctor perhaps a sizeable cut above those other two gentlemen? And are you indeed the professional man to do Bradshaw in?

BRADSHAW-AS-FERRAGAMO: They lack the one thing that I have more than anything else—looks. I'm good-looking. . . . See, Bradshaw is so ugly that when he drops back, the guys are laughing and he luckily gets passes off that are caught. Me, I'm good looking and they stand and amaze at my beauty.

As a capper, "Ferragamo" said that after the Rams won the game, he'd personally autograph eight-by-ten glossies of himself and send them to each Steelers player and member of the press. "So you can have it framed. *That's* the kinda guy I am," he said.

Myron interjected: "Is that the one in the surgeon's gown?"

About the only thing that stopped the fun and games were the commercials. According to the station's rate card, WTAE in 1975 charged sponsors between $110 and $210 per week to advertise on the show, the exact figure depending on the length of the spot (usually thirty or sixty seconds) and frequency (usually three times per week or nightly). The rates would only go up in subsequent years, as Myron's audience and general popularity grew.

"Our sales department charged high advertising rates in so-called 'drive time,' which ended at seven o'clock, but because my show was a hit, the sales staff found itself able to continue commanding drive-time rates clear to eight o'clock," Myron boasted. Notably, by the mid-1980s, when Myron's show expanded to two hours per day, WTAE tied 50 percent of his contract to the value of the show. Evening talk, not the commentaries or Steelers broadcasts, was Myron's biggest contribution to the station's bottom line.

ONLY ONCE DID another talk show host seriously challenge Myron's status as king of local sports talk radio. The competitor appeared out of the northwest, from a location seemingly incompatible with the Pittsburgh sports world. "I grew up in Cleveland, but don't say that too loudly! It was a bone of contention my first couple of years here," joked Stan Savran in 2022, as he proceeded through his forty-sixth year on the Pittsburgh airwaves. At the time, Savran had the relative upper hand on the lung cancer and diabetes that were gnawing away at his health, and he was able to host a daily talk show on the local ESPN radio affiliate. He still sounded energetic on the phone and was ready to talk about his old colleague Myron Cope—though in truth, Savran was always ready to yak about sports.

Attending Mayfield High School east of Cleveland, Stanley George Savransky played baseball and football, as well as saxophone and oboe. But he realized that his gregarious nature and deep, detailed knowledge of sports were his ticket to success. Graduating from Miami University (Ohio) in 1969 and shortening his name, Savran threw himself into the radio world, working at stations in Ohio, Oklahoma, and Florida. He first won attention on New Year's Eve 1971, when with his station's permission he downed ten ounces of 100-proof whiskey during a two-hour broadcast to demonstrate the perils of drunk driving. With a highway patrolman in the studio to monitor his progress, Savran was soon mispronouncing names and slurring his words; by the end of the show, he could not walk in a straight line or touch his finger to the end of his nose. The stunt was soon copied by other broadcasters and in time helped inspire an episode of the TV sitcom *WKRP in Cincinnati*. (In that hilarious episode, DJ Dr. Johnny Fever takes shots of bourbon on air only to see his reflexes get *faster*.)

On-air stunts were not Savran's modus operandi, though. Within in a few years he distinguished himself as both a solid play-by-play announcer, calling games for Ohio State football and the Florida Blazers of the short-lived World Football League, and a very capable talk show host, armed with strong opinions, a bottomless well of information, and a knack for pulling callers into lively debate. "I take sports seriously. It's not a hobby to me, it's what I do," he once explained.

He was working in Orlando in late 1975, when he answered a blind want ad for the sports director's job at an unnamed northeastern radio station. The station turned out to be WWSW, then a solid number two in the Pittsburgh radio market. Savran had grown up rooting for Cleveland-area teams, mainly the Browns and Indians, but after landing the job, he quickly got a fix on what Pittsburghers care about. "They are absolutely berserk about the Steelers. As the sun rises so do the Steelers," he reported back to a Florida columnist soon after his arrival.

Around that time he met Myron. His reaction was about par for the course. "I had been told about him, that he did color on the Steeler games and had a talk show and so forth, and all the caricatures I had been told about were true! The voice, and the—I don't mean this in a negative way—the histrionics, and you know, Myron being Myron," Savran said. Like many going through their first Cope encounter, he was slightly puzzled. "I did wonder about this; this was not something I had heard before," he said. "But of course, I grew to understand the nature of the Pittsburgh sports fan, and why Myron did what he did so well and so wonderfully."

Soon after coming to WWSW, Savran launched a Sunday night "Sports Rap" program that proved popular and expanded to five nights per week the following year. Savran really gained steam after shifting to news station KQV in 1979. The station gave him a nightly one-hour talk show at 6 p.m. and saw its audience in the time slot double, to nearly twenty thousand listeners. Encouraged by his success, the station extended Savran's show to 7:30 p.m. in early 1980—up against the first half of Myron's show on WTAE. "He's going dial tone to dial tone, busy signal to busy signal with Myron Cope, who despite his diminutive size is the Big Guy in the Pittsburgh broadcast market," wrote Bob Smizik in a preview of the matchup.

Myron neatly outlined the difference between himself and his new rival. "His show appeals to the hard-core sports fan. My show does too but I have more of an inclination toward humor," he told Smizik. "I have a perspective that sports is fun and should be fun. His perspective is that sports is serious business."

Savran didn't disagree. "I like to crack a joke," he said, "but my foundation is based on solid knowledge."

The story was notably free of good wishes and best-of-luck clichés. Savran had possibly ruffled Myron's feathers a couple of times, once when the *Press* reported that he wanted to take Cope's place as the color guy on Steelers games and again in the run-up to Super Bowl XIII, when he said, "I don't work with towels and all that."

Speaking in 2022 Savran acknowledged that he and Myron felt a rivalry. "I'm a competitive guy," he said:

> Look, as far as keeping score in terms of popularity and ratings, Myron was ahead 8–3 in the third inning, know what I mean? So, it wasn't as

> though I was challenging him. . . . But yes, I did feel a sense of competition. Frankly, if I may say, I think Myron felt it more than I did. I felt like he was resentful that I dare enter the field. How dare I enter the talk show market, a field that he owned. I don't think he liked me very much to be honest. I think he, I don't know, maybe he was resentful of a younger guy coming and horning in on his territory.

If Myron bore any ill will toward Savran, he kept it out of his autobiography, a place where he voiced his ire toward several other Pittsburgh-area media folk he felt had tried to undermine him, especially Sam Nover and Mark Madden. In 1980 he claimed not to be worried by the upstart. "Competition is part of the business," he said. "I'm not about to be greatly concerned about it. All I can do is do my show. If my ratings were in trouble, I'd be concerned. But my ratings have never been healthier."

In a different universe, perhaps Cope and Savran became like Ali and Joe Frazier, or Tom Brady and Peyton Manning, duking it out for years in a battle for supremacy. In this world, the head-to-head rivalry lasted only a few months. The spring 1980 Arbitron ratings showed both men increasing their audiences, though Cope's remained significantly bigger. At the same time, WTAE-TV was looking for another sports anchor for its evening newscasts. The station opened negotiations with Savran, who held out for a package radio-TV deal that included a nightly talk show. As a courtesy, station managers asked Myron if he minded Savran joining the team. "Fine with me," Myron said. "Stan was developing a following and could add strength to our broadcast format."

"I do know that when they were going to hire me, they went to him and said, 'Do you have a problem with him?'" Savran said. "And he said, magnanimously, that whatever helps the radio station I'm all for." Savran came aboard in January 1981, taking over the 8 to 9 p.m. slot, right after Myron. Ted Atkins said the lineup gave WTAE "the best one-two sports punch in the nation."

He wasn't exaggerating. Prior to Savran's arrival, WTAE had experienced a sharp drop-off in listeners after Myron's show. Savran helped buoy the ratings, and by the fall of 1981, the station ranked as the number-two station in the Pittsburgh market. Two years later WTAE did something previously thought impossible, surpassing the mighty KDKA in total listeners ages twenty-five to fifty-four, the key demographic sought by advertisers. Ted Atkins called it "the most thrilling moment" of his twelve-year reign as the station's general manager.

Savran would follow Cope in the WTAE lineup until he was let go amid disputes with management in late 1991. Periodically, the two worked together, interviewing Steelers draft picks on draft day or taking part in the annual five-hour sports talk marathon that the radio station held at the end of every year. Occasionally, reporters would ask how he and Myron got along, and Savran would answer truthfully that the relationship was fine, though not chummy. "Our relationship was professional, cordial. It was never personal. We didn't socialize or anything like that," Savran said.

He could recall only one real incident of tension with Myron. "He had said something, as I recall, about the Pirates, but he said some negative stuff about me on his show," Savran said. "And he later sent me a personal letter, apologizing. He said, 'That's not my style,' and I appreciated that. I didn't say negative things about him on my show. David doesn't talk badly about Goliath!"

But the two complemented each other nicely at times. In December 1984 Myron recorded a new version of his high-volume, ear-maiming "Deck the Halls" Christmas carol, aiming it again at the Denver Broncos, who were to face the Steelers in a playoff game the following week. Savran was tasked with presenting the video of the clip on the six o'clock news. "I had to write a lead-in to it," he recalled. "I didn't want to go Associated Press style, and go, 'Here's Myron Cope,' so I tried to come up with something a little bit creative."

Actually, he came up with something perfect for a roast. The graphic showing Myron's face was captioned "Yuletide Cheer?" And in the intro, Savran needled Cope about his singing. "By the way," he said with a mirthful smile, "Leontyne Price turned down the opportunity to sing harmony—mainly because Myron sometimes has trouble finding the melody. The following is *not* close captioned for the hearing impaired, for obvious reasons."

Myron left the intro intact when he put the song on a DVD of his favorite broadcast moments in 2007. He could be sensitive to criticism at times—

but also knew a good sport and another top-flight broadcaster when he saw one.

THE ONLY PERSON who had the power to stop *Myron Cope on Sports* was an individual who had nothing to do with WTAE or its competition. That person was Mildred Cope.

During his magazine writing days, Mildred had never objected to Myron's travels—heck, she said, it was nice to get him out of the house now and then. But after he started working at WTAE and the couple had children to raise, Mildred wanted him home more often, and hosting an evening talk show five nights a week threw a Mean Joe Greene-sized monkey wrench into those plans.

"It was not too long after I started the talk show that I noticed that Mildred began to get a little irritable with what had become very wacky hours," Myron recalled when he ended the talk show in 1995.

> I'd finish the talk show at eight, get home no earlier than a quarter to nine, and that's when I wasn't going to a baseball game or to a hockey game, in which case I might get home after midnight. I was suddenly leading a life in which I worked very long and very weird hours. After a while, I noticed it became an irritation to my wife. She'd complain about, you know, the neighbors want us to go out to dinner with them, but we can never do that . . . and she'd see the other men [in the neighborhood] arriving at home 5 or 6 in the evening, besides which, she was on her own to raise the children, with very little help from me. There are crucial times in people's lives when things could go one way or the other. It could have been the end of the talk show, really. I could've said, "Gee, this won't work." She had legitimate beefs.

But in the end, Myron said, Mildred chose to let it go.

"All of the sudden, I stopped hearing about it," he said. "And we never talked about it. Why did it disappear? I knew darn well why. Because Mildred had said to herself, I'm sure, 'Wait a minute lady, this guy is out there earning the bread, he's doing the best he can for us, and everything in life can't be perfect. And I'm just gonna lay off and adapt myself to this strange life.' . . . She quit beefing about it, and I just don't know how I could've made this show a success had that not occurred."

But occur it did, and a success it was. The talk show gave Myron and the city of Pittsburgh a few more hours each week to discuss a team that had already gone from good to great and was about to reach heights that no fan, not even Myron, could have envisioned in their wildest black-and-gold dreams.

10

Super-Steelers Years

In the run-up to the 1974 season, Chuck Noll went on a minor trading spree, dealing away several veterans, including Pro Bowl right guard Bruce Van Dyke, for nothing more than a few low-round draft picks. Other familiar faces were simply cut or placed on injured reserve. In their place Noll installed more than a dozen rookies, eager but raw twenty-two- and twenty-three-year-olds. Yes, it had been an unusual preseason, as a brief, failed players' strike had sidelined many veterans and given the youngsters a chance to shine during the exhibition games. But the Steelers had finished a strong 10-4 in 1973 and came within a touchdown of the Super Bowl the year before, so some NFL observers looked at Noll's overhaul and thought, "What gives?"

Myron gave voice to the surprise in a commentary three days before the season opener. He noted that another respected coach, George Allen of the Washington Redskins, looked at rookies as a risk akin to holding a day for kleptomaniacs in a department store:

> "Yet here are the Steelers," he said, "with visions of a Super Bowl, and there's Chas Noll choosing his forty-seven-man squad yesterday and

keeping fourteen rookies! That's even one more rookie than he kept in 1969, his first year as a Steelers coach, when he tore apart the club to rebuild. Yes, almost one-third of the squad is rookies, and if the Steelers win the Super Bowl, it will be like a kindergarten class beating up on the twelfth grade."

But that's exactly what this kindergarten class proceeded to do. The group of rookies included five future Hall of Famers—linebacker Jack Lambert, center Mike Webster, receivers Lynn Swann and John Stallworth, and safety Donnie Shell. A team already loaded with talent was now filled to the brim, and the supercharged Steelers embarked on a run still unsurpassed in NFL history. From 1974 to 1979, the team won 80 out of 103 games, including postseason contests, capturing six straight division titles and an unprecedented four Super Bowls. The defense was all but bulletproof, routinely leading the AFC in fewest yards and points allowed. In its peak year, 1976, the Steel Curtain pitched a record-setting five shutouts and allowed opponents just twenty-eight points over the final nine games. In one game against expansion Tampa Bay that season, the Curtain held Buccaneer quarterbacks to *11* net yards passing. Lambert was named NFL Defensive Player of the Year after the season—the third straight Steeler to win after Mean Joe Greene in '74 and Mel Blount in '75.

The offense wasn't quite as overwhelming but was powerful just the same. The '76 team was the second (and last) in league history to have two 1,000-yard runners in the same backfield, Franco Harris and Rocky Bleier. In '78, after passing rules were liberalized, Terry Bradshaw became the league's top passer and won NFL MVP. The '79 offense was the best yet, becoming the first in franchise history to lead the league in points scored and total yards gained.

Like other longtime Steelers fans, Myron was elated to see the team soar so high after so many years of losing—doubly elated, as he got to see every game live and to announce them to the suddenly vast Steelers-hungry public. "They won all those Super Bowls, and I got to broadcast them all," he said in a 1999 interview with WTAE's Andrew Stockey. "I was just so fortunate, cause I coulda spent thirty years with some average team, or a lousy team. But I happened to ride the coattails of an outfit that just captivated everybody—across the country, not just here [in Pittsburgh]."

"Captivated" is almost an understatement. For those who weren't there, it's hard to explain just how popular and ubiquitous the Steelers were in the late 1970s, not just in Pittsburgh but nationally. At one point, Noll's men graced the cover of *Sports Illustrated* three times in five weeks. On the tube, Steelers could turn up anywhere: Bradshaw on Johnny Carson's *Tonight Show*, Lynn Swann on *Mr. Rogers Neighborhood*, and offensive lineman John Kolb in the World's Strongest Man competition, where he carried a refrigerator on his back and bent steel bars using his head. Bradshaw, an aspiring singer, even reached the top twenty of the *Billboard* country chart with an old Hank Williams tune.

In 1980 ABC turned Bleier's Vietnam-to-Super-Bowl story into a TV movie, *Fighting Back*, starring Robert Urich as Rocky. It cracked the top ten of the national ratings. The following year, Greene starred in an NBC movie, *The Steeler and the Pittsburgh Kid*. That one finished in sixtieth place. Not everything Steelers-related was scintillating.

It was in commercials that the players really made a killing. Greene made the biggest splash with his Clio Award–winning Coca-Cola ad, the one where Mean Joe, hobbling down a stadium tunnel, tosses his jersey to a young boy who had given him a Coke ("Hey kid. Catch"). But that was merely the tip of the football. Bleier and Mean Joe promoted Swanson TV dinners. Lambert touted Pittsburgh Paints. Bradshaw dashed across the screen for Spalding shoes. Greene, Bradshaw, and Harris shilled for Mattelvision football, an early (and lame) handheld video game. The Uniroyal tire company rolled out a Steeler Radial and naturally hired Greene, L. C. Greenwood, and four other Steelers to vouch for its toughness. Even obscure players got a piece of the action. After just one year as the Steelers' kicker, Matt Bahr starred in a national commercial for Kentucky Fried Chicken. Three years into retirement, Bradshaw's former backup Terry Hanratty got a Miller Lite ad.

According to Elizabeth Cope, Myron, too, was offered a national commercial but turned it down—a decision she laments to this day. "It was Pepsi," she says. "Pepsi contacted my dad and they wanted to do a spoof on Joe Greene's Coke commercial, and they wanted me in it. They wanted my dad to throw a Pepsi can to me, like making fun of the [Coke] commercial. But my dad turned it down, and I was upset about that when I found out. He had this antiquated value that he didn't want his children to be exploited. But any kid would love that! That's not being exploited!"

In Pittsburgh the Steelers won fans like no team before, not even the highly popular 1960 World Series champion Pirates. As late as October 1972, a Steelers fan could stroll up to the Three Rivers Stadium box office an hour before kickoff and buy a ticket; there were always plenty of available seats. By the following year, after Franco's miraculous catch, one needed to know somebody who knew somebody, as season ticket sales leaped from twenty-six thousand to forty-six thousand per year, more than 90 percent of the stadium's capacity. An endless streak of sellouts began, one that stretched into the 2020s (as of this writing).

Those unable to get in could at least watch from their homes or neighborhood bars, as the NFL finally gave in to public protest and dropped its despised local blackout rule. But televising the home games did little to slacken demand to see games in person. The waiting list for season tickets grew to a reported five thousand people in 1975, ten thousand by 1978.

By decade's end the Steelers had not only supplanted the Pirates as Pittsburgh's most popular team; they had become a core part of the city's identity. Football, as a rough-and-tough contact sport, had always excited Pittsburgh's steelmaking workforce more than baseball, and to finally have a champion pro football team in town made locals feel ten feet tall. Kevin Cherilla was the son of a union truck driver who watched the '70s Steelers on a little black-and-white television set—with the sound turned down so Cope and Fleming could narrate the action, of course. "We just thought we were the greatest city," says Cherilla, who was eight years old when the Steelers won their first Super Bowl. "Here we were such a small city, blue collar people, and we're kicking these bigger cities' asses!"

So strong was the team's grip on Cherilla's soul that most of his outfits were Steelers black and gold. "Wintertime was the time we all bought jackets and hats and gloves and it was always Steelers season," he recalls. "Most of my wardrobe as a kid, especially in the warm winter clothes, was

Steeler stuff, and that's all I wanted—like, don't give me anything else, don't give me fashion. From the time I was in third grade through high school, it was always Steeler stuff." Cherilla would carry his fandom into adulthood and his professional life (see chapter 11, "Enter the Towel").

When I was nine years old, I attended my friend Marc Feldstein's birthday party, a Sunday afternoon affair. There were about six of us riding in his dad's station wagon, probably coming back from the Carnegie Museum. Marc's dad turned on the radio and said, "Who do you want to hear, the Pirates or the Steelers?" I immediately piped up: "The Pirates!" They were driving toward the '79 pennant. But instantly my voice was drowned out. "Steelers! Steelers!" shouted the other kids, including the birthday boy. Marc's dad humored me by turning on the Pirates game for a minute so I could hear the score. Then it was over to 1250 AM for Steelers football. I think if you had polled a hundred other station wagons that day, the vote would have been the same.

MYRON SPENT A total of thirty-five years in the Steelers' radio booth, broadcasting 575 regular season and postseason games in all. He began when the roster still had '60s holdovers like J. R. Wilburn and Gene Mingo and endured long enough to call games with players who'd last well into the 2010s (Troy Polamalu, James Harrison) and even the 2020s (Ben Roethlisberger). But it's fair to say that throughout his career, Myron was identified most closely with the Steelers of the '70s. In no small way, Myron had contributed to the strong connection those players enjoyed with the public.

It helped that for the most part, he had a strong connection to many of the '70s Steelers on a personal level. Some announcers—especially ones who, like Myron, never played tackle football—might have trouble winning trust or fitting in among the players. He was also now a generation older than almost everyone on the roster. But from the moment he joined the radio booth in 1970 and began accompanying the team on road trips, he had no problem.

"They accepted me very well," he said in 2004. "In fact, they had a good time with me, like walking up the airplane aisle and batting me on the top of the head—hard—or grabbing my cheek. Mike Webster used to do it and pinch like crazy. Bruce Van Dyke used to bang me on the head. I went to parties where they were at, I loafed in bars where they loafed and you could get to know the ballplayers much better that way."

Speaking at Point Park University's Myron Cope Day in March 2023, Bleier and former Steelers publicist Joe Gordon confirmed Myron's good relationship with the players. "I would say, and Rocky would probably agree, he was by far the most popular media person who ever covered the Steelers," Gordon said, as Bleier enthusiastically nodded.

"Myron was received well in the locker room," Bleier explained. The players liked him just for the fact that he broke up the monotony of press conferences. "With all the media people—everybody had a question, and then a stupid question, and then a *more* stupid question, or the same one that somebody asked before by somebody else," he said. "But Myron always came up with a unique question of one nature or another. He wasn't trying to beat [a competitor]; he didn't have to write a story. But it was part of what he wanted to get accomplished."

Steelers players considered it an honor to be invited to appear on his talk show, Bleier added. "When Myron had his radio show, and he asked you to be on, that was a great privilege, to be recognized," he said.

In terms of bars, the '70s Steelers didn't have a headquarters like Dante's, mainly because few of the dynasty players were heavy drinkers. Myron still tossed back plenty of beers and cocktails with the players on road trips. One of Myron's favorite stories involved a 1975 visit to Los Angeles to broadcast a Steelers-Rams matchup. Myron had just flown into LA, and his body was still on East Coast time. After sharing a drink at a hotel bar with some reporter pals, he announced that he was tired and heading upstairs to bed. He walked into the lobby and ran into Steelers defensive tackle Ernie Holmes, a three hundred pounder also known as Fats.

Holmes's personality had two sides—lovable and eccentric when sober, moody and dangerous when drunk. Myron was a fan; the showman in him loved it when Holmes had his hair styled into the shape of arrow "to point the way to the quarterback." But he was also aware of Holmes's darker side, such as the time his speeding car was chased by police on the Ohio turnpike and he fired shots at trucks and a helicopter. The only reason Holmes stayed out of jail was that the Steelers had him committed to Western Psychiatric Hospital in Pittsburgh.

On this occasion, Myron had just pressed the elevator button when Holmes approached him and, as Myron described it, "firmly placed a large, meaty hand on my shoulder." "Cope," said Holmes, "let's go down to the bar and have a Courvoisier."

Courvoisier, a French cognac, was Holmes's favorite after-hours drink. To deny him the pleasure of company seemed inadvisable.

"Sounds good to me, Fats," Myron said.

Upon Myron's return to the bar, sports columnist Phil Musick of the *Press* strolled up to him and said, "I thought you were tired and going to bed."

Myron replied, "I am tired. But if Fats had said to me, 'Cope, let's go down to the bar and have an enema,' I'd be down here having an enema."

As for parties, Myron went to plenty, but none quite so memorable as Andy Russell's thirtieth birthday celebration at the linebacker's home in Upper St. Clair. After much food and cake and liquor were consumed, the birthday boy began to open the presents, most of them gag gifts like canes and Geritol, a vitamin pill marketed to older folks. For the finale, center Ray Mansfield and Russell's pal Sam Zacaharias lugged in a huge cardboard box. A curious Russell could tell that it was heavy, and as he approached the box, it occurred to him that there might be a person inside, like a stripper.

"As I tore off the large bow," Russell remembered, "the box moved, and I heard someone grumble, 'Get me out of here.' Looking down into the box, I was absolutely dumbfounded to find Myron staring up at me."

Myron then delivered the topper, declaring, "Kiss me, I'm yours!"

For the record, Myron was clothed and Russell did not take him up on the offer.

Having such a good rapport with the players, Myron felt no compunction about promoting their special quirks and qualities or tagging them with nicknames when he felt inspired. He highlighted L. C. Greenwood's gold shoes. He played up Frenchy Fuqua's Count Frenchy persona. He devoted commentaries to unheralded rookies like John Banaszak. He insisted on referring to Chuck Noll as Chas (pronounced "Chaz") and stuck Jack Lambert with the descriptive moniker Splat.

In September 1974 he was also the first to publicize a line attached to Lambert for the rest of his career.

> As for the defense, it has gained a smashing rookie in hard-hitting middle linebacker Jack Lambert. Jack Splat splatters 'em. Or as J. T. Thomas put it, "That man's so mean, he don't even like himself."

Judging by the number of tapes and commentary scripts he saved from that season, the '74 team was especially near and dear to Myron's heart. He had a particular soft spot for one of the less celebrated rookies, Randy Grossman. Grossman was a six-one, bushy-haired tight end who had grown up outside Philadelphia and distinguished himself at Temple University, where he led the team in catches as a senior while the Owls ran up a surprising 9-1 record. The Steelers grabbed him as a free agent after the draft, and he'd play a small but key role in the team's success throughout the Super Bowl years, blocking effectively for Bradshaw, Harris, and company and catching passes when called upon.

But Myron didn't like him just for his play. Grossman, like Cope, was Jewish, one of the very few Jewish players in the NFL at the time.

Grossman first encountered Myron when he arrived for Steelers training camp in July 1974. He might have read one or two Myron's magazine articles, he says, but had no previous exposure to Cope the broadcaster. "It's important to put in perspective what limited exposure you had back then to different areas," Grossman says. "I was wondering who this maniac was! He was obviously very much a character, he was a one-off character, and it's an overworn expression, but he had a face made for radio. It's a shame that we don't have people like him anymore. Everybody else was trying to be so professional, basically much of a bland character, and he was himself. And he reveled in himself."

A year earlier, in July of '73, an outfit called the Jewish Defense League had protested the lack of Jewish players on professional sports teams. The protest inspired Myron to create a hilarious commentary in which he recounted the attempt of a Jewish receiver, Dana Whitten, to make the Steelers squad. Imagine, if you will, the sound of Cope belting out the script against an up-tempo, wailing version of "Hava Nagila."

> Whitten made the Jewish All-America team and had been described by the *Miami News* as the Jewish Paul Warfield! [He] showed up for training camp and this reporter watched him in pass-catching drills and saw him make a sensational diving catch, and in unison with Art Rooney Junior we cried out, "Nice going, Jewish hope!" But that was Tuesday morning, and on Wednesday afternoon, coach Chas Noll, after reviewing reports from ends coach Lionel Taylor, unceremoniously cut Dana Whitten from the squad. "I am not anti-Semitic," declared Lionel Taylor, "but I am prejudiced against receivers who run slow!"

A year later Myron devoted another commentary to a Jewish pass catcher trying to make the team. The tone of the piece, aired August 12, 1974, suggests that Myron had confidence that Grossman would win a roster spot: "In the Steeler training camp, the coaches have been saying, 'Nice moves, good hands.' So who knows? Randy Grossman could still be a Steeler come Yom Kippur and for many more Yom Kippurs to come."

The prediction was on target, as Grossman would stick around for eight Yom Kippurs in all, racking up 134 receptions, including some key postseason catches, most notably the Steelers' first touchdown in Super Bowl X. In a postgame interview that day, Myron greeted Grossman with a hearty "Mazel tov," Hebrew for congratulations. On several other occasions, he worked references to Grossman's Jewish heritage into his in-game comments or his talk show.

Grossman says Myron generally didn't belabor their mutual Jewishness, but "obviously, he knows my background, I know his background, so yeah, it's nice. It was like anybody pulling out of their background things that are a personal connection."

Myron, as noted, didn't hesitate to criticize players' performance during a game. But he also stuck up for them at key moments, too. During the '74 season, the Steelers were embroiled in a season-long quarterback controversy. Third-year man Joe Gilliam had seized the starting job with outstanding play during preseason, displacing Terry Bradshaw. Bradshaw was not exactly a Pittsburgh favorite at the time. When a Bengals linebacker slammed him to the turf in a 1973 home game, giving him a separated shoulder that forced him out of the game, a good chunk of the crowd cheered. ("Idiots disguised as Steeler fans," was Myron's description of the applauders.)

But Bradshaw was white and Gilliam was black, and the debate over who should start took on racial overtones, with Gilliam becoming the target of hate mail, death threats, and epithets hurled from the stands.

"It became a race issue, and things started to get nasty," Myron remembered in 2000. "[On my talk show] we took all kinds of calls from people who were upset that Joe was playing and he was black. It wasn't a time to be proud of."

In an October 28, 1974, commentary, ahead of that week's Steelers game, Myron made a plea for racial tolerance and general sanity. In retrospect, the plea feels too soft, too evenhanded given the hostility that Gilliam had to endure. Nonetheless, it was a well-intentioned appeal:

> The game itself is almost overshadowed by the senseless mood that prevails among many Steeler fans as a result of the Gilliam-Bradshaw controversy. Pittsburgh just two years ago was a football town that was all America's delight . . . a merry as scene as could be found in pro sports. Yet in just the past few weeks, thanks to extremists on either side of the quarterback argument, Pittsburgh has become a sullen football town.
>
> We do not simply lament that there are noisy racists clamoring for each of their quarterbacks—certainly many fans argue for their man from honest conviction unsullied by bigotry. But what we are saying is that the controversy is out of all proportion to its worth. It's just football, that's ALL it is, and yet the municipal obsession has reached proportions that would lead one to believe the fate of the nation were at stake.

The QB controversy simmered all season, as Noll started Gilliam for six games, played Bradshaw for three, tried Terry Hanratty one week, then used all three at times down the stretch, with Bradshaw finally emerging as the starter. In Hanratty's lone start against the Browns, he and Gilliam combined for just three completed passes on the day, but the Steelers still won 26–16 through a single touchdown pass, a J. T. Thomas fumble return for another score, and four Gerela field goals. "I'm through trying to make any sense of Steeler quarterback situations," Myron exclaimed in the third quarter when Gilliam replaced Hanratty. "I give up! I've had it!"

Myron instead focused his attention on the Steelers' running game, specifically the status of Rocky Bleier. Bleier, then twenty-eight years old, entered the '74 season five years past the leg and foot wounds he had suffered in Vietnam, wounds that required multiple surgeries and had threatened to end his football career. After three years playing almost entirely on special teams, Bleier pushed himself harder than ever that preseason and began earning time in the backfield. When Harris and Fuqua went down with early season injuries, the Rock (as Myron called him) filled in capably against Houston, opening holes for fellow backup Preston Pearson and carrying the ball eight times himself for 37 yards.

In his commentary the next day, Myron began calling for more Bleier in the Steelers' game plan. "Bleier," he said, "a guy who has had to battle to make the roster every year, is a willing blocker, and it just may be that as the Steelers strive to fashion a ground game, Rocky's a guy they'll need—in the starting lineup."

Once Noll did make Bleier a starter, Myron advocated for the Steelers to stop rotating four or five running backs per game and to make Harris and Bleier the workhorses. It took a while, but by playoff time, that's what Noll was doing, and the combination helped carry them to the Super Bowl.

Myron forever after claimed, half-jokingly, that he was responsible for Bleier's success. When Bleier made light of this claim at a 1999 roast, Myron shot back, "He glossed over it, seeking to run around the truth, but the fact of the matter is: I MADE HIM!" The crowd, including Bleier, laughed hard—though Bill Hillgrove today throws cold water on Myron's claim. "Noll was a stickler for finding his own path," he says. "He would listen to his coaches, but the rest of the world's opinion didn't matter to him."

The last Sunday in December, the Steelers reached their first Super Bowl with a 24–13 beatdown of the Raiders in Oakland, limiting Al Davis's men to just 29 yards rushing. As the Steelers winged home that night, Myron decided to borrow Jack Fleming's tape recorder and conduct quickie interviews with the happy passengers, presumably for his commentaries and talk show. The surviving thirty-minute tape is an interesting fly-on-the-wall document of a franchise on the precipice of greatness and several beers in the bag. Steelers great Bullet Bill Dudley, along for the ride at the invitation of Art Rooney, tells Myron that the Steelers dominated the game on both sides—"offensely" and "*dee*-fensely." Defensive tackle Dwight White, never a shy sort, strolls up to Myron with a bottle of champagne in one hand, a fat cigar in another, and announces, "I'll take the mic from here, Myron. Would you just get lost in the shuffle, please?" He goes on to declare that this fine group of ath-a-letes, this fine group of competitors, is going to bring the Super Bowl crown back to Pittsburgh, P-A! Other Steelers respond with cheers, shouting, "Right on! Right on!"

Myron's favorite moment came from a very hyped-up Lynn Swann, who had caught the go-ahead touchdown in the fourth quarter. Myron began by telling Swann that he looked like he owned the world. Swann, sounding like he'd taken a few swigs of White's champagne, shouted, "That's right. In Pittsburgh, we own the world. The Steelers are on top, and we are going to have Super Bowl rings for the rest of the year!"

Swann proceeded to explain how he had told Noll, on the sidelines, that he could beat the Raider secondary by running a route called the "I-cut." The Steelers ran a couple of plays and didn't score. Noll sent Swann into the game and told him to run the route.

> I run in the game and say, "Terry, I can beat him on the I-cut." Terry said, "WHAT? WHAT?" I said, call four split right forty-two, He called the play. I made two steps outside, broke across the middle, ran to the back of the end zone. Terry's poised, waiting, waiting till the last minute, fires one over the linebackers. I leaped up and caught it in my hand, looked down at the ground, tapped two feet in and it was a touchdown. From that moment on, victory was ours! Pittsburgh was the happiest place in the world. There are fourteen rookies on this team, and we started the season [with an exhibition game] in New Orleans, we went back again this year, we beat New Orleans in New Orleans, and we are going back a third time for the Super Bowl and the ring shall be ours!

Myron kept the tape of that plane ride home to the end of his life, and when he celebrated his twenty-fifth anniversary on WTAE in 1993, he replayed Swann's speech. Every time he listened to it, he said, he was right there back on that plane, reliving the moment when the Steelers, after so many years of futility, finally got over the hump and reached the championship tier of the NFL.

FITTINGLY, IT WAS Bleier and Swann who were responsible, indirectly, for one of the great leaps forward in Myron's career. Late in the second quarter of Super Bowl XIII in January 1979, the Steelers drove down to the Dallas 7-yard line. On third down, Bradshaw scrambled right to avoid the pass rush. Looking for a receiver, he spotted Bleier a few yards deep in the end zone and tossed the ball his way. The throw came in high but Bleier jumped, stretched his 5-foot-11 frame, and caught the ball for the touchdown, giving the Steelers the lead.

In the WTAE radio booth, Myron all but went berserk. At first, he told listeners, Bradshaw looked like he might run for the first down: "Then he spotted the Rock and said, 'Here, play Lynn Swann, Rocky Bleier,' and put that ball up the air and the Rock went up there like some Russian high-jumper. YOI!"

The last word wasn't a word at all; it was an exclamation, a sound that leaped out of his voice box in a moment of sheer elation. Was it Bleier's touchdown that brought it into being? Hillgrove says no; he remembers hearing it earlier on Myron's talk show. But this was possibly Myron's first "Yoi!" during a Steelers game. In time it would become his signature word.

Myron shed light on the origins of *yoi* during an interview to promote his autobiography. "I am known for uttering things that make no sense, among them various kinds of exclamations," he said. "One night, the word 'yoi' popped out of my mouth. I was startled by something, I guess. I can't remember what it was. I says, 'YOI!' And when I did something like that, it would somehow become habitual for a while. . . . So yoi became a permanent part of my jargon, because advertisers for whom I did commercials would start writing it into scripts. They'd almost insist on having a yoi in there."

The word, he explained, could be used to express surprise or dismay, depending on context. For Steelers games, Myron almost always used it to put an exclamation point on a big Steelers touchdown or turnover. If the play was a game winner, he added, he might amend the call to "double yoi!" or even "triple yoi!" though the latter was used only for extreme circumstances.

Back to Super Bowl XIII. A minute after Bleier's touchdown, waiting for play to resume, Myron and Jack Fleming were killing time when this dialogue unfolded:

COPE: Would you have expected Rocky Bleier to turn into Nijinsky?

FLEMING (after a slight pause): Who's Nijinsky?

COPE: Nijinsky was a great ballet dancer.

FLEMING: I thought he was a defensive tackle at Notre Dame in the '20s.

This was almost definitely the first time Myron invoked the name of Vaslav Nijinsky, a Russian ballet star of the early 1900s known for his gravity-defying leaps and his gradual descent into insanity. Nijinsky was long dead by the Super Bowl era, and Myron was not known to be a fan of ballet. However, the dancer had reentered the news in late 1978 as two contemporary ballet stars, Mikhail Baryshnikov and Rudolf Nureyev, announced competing attempts to bring his life story to the screen. When Myron saw the Rock leap for Bradshaw's pass, he reached for a comparison and pulled Nijinsky's name off his mental shelf.

"I didn't even know who Nijinsky was at that time," Bleier told the Myron Cope Day crowd. "It will always be one of the things I treasure, because [that clip] will always be played somewhere down the line, when someone talks about Myron and his terminology."

That Steelers-Cowboys showdown marked something of a watershed for Myron as a broadcaster. In games from the early and mid-1970s, as mentioned, he generally let Fleming be the dominant presence, keeping his comments uncommonly brief, like a dog pulling on his own leash to restrain itself. But as the decade and the dynasty unfolded, he gradually loosened up—claiming more airtime, allowing himself to get more animated, and uncaging his creativity. Now, in the span of two minutes at the Super Bowl, he had unveiled two of his soon-to-be-signature Copeisms. Elsewhere throughout the game, he spat out his comments in fast-paced, high-decibel outbursts. If Fleming was bothered at being upstaged, he didn't utter a word of complaint.

The game was the final step of Myron Cope bursting out of his broadcasting shell. From this point on, there was no holding him back. Steelers fans were going to get the full Myron—or as Pittsburghers would say it, *Mahrn.*

1. Myron as a one-year-old, 1930. He apparently disliked this picture, saying, "I look like a girl!" Courtesy of Elizabeth Cope.

2. OPPOSITE TOP: Myron in writing mode as sports editor of the *Pitt News*, 1950. Yes, college sportswriters routinely wore suits and ties back then. Courtesy of Elizabeth Cope.

3. OPPOSITE BOTTOM: In the era before computers and smartphones, newspaper staff working the late shift often played cards to pass the time. *Post-Gazette* writer Ed Jensen (*top right*) and another staffer wait for Myron to make a move, 1955. Courtesy of Elizabeth Cope.

4. ABOVE: Tanned and fit, Myron enjoys the beach and the company during a vacation in Jamaica, mid-1950s. Courtesy of Elizabeth Cope.

5. A studio shot taken in the late 1950s, about the time Myron embarked on his freelance writing career. Courtesy of Elizabeth Cope.

6. RIGHT: A very happy Myron Cope and former Mildred Lindberg cut the cake after their wedding in December 1964 in Charleston, West Virginia. It was the first marriage for both. She was thirty-three; he was thirty-five. Courtesy of Elizabeth Cope.

7. LEFT: December 1965, around the time of Myron and Mildred's one-year anniversary. Although Cope was Jewish, the couple always celebrated Christmas. Courtesy of Elizabeth Cope.

8. ABOVE: A highly successful writer wearing his favorite orange sweater, mid-1960s. Myron wrote around 130 magazine articles during his freelance career and was the author of three books plus his autobiography. Courtesy of Elizabeth Cope.

9. OPPOSITE TOP: A proud father holds his happy son, 1968. At this point, Myron and Mildred didn't know that Danny Cope was born with serious mental and developmental disabilities. A few years later, they had no choice but to place him in a home for special-needs children. Courtesy of Elizabeth Cope.

10. OPPOSITE BOTTOM: Elizabeth Cope and her older brother, circa 1975. Though Danny was prone to tantrums, he had (and has) a loving relationship with his sister. Courtesy of Elizabeth Cope.

11. ABOVE: Myron plays weatherman with WTAE Channel 4 anchor Paul Long and the station's real weatherman, Joe DeNardo, in 1971. All three were fixtures on the station's evening newscasts for decades. Courtesy of WTAE-TV Pittsburgh.

12. OPPOSITE TOP: Myron gets a laugh from Franco Harris before they play at the "Iron City Tennis Classic" in Pittsburgh's Civic Arena, July 1973. Courtesy of Elizabeth Cope.

13. OPPOSITE BOTTOM: Myron began doing commentaries for WTAE radio and TV in 1968 and began providing the "color" for Steelers radio broadcasts two years later. In 1973 WTAE gave him a radio show that helped pioneer the sports-talk format and ran for twenty-two years. Courtesy of WTAE-TV Pittsburgh.

wtae
radio 12-5-0
KENT

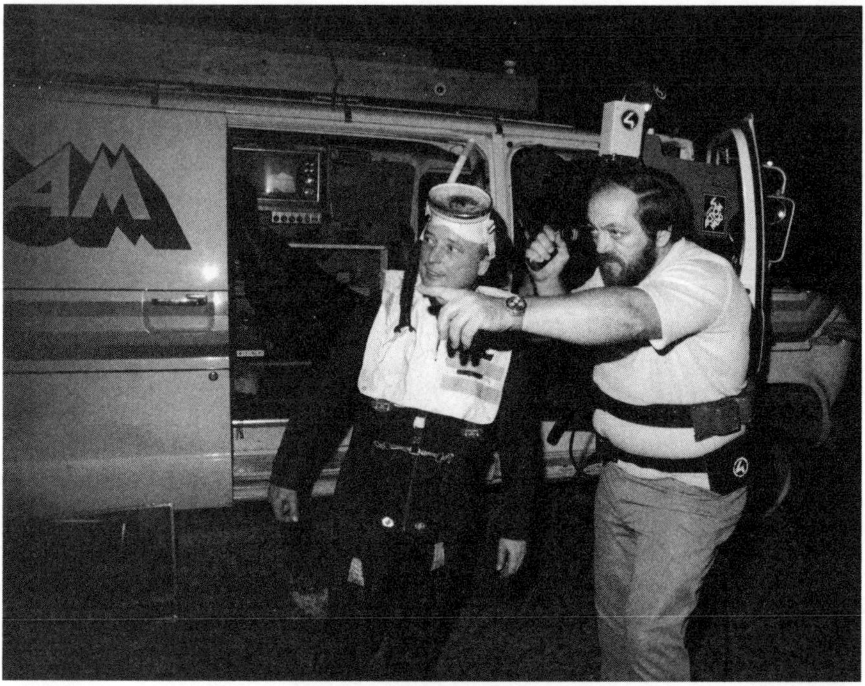

14. OPPOSITE TOP: In 1976 Myron remarked on the air that he'd swim the Monongahela River if the Oakland Raiders beat the Steelers' division rival Cincinnati. The Raiders won, and ten months later, Myron donned a wet suit to make good on his promise. Here, he plans his route with a WTAE-TV cameraman. Courtesy of WTAE-TV Pittsburgh. All rights reserved.

15. OPPOSITE BOTTOM: Mildred and Myron in the living room of their home, 1979. Photo by Michael Robinson. Courtesy of Elizabeth Cope.

16. ABOVE: Elizabeth registers disapproval of an early Terrible Towel cake, circa 1979. Courtesy of Elizabeth Cope.

17. Steelers linebacker Jack Lambert prepares to dump another helmetful of water on Myron, 1985. The two were filming a water-logged commercial for Kennywood's Raging Rapids ride. The writers allowed Myron to give a plug to his beloved creation, the Terrible Towel. Courtesy of Elizabeth Cope.

18. Myron broadcasting a Steelers game, mid-1980s. At one time, an estimated 50 percent of Steelers fans watching their team turned down the TV sound and turned up the radio to hear Myron call the game with play-by-play man Jack Fleming, later succeeded by Bill Hillgrove. Courtesy of WTAE-TV Pittsburgh.

19. Having a ball at a golf outing in 1991. Myron was a legendarily bad golfer, failing to break 100 for his entire lifetime, but he was fun to watch. Columnist Jim Murray said he saw Myron swing and miss the ball four times in a row on a par-three hole. Courtesy of Elizabeth Cope.

20. Myron with his late-career broadcasting partners, former Steelers offensive lineman Tunch Ilkin (*left*) and Bill Hillgrove, circa 1998. He broadcast the team's games for thirty-five years and was invited back to help call Super Bowl XL in 2006, but he had to decline due to poor health. Courtesy of Elizabeth Cope.

11

Enter the Towel

The temperature hovered at forty below zero, cold enough to drive the most rabid Green Bay Packer fan inside. Wind howled through the sky like a runaway train, and every surface in sight was a jagged, snow-covered rock. This was a place fit for neither man nor beast nor towel.

But there they were, Kevin Cherilla and the Terrible Towel, at the peak of Mount Everest on June 5, 2007. Everest is the world's tallest mountain, towering more than twenty-nine thousand feet above sea level. Cherilla had trained years for this moment and spent six weeks gradually ascending the mountain with a team of Sherpa guides and fellow climbers, letting his body adjust to the altitude and lower oxygen levels. When he finally reached the summit at 7:15 that morning, he pulled out his camcorder (this was before smartphones) and took a 360-degree video of the Himalayan splendor around him, letting out an excited "Wooo!" and shouting, "I'm on top of the world!"

The Towel was in his backpack, poised to make its Everest debut. Unfortunately, it never got a chance to fly. Cherilla's camcorder froze and stopped working. His digital camera did the same. At that point,

Cherilla decided he'd better start his descent, unless he wanted to freeze and stop working too.

"Do I wish I had the iconic photo of me waving the Terrible Towel on the summit? Yeah, I do," Cherilla says today from the warmth of his Scottdale, Arizona, home. He has the consolation of a picture taken that June day by another climber, showing him standing on the world's highest peak and wearing a pair of shin-high, heavy-duty black-and gold-boots outfitted with spikes the length of fingers. The boots don't qualify as true Steelers paraphernalia, as they aren't licensed by the team or NFL Properties. Still, the color scheme speaks loud and clear.

Cherilla has prominently carried the Towel on his international travels since the 1990s, when he left his native Pittsburgh to embark on what became a professional climbing and hiking career, leading adventurous souls on rim-to-rim treks through the Grand Canyon, up the slopes of Mount Aconcagua in the Andes and to the summit of Africa's highest peak, Mount Kilimanjaro in Tanzania. His Kilimanjaro clients have included former Steeler Jon Kolb, a hulking offensive lineman on all four Super Bowl teams in the '70s and a successful competitor on TV's World Strongest Man competition, where he finished fourth two years in a row. When Kolb reached the summit, he let Cherilla put on all four of his Super Bowl rings. "Not one of them even came close to fitting my fingers," Cherilla jokes.

Originally, the Towel was simply a symbol of Cherilla's attachment to the Steelers. "Back in the day," he explains, "I remember people putting the Terrible Towel on golf bags and just letting it hang, and I always thought that was pretty cool. So, when I started carrying a backpack, I just said I'm going to carry a Terrible Towel." But in time he began to identify with the Towel and its creator in a different way. Not long before Cherilla went on his first international climbing trip, to South America in 1997, he saw news that Myron had directed the proceeds from Terrible Towel sales to the Allegheny Valley School for people with mental and physical disabilities. The move struck a chord in Cherilla, whose own grandfather had a disability. And as he traveled the world, ascending mountains and walking through valleys, Cherilla became a volunteer ambassador for the Towel.

"On my first international trip, I carried it down to Argentina when we climbed Aconcagua, the highest mountain in the Western Hemisphere, and I ran into some people from the U.S., in the middle of nowhere, and they made a comment about the Terrible Towel," he explains. "I thought that was fascinating to hear. So, I carried it everywhere—thousands of miles through the Grand Canyon, I swear. One towel I have, that one alone has been to the top of Kilimanjaro over thirty times, went on three Aconcagua trips, went to the summit of Everest. And every time I would carry it, it would strike up a conversation. Somebody would ask about it. And then, if I got into a good conversation, I could tell people, 'Do you know that the proceeds of what this goes to is a really good cause?'"

In 2009 Cherilla co-led an expedition of twenty-five people, eight of whom were blind, to the top of Kilimanjaro to raise money and awareness for people with disabilities. The climb generated $200,000 to assist visually challenged individuals in Arizona and an orphanage in Tanzania for blind children and albinos, who are shunned and persecuted in parts of Africa. Afterward, Cherilla and a partner launched the K2 Adventures Foundation. The nonprofit helps people with disabilities get the equipment, supplies, and medical care they need to live better lives. Travel clients are asked, not required, to donate to the foundation. The majority give something, and over the last six years, the foundation has raised close to $2 million. "We give back between eighty-seven and ninety cents on every dollar," Cherilla says.

Sales of the Terrible Towel, meanwhile, have generated around $8 million for the Allegheny Valley School. Myron called the school a godsend. It's safe to say the school's officers think of Myron and the Towel the same way.

And to think, it all started with a hand towel that Myron Cope insisted had magical powers. "The Terrible Towel is a force that carries the Steelers to heights mortals scarcely can conceive!" he once boasted. Maybe that's why Cherilla has enjoyed so much success climbing the world's most skyscraping peaks.

He still considers reaching the top of Mount Everest his greatest achievement. "Only 10 percent of those who attempt Everest ever stand on top," he says. "Myron must have been with me!"

THE BEGINNINGS OF the Steelers Nation's banner are no secret. In mid-December 1975 Myron was called into Ted Atkins's office at WTAE, about twelve days before the Steelers were to host a first-round playoff game at Three Rivers. Atkins got right to the point. We want a gimmick that will get fans more involved in the game, he told Myron; come up with something. Myron protested: "I ain't no gimmick guy." WTAE sales manager Larry Garrett spoke up, saying a good gimmick would demonstrate the station's influence and make Myron's talk show more attractive to advertisers. Besides, wasn't Myron's contract up for renewal soon? Myron said, "I'm a gimmick guy."

Brainstorming followed. We need something the fans can wave in the stands, Myron said, something lightweight and portable. Garrett piped up: "How about towels?" Inspiration hit Myron like Jack Lambert decking a Cleveland quarterback. "We could call it the Terrible Towel. I could say the Terrible Towel is poised to strike!" he exclaimed. Atkins and Garrett liked it. WTAE top boss Franklin Snyder liked it. When Myron asked the Steelers' players about it, several disapproved, especially Andy Russell. "What's this crap about a towel?" he growled. Myron forged ahead and promoted the idea in his commentaries, telling fans to bring gold and/or black towels to the playoff game. Think of all the practical uses, he said. "You can use it as a muffler against the cold. You can drape it over your head if it rains."

Game day arrived, and Myron felt a wave of concern when he didn't see many fans lugging towels into Three Rivers. But right before kickoff, as the Steelers were being introduced, towels seemed to come out of nowhere, thirty thousand of them by his count, whirling in the December air. Better still, the Steelers beat the Baltimore Colts 28–10, with the chief Towel objector himself, Andy Russell, scoring the game-clinching touchdown on a 93-yard run after picking up a fumble.

That, in a nutshell, is the Towel's origin story. Myron recounted the tale dozens if not hundreds of times. And you know what? By all available evidence, it's correct. Atkins confirmed the legend to an online interviewer a few years before his passing in 2012. "My original idea was to buy 50,000 Lone Ranger masks to pass out at the game (Stealers, get it?) but it was cost prohibitive (15 cents each)," he wrote.

> Larry then suggested that we go for something that everybody already had . . . like a rag or a towel to wave. Myron jumped right in, saying it had to be gold or black and then said, for the first utterance EVER, 'We can call it the Terrible Towel.' Garrett and I just looked at each other. Terrible, in this instance, according to Myron's rationale, was a good thing. It would be a terrible omen for the opposition. We ran with it, and for a full week, Myron plugged the idea on his nightly radio show and on WTAE TV. Credit Larry Garrett for the towel idea and Myron for naming it. I was just a spectator in that slice of life.

Atkins added to the story:

> Garrett and I remained somewhat skeptical but bought a bunch of gold towels (there was no lettering on them back then) to pass out to staff members in the WTAE box at the game. It was a bitterly cold day, and driving to the game, I was a little depressed to note crowds heading into the stadium with nary a towel in sight. However, as the team was introduced on the field, from under parkas and overcoats, there was an unbelievable sight. Estimates have it that over 30,000 fans whipped out towels and began waving them. As I watched Myron in the broadcast booth, I thought he was going to fall out the front.

Starting that day—December 27, 1975—the Terrible Towel was the go-to object that Steelers fans used to demonstrate their passion. Towels flew again the following week at Three Rivers as the Steelers beat the Oakland Raiders in the AFC Championship Game. In the midst of the postgame celebrations on the field, two fans carried a ten-foot-long banner through the end zone that simply read "The Terrible Towel." Many Towels followed their owners down to Miami as the Steelers won Super Bowl X, and Terrible Towels were a presence at Steelers games forevermore, even though Myron did not resume heavily promoting his creation until the Steelers hosted another playoff game in 1978.

In Myron's creative hands, the Towel eventually developed an entire persona—it was male, he explained, it lived in his home, and it ate breakfast. ("It is very picky about the way its eggs are done.") More pertinent for Steelers fans, the Towel as defined by Cope had extraordinary powers, ones that could enable a Steelers receiver to outjump an opponent in the end zone or bounce a fumbled football directly into a Pittsburgh defender's hands. "Mind you, I did not see the Towel as witchcraft to hex the enemy," he explained in a July 1979 *Sports Illustrated* article. "It would be a positive force, driving the Steelers to superhuman feats."

A half century later, the Terrible Towel is ubiquitous in Pittsburgh and shows up wherever Steelers fans roam. It went up Everest with Cherilla. It's flown aboard the International Space Station with three separate astronauts. It's twirled in the hands of at least three U.S. presidents. The Towel even turned up in Afghan and Iraqi war zones with American soldiers, though it did no documented fighting against the Taliban or Islamic State. At home, the Towel is frequently incorporated into births (think newborns in blankets), bar mitzvahs (Terrible Towel yarmulkes), graduations, birthday parties, weddings, political campaigns, Christmas decorations, even funerals.

Many a Towel has accompanied its owner into his or her final resting place. "It's very traditional for families to bring the Terrible Towel in, to place inside the casket with their loved ones," funeral home director Scott Beinhauer told WTAE-TV in 2022. "We've had families wave the Terrible Towel as they persist into the cemetery. And then, if you take it to the next level . . . as a final tribute to the family's loved one, having everyone place a Terrible Towel on top of a casket just prior to burial."

But as with any success story, there's a backstory, a long series of other ideas and inventions that led to the great breakthrough. The Terrible Towel, and the very notion of a gimmick to get the fans more involved, did not materialize out of thin air.

There was a time, long ago, when sports fans didn't wave much of anything in the stands. When Joe Namath and the New York Jets pulled off their legendary upset in Super Bowl III, they did it without a single green rally flag, pom-pom, or giant foam finger cheering them on. Then, in November 1971, Miami Dolphins announcer Rick Weaver and the team's flagship radio station decided to conduct an experiment. Weaver was in his first year as the Dolphins' play-by-play man. He and the station wanted to show advertisers that fans were listening, particularly on the pocket transistor radios that many carried to games in that era. Ahead of the Dolphins' showdown with the defending Super Bowl champion Baltimore Colts, Weaver urged fans to bring white handkerchiefs—a pure, beachy white being one of the Dolphins' primary colors—and whirl them around whenever the home team scored. A reported fifty thousand Miami rooters did just that, as the ascendant Dolphins beat the Colts 17–14. Thereafter, whirling hankies became a standard sight at the Orange Bowl as Don Shula and company went on to win the AFC title.

The following year Weaver tried to monetize his idea and had a printer make five thousand white handkerchiefs for Dolphins fans to purchase and wave. "For some reason, we couldn't sell a single one," he recalled years later, with a laugh. The problem was likely his hanky's dull design, dominated by a generic red football, with a drawing of Weaver off to one side and the words "hanky power" in small print at the top. There was nothing on the handkerchief that explicitly tied it to the Dolphins or Miami. It looked like a cocktail napkin.

Myron, for the record, believed that hankies were too dainty for football and deemed white a bad color for a rally flag. "Can you imagine a white towel?" he said. "It's anemic to begin with. It obviously has tired blood and is incapable of performing any services."

Miami fans nevertheless kept bringing hankies to games and whirling them in large numbers as the Dolphins rolled to consecutive Super Bowl wins in the 1972 and 1973 seasons. All the hanky waving got under the skin of the Oakland Raiders, whom the Dolphins beat in Miami to win the AFC title in '73. When the teams met in the playoffs again a year later, this time in Oakland, Raider defensemen Gene Upshaw and Horace Jones called on fans to wave *black* handkerchiefs, reflecting the Raiders' silver-and-black color scheme and the team's tough-guy image, cultivated by owner Al Davis. Black handkerchiefs being hard to find, an Oakland radio station urged people to simply wave black socks instead ("Sock it to the Dolphins!"). Fans gladly complied, and the energized Raiders defeated the Dolphins 28–26 in the famous "Sea of Hands" game, ending Miami's brief dynasty.

The socks made it onto Myron's radar, and he took note of them in a commentary as the Steelers headed to Oakland for the AFC Championship Game:

> When you think of California, you think of the beach at Santa Monica or the bright lights of San Francisco or a game of golf in the desert air of Palm Springs. But Oakland? Well, Oakland is to California what a bowl of lumpy oatmeal is to a gourmet dinner, or maybe it just seems that way because Al Davis and his shifty-eyed lieutenants scheme twenty-four hours a day to make things uncomfortable for the visiting team. For the playoffs this year, Al Davis came up with a new twist. Oakland fans were urged to carry black socks to the game and wave them to taunt the visiting team. As we heard it, Davis told the fans, "I'm not asking you to buy anything special. Even an OLD pair of socks with holes in 'em will serve the purpose nicely." So, Oakland fans then took off their socks and were ready for the kickoff.

Even before the '70s, Myron was familiar with gimmicks to rally the fans. In 1966, as the Pirates made a push for the National League pennant, they were aided by the Green Weenie. The Weenie was the creation of the team's trainer, Danny Whelan, who had a Cope-like knack for unique ideas and expressions. One of these was his habit of shouting "Green Weenie!" at opposing players from the top step of the dugout. The term originated with the Marines during World War II, as a euphemism for being denied a promotion or otherwise "screwed over" by military bureaucracy. Whelan, a navy veteran, repurposed the phrase to place a hex on the other team. It seemed to work well during the Pirates' magical 1960 season, and that summer, Whelan took the concept a step further by buying a plastic hot dog, painting it green, and aiming it at selected players. If pointed at the opposition, it worked as a jinx; if directed at a Pirate, it delivered good luck. The Pirates players loved it and even concocted a ceremony where the hot dog was locked in a medicine cabinet after each game so the Weenie could not be stolen, tampered with, or damaged.

After the Pirates won the World Series, the Weenie was retired for a few years. "I just put it away and let it rest," Whelan explained. But in June

1966 he brought it back as the Pirates were trailing in Houston. Pirates announcer Bob Prince, helming the telecast, spotted Whelan deploying the Weenie in the dugout and pointed it out to viewers. The Pirates rallied to win, and the Green Weenie became an overnight star. The ever colorful Prince assumed command of Whelan's creation and began calling on its power at key moments during games—judiciously, so as not to burn it out. During one game against the Phillies, Prince's radio partner Don Hoak urged him to use the Weenie in the seventh inning with the Pirates down by two runs. No, not yet, Prince said; it's too early. But with a rally brewing in the eighth, the Gunner finally put the Weenie to work, and the Bucs scored four times to win the game.

"Never," Prince cautioned, "waste the power of the Green Weenie."

The Weenie's effectiveness faded quickly; the Pirates slumped in September, finishing third, and local companies that had hoped to cash in on the craze were left with thousands of unsold Weenies. Still, the Weenie proved that Pittsburgh was fertile territory for a sports-team gimmick—if the right one came along.

Prince had another trick up his sleeve. After a World Series win in 1971, the Pirates' attendance slumped despite regular division championships. The death of Roberto Clemente was one likely cause; the growing passion for the Steelers was another. But the Pirates front office seemed clueless on how to reverse the decline. "I covered the Pirates from 1972 to '77 and never saw any concern or even recognition from them about the Steelers' surging popularity," says longtime Pittsburgh sportswriter Bob Smizik. "Marketing was something the Pirates never heard of or chose not to employ. Their basic philosophy was 'open the gates.'"

Early in the '75 season, with home games regularly drawing just seven or eight thousand fans, the front office turned to Prince for ideas. The announcer came up with a doozy—Babushka Night. More precisely, Babushka Brigade Ladies Night. Ladies wearing the traditional headscarf, usually associated with older women from Eastern Europe, would be admitted at half-price to the Pirates' July 8 game against the Dodgers. The odd promotion drew nearly thirty thousand fans, the Pirates' best Tuesday night attendance of the season. For a follow-up promotion three weeks later, the Pirates handed out headscarves emblazoned with the team's logo and the slogan "Babushka Power." Forty-three thousand turned out.

At Prince's urging, the women also whirled their babushkas whenever the Pirates rallied—a scene that would be repeated with another team and another object in the near future. Myron never mentioned any connection, but Prince believed his creation was an inspiration for the Terrible Towel. "I don't want to take anything away from Myron Cope," said Prince in 1982, "but his Terrible Towel is what I call the illegitimate son of Mother Babushka."

The babushka gimmick helped lift the Pirates' overall 1975 attendance by a hundred thousand, the first increase in four years. So it was a stunning move after the season when the Pirates and KDKA fired Prince, reportedly due to friction caused by Prince's tendency to second-guess manager Danny Murtaugh on the air and an even stronger tendency to tell rambling stories and ignore the action on the field. The station fired Prince's sidekick and analyst, Nellie King, too. A few commentators suggested that as King's replacement, the Pirates consider their old hot dog vendor. Myron never expressed any interest, though—and frankly, it's hard to picture him shouting "Yoi!" after a double play or two-run single.

Why did the Terrible Towel catch on so quickly and permanently, while other sports team gimmicks faded away? Myron touched on that topic in the 1979 story about the Towel that he wrote for *Sports Illustrated*. Steelers president Dan Rooney had given him an article from a now-defunct newsletter called *Sports Business*, he said. The article surmised that the keys to any successful sports gimmick were (1) color and (2) motion. "Crowds dressed in the same color clothing can make an impact," the newsletter said, "but it is passive. Color plus motion in the stands creates a kind of framework for the contest itself, making the entire experience more memorable for the spectator."

Myron wrote that he could not decide which impressed him more—the newsletter's astute observation or the fact that he had created the Terrible Towel in total ignorance of the magic formula.

The fact is that Myron, with an assist from Larry Garrett, had instinctively sidestepped the other gimmicks' flaws. The Dolphins' white hankies and the Raiders' black socks had motion but no color. The Green

Weenie had color but no real motion. If designed properly, Bob Prince's babushkas could have had both, but their association with Old World grandmas may have reduced their overall appeal. The Towel was age- and gender-neutral. In its gold form, it was perfect for brightening up Three Rivers on Sundays when the Pittsburgh weather brought clouds and rain. And being bigger than a sock, hanky, or babushka, it was also a little more fun to twirl.

Dan Rooney, a longtime friend of Myron's, couldn't help but needle him about the Towel's almost accidental success. "Your ideas were pure genius," he told Cope. "But you were too stupid to know what you were doing."

Myron wouldn't have termed himself a genius but no doubt fired back at the suggestion that he was dumb. He was a smart guy, smart enough to see how his creation was connecting with Steelers fans—and wise enough to know there might be dollars to be made, given the right circumstances.

ON DECEMBER 20, 1978, readers of the *Pittsburgh Press* who opened the sports section found an ad touting a new product from Gimbels, a department store chain with six locations in the Pittsburgh area. "Here it is, Steeler fans!" proclaimed the ad. "Myron Cope's secret weapon that strikes fear in the heart of opposing teams. Wave it high as the Steelers march to victory in the play-offs and Super Bowl XIII." Above the text was a black-and-white photo of a hand towel bearing three words rendered in a fashion that made them look stamped out of pure steel.

For the first time, the Terrible Towel was poised to sell.

During the first three years of its existence, the Towel was strictly a not-for-profit, do-it-yourself affair. Most Terrible Towels waved at Steelers games were ordinary gold or black towels purchased at department stores and hand decorated with iron-on decals, embroidery, or other means. Myron, or someone around him, did make one attempt at a formal printed design. After swimming the Monongahela River for Channel 4 in September 1977, Myron dried off with a gold bath towel that featured the word "STEELER" running down the left side, the words "Terrible Towel" in the center, and below that, the heads of three anonymous football players, one with a Steelers hypocycloid on his helmet. At the bottom right was a bold, black MC logo, standing for Myron Cope. A terrible design it was not, but overall, it looked somewhat amateurish. This towel may have ended up in the river, as Elizabeth Cope doesn't have it in her collection.

About a year later, in the summer or fall of 1978, Myron got a call from Bernard "Bernie" Pollack. Pollack was a merchandising manager for the Pittsburgh division of Gimbels. We've got an idea, he told Myron. What if we create a Terrible Towel logo and put it on gold hand towels? We'll sell 'em in our stores, at maybe $5 apiece. You'll get a royalty, we'll make money too, and it'll promote both your station and the team.

A Terrible Towel logo? Sure, said Myron. One question: Who does the design?

Fifty years on, it is surprisingly hard to determine who created the logo that has graced, at minimum, eight million Terrible Towels. It certainly wasn't Myron, a creative mind with words but not with art. Nor was it anyone with the Steelers, who had no official connection to the Terrible Towel until the mid-1990s, or anybody at WTAE. The best guess comes from Michael Lisicky, an expert on the rise and fall of America's once grand department stores and the author of *Gimbels Has It!*, a history of the retail company that operated stores in New York, Pittsburgh, and other cities for well over a century before closing in 1987.

Lisicky's view: it was the Gimbels staff, in a team effort.

"Since Pollack was a district merchandising manager, he would have not designed the logo," Lisicky says. "There is a mention [in a newspaper article] about Pollack getting the Gimbels buyers involved but they would have had no creative design with the towel. Considering the size of Gimbels in 1978, the design was ninety-nine percent most likely done in-house. . . . It would've gone to the art department, promotion and marketing, on a local in-store level."

Getting a more precise answer is just about impossible, he says, given the passage of time and the disposal of most of Pittsburgh Gimbels's paperwork after the stores closed in the mid-1980s. Lisicky also notes that the original trademark application for the Terrible Towel logo, filed with the state of Pennsylvania in 1979, does not list a creator.

Whoever the artist or artists were, they did an outstanding job. The original logo stacked the three words (including *the*) atop each other, with each word the same height, all letters in lowercase. Everything was written in a stenciled, industrial-style typeface, similar to the one used by the Steelers on their helmets. The typeface was the key element. The Steelers had borrowed their lettering style as well as their distinctive logo from the U.S. steel industry's trademark in the early 1960s. By reusing that style for the Terrible Towel, the logo creators gave Myron's creation an overt connection to the team, an equally strong connection to the city of Pittsburgh, and, crucially, they imbued the Towel with an aura of strength and toughness, even a hint of brute power—qualities not usually found in bathroom towels.

Myron saw the logo and gave it a thumbs-up. Gimbels contracted with Fieldcrest, a manufacturer of home goods, to produce an initial batch of six thousand towels, the majority of them dyed a Steelerish gold with black lettering, others black with the lettering in gold. The store put them on sale ten days before the Steelers' divisional-round playoff game against Denver. The Towels sold out almost immediately—sold out within four hours, the way Myron later told it—and Gimbels realized it had a big hit on its hands.

The company quickly ordered up a second batch of six thousand in time for the December 30 playoff game at Three Rivers and ran new ads announcing that a fresh supply had arrived at the chain's Pittsburgh-area stores. "If you can't get to the game, hang it on your TV," said the new ad. "Its power is awesome."

If Pittsburghers needed any convincing of that, they got it in the playoff game. The last player introduced, Lynn Swann, ran onto the field whirling the Terrible Towel above his head. The entire stadium roared, and the fans vigorously spun their own towels, some of them with the new logo, others deemed Terrible for the occasion. Myron, writing for *Sports Illustrated*, said the Broncos were utterly intimidated by the spectacle. "[They] found themselves trapped in a vortex of yellow, gold and black terrycloth whirling against the bitter December sky like the swords of fifty thousand Cossacks," he said. The proof was in the final score: Steelers 33, Broncos 10.

Not surprisingly, Gimbels's second batch of Terrible Towels also sold out—this time in just *two* hours, Myron claimed—and even more towels were flying at Three Rivers Stadium the following week when the Steelers hosted Houston for the AFC Championship Game. This time, safety Mike Wagner had the honor of leading the towel whirling, and again the Steelers cruised, scoring 17 points in just over a minute right before halftime en route to a 34–5 win. While it was a question of who was carrying whom, the Steelers and the Terrible Towel were going to the Super Bowl.

With the Steelers returning to the big game for the first time in three years—for a rematch against the Roger Staubach and the Cowboys, no less—the Towel emerged as a focal point in the pregame media coverage, with newspapers from Philadelphia, Miami, and New York running features on its origin and impact. WTAE-TV produced its own half-hour special on the phenomenon, which opened with Myron, clad in trench coat, addressing the camera like a cop in a low-budget noir movie, ominously warning the Cowboys that they faced a force "as mysterious and deadly as the Bermuda Triangle."

NBC, which was televising the game, arranged for Myron to do a live interview with reporter Mike Adamle about a half hour before kickoff. The young, enthusiastic Adamle, just three years removed from his NFL career, could not wipe a goofy grin off his face as he talked to a plaid-suited Cope:

ADAMLE: And Myron I understand, as we look at the Terrible Towel, you're also an inventor.

COPE: Well, I created the Terrible Towel. It last flew in 1975, which was the last time the Steelers, as they did this season, had two playoff games at home. The towel carried them all the way through the playoff games and to victory in the Super Bowl. It is not a good luck charm, mind you, it is a FORCE. It gives the Steelers tremendous strength. It is not a curse on the opponent. But, if need be, it will pose mysterious difficulties for the opponent.

ADAMLE (putting a hand on Myron's forehead): Can it grow hair?

COPE: It can do anything if it puts its mind to it. It doesn't like to travel cause its strength is in numbers and you can't get enough Steeler people into the Super Bowl, tickets being limited. But it'll come through.

ADAMLE: OK, you crazy man.

Twenty minutes later, Swann charged onto the field during pregame introductions waving the Towel above his head in front of a national TV audience. "He's got his own Terrible Towel!" Cope exclaimed on the Steelers radio broadcast.

Swann wasn't the only one. Center Mike Webster had agreed to wear the Towel, tucked into the side of his pants, for the first couple of plays of the game. The Steelers scored a touchdown on the drive, and Webster decided to leave it on. The Steelers dominated on offense throughout the game, piling up five touchdowns, and with seven minutes to go, the Steelers led 35–17. Myron, as always, left the booth midway through the fourth quarter to get down to the locker room for postgame interviews. But first he made a stop on the Steelers' sideline and ran into Webster, who handed him the Towel. Myron accepted.

Bad move. The Cowboys went 90 yards for a touchdown, recovered an onside kick, and quickly scored a second TD. With twenty-two seconds to play, the score was 35–31, and the Terrible Towel was in no position to strike. Fortunately, Rocky Bleier recovered the Cowboys' last onside kick to seal the win, the Steelers' third Super Bowl triumph.

After interviewing a number of players in the locker room, Myron confessed his faux pas with the Towel to defensive lineman John Banaszak.

COPE: I come down on the field just after you guys had taken an eighteen-point lead, and Mike, I guess, figured it was over with, and he hands me the towel, he says you can have it now. He hands me this wet soaking towel and I stuff it in my briefcase and then the Cowboys proceed to stage a, a frightening comeback.

BANASZAK: It was very frightening, Myron. . . . I can't understand it. I blame you, Myron Cope. You shouldn't have taken the Terrible Towel, there's no doubt about it. It's your fault.

COPE: There is absolutely no question. I was kicking myself! And I felt like giving it back to him, but that seemed awkward, ya know, having stuffed it in the briefcase.

BANASZAK: What do you want me to do, knock you out for doing it? Hell no Myron, we're still happy! We're happy. We'll take it.

Several months later, Myron chastised himself again: "I realized later that the towel was crying to be turned loose from my briefcase, but I did not hear it above the din that filled the Orange Bowl."

Two weeks after the game, the city held a victory party for the Steelers on a Friday afternoon in Market Square. The odd timing and sub-twenty-degree temperatures held down the crowd to about five thousand, but Myron, serving as MC, was still able to whip them up to a fever pitch, yelling "All hail the dynasty!" and formally proclaiming Chuck Noll as "the Emperor Chas." Noll, rarely the jovial type, got into the spirit of things by donning a ten-gallon cowboy hat and draping it with Myron's creation. Jack Ham, taking his turn at the microphone, informed the crowd that the Steelers hadn't won the Super Bowl because of the Steel Curtain or Bradshaw's arm or Swann's pass catching. "We won," he said, "because of the Terrible Towel."

A little more than three years after its creation and its near rejection in the Steelers' clubhouse, the Towel had woven itself into the fabric of Pittsburgh. Or had become the fabric of Pittsburgh. Or something. It was big. And plans were underway to make it even bigger.

IN THE TWO weeks leading up to Super Bowl XIII, Gimbels milked the Terrible Towel for all it was worth, rolling out a limited Super Sunday edition ("There are only 4,000 of these collectors' items!" blared the ad) and introducing Terrible Towel cakes in its bakeries. It also quietly hiked the price from $5 to $6. By the end of January, the chain had grossed more than $80,000 in towel sales. Pollack and company began to think ahead to next season, to the Steelers' next run at the Super Bowl.

Myron no doubt liked the sound of the cash registers ringing as much as Gimbels, but for a different reason. Before the towels went on sale, he decided that a portion of his proceeds would go to a charity. The charity, naturally, was the cause closest to Myron's heart, the Pittsburgh chapter of the National Society for Autistic Children. On Myron's talk show, a caller offered to give $100 to the group if Mike Webster agreed to wear a Terrible Towel for two plays in the Super Bowl. "If Webster autographs it, will you give a hundred twenty-five?" Myron asked him. The caller said yes, Myron got the check, and Webster and Noll went along with the scheme; that's how the Towel wound up in the trenches of Super Bowl XIII.

In early January Myron turned over a check for $4,000 to the society. It could have been more, but Towel production was limited ("the manufacturers were tied up with their annual white sales," Myron explained) and Gimbels was losing some business to competitors. Once the Towel's popularity exploded in late December, various individuals had begun to make and sell knockoff towels, inferior in quality and design to the original but still boasting the magic words that struck fear in Steelers opponents souls. One Pittsburgh car dealership offered a free—and fake—towel with every purchase. A bakery chain, Rhea's, even horned in on Gimbels's cake business, selling hundreds of unauthorized Terrible Towel cakes at $11 apiece.

As winter turned into spring, representatives for Gimbels and Myron decided it was time to do something about it. First step was to file for trademark protection with the state of Pennsylvania. Next was to go after the imitators. A lawyer friend of Myron's, Arnold Silverman, went on a scouting expedition to Mike Feinberg & Company, a popular novelty/party supply store located on Penn Avenue downtown. In May 1979 he sent Myron a towel he had purchased at the store. "While I am not an expert on the subject of the Terrible Towel," he wrote in an accompanying letter, "I do not recall ever having seen one like the enclosed."

Discussions ensued, and the following month, Silverman sent out a form letter to Feinberg, Chatham Sports, the S. W. Randall toy store, and at least ten other establishments. "It has been brought to our attention that without authorization you have been marketing a towel bearing the mark 'THE TERRIBLE TOWEL,'" he wrote. Such activities could confuse consumers, Silverman said, and amounted to an infringement on his client's trademark. He asked each recipient to immediately stop using the phrase or any similar words on their products. "In the event that you fail to do so," he added, "litigation may be entered against you without further notice."

The letter was the opening shot in an extensive, expensive legal battle to stop the sale of illegitimate Terrible Towels. Myron never objected to fans making towels for their own use, but when businesses tried to profit from his creation, he unleashed the lawyers.

Shortly after the letters went out, Myron, WTAE, and Gimbels also finalized a contract on the ownership and licensing of the Towel. The late '78 to early '79 sales had been done on an ad hoc basis, with no formal deal in place. Now, all parties signed an agreement that established Cope and WTAE as co-owners of the trademark for the Terrible Towel and any other product labeled and sold as "Terrible," such as T-shirts, shorts, and tote bags. Gimbels was given a one-year, exclusive license to sell such products, with a requirement that the company set up a clearly defined Terrible Towel shop in all of its Pittsburgh-area stores and launch an extensive advertising campaign. This Gimbels did, placing full-page ads in the *Press* with a picture of Myron, an explanation of the Towel's powers ("The Terrible Towel is not an instrument of witchcraft") and a catchy tag: "Nationally Known, Uniquely Pittsburgh."

This contract helps answer a question that Myron was asked from time to time but never definitively addressed: How much money did he make off the Terrible Towel?

Paragraph six laid out the first royalty structure for the Towel. "As compensation for Cope's services with respect to his advisory and consultation duties," it read, Gimbels agreed to pay Myron a sum equivalent to 12 percent of the gross retail sales of "Terrible" products, minus deductions for returns. The amount would be calculated and paid monthly. In addition, Gimbels agreed that Myron's minimum compensation for the one-year deal would be $20,000, to be paid upon all parties signing of the contract. The company made the payments in two equal installments in May and July 1979.

But that was just the beginning. As the Steelers romped toward another Super Bowl in the fall of '79, Gimbels put the Terrible Towel logo on every conceivable type of product—baby bibs, tablecloths, napkins, ashtrays, shot glasses—and sales went through the roof. According to Gimbels's own accounting statements, the company netted $360,000 in "Terrible" sales between July and late December that year. Nearly half of that revenue came during the run-up to Christmas, mostly from the store's downtown, South Hills, and Monroeville locations.

Lisicky says that the Towel helped turn around the fortunes of Gimbels, at least in the short run. "It was a great marketing move on Pollack's end," he says. "In the late '70s, Gimbels had fallen way behind in all of its markets, except Milwaukee. It was a very distant third in the Pittsburgh market [behind Kaufmann's and Horne's]. Their Terrible Towel Shop became pure gold."

Myron got a fair share of that gold. The $20,000 Gimbels paid him upfront was essentially an advance on future royalties. If the Towel hadn't sold, he wouldn't have received another dime. But because it did, he started getting big checks in the mail: one for four thousand bucks in December '79, another for nineteen thousand the following month.

When the Steelers cruised through the playoffs and beat the Rams in Super Bowl XIV, Gimbels did an additional quarter million dollars in post-holiday "Terrible" business. The surge earned Myron his biggest royalty check yet, $29,500—more than the minimum annual salary for a Major League baseball player at the time and enough to buy a cabin in the mountains or a '79 Lincoln Continental town car the size and weight of a tank.

Many a sportscaster in his position would have done exactly that. Not Myron, though. According to contemporary news accounts, he put some of the money into a fund for legal expenses and then used it, filing a lawsuit against both Feinberg and S. W. Randall in January 1980 for continuing to infringe on the Terrible Towel trademark. (Both stores agreed to stop selling their version of the Towel after a court injunction.) More charitably, he also turned over sums of money to the Autism Society of Pittsburgh throughout 1979: the initial $4,000 in January, another $2,000 in April, and $6,000 more by year's end. While there were no reports on specific contributions thereafter, there is no reason to think the donations stopped, especially given that in 1981, Myron started an annual golf tournament to benefit the society and would later donate tens of thousands more he earned from speeches and commercials—without fanfare, for the most part, other than passing mentions in newspaper and magazine profiles.

That didn't stop at least a few individuals from questioning Myron's intentions with the Towel. In August 1979, after Gimbels began its preseason promotional push, Myron received a testy call on his talk show.

"There's a super big ad for the Towel in the Sunday paper, and I noticed there was no charity. Did you drop the charity?" the caller demanded.

"No, I have not dropped the charity. You, ah, want me to tell you what I'm doing?" Myron replied.

"I thought you were gonna put it all your pocket, that's what I thought," the man said.

A slightly agitated Myron went on to explain that to that point, he and "the department store" had given $7,000 to "the charity." (Myron often declined to refer to companies and other entities by their proper names on-air, presumably to avoid free advertising.) "Does that pass muster with you?" he asked. The caller said it did, though at the end of the call, he added, "I think [the Towel] is a rip-off and I hate the whole concept of it." Myron said he was certainly entitled to his opinion—then cut him off for the hourly news.

Myron stated on that show and other occasions that he might keep "a few bucks" from towel sales for himself. He likely did, but not necessarily to buy himself some toys. In 1982 he was finally able to bring Danny home from the Devereux school in Philadelphia and place him in what was then known as the Allegheny Valley School for Exceptional Children, which had begun to accept kids with Danny's type of disabilities. The home was about a half-hour drive from the Cope home in Upper St. Clair. He still dispensed funds beyond insurance to ensure that Danny was well cared for, but now his son spent every weekend at home.

The '79 season was the early peak for Myron's creation. That December students at Edinboro University in northeast Pennsylvania constructed the world's largest giant Terrible Towel, measuring ninety-three feet long and fifty-four feet wide. It was unveiled on the field during the Steelers-Dolphins playoff game. The week of the Super Bowl, a University of Pittsburgh researcher, William Cassidy, planted the Towel on a stake at the South Pole. And one month later, the Towel wound up in the hands of President Jimmy Carter as he congratulated both the Super Bowl champion Steelers and World Series–winning Pirates at the White House. The president grinned his trademark broad grin as he raised the Towel for the cameras, with the beaming mayor of Pittsburgh, Richard Caliguri, on one side of him and a slightly bemused-looking Rocky Bleier on the other.

The Terrible Towel had become a symbol not just of a team but of a tribe. The Steelers' official 1978 highlight film named them. "During the week, Pittsburgh, Pennsylvania, makes the nation's steel," intoned deep-voiced narrator John Facenda. "But on Sunday, they become the Steeler Nation."

That made Myron a modern-day Betsy Ross. After all, hadn't he created the new nation's flag?

A NEW PROMOTIONAL campaign prior to the 1980 season saw Myron in full mystical-towel mode: "The Terrible Towel, having performed its wonders in the 1970's, is flying zestfully into the 1980's, committing its total support to the powerful Steelers!" blared a full-page ad in the *Press*. But either the Towel or the Steelers lost their touch that season, with the team missing the playoffs for the first time in nine years. Sales of "Terrible" merchandise cratered, and Gimbels, which had paid Myron a $40,000 advance ahead of the '80 season, took a heavy loss.

In February 1981 the company sent him a terse letter, saying due to the lack of sales, it would no longer send checks each month. "We will continue to send a statement which will include a cumulative amount due," it said. "When this amount reaches $10.00, we will send a check." A year after being held by the president of the United States, the Terrible Towel was being hung out to dry.

It was the start of the lean years, as Myron later called them, when the Towel got little attention from Steelers fans. Gimbels agreed to one more go-round with the Towel ahead of the '81 season, giving Myron an advance of $10,000. But the Steelers missed the playoffs again, and sales were negligible. For the next few years, as the stars of the '70s retired, most Terrible Towels lay untouched. Fans who whirled the Towel for Terry Bradshaw and Franco Harris were less inspired to pick it up for the likes of Mark Malone and Walter Abercrombie.

The Terrible Towel wasn't finished, and Myron would make sure it never totally left the public consciousness. But it had gone into storage, or perhaps a rest and regeneration period like the Green Weenie had enjoyed. It was waiting for better times. When it reemerged, it would come back bigger, more popular, and more iconic than ever.

12

The Eighties

The fall of the Steelers dynasty commenced October 12, 1980, an overcast day with an ominous wind blowing at Three Rivers. A few years earlier Myron had started referring to the Cincinnati Bengals as the Bungles, in honor of late-season losses that cost Cincy playoff spots in 1976 and '77. But in week three of the '80 season, the Bengals upset the defending champion Steelers in Cincinnati, with kicker Matt Bahr missing a last-second 51-yard field goal try that would have won the game. Hoping to exact revenge three weeks later in Pittsburgh, the Steelers instead came out flat, fumbling six times, allowing sack after sack of Terry Bradshaw, and losing punter Craig Colquitt to injury in the first quarter, forcing Bradshaw to take over the punting duties.

Somehow, Noll's men trailed by only a single point as Bradshaw drove them to the Cincy 22 with nine seconds to play. With the game riding on his right foot, Bahr trotted out to try again for a game-winning field goal. The snap was fine, but Bahr missed—missed badly to the left, the ball failing to even reach the goal post. One could almost hear a *sssssssss* as air leaked out of the Steelers' balloon. The Steelers would drop their next two games as well en route to a 9-7 finish, good for third place in the AFC Central and nothing else.

Over the next few years, the giants began to retire—Bleier after the '80 season, Greene after '81, Ham and Swann after '82, along with a slew of others who had carried the Steelers to four Super Bowl titles. A total of twenty-two men had played on all four of those teams, and nearly every one of them chose to end his career with Pittsburgh rather than hang on someplace else, a testament to their respect for Chuck Noll and the Rooneys.

Myron was just as sad as the fans to see the Super Bowl champs depart. In the fall of '83, he even tried an intervention to keep one player's career going. Terry Bradshaw had been sidelined all season with an ailing right elbow. Rest didn't seem to be helping, and doctors weren't sure what to do. Then one day Myron got a phone call from a man in Toronto, a curly-haired, middle-aged gent named Colin Kerr. Years later, he recounted what happened next.

> A guy calls me. . . . He says, "I got two magic mynah birds that'll heal Bradshaw's elbow." I say, "Well, I'll ask him if he'll let them try. But you pay your own expenses coming down here. I ain't paying a dime of it!" And Bradshaw, I propose this to him. He says, "That's terrific, yeah let's do this." So the guy takes one of these birds out of the cage. I think they were green fluffy birds, they're both squawking like crazy. He says to Bradshaw, "Hold your elbow out." He puts the mynah bird on his elbow, see? And Bradshaw says, "Woooooo. I feel the power. I feel the power of the mynah bird. Mynah bird, can you help me lower my alimony?"

The bird got its two minutes of fame on the Channel 4 news but was unable to heal Bradshaw's arm or financial woes. The quarterback appeared in only one game in 1983, a late-season contest against the Jets in which he threw for two first-half touchdown passes, helping the Steelers get a win that clinched the division title. The second score was the last pass Bradshaw ever threw in the NFL. Without him in the playoffs, the Steelers were crushed by the Raiders, 38–10. The team rebounded to win a division title at 9-7 in 1984, then endured four straight years out of the postseason as the Chuck Noll era neared its end.

The Steelers' decline to a .500-caliber squad in the '80s was a minor tragedy compared to the economic catastrophe unfolding across the Pittsburgh area. The U.S. steel industry—the bedrock of the Western Pennsylvania economy for a century—had been on a slow decline throughout the '70s, dragged down by outdated mills, rising foreign competition, and high-wage union contracts. When the American auto industry slumped at the turn of the decade and the country was hit by sharp, back-to-back recessions, the big steel companies took a chainsaw to costs in order to survive, shutting down dozens of mills and laying off tens of thousands of workers. The ripple effect on the regional economy was enormous, and by end of 1982, unemployment in the greater Pittsburgh area had spiked to an alarming, Depression-like 17.1 percent. In outlying counties, up to one in every four workers was unemployed.

Steel workers who had toiled steadily in the mills for ten, twenty, even thirty years were suddenly reliant on food banks and unemployment checks. When the checks ran out and the jobs didn't come back, people began to move away, tens of thousands of them, turning some western Pennsylvania towns into hollow shells. To many, it felt like an entire way of life was ending. "People who took pride in their jobs, their families, in educating their children, are being wiped out," Myron's friend Roy McHugh quoted a McKees Rocks woman in a 1983 column. "It's an industrial holocaust."

About the only Pittsburgh business immune to the downturn was the one that had borrowed its logo from the steel industry twenty years earlier. Attendance at Steelers games never dipped. If anything, the pregame tailgate parties outside Three Rivers got bigger. Those who weren't at the parties watched on TV—often with the sound turned down and the voices of Cope and Fleming turned up high.

"I remember guys coming up to me and telling me, 'In the '80s, you can't believe what it meant to me to watch the Steelers,'" says Craig Wolfley, then a Steelers offensive lineman, now the commentator during radio broadcasts of Steelers games. "These are the steelworkers. The industry had just bottomed out, and they said, 'I didn't know if I could put food on the table for the coming week, but I had the Steelers to look forward to on that Sunday.' And it was highlighted by Myron. You know, Myron just drew the highest ratings on the radio over the TV."

Wolfley met Myron in 1980, when the Steelers drafted him out of Syracuse University to replenish an aging offensive line. He had grown up in Buffalo precisely two-point-four miles from Rich Stadium, home of the Bills, and had barely heard of Myron Cope let alone heard his voice. That changed when he got to the Steelers' training camp at St. Vincent's College in Latrobe that summer.

"You want to talk about a spartan existence—you checked into Bonaventure Hall, and it was no air conditioning, horsehair stuffed mattresses, and you were a prisoner of football, Chuck Noll and cornfields," Wolfley remembers. "Radio was the only thing available. You'd turn on the radio at night, and you'd get some version of Myron." As always, Myron made an immediate impression, something Wolfley recalled when he spoke at a postseason banquet later that year: "I was kind of rippin' on Myron and going, 'When I first came here, [I thought] who was this little scrawny guy with this crazy voice, who said oy, yoi, double yoi and mmm-hah, these catchphrases, and never even played the game? I mean, the man needed a brochure to figure out how to put on a jockstrap.'"

Myron, listening to Wolfley's remarks, laughed heartily.

"Myron loved when you went after him, he loved the give and take of you know, guys just being guys," Wolfley says. "So, I sat down and he got up and proceeded to rip me a new one. I mean he just took me up and down about being a rookie, my bad haircut and everything. I remember him looking at me with a smile, a smirk on his face, and he said, 'Wolfley, let that be a lesson to ya. You never mess with the man who's got the microphone last!'"

Wolfley played ten seasons with the Steelers, and before ascending to the radio commentator spot, he spent several years as the team's sideline reporter, working with Myron during his final seasons in the broadcast booth. Every so often, he's known to break into a Myron imitation on the air, and he gives Myron significant credit for his broadcasting career.

"He made a way for people like me," Wolfley says.

> I am not a gifted broadcaster by any means. He opened that pathway for the lesser-schooled like me. Somebody asked me, "Do you try to be like Myron?" I said no, but I said, "How can you not be influenced by a man who showed you how it's done?" It's the same way with [Steelers offensive linemen] John Kolb and Mike Webster. I never could be Mike Webster, I could never be John Kolb, but was I influenced by them? You bet I was! I wanted to be like them. I wanted to have that same proficiency and be that professional. And with Myron it was very much the same way.

In the early '80s Cope and Wolfley were among the few Pittsburghers not going through tough times. Myron's talk show remained highly popular, drawing between twenty-five and thirty-five thousand listeners per night, even as a general audience shift from AM to FM radio gained speed. The fall 1981 Arbitron survey found that Myron commanded nearly one-fourth of adult male listeners in the 7–8 p.m. hour—exactly whom his show was designed for and far more than his direct competitors, Roy Fox on KDKA and Sam Nover on KQV, even though KDKA maintained its overall audience lead.

His Steelers broadcasts with Jack Fleming—long the dominant sound of Sunday afternoons in Pittsburgh—were now reaching an even larger audience. WTAE was now the flagship of a game-day network run by Mutual radio that encompassed more than one hundred stations across eight states. Many in the listening audience were former Pittsburghers who had gone elsewhere to find work.

"People say Steeler Nation travels well—well, they don't travel well, they just live there," joked Rocky Bleier during Point Park University's "Myron Cope Day" in March 2023. "They don't travel to go to games, but they live all over. And Myron gave them that sense of being in Pittsburgh. You talk about a Pittsburgh guy. . . . It's somebody they could be proud of. They're listening on the radio, wherever they may be, and it's a part of home."

Between his radio work, the never-ending flow of commercials, and his association with the Terrible Towel, Myron was no longer just a popular sportscaster. He had become famous, virtually a household name in

Pittsburgh and known to dedicated football fans elsewhere. When fans swarmed the first day of the Steelers' 1980 training camp in Latrobe, six months after the team's fourth Super Bowl win, they chased Myron as much as any of the Steelers' stars. "I needed a cop to get me back in the building," Myron told a reporter. "One of the kids said, 'There's Myron Cope' and the next thing I knew three hundred kids had me backed up against the wall."

"All you have to do is refer to him by his first name," Myron's pal Jerry Finn aka Zivko Kovulcheck said. "Nobody ever asks, 'Who's that you're talking about?'"

Pittsburgh sports columnist Gene Collier remembered driving with Myron to Cleveland the night before a Steelers-Browns game: "We walked into a hotel full with Steeler fans with Myron on a Saturday night and you could not have walked in there with Beyonce and created any more of a stir. It was crazy. I remember saying to him, I'll see you at the bar later, Myron—if you get there."

"We couldn't go anywhere without people asking for my dad's autograph," Elizabeth Cope confirms. "Even in Florida, wherever we went, people recognized him. Hard to believe when you're not even in Pittsburgh."

Myron's popularity led to some unusual offers. In November 1981, outlandish boxing promoter Don King, he of the gravity-defying hair, brought a heavyweight title bout to Pittsburgh, with champ Larry Holmes taking on challenger Renaldo Snipes. Guess who he hired as the ring announcer?

"Welcome to the Civic Arena and tonight's world heavyweight cham-*peen*-ship card," a tuxedoed Cope shouted at full blast as the crowd of fourteen thousand roared in recognition of who was speaking. Howard Cosell, calling the fight for ABC television, chuckled and suggested that Myron, a lifelong boxing fan, was living out a childhood dream. Myron did a fine job, although his short stature made him invisible in the crowded ring when he announced Holmes as the winner on an eleventh-round TKO. He wisely stayed away from a post-fight scrum between Holmes and a bitter Snipes, who thought the referee shouldn't have stopped the fight and fired some punches toward Holmes over the head of a seated Cosell (Cosell, characteristically, talked nonstop throughout the exchange).

In 1983 a local theatrical producer, Dan Fallon, staged a revival of the 1961 Broadway musical *How to Succeed in Business without Really Trying*, reimagining the show to set it in Pittsburgh. He needed an offstage voice to play a talking advice book. After mulling possibilities for several days, "it just came to me in the middle of the night," said Fallon. He called the most familiar voice in the city. Myron professed to not being an actor but agreed to play the part because it would be recorded in advance. The play ran for three weekends that August, with the *Press* saying Myron, among others, gave a good performance.

In 1985 Myron got another call, this one from a local ad agency, Marc Advertising. The firm had scored a big success two years earlier when it put Steelers linebacker Jack Lambert in a commercial for Kennywood, western Pennsylvania's most popular amusement park. The ad, which featured the fearsome-looking Lambert reduced to child-like fright when he rode Kennywood's roller coasters ("Get me off of this thing!"), won several advertising industry awards and was a finalist for the Clio, the industry's Oscar. Now Kennywood wanted to do a follow-up promoting its new ride, Raging Rapids, a white-water course packed with spouts, geysers, and waterfalls to thrill and cool down riders on hot summer days. Would Myron be interested in filming a commercial with Jack Splat? Myron, expecting a regular half-day TV shoot, the kind he had done at least a dozen times, said yes.

It wasn't a regular shoot. Raging Rapids hadn't been installed at Kennywood yet, so that April, the company sent Cope and Lambert down to King's Dominion, a park in central Virginia that had the same ride. Director Rip Charbonnet placed the pair in one of the ride's huge circular rafts and filmed them cascading down the fast-moving, fast-soaking waterway—thirteen times. Each take, Cope and Lambert mock-shrieked in terror for the camera as they were pummeled by water, some of it from the ride, some of it dumped on their heads by crew members positioned just off camera. It was funny stuff, made funnier by the yellow kiddie rain hat on Myron's head and the floatation device he wore, a yellow inflatable duckie.

Off camera, Cope and Lambert weren't in such playful moods. The day was thankfully warm, at least eighty degrees, but the water was still springtime cold, and there was no time to dry off between takes. "It's miserable," Myron complained. "I'm so cold I can't even hear the falls because my teeth are chattering."

Between takes, an equally chilly Lambert looked down at Cope and said, "This is a lot of shit."

Myron kept his eye on the money the duo were being paid. "Listen, Splat," he said. "This is like robbing a bank."

Lambert agreed, and the two braced themselves for another drenching.

The writers did allow Myron a self-serving plug. In the last shot, Myron faces the camera, trying to wipe himself dry, and says, "Good thing I brought my Terrible Towel." Standing behind him, a grinning Lambert says, "It sure is, Myron"—and uses his Steelers helmet to dump yet another gallon of water on Myron's head. The shot required eight takes, after which Myron finally got to dry off after nearly thirteen hours of filming.

He was last seen with his sopping wet pants draped over his arm and an orange towel wrapped around his waist, exposing the lower half of his bony legs. For some reason, he was still wearing his white socks and brown leather shoes.

Lambert declared, "I just hope I don't dress like that when I'm sixty."

The commercial was a hit, generating stories in the local press and TV, and led to the same pair starring in a series of radio and print ads for Budweiser. "Advertisers saw me and Lambert as a team," Myron said, "perhaps because the image of the tall, lean, furious linebacker contrasted comically with that of a loud-mouthed runt."

AS IF HE didn't have enough to do, in 1983 Myron was named to the Pro Football Hall of Fame Board of Selectors. Joining the board was both a privilege and a responsibility. The selectors choose the handful of men who are enshrined at the Hall of Fame in Canton, Ohio, each year. It was a highly exclusive committee at the time, consisting of just twenty-nine voters, one for each NFL team that existed then, along with the head of the Pro Football Writers' Association. Myron, with his history of interviewing early football stars and broadcasting Steelers games, was a logical choice to represent Pittsburgh. He replaced his newspaper pal from the *Press*, Pat Livingston, who in turn had replaced Myron's old *Post-Gazette* colleague Jack Sell.

At the time, the Steelers were barely represented in Canton. Only two players primarily associated with the team, defensive tackle Ernie Stautner and two-way star Bill Dudley, had ever been elected to the Hall. "That was very understandable, because the Steelers weren't any good!" says the team's longtime publicist, Joe Gordon. During their first thirty-nine years, the Steelers won no titles of any kind and had only seven winning seasons, most of those just a game or two over .500. This effectively blocked most Steelers from serious consideration by the electors. "Obviously, someone who plays on winning teams is going to get more support than somebody who played on losing teams," Gordon says.

Livingston learned this the hard way when he tried to convince the board to elect two Steelers in particular, 1950s safety Jack Butler and 1960s running back John Henry Johnson. "Johnson and Butler certainly had the credentials," he wrote in the *Press*. "[But] for the life of me, I could not persuade those electors that if anyone belonged to posterity, either as athletes or as warm human beings, these men did." His frustration led Livingston to quit the board after the 1982 vote, paving the way for Myron.

Myron, ironically, didn't take the Hall of Fame all that seriously at one time. "I used to think it was nonsense," he said soon after joining the board. "I mean, what does it matter when we are all six feet under? But I became acutely aware of what it means to these players, and [now] I take it very seriously."

While the size of the board and the voting process has been tweaked over the years, selectors in the 1980s did essentially the same thing they do today—take a large list of Hall of Fame nominees, whittle it down via preliminary ballot to a group of fifteen to twenty finalists, then debate their merits at an in-person meeting, usually held the weekend of the Super Bowl. To win a spot in the Hall, a candidate needs "yes" votes from 80 percent of those in attendance.

In the meeting, "the representative for the local team generally campaigns for players from his particular area," explains Gordon. "It becomes at times political. There's some vote trading, no question about it." There's also some loud arguing, he says, "because some people on that board take a personal approach to a nominee, rather than professional. There can be some animosity, because one of the electors didn't support somebody that another was campaigning for. There can be some hard feelings." Myron, however, excelled at campaigning and arguing, making him an ideal person to represent the Steelers in such a forum.

He kept a low profile his first few years on the board, until Raiders owner Al Davis came on the ballot in 1986. The combative Davis had approximately zero fans in Pittsburgh, mainly due to the mid-1970s Raiders targeting Lynn Swann with blows to the head and a lawsuit that Davis instigated against Chuck Noll in 1977 after Noll spoke, figuratively, of a "criminal element" on the Raiders. Davis had also made enemies around the NFL by suing the league and moving his team from Oakland to Los Angeles in 1982 against other owners' wishes.

"I had a visceral reaction when I read his name, but you don't vote on the basis of that," Myron told a reporter ahead of the '86 vote. "I haven't made a decision yet. But you have to consider the fact that the man sued his partners, moved a team from a town that was supporting it. Has he been good for the league or a liability?" The tone of the question gave away Myron's answer. Perhaps he persuaded some fellow voters to vote nay, because Davis, despite the Raiders' long record of success, didn't win election that year. He wouldn't get in until 1992, his seventh year as a finalist.

Starting the next year, a surge of Steelers hit the Hall of Fame ballot, and Myron became their passionate advocate. The results spoke for themselves. In 1987 the board elected Mean Joe Greene and John Henry Johnson. In 1988 Jack Ham got in. In 1989 it was Mel Blount and Terry Bradshaw. In 1990 it was Franco Harris and Jack Lambert.

Except for Johnson, every man was elected in his first year of eligibility.

Greene, Ham, Blount, Bradshaw, Harris, and Lambert were all four-time Super Bowl champs with numerous awards and all-pro designations, so no one begrudged their entry into Canton. Still, for six Steelers to go in on their first ballot—that was extraordinary. Even Myron was surprised. "Greene and Ham made it, but it's too much to expect it to keep happening like that," he said in 1988. "And there would, I suppose, be a reluctance to put them in bing-bang-bing."

However, that's exactly what happened, and Dan Rooney, among others, gave Myron credit for convincing the selectors not to make the players wait. "He did a great job when we had all those players eligible for the Hall," the

Steelers' owner and president said. "I know other guys among the selectors would get mad at him, that he would come on so strong for Joe Greene and Terry Bradshaw, but they belonged and let them know it, with so many of our other guys too. They're in there, in part, as a result of Myron."

There was one Steeler whom Myron couldn't seem to push over the finish line. For fourteen straight agonizing years beginning in 1988, Lynn Swann was a finalist for the Hall. Each year, Myron argued his case, pointing to his production in the Steelers' playoff runs and the spectacular catches he made in the Super Bowl, especially the diving, juggling grab he made in Super Bowl X, still considered one of the best in the game's history. But year after year, Swann came up short in the vote. The biggest stumbling block was statistical. His career total of 336 catches looked puny compared to receivers who had arrived in the league after him—no matter that the '70s Steelers were a run-first team or that Swann played part of his career before the NFL liberalized its passing rules.

Swann also faced a general feeling that too many of his teammates were already enshrined, especially after Chuck Noll and Mike Webster were elected in the '90s. "I have a hard time putting nineteen Steelers in the Hall of Fame," said Hall elector and *Sports Illustrated* writer Peter King.

But in the meetings, Myron argued, vociferously, that Swann's contributions to the Steelers and the NFL were so profound that he deserved induction. "He raised the bar for receivers. Swann affected the game. He changed it with his acrobatic catches," Myron said. "When kids on the playground would make a good catch, they'd call it a 'Lynn Swann catch.' That's what the Hall of Fame should be about. . . . He should have been a shoo-in, but so much of what they go by is numbers. [Hall of Famer] Charlie Joiner couldn't carry Lynn Swann's jockstrap, and he's a good receiver."

Myron eventually got his way; the board finally elected Swann to the Hall in 2001. Swann graciously thanked Myron at the news conference announcing his induction.

But by then, Myron was off the selection board. With his pleas going unheard, Myron got fed up after the 1995 meeting and gave up his vote. "I got emotional in arguing [Swann's] case," Cope recalled. "After one meeting, I bumped into a friend in the hotel lobby who overheard another one of the selectors say I was ridiculous. I started thinking I was hurting his chances with the board, so I resigned the seat.

"The guy who said it . . . he was a jerk anyway."

EXTROVERTED AND ENERGETIC as he was, at times Myron got his fill of life in the public eye. Elizabeth Cope says that whenever her dad went to South Hills Village, the big shopping mall in Upper St. Clair, "he'd walk with his head down, with his hands in his pockets, if he just wanted to run and get something really quick. You don't always want to be recognized and have people point and whisper and come up to you and ask questions. He'd try not to make eye contact with people. In fact, he could be . . . I don't want to say shy. He had to be 'on' when he was in public. He knew people expected him to tell stories and funny jokes, and I'm sure that gets exhausting."

"Whenever we were invited to dinner or any kind of event," she adds, "my mom would say, 'We're not going to be the first person to leave.' She's like, 'Just keep that in mind, we're not going to eat and run, that's very rude!' Because my dad always wanted to leave early, even with relatives for Thanksgiving dinner. He'd always use my brother as an excuse. He'd say things like, 'We have to get Danny back to school.' My mom would say, 'No we don't.'"

Former Steeler Randy Grossman ran up against Myron's privacy wall one day while motoring down the Parkway. "We were driving down the road, going the same direction, and he's driving the car next to me, and I'm honking at him and waving at him, and he's doing this whole celebrity thing, like he doesn't want to look over and acknowledge me," Grossman remembers. "And finally, I get his attention and he's embarrassed that he wasn't paying attention. It was pretty funny. But being a celebrity is tough, and he was a significant celebrity."

Friends say Myron, unlike some celebrities, was able to put his on-air persona to the side when the lights and microphones were off. "When you went out and had dinner with him, he was just a normal guy," says longtime pal Sam Zacharias. "The on-air Myron, and the off-air, they weren't the same. When he was on the air, he was a performer, and he was good at it. When he was at home, or having a drink, he was just like you and I talking."

"Off camera, off microphone Myron was definitely not as flamboyant," says niece Marcia Grodsky. "He was always sociable, always had a story to tell, but he was never flamboyant off the air. My grandfather, you couldn't shut him up, he was just always talking. Myron wasn't like that. Myron was more conversational. It would be a two way or more street. He was a listener as well as a talker."

Overall, Myron liked being a celebrity, as evidenced by the number of speeches, commercials, and personal appearances he made on top of his Steelers and WTAE duties. Given the scope of his success in Pittsburgh, one may ask, Did Myron ever consider taking his act to a bigger market, or going national? It's not hard to picture him in the boisterous Miller Lite commercials that boosted the popularity of John Madden and other sports figures in the mid-1980s ("Tastes great! Less filling!"). Myron was certainly on the big networks' radar; Bob Costas profiled him for NBC's NFL pregame show in 1985. And Myron acknowledged that he harbored network dreams. "I used to think I could do *Monday Night Football*, 'cause of Cosell's value to them," he said in a late-career interview. "He was not your normal broadcast or jock type. Nor was I. So I felt in my own way I could do *Monday Night Football*, if ever asked."

The question of why Myron stayed in Pittsburgh came up even before he broadcast his first game for the Steelers. In July 1970 a *Pittsburgh Press* writer suggested that Myron had sufficient credentials to get a sportscasting job in the Big Apple. "Who the hell wants to live in New York?" he replied. "I could have made, I suppose, more money by going there, but I like Pittsburgh. I guess I'm a born provincialist." Myron allowed that he visited New York several times a year on business and knew that some people liked how big and fast it was, but added, "If I stop and ask directions, I like to get a friendly answer."

He addressed the subject at greater length years later in *Double Yoi*. In his mind, getting a job with one of TV's twentieth-century big three—ABC, CBS, and NBC—would have been a cinch. "I knew that all I had to do to join a network was send them a history of my ratings—year after year at the top . . . and doing it with a weak 5,000-watt radio station whose signal disappeared at dusk from a vast area to Pittsburgh's north. The networks could not ignore such data," he wrote. He acknowledged that none of the national networks had actually called him, but he said he received feelers in the '80s from Ted Turner's operation in Atlanta as well as representatives for radio stations in Cleveland, San Francisco, and New York. Had he made the leap, he said, he could have broadcast games for the Browns, 49ers, or Jets.

Myron ultimately stayed put with the Steelers. That's the team he had rooted for since childhood, he explained; that's the team that owned his heart. However, Elizabeth says that privately, her dad boasted that he could connect with audiences anywhere. "He'd say, 'People don't realize this, but I'm very adaptable.'"

Myron's friends and colleagues aren't so sure his Pittsburgh way of talking and his Steelerized shtick would have played well in other cities. "I always believed that Cope's style was unique to Pittsburgh," says Joe Gordon. Stan Savran concurred: "I certainly don't think it would have translated to the big markets—New York, LA, Chicago, Boston. . . . Some of the things Myron did were pure Pittsburgh, because he was pure Pittsburgh. I don't think it would have worked in Detroit or Baltimore. And I'm sure there are people in those markets who wouldn't make it in Pittsburgh."

"Would it have worked in another city? I rather doubt that," says Hillgrove. "Myron was a Pittsburgher through and through and I've always believed that Pittsburgh is a different market. Why? I can't put my finger on it. It could be the blue-collar, hardworking, appreciate-defense mentality that comes through. Also, we're a big little town, whereas other cities are big cities, and they're not little towns. That's what makes us unique."

Hillgrove believes that Myron may have also noticed the misfortune suffered by another Pittsburgh broadcasting legend who sought out wider vistas: Rege Cordic. Far more formal and restrained than Myron but every bit as funny, Cordic helmed a magnificent radio ship of the absurd for a decade on KDKA, presenting satires of popular shows ("Father Knows Less"), fake commercials ("Nothing holds your hair in place like GLOO!"), and characters like the painfully bad punster Carmen Monoxide and local trash collector Louis Adamchevitz (featured in the magazine *Better Homes and Garbage*). The humor contained a helping of Pittsburgh-centered bits such as a daily pigeon count in downtown's Market Square and a recurring segment titled "What the Outside World Thinks of Pittsburgh . . . When and If They Do!" So popular were the show's commercials for fictional beer Old Frothingslosh ("the stale pale ale with the foam on the bottom") that they inspired a real-life seasonal brew that the Pittsburgh Brewing Company manufactured for decades.

At its peak in the early 1960s, *Cordic & Company* loomed over competitors like a redwood blocking out the sun, capturing a reported 80 percent of the morning audience. Cordic was a born-and-bred Pittsburgher, but like anyone enjoying that kind of success, he started entertaining offers. In 1965 he accepted a job as the morning man on one of Los Angeles's top stations, KNX, replacing actor Bob Crane, who had left the job to star in the sitcom *Hogan's Heroes*. Unfortunately, something got lost in the move. "His act, which was purely Pittsburgh, didn't fly in LA. And the job failed miserably," says Hillgrove. Within eighteen months, KNX changed formats, and Cordic was off the air. He decided to stay in California and eventually carved out a new career performing small parts on TV shows and doing voice-overs for commercials. But he never found the same kind of success he enjoyed in his hometown. "Not even close," Hillgrove adds.

In 1969 Cordic made a semi-comeback on Pittsburgh radio, doing four hours every Sunday for WTAE. He taped most of the shows in Los Angeles but flew in for occasional live shows from Ardmore Boulevard. During one such appearance, somebody convinced Myron to lend his voice to the fun, and for three minutes, WTAE boasted the comedy team of Cordic & Cope. The tape still exists, and one can hear Myron rattling off a report about fictional Pittsburghers living on the West Coast, such as bartender Clifton McBourbon and bank teller Samantha Poppenperk. At one point, Myron gets lost on the page and blurts out, "What do I do next?" Cordic steers him back on script to read an update about a former Pirates pitcher taking "saliva therapy" in hopes of revitalizing his spitball.

At the end of the bit, Rege thanks his guest and intones, "Ahhh, a star is born." But overall, Myron sounds a trifle unenthused. Perhaps he could sense that Cordic's once-brilliant star was on the decline. Myron's, at that point, was just beginning to rise.

ONLY TWICE IN Myron's thirty-plus year relationship with WTAE did he seriously consider leaving it. The first came in 1969, before he had signed a full-time contract with the station. The other came in early 1985 and resulted in a deal that would've satisfied the average NFL linebacker.

After decades as the king of Pittsburgh radio, KDKA was beginning to slip. The audience shift from the AM band to FM was one factor. The failure to find talk show hosts to replace the popular Roy Fox and John Cigna was another. Add in the troubles of the money-bleeding Pirates, who many saw as doomed to leave town, and executives at Gateway Center were starting to sweat. Searching for ways to bolster the ratings, KDKA executives settled their sights on two big targets: the Steelers and Myron Cope. Both targets were in a listening mood, as the Steelers' contract with WTAE radio had ended after the '84 season, and Myron's was due to expire the following April.

KDKA quickly realized that landing one quarry depended on getting the other. "When we first started talking to the Steelers they gave us a list of four things they wanted," said KDKA radio's general manager at the time, Rick Starr. The first three—more money, heavy promotion, and operation of the Steelers' radio network—were no problem. "The fourth thing on the Steelers' list that they wanted was for Myron Cope to remain part of the broadcast team," Starr said. "That was fine with us, especially since we were going after him on our own."

Myron was already making good money at WTAE. His salary had risen steadily over the years, passing $70,000 per year in 1979, $80,000 in 1982, and $90,000 in '83. At the same time, his workload had gotten heavier. At its peak in the fall of '83, he was broadcasting Pitt games with Bill Hillgrove on Saturdays (filling in for an ailing Johnny Sauer), Steelers games with Fleming on Sundays, doing his talk show five days a week, and giving multiple commentaries per day for radio and TV. Myron was a workaholic, high-energy guy, even as he moved through his midfifties, but he was beginning to feel shortchanged. When WTAE opened negotiations to renew his deal in January 1985, he talked to his friend and de facto agent, Sam Zacharias.

"His contract was up," Zacharias remembers. "He was offered X number of dollars again from Channel 4 and the radio station, and he said to me"—

here, Zacharias slips into a Cope imitation—"'You know, they're not paying me enough!' I said, let me get involved, no charge, I'm your friend, I'll go talk to other TV stations here in Pittsburgh. He said, go ahead and do that. So, I did, and KDKA, they wanted him badly, and they offered him more money than what he would get at Channel 4."

"More money" was an understatement. KDKA's offer, outlined by Zacharias to Cope in a February 1985 memo, was for a three-year contract at a salary of $200,000 per year—more than double what Myron was making at WTAE. The proposal included improved travel and dental insurance plus options for life insurance and matching contributions to a savings plan. Left unsaid was KDKA's stronger radio signal, which would give Myron's nightly show greater exposure, providing expanded opportunities for commercials and in-person appearances.

It was a "whopper" of an offer, Myron said. He met with KDKA executive Carolyn Wean and told her he'd give WTAE a chance to match the offer. If they did, he'd stay where he was. If not, he'd make the move.

WTAE execs now had tough decisions to make. Letting Myron jump to KDKA would encourage the Steelers to make the same leap, effectively waving goodbye to a good chunk of the station's audience. But keeping both would cut deeply into the profits. The Steelers, trying to stay competitive in terms of player salaries, wanted a big bump in pay for their radio rights.

In the end, WTAE, backed by the deep pockets of the Hearst Corporation, decided it had no choice but to pony up. "We are a business and it's a business risk," Ted Atkins told a reporter. "But the Steelers, coupled with the re-signing of Myron Cope, are something we had to have."

Under the new deals, completed in March 1985, WTAE agreed to pay the Steelers $1.5 million—double the previous amount—to broadcast the team's regular-season games on radio and its preseason games on both radio and TV. Myron got a three-year contract that started at $187,000 per year and rose to $217,000, essentially averaging out to the same figure KDKA had offered. WTAE threw in a raft of additional perks, including a $2,000 annual clothing allowance, a $1,500 annual restaurant allowance, and a three-year golf membership at the Rolling Hills Country Club in Mt. Lebanon. To help offset the increased salary, Myron's talk show would expand from one hour per day to two, but Myron now had the right to broadcast from home two nights per week and no longer had to record afternoon commentaries.

Myron was highly satisfied with the outcome. Details of the contract were not reported at the time, but in a later interview, he couldn't help but let his pleasure show. "I ended up staying put—but I do thank KDKA for improving my circumstances," he said, with a chuckle.

It wasn't just money that made him stay, however. "What it boiled down to," he said, "was that I was very comfortable at WTAE and really like the people I've been working with for so many years. It would've been tough to leave."

Zacharias admits that he thought Myron might make the jump but understands why he chose to stay with WTAE. "Any problems or situation he had with his family—his son had problems, and his wife [later] passed away—I think whatever was going on, they let him do whatever he had to do. They said, 'take the time.' They were very loyal to him and vice versa."

Subsequent correspondence suggests that after 1985, WTAE radio carried on with relatively thin profit margins. It may be no coincidence that Ted Atkins, after a twelve-year run as the station's general manager, decided to resign that summer to pursue a personal business venture, buying some television stations in California. But given what Myron had done for WTAE—and all that still lay ahead—it seems that all parties were satisfied that the deal was fair. That includes John Conomikes, who was then the Hearst Corporation's general manager for broadcasting and was involved in the negotiations. "The bottom line, I had to pay a fair amount of money to keep [Myron], probably more than it was worth, but KDKA really wanted him," Conomikes says. "So, Myron ended up with a wonderful contract with us, and I will never feel bad about it, 'cause he just did a great job for us."

Proof of that came a year after the new contract was signed. In the spring of 1986 the *Pittsburgh Press* conducted an unscientific survey to measure readers' feelings about the twenty-five or so sportscasters working at the city's radio and TV stations. More than 1,400 people mailed in responses. Several of Myron's associates—Hillgrove, Fleming, Savran—scored high. But there was no doubt as to who ranked number one. Myron pulled off a hat trick, winning the counts for favorite talk show host, favorite Steelers announcer, and favorite radio or TV personality.

A few months later, the *Press* published a long feature on Myron, this one written by sports media beat writer Bill Modoono. Modoono argued that with the decline of the Steelers and the then ongoing futility of the Pirates and Penguins, Myron was filling a void in the Pittsburgh sports world. "In case you hadn't noticed," he wrote, "Myron is no longer just a talk show host, or just a football analyst, or just a guy who does sports commentaries on radio, or just another media personality. He has become the city's sports superstar."

The last was a nice compliment to a great broadcaster. But Myron stated on many occasions that it was the Steelers who made him, not he who made the Steelers. Probably, he dismissed Modoono's comment as a bunch of gorgonzola.

AMID HIS MANY duties, Myron occasionally had to anchor the sports report for the Channel 4 news if Hillgrove, Stan Savran, and John Steigerwald were otherwise engaged. As anchor, Myron played down his personality quirks and delivered the news straight, though he wasn't above a little mischief off the air, according to Hillgrove.

"Myron, he knew what Pittsburghers like," Hillgrove remembers.

> He did the sportscast one night and got a call afterwards in the sports department from an irate viewer, who said, "You didn't tell us anything about the big car race," the Indy car race at such and such. Myron said, "Well, I didn't think it was that important and I don't think people 'round here are that much into auto racing, so I used my best judgment."
>
> And the guy became irate, to the point where Myron had had enough and said, "Well pal, if you feel that strongly about it, why don't you come meet me outside the Channel 4 main entrance." And the guy said, "Well, who is this?" And he said, "Bill Hillgrove!"

TIME WAS MARCHING on, and with it came inevitable losses. Myron's dad, Ellis Kopelman, passed away in July 1983, thirteen years after his wife. Art Rooney died in August 1988, about three weeks after he gave

Myron what turned out to be his final extended interview. Both were in their late eighties. More surprising was the death of Jerry Finn, known to the larger world as Zivko Kovulcheck, who passed away in July 1988 at the age of fifty-six at Montefiore Hospital. Zivko had been fighting leukemia but had called in to the talk show as recently as three weeks earlier from his hospital bed, chastising Myron for being too hard on umpires.

Myron's own health was fine, but as he advanced through his fifties, the long hours he maintained were beginning to wear on him. The daily commentaries, daily talk show, and weekly Steelers broadcasts would have been a full load for anybody. On top of that, Myron insisted on seeing numerous Pirates, Penguins, and Panthers games in person, of attending midweek luncheons and press conferences, of getting as much information as possible firsthand.

"I've asked him, 'Why not find out things from somebody else?'" Mildred said in a 1986 interview, voicing a rare public hint of complaint with her husband's working habits. "But he's never been that way. He feels like he should be there and see for himself."

In time, however, Myron's perspective shifted closer to Mildred's. With cable television showing more and more local games, he felt less and less need to drag himself down to Three Rivers Stadium or the Civic Arena after finishing his talk show. He went to fewer of the teams' weekly press luncheons, too. He wasn't a young buck anymore. "I've always prided myself on being one of the hardest workers in my profession, but I find as I got to nearly sixty I couldn't work those sixteen-hour days anymore. It's simply nature," he explained.

Still, WTAE execs wanted as much Myron as they could get. With his contract set to expire in April 1988, the station proposed a new three-year deal that called for him to maintain the same schedule of talk shows, commentaries, and Steelers broadcasts. His pay would escalate about 3 percent per year, ending at $240,000. It was a modest raise, station executive Michael Flinn acknowledged in a letter sent to Myron's lawyer, Lester Zittrain. But the station couldn't afford more, Flinn said, given the economics of the Pittsburgh market and the fact that WTAE radio—now a full-time sports and talk station—paid 40 percent of its revenue for sports programming.

In a handwritten response sent to Zittrain, Myron voiced no objection to the proposed salary but suggested that he might want to quit the commentaries and talk show after another year. The sides finally agreed on a one-year deal at $225,000.

When that contract expired the following spring, Myron made more noise about wanting to retire or at least work less. Mildred's health was starting to get shaky. She was hospitalized for a time in early 1989, and according to a Bob Smizik story in the *Press*, "Cope was exhausted going from job to hospital to home." Wanting to keep their star happy ("We are so determined to keep Myron," wrote station manager Jim Carter in a letter to Zittrain), WTAE initially agreed to let him take an eleven-week vacation beginning May 1, 1989, with the understanding that he would come back to his usual daily talk show at the start of Steelers training camp.

But during the vacation, Myron, enjoying the freedom to rest and golf as he pleased, exercised a walkout clause in his contract; he was tired of the daily grind, he said. Somewhat reluctantly, Carter agreed to limit the talk show to Mondays and Tuesdays, along with a single radio commentary each of those days. He'd tape three commentaries per week for TV and continue with his Steelers broadcasts as before.

The reduced workload came at a significant financial cost. Myron's WTAE salary was cut to $90,000 per year, though he could (and did) enhance that with commercials and personal appearances. For him, the time off was worth the lost salary. "I decided I wanted to smell the roses," he said. "Play golf. I wanted to eat dinner with my wife and be home evenings. I cut back, and I'm glad I did."

As for his employers, Bill Modoono of the *Press* summed up their position: "I suppose the station's attitude," he wrote, "must be that a little of Cope is better than none at all."

13

Myron the Contrarian

In the late 1980s, amid growing evidence of the harmful effects of secondhand smoke, the Pittsburgh City Council and the Pennsylvania state legislature passed laws that banned smoking inside most public and commercial buildings. "No Smoking" signs went up in the WTAE building on Ardmore Boulevard. There was some grumbling in all departments, but employees learned to step outside if they wanted to light up. With one notable exception.

"I saw Myron with cigarettes all the time," says Sally Wiggin, Channel 4's most prominent news anchor for over three decades. Station management sent out multiple memos reminding employees not to smoke indoors. "Myron was someone who would do it anyway. And nobody would tell him not to," Wiggin says.

Former WTAE-AM news director John Poister confirms: "Ultimately, the building became totally non-smoking except for Myron." Myron was discreet enough to smoke only in his office and radio studio, Poister says, but higher-ups never demanded a full stop: "Myron was such an important part of the radio station, they weren't going to turn up at 6 p.m. [the start of his show] and say, 'Myron, stop smoking.'"

So brazen was Myron about smoking at WTAE that when a local public TV channel profiled him in 1992, he took an on-camera puff in the radio studio and kept an open pack of Marlboros and two smoldering ashtrays on his desk.

The message was pretty clear: no smoking, my ass.

No one who knew Myron would have been surprised. From the start of his career, Myron had a streak that could be defined, depending on one's view of him, as indomitable, independent, libertarian, feisty, temperamental, or just plain bullheaded. He didn't mind if someone had a different take from his on a sports-related matter. But woe to the fool who tried telling him how to behave, what to think, or what to say. An act of opposition was almost sure to follow, often accompanied by a lashing either from Myron's tongue or his typewriter.

This tendency flared especially strong if tobacco was involved. Myron began smoking in the 1940s, an era when cigarette commercials were inescapable and tobacco companies tried to blot out any hint that their products were harmful. (A typical ad: "What cigarette do you smoke, *doctor*?") Like millions of others, he maintained the addictive habit despite mounting, irrefutable scientific proof that linked smoking to cancer and also found secondhand smoke to be a threat. Elizabeth Cope says that at one point, her dad smoked four packs a day. "I hated it," she says, and she tried reasoning with Myron, to no avail. "He'd smoke in the car and wouldn't put the windows down," she remembers.

Poister describes himself as a vehement anti-smoker. "I tried to avoid going into Myron's studio if I could," he says. "It smelled like many, many Marlboros. It seeped into the walls." But like everyone else at the station, he refrained from asking Myron to put out his cigarettes. "There were so many things Myron did so well, you just weren't going to say that stuff to him," he says. "You wanted him to be happy. He was already a legend. Thinking back to this time, he really did kind of walk on water at WTAE. There's no other way to put it."

Free to smoke at Ardmore Boulevard, Myron challenged smoking bans elsewhere, with varying degrees of success. Initially, he could get away with it at Three Rivers Stadium, where no one dared tell Steelers owner Art Rooney to put out his ever-present cigar. In 1988 Pittsburgh mayor

Sophie Masloff tried to confront Rooney about the city's no-smoking law. "He never said a word. He just waved his hand and blew smoke at me. He didn't think that question was worthy of an answer," she recalled with a laugh when Rooney died.

But after Rooney passed away that August, the Steelers started enforcing the law. Myron resisted. One day he was strolling down a hallway at Three Rivers with a cigarette in hand. The Steelers' head of football operations, Tom Donahoe, saw it and said, "No smoking, Myron." Myron happened to be standing outside the Steelers' library, which had a portrait of the late Rooney clutching one of his beloved stogies. Cope gestured toward the painting and told Donohoe, "Why don't you go in and tell the Chief to put out that cigar?"

Bill Hillgrove says that for years thereafter, Myron smoked in the radio booth at Three Rivers during Steelers games, though when the team moved to Heinz Field, he finally compromised and went to an outdoor ramp before lighting up.

In time Myron launched something of a one-man campaign against smoking restrictions, devoting a chapter to the topic in his 2002 autobiography. His campaign only intensified after he was diagnosed with throat cancer, a condition undoubtedly brought on by his consumption of Marlboros and his other source of nicotine, Mail Pouch chewing tobacco. In July 2006, shortly after a twelve-day stay in the hospital, he wrote a column for the *Post-Gazette* titled "The Smoke Nazis Are After Us," in which he ranted against the paper's call for a county-wide indoor smoking ban to close gaps in the state and city laws. None of the arguments he made held much water, though as always, he turned out several funny lines. "For all I know," he wrote, "the PG fears smokers will cause an outbreak of beriberi or mad cow disease."

In 2005 he flouted Pittsburgh's smoking ban at a city council meeting, puffing on a Marlboro as the council honored him for his broadcasting career. "I light up a cigarette in defiance of the health Nazis who would have us go down into a sewer to have a smoke," he said with a smile. Council members indulgently laughed.

Pittsburgh police were not as indulgent in May 2001, when Myron got into a fender bender and was slapped with a charge of driving under the influence. The way Myron told the story, he was driving home from a charity party where he had stayed too long, chatting with former Steelers Frank Lewis and Frenchy Fuqua, and had imbibed too much alcohol. As part of his "rehabilitation," he was ordered to attend classes on the dangers of drunk driving. On a December afternoon, he drove to Pittsburgh's South Side for his first class. Then the defiant side of him flared up. Walking to class, he passed a pub. Inside, several fans recognized him and called out, "Hey, Myron. Come on in. We'll buy you a drink!" Myron thought to himself, "Why not?"

One vodka martini on the rocks later, he reported to "drunk class," as he called it, in an old converted rowhouse. To his horror, he was asked to take a breathalyzer test. "I can't take this test," he told the instructor. "I just had a drink down at the corner saloon."

The room erupted in laughter. Fortunately, his popularity protected him again. The instructor allowed him to wait until the end of the four-hour class to take the breathalyzer test, by which time the alcohol had departed his system.

SOMETIMES, WHEN HE felt aggrieved, Myron didn't bother to sugarcoat his pushback with a laugh and a smile. Take the incident that began the third week of October 1971, when he served as master of ceremonies for a smoker—an evening of food, drink, sports talk, and yes, smoking—at the University Club, a popular private social club located near the Pitt campus.

The speaker list for the event was nothing controversial, just an assortment of figures from the Steelers, Penguins, and Pitt athletic program, and the evening went off without a hitch. But there was controversy to come. The club, unbeknownst to Myron, had a longstanding policy of barring Jews from membership. Myron could visit the club's grand eight-story facility to speak, but his check would be politely declined if he tried to pay dues.

Two weeks after the event, Milton K. Susman, a columnist for the *Pittsburgh Jewish Chronicle*, decided Myron had crossed a line and deserved a public talking-to.

"Myron Cope is a young man with an acid tongue and an ample supply of salt which, when he is so minded, he generously pours into open wounds," wrote Susman, evidently not a fan of Myron's commentaries. He said if Myron wanted to air his "caustic" observations on sports, that was his right. But since Myron was Jewish, Susman said, "how he comports himself publicly . . . is of vital concern to every Jew in this community. That is why it was a miscarriage of judgement for Mr. Cope to mc a sports smoker recently at the University Club in Oakland which, since the day its cornerstone was laid, has denied membership to Jews." Myron, according to Susman, should have followed the lead of a judge who, when asked to chair a testimonial dinner for a colleague, refused to take part until the affair was moved out of the Duquesne Club, another social group that barred Jewish members.

It was only three paragraphs on an inside page of the paper. But to Myron, the column was like a bomb that had exploded in his front yard. The day after it was published, he took a page of his personal stationery, rolled it into his manual typewriter, and began composing a reply to the column—a reply acid enough to burn through the lens of Susman's glasses:

> If Milton Susman finds my commentaries on television and radio "caustic," so be it, but unlike him, I try to work within the limits of good taste and would regard myself with horror were I to neb willy-nilly into the religious life of another man. That is precisely what Mr. Susman has done in his objections to my serving as toastmaster at a dinner held at the University Club.
>
> First of all, if it is true that the University Club bars Jews to membership, as Mr. Susman says it does, I find it impossible to be indignant. I have the old-fashioned notion that people in their private lives ought to have the freedom to select those with whom they would socialize. Further, I am personally acquainted with many persons who, while not bigoted, belong to such clubs because they find them a convenient place to get a drink or a good meal or to transact business. I am speaking common sense, although by now Mr. Susan probably is up on his high horse and galloping in furious circles.
>
> But let's get to the meat. If Mr. Pious had given me the elementary journalistic considering of allowing me to present my side before he took it upon himself to act as my religious conscience, he would

have learned that a) I had no knowledge of the University Club being restricted, thus had given it no thought, and that b) public speaking is in part my profession—I make my living doing it.

I am invited to speak by a great variety of groups or clubs, and I think I would find it tedious if on each such occasion I first made an inspection of the buyer's morals. Let's put it this way: I am certain that Mr. Susman, who used to hustle advertising and public relations, did not receive a new client by demanding that he give him a list of his club affiliations. And I would bet my house that he transacted business with persons belonging to restricted clubs. So come on, Susman, don't give me that conscience garbage.

By innuendo, what Susman has done was to hang the "bad-Jew" label on me. If, as a pretender to journalism, he has the slightest knowledge of the impact of words, then he knew this would be the effect of his miserable paragraphs and that a public figure can never totally shed that label once it has been fastened. However, I shall choose to be kind and assume that Susman did not have the expertise to foresee what he was doing.

That was the letter as published by the *Chronicle* in its November 11, 1971, issue. But it was not the complete response. The paper's editors chose not to print the last couple of lines. Myron had actually concluded the letter by writing, "I shall assume that Susman . . . is not a vicious gossipmonger but was merely playing the role of ignoramus. Finally, I only wish that he were a younger man, in which case I would look him up and *bust every tooth out of his mouth* so he would pause when it occurs to him to butt into my private life" (emphasis added).

Elizabeth Cope says "ignoramus" was a favorite insult of her dad's, usually deployed when he was angry. As for the threat of violence, that might have gotten another man fired. Myron got away with it, maybe because of his growing popularity, maybe because the *Chronicle* wanted to spare his reputation (or Susman's), or maybe because of his 5-foot-4 stature, which made any threat from him seem . . . unthreatening. Susman was twenty-three years older than Myron but also taller and broader, and had the two exchanged blows—well, who knows? Maybe it's Myron who would've lost a tooth or two.

ON AT LEAST ONE occasion, Myron's penchant for mouthing off got him into an actual fistfight. The topic of the argument is lost to time. What's known is that it happened one evening in the early '60s, when Bobby Layne and a crowd of Steelers had commandeered their favorite watering hole, Dante's. Myron got into a loud argument with a drunk man at the bar, according to *Pittsburgh Press* columnist Pat Livingston, himself a Dante's semi-regular. "Words led to hot words, the hot words to nudging, and the nudging to punching," Livingston wrote. "Because of the mismatch—Cope barely came up to the drunk's chest—a bespectacled peacemaker stepped between the brawling pair."

But that wasn't the end of it. "Wham, the drunk landed a roundhouse right squarely on the left eye of the conciliator, shattering his glasses into a thousand shards," wrote Livingston. "Miraculously, the shattered slivers did no physical damage but while a doctor escorted the victim to the washroom to examine the eye, Cope, unharmed but in high dudgeon, turned to the bartender in a rage. 'Lou, that bum spilled my drink,' said he."

Myron nearly got into more fisticuffs a few years later in Lewiston, Maine, where he traveled in March 1965 to watch Muhammad Ali defend his heavyweight crown against the former champ, Sonny Liston. This time he was sitting at a long table with about a dozen other writers, knocking back some drinks the night before the fight. At the other end of the table was the Pulitzer Prize–winning journalist and novelist Norman Mailer. A decade later Mailer would write a well-received book on Ali's famed fight in Zaire against George Foreman. However, in 2007, Myron told his old broadcasting partners Tunch Ilkin and Craig Wolfley that he was not impressed with Mailer's knowledge of "the fight game."

"Mailer's there [talking], because he always thought he knew something about boxing," Myron remembered. "I had boxed a little, but that's another story. Anyways, I looked up, and I'd had it, and I said, 'Mailer, why don't you shut up, you don't know *nothin'* about boxing.' Whaaat? The great Norman Mailer?! He gets up, and I get up, and we're crawling down the table between everybody. And of course, they broke it up, which I regretted, because that's one fight I coulda won!"

Ilkin broke out laughing, while Wolfley interjected, "You think you could've whipped Norman Mailer?"

Myron dropped to a low voice and said, "He was a stiff. You just look at him and knew he couldn't fight."

It was a real boxer who, indirectly, landed Myron in the only semi-hot water incident of his career. In July 1991 Mike Tyson was arrested for allegedly raping an eighteen-year-old beauty pageant contestant, Desiree Washington, in an Indianapolis hotel room. The arrest and the subsequent trial were hugely publicized affairs, not least because Tyson's ex-wife had previously accused him on national television of being abusive and violent in their marriage.

The case became fodder for many a newspaper columnist and talk show host, including Myron, who gave his two cents when the official rape charges were filed in September. Without being pro-Tyson, he showed a startling lack of sympathy for Washington. "Any woman who enters a man's hotel room thinking they'll merely share the wisdoms of the Gideon Bible or watch the 11 o'clock news is in need of a new cranium," he said on his talk show.

Several listeners immediately called WTAE to protest, calling the comments sexist. A *Pittsburgh Press* reporter called Myron after the show to see if he wanted to retract anything. The answer was a firm no. "I don't think it was a bit sexist at all," he said. "I think it refers to the need for people to be responsible for their own stupid decisions, whether they be women or men." He added that if Washington went into a hotel room with a guy "who is a known thug and gorilla" and expected harmless activity, she should be responsible for her own stupidity.

In the age of social media, comments like that would likely generate a tsunami of online outrage. At minimum Myron would be accused of racism for calling Tyson a gorilla and for extreme callousness for suggesting that Washington was responsible for her own rape. No greater wave of protests materialized in 1991, and WTAE stayed silent about its top-drawing card's remarks—until Myron essentially repeated them in March of '92, when Tyson was convicted of rape and sentenced to six years in prison.

This time, he said, "You have here a girl who was an honor student, on scholarship, and a bright person, and she's entering the hotel room of a world-famous brute not knowing what could be in store for her? If that's not relevant, then my name is Boris Yeltsin."

Some people thought Myron had a point; others thought, again, that he was being a sexist pig. WTAE refrained from suspending or firing Myron but took the unusual step of rebutting his comments in an on-air statement. The statement, read by newscaster Paul Long, said that Washington's actions in no way absolved Tyson of guilt, regardless of what "voices on the sidelines"—a.k.a. Myron—were saying.

That might have been the end of it, except that Myron went on the six o'clock news for a live commentary during which he denounced his critics as insipid children and, in a silly but pointed gesture, stuck out his tongue at them—*nyaahhh*—on camera.

That might have been the end of it, except another WTAE talk show host, Bruce Keidan, went on the air the next day and said that Myron had a Neanderthal point of view and was talking "drivel."

That was almost the end of it, except that Myron told the press that "I don't worry about [criticism], especially not from people who talk drivel themselves."

That was the end of it.

Elizabeth Cope acknowledges that her father's comments on Tyson and Washington would likely get him fired today. "He knew what he could and couldn't get away with. I don't think he'd get away with it now," she says. "Those comments were risky then, but they would really be in bad taste now. You'd never do that now, unless you were nuts, and he wasn't nuts."

Still, one can't say for sure that Myron would have backtracked. "He didn't like to apologize," Elizabeth says of her father. "I've known him to apologize, but not often. He usually thought he was right."

IF THERE'S ONE incident that epitomizes Myron's intractable don't-tell-me-what-to-do streak, it's the one that unfolded during the Steelers' final game at Three Rivers Stadium, December 16, 2000.

The Steelers were playing the Washington Redskins, with both teams at .500 and trying to hang onto faint playoff hopes. The season had been a major disappointment for Washington, whose then new owner, thirty-six-year-old Daniel Snyder, had coughed up tens of millions of dollars to acquire aging stars like Deion Sanders, Bruce Smith, and Jeff George in hopes of vaulting the team to the Super Bowl. Maybe in an attempt to fire themselves up, some of the Redskins had gone to the center of the field during warmups and jumped up and down on the Steelers' logo. The act caught Myron's attention, and he wasn't pleased.

He said, "Those overpaid stiffs standing over there . . . they should be called the Washington Redfaces," a reference to the embarrassment he thought they should feel for their contracts and their behavior. He then used the name several times during the broadcast, with obvious glee.

Myron rubbed salt in the wounds during the third quarter, when he said that every time Snyder visited the high-priced restaurants in Washington where senators and big shots gather, he had to know that his fellow diners were whispering, "That's the kid who spent a hundred million dollars and stuck his face in a can of paint!"

The *Post-Gazette* sports media writer, Chuck Finder, was in the radio booth that day, chronicling the last broadcast from the not-quite-venerable stadium. During the third quarter, with Finder standing nearby, a dark-suited representative from the Redskins entered the Steelers' radio booth and spoke to the producer, Greg Weston. The young man asked Weston if Myron would kindly cease and desist from referring to the Washington team as the Redfaces.

"I can still picture the young guy, probably in his late twenties," says Finder. "He said, 'Mr. Snyder would like you to stop doing that.' . . . You could tell he was something like a personal valet to Dan Snyder, and he didn't want to carry out that duty. And he didn't know who Myron was. But I thought: 'Ohhhh, you just threw gasoline on a fire, young man.'"

"I was giving this guy a bit of an incredulous look," Weston told the *Athletic* in 2020. "I was like, really? I don't think he said [the order] came from Dan Snyder. Or maybe he did. But we inferred that it was coming from on high. I said, 'Well, I'll pass the message along, but Myron's going to say what he wants to say.'"

Minutes later, during a commercial break, Weston told Myron about the Redskins' request. Finder says Myron's face clouded with disbelief and anger. “It was a look like he was twenty-two years old and somebody took away his typewriter and said you can never write again,” Finder says. “You could probably say he turned a little crimson.”

When the break ended, Myron and his boothmates immediately shared the development with listeners. Hillgrove said, in a tone of disbelief, “We just got word from the press box that references to the Washington Redfaces are to cease and desist!”

Cope chimed in. “Well, they didn’t put it that way, but they said there are people who want me to cease calling them the Redfaces. I never heard of anything like that!” In his thirty years of broadcasting, he sputtered, neither the Steelers nor any other team had tried to censor him. Ilkin pointed out that Myron had referred to the Cincinnati Bengals as the Bungles for twenty years without a word of complaint from team owner Mike Brown. “Yeah,” Myron replied, “Mike Brown shook hands with me and said, ‘How’re you doing, Myron,’ not too long ago. This is preposterous!”

In the end, Myron was a good boy and complied with the Redskins’ request. “From Three Rivers Stadium,” he announced at the next commercial, “the score is the Steelers 24, the Red . . . skins 3.” The pause and the reluctance to say “skins” threw Hillgrove and Ilkin into hysterics.

The incident made the papers the next day and made a laughingstock of Snyder, who eighteen months after buying the Redskins was already starting to earn a reputation as one of the most meddlesome, thin-skinned, and shortsighted owners in the NFL, if not all of professional sports. For the record, the Redskins said it was club president Steve Baldacci who sent the young man into the lion’s den of Myron’s radio booth. That didn’t stop columnist Thomas Boswell from lacerating Snyder and the Redskins two days later in the *Washington Post*. Even if Snyder didn’t directly order Baldacci to act, Boswell said, he had been responsible for one bad decision after another during his short tenure as owner.

“The Redskins need to realize that far too much of their behavior under Snyder has made fans all over the country want to tell them to go stick their head in a can of paint,” Boswell wrote. “Like it or not, Myron Cope was speaking for America. And the Redskins should listen.”

Apparently, Snyder never did. The Redskins suffered through more than two decades of losing football, constant coaching turnover, severe fanbase erosion, and accusations of a toxic workplace culture before Snyder sold the Redskins, by then known as the Commanders, in 2023.

The incident did teach a lesson to Snyder and any other NFL bigwigs who thought they could influence Steelers radio broadcasts. Not one ever tried to control the mouth of Myron Cope again.

14

Rolling with the Nineties

Throughout his first twenty-four years in the Steelers' radio booth, Myron had two reliable partners—Jack Fleming during the games and Mildred Cope every night at home. Within a matter of months, he lost both.

In Fleming's case, Myron lost a close colleague. Long considered one of the most engaging, sharpest play-by-play men in the business, Fleming's on-air work declined during the 1980s. Too often, he seemed a beat behind the action, slow to identify the ball carrier, the type of play being run, or the outcome. With increasing frequency, Myron would have to fill in the gaps so the listening audience wouldn't be confused. In one game, when Fleming got lost in his description of the action, Myron jumped in and shouted, "It's a touchdown!" Without that, fans wouldn't have known that the Steelers had scored.

Bill Modoono, the sports media reporter for the *Press*, became a Fleming critic and called for him to step down. "He is no longer capable of doing radio play-by-play for a pro football team," Modoono wrote in November 1991. "Cope has become quite adept at covering for Fleming. . . . Why should Cope, a bright and inventive broadcaster, be forced to spend so much of his time reporting things that a play-by-play man could (and should) have covered?"

Why? Because Myron would rather cover for his friend than see him fired. Fleming, then nearing his seventieth birthday, had two young daughters from his second marriage in addition to grown children from his first. He needed to keep working, needed the money. Elizabeth Cope says Myron used his clout with WTAE and the Steelers to ensure that Fleming stayed behind the mic. Both parties accommodated Myron for a while, until the announcer's shortcomings could no longer be ignored. At his bosses' request, Fleming resigned from his Steelers gig in February 1994, at age seventy-one, after spending half his life calling the games.

WTAE general manager Jim Carter made it clear that the new announcer would need to be compatible with the color analyst. "We want to find the best possible person," he said, but added, "He'll have to be able to work with Myron Cope and understand and appreciate the contributions Myron makes to the broadcasts." Within a couple of months, the station and the team found their man: Bill Hillgrove. Hillgrove was a native Pittsburgher, had called Pitt football games for more than twenty years, had worked frequently with Myron at WTAE, and was simply a colorful, captivating announcer. He and Myron had even called Pitt games together in 1983, when the usual Pitt analyst, Johnny Sauer, had a heart attack.

Joe Gordon, who listened to audition tapes from more than a dozen applicants for the job, said the choice was easy. "Why go out of the market when you've got someone right here?" he says. "It was a natural. Bill was the logical guy."

He was also known as a genuinely nice guy with little ego, one secure enough in his own talents to share the spotlight with a noisy, attention-grabbing partner. Myron was all for the hire, and he and Hillgrove were soon operating smoothly as a veteran vaudeville duo. "I can't imagine anyone being easier to work with," Myron said that November. After Fleming's increasingly fuzzy play calls, listeners also appreciated Hillgrove's on-spot description of the action. "It's nice to know where the ball is after all these years," wrote Bob Smizik.

But even as one partner was replaced, Myron was losing another, one impossible to replace. For years, Mildred's health had been shaky. She suffered injuries in a 1978 car accident. She dealt with autoimmune conditions like scleroderma, a thickening and tightening of bodily tissues, and Reynaud's disease, a condition that turned her hands and fingers icy and blue. Most seriously, she battled brain cancer. It was Mildred's hospitalization for the cancer that prompted Myron to cut back his schedule in 1989.

As Mildred's health declined, Myron made a point of occasionally bringing her into the spotlight that she had long shunned. When WTAE honored him in 1993 for his twenty-fifth anniversary with the station, he told the dinner crowd, "I've been around a lot of guys who have been heroes to many people, but—I'll have to make this real short—I ain't got no heroes, I got a heroine. Her name's Mildred, and she's sitting down there." He pointed at his wife, and the crowd applauded her as she beamed.

By September 1994 the tumors in Mildred's brain had returned. Doctors gave her only a year to live. She began renewed radiation treatments, and the Copes made plans to install a bedroom on the first floor of their house so she wouldn't have to climb the stairs. They never got to set it up; Mildred was taken to Allegheny General Hospital early that month and died there of sudden heart failure on September 20, only sixty-three years old. Elizabeth says she was getting a diet Coke at a vending machine two floors below when she heard a code blue alert for her mother's room over the hospital PA. She dropped the Coke and raced upstairs to see her father in the hallway, head buried in his hands, and medical staff crowded around Mildred's bed, trying to save her. The staffers could only do so much; Mildred had written a do-not-resuscitate order saying that no extreme measures should be taken to preserve her life.

Myron somehow composed himself to talk to the *Post-Gazette* the next day for his wife's obituary. "She was a selfless person and a good mother to her children," he said. Regarding her illnesses, he said, "She was the most amazing battler. She always wore a smile on her face."

Two days later Mildred was buried at Chartiers Cemetery in Carnegie, south of Pittsburgh. WTAE anchor Sally Wiggin was among those at the funeral. Up until that point, she had mostly seen Myron in his professional roles—the commentator, the commercial pitchman, the Steelers' hyper, somewhat goofy rooter-in-chief. She was struck by how solemn and sad he suddenly was. "Seeing him and watching him at the funeral, you could tell he adored her, he *adored* her," Wiggin says. "I remember that impacted me. I remember seeing him so broken hearted. That showed me there was a whole 'nother human being that was behind the curtain."

Grief stricken, Myron chose not to accompany the Steelers on a road game to Seattle that weekend. It was the first game he had missed since joining the radio team in 1970. But he was back in the booth for the following week's game and soon returned to hosting the talk show on Mondays and Tuesdays. "Working kept him focused, it gave him a schedule," says Elizabeth. He made an effort to act like the usual energetic Cope, and while he did acknowledge Mildred's passing on air, the average listener could not necessarily tell that something was wrong.

Only Elizabeth got something close to the full picture. "He didn't talk that much about his emotions, but I heard him crying late at night in his office. He didn't know I could hear him," she says.

Elizabeth was deep in mourning too, but her father, characteristically, encouraged her to go back to college at West Virginia University. "I wanted to drop out, but he begged me not to do that," she says. "He said, 'If you drop out, you'll never go back.' So I went back. He threw himself into his work, and I threw myself into my studies. I wound up getting straight A's that semester."

One of the things that sustained Myron that fall, besides broadcasting, was a conviction that while Mildred's body had passed on, her spirit was still alive. His belief originated in a discovery he made outside their home a few days after Mildred's funeral. He wrote about it in his autobiography, in a chapter where he talked directly to his late wife:

> I glanced out the window of my study, which looked out onto the front lawn. You had told me early on, about twenty years before, "You're the gardener." I was a lazy gardener, so our three rose bushes dwindled to two, and those two became scraggly. Only in spring and early summer would they pop up a few yellow roses. Yellow was your favorite color, so I yelled for you whenever I saw a rose coming into bloom.
>
> Now I noticed through my office window in late September that a single rose had begun to bloom on the tallest branch of an otherwise

bare bush. That rose fairly burst into fullness, huge and glorious. I beckoned Elizabeth, Mom, and you surely must know that as close as the two of you had been, she had reacted to your death horrendously, unbelieving.

"Look," I said. "Do you suppose Mom is speaking to us through that rose? Do you think she's telling us to hang tough?"

Through the rest of September and through October—a brisk, sometimes downright cold October, he said—the lone rose stood atop the branch. It finally wilted and died on the last day of October, but its brief life had made a lasting impact on Myron. Previously, he had been agnostic; "I wasn't sure that God existed," he said. After watching the rose, he said, his agnosticism was a thing of the past.

Regarding Mildred herself, he wrote, "I know you're there."

It probably gave Myron a small lift that the Steelers, after getting thumped 30–13 in the contest he missed, reeled off ten wins in their next eleven games. If nothing else, winning football is easier to broadcast than losing football. Come December he was able to crank out his annual "Deck the Halls" Christmas carol, aiming this version at the Browns and their owner, Art Modell, whom he termed Modell's Meatballs. He even sang a line of the song for NFL Films in their annual Steelers highlight video. If one's eyes were closed, it sounded like the regular, caterwauling Cope. But the film showed the truth. Myron's brown eyes, usually filled with life, looked atypically glassy and unfocused, betraying the grief that had taken residence in his soul.

EVEN BEFORE FLEMING'S departure and Mildred's death, Myron's world had undergone some significant changes. Elizabeth, now in her early twenties, was away from home at WVU in Morgantown, though she had returned frequently when her mother was ill or, more happily, for Steelers home games. Meanwhile, WTAE 1250 had transitioned from a "full-service" station to an all-talk outlet with a heavy side of sports. Stan Savran was let go in November 1991 amid ill will with management, leaving Myron as the station's biggest hitter in the ratings—one of the factors, no doubt, that allowed him to get away with smoking in the radio studio.

In a broader sense, the broadcast business was changing in ways that Myron found hard to accept. Radio stations fighting for attention were giving on-air personalities far greater latitude in terms of topics and language, some of which struck veterans like Myron as crude and tasteless, especially when deployed by "shock jocks" who made offensive content their calling card. Myron had tried to avoid even mild swear words like *hell* and *damn* on his shows, and mostly stayed away from jokes or topics of a sexual nature (the Mike Tyson rape trial was an exception), knowing that some children were in his audience.

"I rather would forfeit a week's pay than intentionally utter vulgarisms on radio or television," he wrote in 2002, and he meant it. His argument was that if people heard profanity on the airwaves, it would become more acceptable in public, creating what he called "social meanness" that in turn would produce "hardened and irresponsible citizens." From the perspective of twenty-plus years on, he may have had a point.

In the early '90s the airwaves were just beginning to get polluted when WTAE began to present periodic "blabbathons," a chance for its talk show hosts to assemble in one studio, sans guests, and yak with each other and their callers for an entire day. One afternoon, three of the station's chief talkers—Lynn Cullen, Phil Musick, and Doug Hoerth—were in the eighth and final hour of the gabfest. The three were using the same studio where Myron did his talk show, and after a full day of tongue flapping, they were getting loopy. Cullen, looking back at Myron's life on the day he died in 2008, said she didn't remember what the trio was discussing but recalled, "We were being outrageous, and maybe a little off-color, and a little over the top, and we were having a heckuva time."

The mood changed abruptly shortly before 6 p.m., when Myron entered the studio, furious. Cullen said she had inadvertently irked Cope some time earlier. "He became a little bit irate, I understand, because [his] microphone started to get a reddish hue on the end of it," she said. "He wondered what was happening, and it turned out of course that it was that *girlie*—that would be me—and my lipstick. Every once in a while, my lips would brush the windscreen on the mike."

But Cullen quickly recognized that the lipstick was not the issue on this day.

"We welcomed him—'Myron! Hi!'—and he *lit* into us," she remembered. Myron had listened to the station while driving into work, and in his view, the trio had befouled the airwaves with their "lack of decorum," a catchall term he used to describe behavior he found inappropriate and unfit for the general public.

"He was fuming," Cullen said. "He was enraged, and he told us that we were everything that was wrong with radio. . . . He dressed us *down*. And I can't imagine Phil Musick, Doug Hoerth, and me sitting still for something like that coming from anybody but Myron Cope—because we didn't argue. We just sat there and took it and we apologized to him."

Channel 4 news anchor Sally Wiggin also got a talking-to from Myron, though with a much less combative tone, when she began to host TV pregame shows for the Steelers' appearances on *Monday Night Football*. Earlier in his career Myron had voiced objections to female sports reporters, saying that they should not be allowed into male athletes' locker rooms. He stuck to his view even as women became sportswriters, sideline reporters, announcers, and studio hosts. "I've got some chauvinism in me, you betcha," he said in 1992. "I'm sorry, I don't understand [a woman] who wants to hold a job which requires them to be in a men's dressing room, no more than I'd want to be in a woman's room."

Wiggin hosted her first Steelers pregame show in 1993. Shortly thereafter, she says, she got a letter from Myron in which he complimented her skills but also said that "he wanted to make sure—some people would be offended by this—make sure that I remained a lady. The medium was loosening up, I guess, but he was very old-fashioned. I think because of that . . . he didn't criticize me for doing the pre-game show, but he wanted to make sure that I didn't forget a sense of decorum. He never said it that way, but that's kind of what he meant."

Wiggin, a fan of Myron's work, acknowledged the sexual stereotype at the heart of the letter. "Some women would be offended," she says, "because they would say, if you you're not expecting [a sense of decorum] from a man, why would you expect that with women? And I remember showing it to somebody and she was irritated. But I wasn't, because I knew from whence it came."

Wiggin says that she, too, heard Myron use words like *girlie* and cringed. "I didn't like some of the terminology he used for women, I admit that," she says. But, she adds, "I took it in stride. It's who Myron was. It's who a lot of people were."

Myron wasn't out of step with every 1990s trend. Much to his surprise, he had become a video star. In 1990, after a decade of mediocrity, the Pirates soared to the top the National League East standings, led by young slugger Barry Bonds, winning the first of his seven MVP Awards, plus twenty-two wins from pitching ace Doug Drabek. As the Pirates prepared for a playoff series against the Cincinnati Reds, WTAE radio's general manager, Jim Carter, gave Myron a request: write and perform a Pirates fight song based on the current hit by the rapper MC Hammer, "U Can't Touch This."

Myron was taken aback. "I says, 'I don't follow those kind of rap guys, those roc 'n' roll guys and everything. I never heard of MC Hammer, I never heard of 'U Can't Touch This.'" An undeterred Carter handed Myron a cassette of the song and asked him to give it a listen. It wasn't exactly up Myron's musical alley. "He was a jazz person," says his niece Marcia Grodsky. "He'd get a kick out of rap music or country, but they weren't things he'd listen to on the car radio."

But ever the professional, Myron did as he was asked, and on a morning in October 1990, Myron's usual commentary was replaced by his first-ever rap. In a growly voice not attuned to any particular rhythm or key, Myron punched out rhymes like "Buccos flyin' / Mets are cryin'" and rapped lines like "Barry Bonds / he's doing it all / don't call Barry Bobby or he'll smack y'all." That was a reference to announcers sometimes referring to Bonds as Bobby, his father, who had been an all-star center fielder in the '70s.

Executives on the TV side heard the rap, liked it, and asked Myron to star in a video. He enthusiastically assented, according to Channel 4 TV director Brian Campbell, who oversaw the production. "Myron got very excited about the opportunity to do a music video," Campbell told writer Brian W. Boyles. "The concept was there for us. We just took Myron's lyrics and, shot-for-shot, developed a treatment that reflected the MC Hammer video as well as the fun that [Cope] generated lyrically." The treatment involved putting Myron in MC Hammer's trademark parachute pants as well as gold necklaces and a black jacket open almost to the navel. He topped the outfit with a black Pirates baseball cap, which happened to be a hat of choice among rappers. Myron then lip-synched, mugged, and pranced while a troupe of four young dancers mimicked the moves from Hammer's video of the song, which was in heavy rotation on MTV.

Played on WTAE's six o'clock news, the video made a big splash. So big that Myron later reprised the general idea for two Steelers-themed videos, one based on the 1992 Billy Ray Cyrus hit "Achy Breaky Heart," the other on the 1996 dance craze from Spain, the Macarena. For the former, he dressed up as a guitar-wielding country-music singer, complete with fringed jacket and cowboy hat, and for the latter, as a cape-wearing Spanish matador, clad in black. WTAE went all out for the Macarena video in particular, hiring four midriff-baring female dancers to bounce and glide through the dance moves while Myron chanted out lyrics extolling new Steelers mainstays like Jerome Bettis, the friendly but bruising running back that he had aptly dubbed The Bus.

Jerome Bettis, Jerome Bettis
He is surely the real thing
He ain't no head of lettuce
He is one tough cuss
All aboard the big bus
Yoiiiiii, Jerome Bettis!

Chuck Finder, the sports media writer for the *Post-Gazette*, got to witness the shooting of the Macarena video over six hours on a Saturday afternoon. By this time, he says, Myron didn't have to be pushed into these musical parodies. "He got to be a caricature of himself, and he enjoyed people laughing at him and having fun alongside," Finder says. "I mean, how many people can really put their ego aside and sing badly? And he's what, five-foot-five, singing the Macarena dressed as a bullfighter? And pull it off, too! I think he enjoyed it."

All three videos can still be found (albeit in low quality) on YouTube. The Macarena parody—retitled "Yoi! Steeler Mania"—proved to be Myron's all-time biggest hit, racking up more than 1.1 million views over the years.

That's peanuts for an old Franco's Italian Army general like Frank Sinatra, but MC Hammer would've been pleased.

PROJECTS LIKE THE Macarena video helped Myron gradually climb out of the hole left by Mildred's passing. Work, as Elizabeth noted, was essential to his well-being. Sally Wiggin had been surprised to see him back in the WTAE studios so soon after Mildred's death but came to understand his motivation. "It was because he loved what he did," she says. "He didn't love it more than his family. It was a different part of life, but it was central, it was part of his core. So was his family. We don't have one core, we have several."

At the same time, Myron was now in his midsixties—the traditional age of retirement for someone of his generation—and regular workdays, even with his reduced schedule, were starting to tire him out. In January 1995, after the Steelers lost the AFC Championship Game, a Pittsburgh columnist wrote, "Myron Cope needs a vacation. I seriously doubt if the little guy's pipes would have held up for another two weeks." That same month, Myron dropped a hint to the *Post-Gazette*: "If I ever retire, I'm going to play golf and put my feet up. I yearn for the day when I get back to reading books that aren't about sports."

Shortly thereafter, he decided the day had come. In early '95 he told WTAE he was giving up the commentaries and the talk show. The decision was announced March 10 in a press release that assured fans (and advertisers) that Myron would continue to broadcast Steelers games and cover events like training camp and draft day. What he was giving up, Myron said, was a life of deadlines and appointments: "The most important appointment now is one that involves a tee time. My highest priority project will be to break 100 for the first time."

Chuck Finder wonders if Myron might have retired too soon, given the exploding popularity of sports talk radio at the time. When Myron started in 1973, his was the only sports-themed talk show in the Pittsburgh area. By fall 1994 southwestern Pennsylvania radio stations aired about eighty-five hours of sports talk per week, according to Finder's painstaking calculations, and full-time sports stations such as WFAN in New York were proliferating everywhere. "If he had stuck with it, ESPN would have hired him," Finder says. "He'd have been Chris Berman."

But WTAE radio news director John Poister says Myron had had enough. "I think he just reached the point where he didn't want to do it anymore," Poister says. "The death of his wife was certainly a major factor, but I think it was the daily grind. . . . When I talked to him, he said, 'I'm not gonna do it halfway. If I'm gonna be on the radio, I have to prepare.' It was him stopping by the Steelers, Pirates, taking in an afternoon meeting, getting that information that made the show must listening for fans. He had info that others didn't have. That wore on him, and he didn't need to do it anymore."

Finder thinks Myron's stable of callers were also ready to hang it up. "Some of those guys in their sixties get tired of calling up talk shows," he says. "At the end of the day, they just wanna sit down and have a drink."

The final edition of *Myron Cope on Sports* on April 3 turned into something of an event, going three hours on a Tuesday night, drawing calls from Pennsylvania governor Thomas Ridge and a caller who somehow picked up the broadcast from Windsor, Colorado. The former congratulated Myron and talked football for a few minutes. The latter asked to be made a Copeanut; Myron turned him down flat.

Local sports reporters covered his every move ahead of the final show, filming him getting in and out of his car, watching him tape his final TV commentary, then joining him at the bar of the Wilkinsburg Holiday Inn for a final pre-show "toddy." He'd continue imbibing as the show unfolded, downing three vodka-infused Jell-O shooters by the halfway point in the show, according to the running count kept by *Pittsburgh Tribune-Review* reporter Joe Starkey. He smoked at least five cigarettes in studio as well.

Many of Myron's regulars called in to say goodbye, but the final call came from a first-time caller and longtime listener named Maureen Marsteller. She explained that years earlier, she had been listening one night with her eight-month-old son as Myron signed off from the talk show. The boy had previously said nothing more than "mama" and "dada," she said. But when Myron announced, "This is Myron Cope" and paused briefly as he normally did, the baby suddenly said, "on sports!"

Myron was thrilled. "Get out! Those were the first two words of his life?" he exclaimed. "That's a yoi. That's a double yoi!" And he made the woman a Copeanut.

"That was perfect," he said later that night. "The kid's first words, 'on sports.' I never could have planned such a perfect last call."

Ending on that high note, however, did not totally eradicate Mildred's absence. At the beginning of the show's final hour, Myron, audibly holding back tears, paid an emotional tribute to her. "The only complaint I have about this show tonight," he said, "is that when it ends, she oughta be out in the lobby, and we should be going to a nice place, and drinking a toast. . . . That's the only beef I got tonight."

He wasn't playing for sympathy, remembered Starkey in a column twenty-five years later. "Once he signed off, Cope seemed so alone, desperately missing his late wife," he wrote. "He gave me all the time I needed for what was a very large assignment."

The end of Myron's talk show marked a turning point for WTAE radio, which plugged Bill Hillgrove into his Monday-Tuesday slot but soon suffered sagging ratings. "Management was very sad to see him go," Poister says. "We took a hit when he retired. It wasn't the same. People sensed that." The station would be sold four times in four years, switching from talk to full-time sports and changing its call letters before finally acquiring steady ownership under ABC, which turned it into an ESPN Radio outlet.

Myron's fans weren't exactly starved of his presence. He continued to serve as color analyst for Steelers games in addition to hosting pre- and postgame shows. In 1997 the latter expanded into more of a postgame party with *Cope's Cabana*, with Myron holding forth in a tent outside Gate D at Three Rivers Stadium, decorated with a thatched roof, bamboo poles, and fake parrots. Fans who hadn't had enough pregame tailgating gathered to drink a few more beers and watch as Myron and guests dissected that day's game. For the theme song, Myron sang a rewritten version of Barry Manilow's "Copacabana" with appropriate lyrics:

You are in Cope's Cabana, sure you are
We're gonna talk about the Steelers game from A to Zanzibar
I'm top banaaaana

In Cope's Cabaaaaaaana
Whaaaaat's on your cranium?

At first Myron was reluctant to do the show. "My reaction to that was not good," he told WTAE sportscaster Andrew Stockey in 1999. "I said, 'Okay, I'll go along with it,' but it seemed to me I'll be in there playing the clown. I know I carry on a lot, but I don't like to play the clown, if you understand what I mean. But now, I love playing the Cabana. It's just a whole different atmosphere and it's been nothing but fun."

But outside game days, Myron in the latter '90s gave himself more time to relax, to take life at a slower pace. Several months after Mildred's death, he began to circulate again, attending banquets and charity fundraisers, golfing with his buddies, even serving as the king for Pittsburgh's 1996 Mardi Gras parade. (The queen was former mayor Sophie Masloff, perhaps the only person in town with a voice as scratchy and recognizable as his own.) He and Elizabeth began an annual tradition of spending Christmases with extended family at Snowshoe, a ski resort in the mountains of eastern West Virginia.

He sold the family's house in Upper St. Clair, where the memories of Mildred hovered in the air, and purchased a three-bedroom home in the Woodridge community of Mt. Lebanon, an upscale, landscaped community with a pool and lots of walking paths. Chuck Finder says he used to see Myron around Woodridge because his parents lived in the same complex. "We used to see him wearing Bermuda shorts at the swimming pool," he says. "He had a nice condo, actually a townhouse, directly across from the condo my parents had. My father used to torture the poor guy. My father was president of the co-op and its lawyer, so he would do co-op and HOA things. Anytime Myron had a question—and Myron always sat in the front row—my father would say, 'Excuse me sir, can you stand up and identify yourself?'"

For a while Myron even had a new girlfriend, a woman with grown children from Upper St. Clair who was his junior by about fifteen years. He met her while at St. Clair Hospital for a procedure. "She was a nurse there, and he had been her patient," Elizabeth says. "When he was discharged, he asked if she'd want to meet him for dinner and she said yes. They wound up dating for about two years." She even spent two Christmases with the Copes at the Snowshoe ski resort before the couple broke up, amicably.

The relationship ended, Elizabeth says, primarily because Myron did not want to get remarried. "He had sat me down some time after my mother died," she says, "and said he would date but would never get married again. My mom was the love of his life."

One night in the late '90s, when not occupied by his girlfriend or HOA matters, Myron went looking for an old friend: Mike Webster. After playing center for seventeen years in the NFL, his body and brain absorbing tens of thousands of violent collisions, Webster spent his post-playing years in a tailspin, suffering from what was diagnosed after his death as cognitive traumatic encephalopathy, a brain disorder caused by repeated head injuries. Within three years of retirement, he had lost virtually all his money to bad investments, left his wife and children, and mostly lived in cheap hotel rooms or out of his truck, drifting between Pittsburgh and his home state of Wisconsin. Sometimes, concerned friends and family didn't know where he was. On one such occasion, according to Joe Gordon, Myron got in his car and went looking, unsuccessfully, for the man once known as Iron Mike. Asked if he could confirm Gordon's memory, Webster's former linemate Craig Wolfley says he can't but adds, "If Joe said it, it's true. He knows things."

The decade ended with Myron getting his first new employer in thirty years. Troubled with constant turnover, WTAE radio was outbid for the Steelers' radio rights by another local station, WDVE. Myron found it funny that his new employer was a rock station; he had been good-naturedly bashing rock and nearly every other non-pop and jazz trend in popular music for decades. "When they got the Steeler broadcast rights," he said, "I told the executives there—I've been saying it for years, and I can't take it back—that rock killed American music, and it did," he said.

WDVE executives didn't care. Myron's critique wasn't going to influence their listeners; they just wanted his voice on the Steelers broadcasts. Elizabeth says the station paid him $10,000 per game—a handsome salary for a man who still prepared thoroughly for every Sunday but was essentially working one day per week. And even there, the workload had eased. In 1995 the Steelers added a third man to the radio team, former running back Merril Hoge, with the stated goal of giving technical football analysis that was beyond Cope's or Hillgrove's experience. Hoge had trouble getting a word in—"Myron had been there for so long, he didn't want anybody else," Hoge told author Jim Wexell—but Myron began to yield airtime when Hoge left for a full-time job with ESPN and was replaced by former offensive lineman Tunch Ilkin in 1998. The more high-spirited Ilkin had better chemistry with Cope and Hillgrove and was adept at giving Myron set-up lines, like the time in Cope's Cabana when a female fan asked Myron to "never, ever, ever retire." Ilkin said, "I think she has a crush on you." Myron replied, "She should."

In fact, by the end of the decade, the bulk of Myron's comments were humorous or emotional rather than informational. With Ilkin on hand to explain the X's and O's, Myron was freer to take entertaining detours or employ his brilliantly unique metaphors, like when he said a Steelers cornerback covered a receiver so closely "he could tell whether the guy used Listerine or Scope."

Other commentators might simply say a linebacker walloped or flattened the ball carrier. Myron, in a 1999 game, spun out this gem: "Carlos Emmons hit him so hard I swear I saw his mouthpiece fly into the third row! An old lady caught it on the fly, checked it for a fit, and put it in her pocket." He also tossed out yois and double yois more frequently, so much that some listeners began playing a drinking game, downing a shot each time Myron uttered his signature word.

Hillgrove says Myron's progression was natural as he aged. "The older you get, you think 'I have to be careful, I gotta make sure I still have my fastball.' So in order to make up for whatever thing nature has taken away from you, you tend to go to your strength, and his strength was getting people fired up, whipped up emotionally. The fact that he did that more later in his career, that's not a surprise."

And yes, nature was beginning to nibble away at Myron. His voice, still operating at full blast as late as the mid-1990s, grew gradually thinner and hoarser, as a lifetime of smoking and decades of broadcasting began to take a toll. Physically, Elizabeth says, he was troubled more often by coughs and colds and other ailments. Not wanting to overcommit himself, Myron insisted on signing only one-year contracts once he joined WDVE. It would be less messy that way, both for him and for his employer, if he decided that he didn't want to, or couldn't, broadcast Steelers games anymore.

STILL, IN MANY ways, life was good. He could golf and travel to his heart's content. He could take speaking engagements whenever he wanted them. He could work on his autobiography, which was published in 2002. And the Steelers were a good though not unstoppable team, making it as far as the AFC Championship Game in the 2001 season, where they lost to a New England Patriots team quarterbacked by a newcomer, a kid named Brady.

People now routinely referred to Myron as a legend or other terms reserved for the highly revered. Myron was only half-comfortable with the praise. "They use that word icon, which c'mon, let's get serious," he told WTAE's Andrew Stockey. "They say, 'You're a legend,' and when I hear that, I think they're putting me six months from the grave, because legends aren't supposed to be alive."

As the new millennium commenced, Myron was very much alive and kicking. And his creation, the Terrible Towel, was doing even better. If anything, it had achieved a kind of immortality.

15

The Towel Returns

Unbelievable as it sounds, the Terrible Towel was once considered a feeble, washed-up old rag.

Oh, Pittsburghers didn't say that out loud. (And if they did, they said it was a *worshed*-up old rag.) But at the start of the 1990s, the Towel was seen as a relic, an artifact of the bygone days when the Steelers reigned over the NFL and the rivers of Pittsburgh were still lined with steel mills. No official Terrible Towels had been produced for nearly a decade. Many people still had the old ones, but they were buried in closets and attics, untouched unless they were pulled out for a tailgate party or to satisfy a nostalgic pang.

The one person who still cared about the Towel was its creator. Myron never stopped promoting the Terrible Towel. When he began giving predictions for Steelers games on the Channel 4 news using his wife's old chemistry microscope—renamed the Cope-ro-scope—the Towel inevitably made an appearance, often in a burst of smoke. When Myron dried himself off after his ride on Kennywood's Raging Rapids, it was with a bona fide Towel. And every few years before the Steelers faced an important contest at Three Rivers, Myron would call on fans to pull out the Towel and wave it high again, to cheer on the Steelers, to psyche out their opponents, to make the football bounce the Steelers' way, just as it had in '78 and '79, when the Towel seemed to have the power of a hundred sorcerers, none of whom liked the Browns.

Problem was, it didn't work. Myron first called for the Towel's resurrection before a January 1983 playoff game against the San Diego Chargers. The Steelers lost, despite recovering the opening kickoff for a touchdown and taking a 28–17 lead in the fourth quarter. He issued another appeal ahead of a key November 1985 contest against the Redskins. The Steelers went down 30–23 and went on to finish the season with their first losing record in fourteen years. *Post-Gazette* Steelers beat writer Ed Bouchette declared the Towel all but dead. "The magic is gone," he wrote.

When Myron made another appeal to revive the Towel ahead of a Steelers playoff game against Buffalo in January 1993, he got some push-back from the sports columnist of the *Indiana Gazette*, a paper northeast of Pittsburgh. "Do we have to, Myron?" wrote Rick Weaver. "Pardon me for coming across as a party-pooper. But this is the 1990s and like knee-high sweatsocks, the Green Weenie and eight-track tapes . . . the Terrible Towel has become obsolete." He suggested fans find a way to cheer for the 1990s Steelers without using a symbol of the 1970s teams.

Myron would have none of it, even after the Steelers lost the playoff game 24–3. In fact, he was making plans to put the Towel on store shelves again. A one-year contract with Kaufmann's department store in 1990 had failed to generate sales, but in 1993 Myron struck a new deal with the Mike Feinberg Company, a popular retailer and wholesaler of novelty items in Pittsburgh's Strip District. In some ways it was an odd choice; Myron had successfully sued Feinberg twice, in 1980 and 1988, to make him stop selling unauthorized versions of the Towel. Now, though, he realized that Feinberg's distribution network was ideal for getting his baby back out to the public. The generous terms Feinberg offered—an advance of $17,000, plus 20 percent of the gross revenue from all sales—undoubtedly helped convince Myron to go ahead with the deal.

Feinberg, in turn, undoubtedly hoped a recent upswing in the Steelers' fortunes would drive a new wave of Terrible Towel sales. Chuck Noll had stepped down as the Steelers' head coach after a losing 1991 season, the sixth time in seven years the Steelers missed the playoffs. To replace him, the Steelers took a page from their 1969 playbook and hired a fresh young face, thirty-five-year-old Bill Cowher. Cowher, like Noll before him, was a backup linebacker for the Browns during a short playing career then distinguished himself as an assistant coach, first on special teams with the Browns, next as defensive coordinator with the Chiefs.

Unlike Noll, Cowher was a native Pittsburgher, from the city's Crafton section, and well before he took the Steelers job, he was highly familiar with Myron Cope. His father had been a dedicated fan of Myron's talk show. Cowher said he still thought of Myron as the voice that blared out of his family's kitchen radio on Hawthorne Avenue in the '70s. "My dad would crack open a beer, listen to Myron's popular show on WTAE, and confirm many of Myron's opinions. 'You tell 'em, Myron,' Dad would say in approval," Cowher remembered in his autobiography.

In certain ways Cowher was more up Myron's alley than Noll ever was—more emotional, less analytical, more willing to laugh or, alternately, to unleash an extended on-field tirade at the referees, epitomized by the 1995 game in which he angrily stuffed an instant replay photo into a referee's shirt pocket to protest an overturned penalty call. He and Myron would work together harmoniously for a dozen years, in pregame shows, press conferences, and assorted other settings, and Cowher would acknowledge that Myron, with his sometimes-manic energy, made him feel young. However, he and Myron never forged a close personal relationship or even visited each other's houses, a fact that Myron blamed on the twenty-eight-year age difference between them.

Truth be told, the era of NFL players drinking and buddying up with media types was drawing to a close. "The players changed," says Chuck Finder. "It used to be when Myron first started, they could loaf together—that was their word for hanging out at a bar and tipping back a few. Players didn't hang out with media anymore. In the '80s and '90s, they became more money-oriented, celebrity-oriented, ego-oriented. Today, they're brand-oriented and they're millionaires or billionaires. I think that affected Myron a little; he wished he had those ties with all the players. A lot of stars still enjoyed spending time with him doing promotions or things like that, but they didn't loaf with him."

While he didn't enhance Myron's social life, the jut-jawed Cowher did inject new energy into the Steelers. Under his leadership, the Steelers in 1992 won their first division title in eight years and hosted their first playoff game in ten. The '93 squad was shakier and slipped back to a wild card spot. But the talent on the roster was getting better year by year, and the '94 team electrified Pittsburgh like no team since the last of Noll's championship squads. The offense was only middle-of-the-league average, but the defense, led by future Hall of Famers Rod Woodson and Kevin Greene, was sack-happy and smothering, giving up the second fewest points in the NFL.

Myron's love for nicknames was triggered, and he tried giving the defense a new handle: the Steel Trap. It wasn't a bad idea—certainly better than his 1971 suggestion of the Anvil Chorus—but the players themselves gave it a thumbs-down, and it didn't catch on.

Sales of the Towel—now known as Myron Cope's official Terrible Towel—crept up during the '94 season, then exploded at year's end as the Steelers beat Cleveland 17–7 at home to clinch the division title. The December 18 game can be considered the day of the Towel's resurrection. For the first time in years, thousands of Towels whirled in the stands of Three Rivers before kickoff and kept whirling throughout a Steelers victory. When the Steelers met the Browns again two weeks later in the playoffs and stomped them 29–9, Feinberg's store was swamped with in-person buyers and huge wholesale orders. Feinberg, who also had taken over manufacture of the Towel, said he was shipping ten thousand per day to meet the demand, some of it coming from "Steelers bars" that had popped up wherever transplanted Pittsburghers lived.

"We had the Terrible Towel last year and lost money on it because they didn't go anywhere and didn't really have stars or heroes," Feinberg explained. "But now. . . . Things have just caught fire."

Even after the Steelers lost the AFC Championship Game 17–13 to San Diego—still one of the most excruciating, gut-punch losses in Steelers history—demand for the Towel remained high. Fans sensed, correctly, that the good times had returned. The Steelers won another division title in 1995 and slipped by the Colts in the championship at Three Rivers to reach the Super Bowl—though a last-second, Hail Mary pass that appeared to deflect into an Indianapolis receiver's arms nearly sent Pittsburgh into mass cardiac arrest. "OH MY G—" Myron started to yell when it looked like the pass was complete, before Bill Hillgrove shouted, "Dropped!" The ball had touched the turf, preserving the Steelers' 20–16 victory.

For the two weeks before the Super Bowl, Feinberg all but devoted his life to Towel sales. A line of customers stretched out the store's front doors and down the sidewalk, and employees worked eighteen-hour days to fill all the orders coming in. Yes, Feinberg's was selling a vast array of Steelers hats, shirts, socks, beer mugs, and what-have-you as well. But the Towel drove the traffic. Feinberg put up a banner declaring his store Home of the Terrible Towel and kept a truck loaded with thirty-six thousand towels parked in a nearby alley.

"It's become a rally point, a gimmick that turned into a cult," said Feinberg's VP, Les Hellman. The owner agreed that the Towel had transitioned into something beyond a fun symbol of team spirit. "It's like a prayer cloth, a religious experience," Mike Feinberg said. "Everybody has to have one."

Not everybody, but at least a quarter million, which was the total number of Towels that Feinberg sold during the '95–96 season. Myron's royalties from Towel sales, a very healthy $38,000 in 1994, spiked to over $150,000 in 1995. They'd climb even higher in 1996, equaling if not surpassing the combined monies Myron earned from broadcasting, commercials, and speeches.

The sales volume caught the attention of the Steelers, who after losing the Super Bowl 27–17 to Dallas—mainly due to two head-scratching fourth-quarter interceptions by QB Neil O'Donnell—were looking for ways to increase revenue to stay competitive. For all of Feinberg's success, Joe Gordon, now the team's director of marketing, thought the team could do an even better job of selling the Terrible Towel through its merchandise catalog, which reached more than a hundred thousand fans in all fifty states, and the team's nascent internet presence. He naturally had an "in" with his best friend, Myron, who could see the advantage of allowing the team that the Towel celebrated to benefit from its popularity.

At the same time, Myron was considering what to do with the sudden influx of Towel royalties. With Mildred deceased, Elizabeth graduated from WVU, and Danny having a permanent home at the Allegheny Valley School, his day-to-day expenses had dropped off considerably. One thing he did was to give more money to Danny's institution. A January 1996 newspaper story said Myron's contributions to AVS had climbed past $100,000.

But Mildred's death and his own advancing age made him think ahead. What would happen to those royalties if he wasn't around to direct them? Would they be assigned to a different charity? Would they get paid at all?

Elizabeth says her dad harbored a deep-seated fear of what might happen to his disabled son. "He was terrified that Danny would be homeless," she says. In the years before institutions like AVS existed, her father had seen people with disabilities similar to Danny's living on the streets, unkempt and hungry. He worried that unless AVS had reliable, respectable funding, there was the real possibility that after he and Mildred passed away, Danny would wind up in the same circumstances.

Myron credited his attorney, Lester Zittrain, with suggesting a solution: gifting the trademark for the Terrible Towel to the school. "He was a brilliant lawyer," Myron said several years later, upon Zittrain's death. "Brilliance by itself is morally worthless, but his integrity matched his brilliance. He believed in good works."

In the summer of 1996 Myron and Zittrain drew up the legal papers to transfer marketing rights to the Steelers and the trademark to the school. They apparently acted without consulting AVS itself, judging from a story told by the facility's CEO at the time, Regis Champ. One day that August, Champ said, he was working in his office when Myron showed up unexpectedly. "He came into my office, and he had a pile of papers," Champ said. "He threw them down on my desk and said, 'Regis, I'm giving you the Terrible Towel.' I said, 'Myron, I have about ten of them. I'll take another one but . . .' He said, 'No, I'm giving you the rights, and you'll be able to get all the proceeds from the Terrible Towels.' I was speechless."

Not long afterward, on August 28, Myron and the AVS chief appeared on Hillgrove's evening talk show to announce the new arrangement. "It's really a pleasure for me to do this," said Myron. "It's right that the Towel should pass on to a permanent institution, a place that not only has permanence, but does wonderful work. . . . It's a great place for the Terrible Towel to unpack his suitcase and I'm sure he's gonna enjoy sitting down to meals with all the kids."

Champ, recovered from his speechlessness, went to thank Myron profusely for his donation. "This contribution is more than just an economic gift, this is a very personal part of the Cope legacy, which we've all enjoyed in Pittsburgh," he said. "We are overwhelmed and honored to be given the role as the caretaker of the Terrible Towel. Nothing has happened to the Allegheny Valley School like this in the thirty-six years that we've been in existence. . . . Myron is a wonderful good-hearted human being, whose sensitivity and caring for handicapped people is unparalleled. Myron, thanks for being there and thanks for sticking with us."

Myron and Hillgrove, radio pros that they were, kept the proceedings from getting too serious. Both noted that the Towel was just a few months away from his twenty-first birthday and would soon be eligible, in Myron's words, to "wander down the street and have a beer." Myron also made clear that while he was giving up his trademark to the Terrible Towel, he would remain as devoted to his creation as ever. "I offered Regis Champ my continued services as the spokesman of the Terrible Towel, or as I like to call it, the high priest," Myron said. "I'm still gonna be out there waving it."

Myron also shared an observation that has held up remarkably well in the thirty years since he made it—the Terrible Towel was now firmly implanted in Steelers culture and lore. "Rather than a sporadic thing that comes to life only when the Steelers are going big," he said, "it's become like the flag of Pittsburgh I do believe—I don't think I'm exaggerating—or the flag of the whole Steeler country, where if you come from Steeler country, wherever you're located, the Towel is your flag, and people carry it to games with pride. It's more now than what it was before, and I think that's one reason that it deserves this permanent home."

The new contracts went into effect at the end of August '96. The Steelers took over responsibility for the manufacture and marketing of the Towel and reaped the bulk of the sales revenue. The 20 percent royalty previously paid to Myron each month now went directly from the Steelers to AVS. The sums received by the school tended to fluctuate—slipping when the Steelers missed the playoffs, spiking when they reached the Super Bowl. But the stream of income never stopped. An official of Merakey, the nonprofit health provider that runs AVS today, said in 2022 that Towel royalties over the years had added up to $7.4 million, an average of nearly $285,000 per year since Myron gave up the rights.

The money is a relative drop in the bucket for AVS, which now serves around eight hundred people with severe intellectual or developmental disabilities across nine Pennsylvania counties. Medicaid covers most basic operating expenses like food, utilities, medications, and staff salaries. But the organization still depends on outside contributions like Myron's to pay for equipment and the upkeep of facilities—"things like updating our homes, putting roofs on buildings," AVS regional executive director Roni Erath told WTAE in 2022. She said Terrible Towel money was also used to open a group home for several individuals in Pennsylvania's Beaver County.

AVS is also still the home of Danny Cope, now a middle-aged man with a paunch, some missing teeth, and softly curled gray hair reminiscent of his father's. He's short like his dad was, with a stockier build. Understanding a football game is beyond him, but he appears to enjoy sporting events. He was smiling broadly when Elizabeth and AVS staff took him to a Pirates game at PNC Park in the summer of 2023. He's also been known to shake a Terrible Towel.

When the *New York Times* did a story on the Towel in January 2009, as the Steelers prepared to play in Super Bowl XLIII, Elizabeth reflected on her brother. "He's never spoken," she said. "Which is kind of funny, because Dad is known for his voice. It's almost like the Terrible Towel is Danny's silent voice."

16

That Terrible Towel

For all his generous deeds with the Terrible Towel, Myron could be highly proprietary about it. From the start, he turned the legal guns on anyone who dared produce an unlicensed version of his baby. Only *he* got to say who sold it and what the proceeds were used for. And the proceeds, he made clear, were to be used to help people with disabilities, like those suffered by Danny Cope.

Elizabeth Cope had just entered elementary school when the Towel took its place as the flag of Steelers Nation, and as a young child she paid zero attention to the issues of Towel-related trademark issues, royalties, and charitable donations that took up a surprisingly big chunk of her father's time. She knew it was popular, however, and so she was taken aback one day when her father abruptly pulled her into a conversation about the Terrible Towel, its purpose, and her future. As Elizabeth writes, that conversation was the start of a simmering dispute between father and daughter that was never really resolved.

When I was ten, maybe eleven years old, my dad sat me down at the kitchen table for one of our "serious" talks. I do not remember how it started, but I certainly remember the gist of it.

"Elizabeth," he stated flatly, looking me straight in the eye. "I want you to know that you are not getting the Terrible Towel."

Remember here that I am no more than eleven years old, so I am a bit confused.

"When the day comes that I am no longer here, I want you to be able to support yourself," he went on. "It is going to be very important that you get a college education and become a strong and independent woman because I intend to leave the Terrible Towel to your brother's school. Your brother Danny is helpless to take care of himself. You, on the other hand, are not."

I stared blankly at him.

"Plus, your husband will earn a living as well," he added.

As if! I wasn't even a teenager yet. Keep in mind, my dad was raised in an era when it was a natural assumption that all women got married. My dad, in particular, seemed to have extremely old-fashioned views. Why my father would want me to be dependent on any man is a mystery to me. That would be a nightmare scenario to me.

What I clearly did understand, as any child would, is that I was not getting something. Naturally, this made me want it.

I do not remember how the conversation ended, but I certainly remember running to my mom that night and privately begging her to change my dad's mind. "Please!" I begged. "Don't let him to do this! I want the Terrible Towel. Mommy, please!"

"What do you want me to do, Elizabeth?" my mom asked. "You know your father. I can't change his mind about anything. If he wants to do something, he is going to do it."

"Yes you can!" I insisted. "I know you can stop him."

The future of the Towel became an ongoing theme and undercurrent in our household as I was growing up. It was rarely mentioned out loud, but it was always looming, like a volcano that could erupt at any time. My dad had said he would leave me enough money to have a solid nest egg and some security in life. But that wasn't really the issue. I felt like I was getting stonewalled.

Over the years my father always gave a portion of the royalties to my brother's school out of the deep gratitude he felt for the care Danny was receiving. At first the school received about one-fourth of the royalties; at some point in the 1990s, it received close to half.

Two years after my mother, who was my dearest friend, passed away just before my twenty-fourth birthday, my father announced to me over dinner one night, "I have gifted all the Terrible Towel royalties to the school."

Yes, he had told me that this was coming. But I was devastated. It felt like my world was falling apart, a feeling heightened when our beloved dachshund, Holly, died that same week.

My father's decision is something I've had to work through and come to terms with. There are some things in life that you just can't change, and we are all powerless over other people's actions, regardless of how they affect us. I have often wondered if he would have done this had I been a son and not a daughter. This has caused me great anguish, and it just isn't worth it for me to be bitter and angry. It only hurts me in the end to have those ugly thoughts and feelings.

I am only human, though, and sometimes when I see people like Paris Hilton or others who inherited great wealth from their family and see what their lives are like, I can't help but fantasize about how mine would be with the over $7.5 million the school has received from the Towel and the royalties it will continue to get as long as the Towel sells.

But perhaps this was just not meant to be. The Terrible Towel was destined for a greater purpose. It was not meant to be owned by a single individual for selfish ends. It is to benefit the many. Would it have been as successful if it had been given to me? Would it be all over the planet? Would it have been taken to mountaintops and outer space? Would the Terrible Towel be buried with people in coffins—their final resting place, for God's sake!—if it benefited only Elizabeth Cope?

The Terrible Towel may truly be the single most popular sports item ever produced. It is nothing less than a phenomenon, a kind of miracle. It demonstrates the love people have for the Steelers, but I think it also demonstrates people's love for others and their innate ability to be selfless. Perhaps it even demonstrates people's love for my dad. I don't know. I do know that the Terrible Towel is in a class all its own. It serves humanity and those less fortunate. That is its legacy. My father's legacy.

When I drive by huge mansions, I sometimes wonder if the owner of the mansion will be remembered after he or she is gone. What have they done with their lives besides accruing a huge fortune and surrounding themselves in luxury? My dad did not live in a big fancy house. In fact, for the last six months of his life, he lived in a small apartment at an independent living facility, and our family always lived in a nice but normal-sized middle-class home.

Perhaps our family was on a higher path, where giving to others was more a priority than keeping it all for ourselves. My father always tried to instill in me those values. "We are responsible for the less fortunate," he would say. "When you are as blessed and lucky as us, you must give back."

I choose to be proud of my dad and all he accomplished in life. I know he loved me and had faith that I was capable of anything I set my mind to.

That is not to say that once in a while, on occasional lonely dark nights, I don't wonder, "What if . . . ?"

17

"I'm Done"

In January 2004 Myron turned seventy-five years old. There wasn't much reason to celebrate. The Steelers were out of the playoffs, coming off a 6-10 season, the worst of the Bill Cowher era. More pertinent to Myron, he was turning into a physical wreck.

He had been looking and sounding older for some time. Years of smoking and drinking and yelling had weathered his voice and stripped it of the ability to "cut through concrete," as he used to say. On some broadcasts, it sounded like his vocal cords were marinating in phlegm. On others, the voice just sounded weak, and it fought to be heard over the crowd noise it once sliced through like butter. Tunch Illkin talked more to fill the gap, and Steelers broadcasts remained highly enjoyable, as Myron's funny bone was still in good condition. Announcing a Subway sandwich promotion—honey mustard melts on sale for $1.99—Myron quipped, "They're on me except you gotta pay a buck ninety-nine!" Both Ilkin and Bill Hillgrove laughed.

"He was still a great Myron," says Chuck Finder. "He was still good at being Myron, which is what Steelers fans wanted first and foremost."

More worrying than Myron's vocal problems were his legs. In the summer of 2002, while at the Steelers' training camp in Latrobe, they began aching every time he walked, especially in the upper leg muscles, the quads. Multiple doctors were unable to determine the cause. Myron didn't miss any broadcasts, but on road trips, he was forced to give up his customary visits to bars and restaurants, settling for room service. Inside stadiums, producer Nik DelGreco hauled his briefcase and cleared a path through the crowd, shouting "Coach coming through! Coach coming through!" After home games—and the postgame drinks Myron often imbibed during *Cope's Cabana*—Ilkin and Craig Wolfley would drive him back to his townhouse in Mt. Lebanon, "you know, to make sure he got home safely," Wolfley says. "He was a very endearing guy."

In 2003 Myron underwent surgery to place a battery in his stomach that could deliver a jolt of electricity to his legs and hopefully relieve the pain. It didn't help. Nor did pain medications, including an experimental round-the-clock morphine drip. His list of ailments began to grow, encompassing frequent nausea, twitching in his hands, and night sweats—all of them likely caused, to at least some degree, by the pain medications.

He told Joe Starkey of the *Pittsburgh Tribune-Review* that by early 2004, the physical discomfort reached a point where he "occasionally went to bed wishing I wouldn't wake up." Many days he struggled to get going. "It was just a miserable existence," he said. "It was never life-threatening, but I'd wake up in the morning in a cold sweat, with my pajamas soaked, and I had no appetite whatsoever. I had pain whenever I would stand up or walk. My quads felt like two bags of cement." So acute was the discomfort that he began to resign himself to retirement and began reading literature for senior homes.

At times he wasn't sure he'd make it to the senior home. On April 8, 2004, he had a major health scare, suffering shortness of breath. Alarmed neighbors took him to the emergency room of St. Clair Hospital in Mt. Lebanon. Doctors diagnosed him with atrial fibrillation—a problem with the heart's electrical system—and he spent four days in intensive care. Myron recovered, returned home, and was put on medication and a low-sodium diet, but he still had trouble getting out of bed or functioning. He was readmitted to St. Clair on April 25. The same night, he was honored in absentia by the Historical Society of Western Pennsylvania in a black-tie gala. News of his hospitalization was kept hush-hush; the local papers said he was sidelined by a back injury.

Myron might have remained stuck in the same hellish loop of health scares and emergency room visits had his friend Sam Zacharias not found a doctor, Michael Finikiotis, who finally figured out the source of his ever escalating ailments. The culprit was polymyalgia rheumatica, a type of arthritis that can cause great muscle stiffness and pain.

He was prescribed prednisone for the pain and sent to a rehabilitation center in Harmarville, northeast of Pittsburgh, where he experienced an almost overnight transformation. "My first day of physical therapy, I was doing things I hadn't done when I was healthy," he told Starkey. "Within a week, I was pumping iron. My physical therapist said to me, 'What are you going to do with all your new muscles?' I said, 'I don't know, I might go into a biker bar and punch a couple of guys out.'"

By the beginning of June he was back to relatively good health and put aside all talk of senior homes, instead getting a new awning installed on his deck. Optimistic that the worst was over, he signed another one-year contract to broadcast his thirty-fifth season of Steelers football.

Then the real problems began.

IN LATE JULY 2004 doctors found a bump on his throat. It tested positive. Cancer.

A UPMC doctor, an older, highly experienced surgeon, assured him that it had been caught at the earliest possible stage and could be safely removed. For the third time in fifteen months, Myron went under the knife. Two weeks later, he met with the doctor for a checkup. "We found a second bump," the surgeon explained, and "thought it was best to remove it and part of your epiglottis too." The epiglottis is a flap in the throat that diverts food down the right pipe, into the esophagus instead of the lungs.

The surgery was life changing, not in a good way. The partial removal of the epiglottis made it harder for him to swallow his food. Removal of the bumps, however well-intended, damaged his vocal cords and made it harder for him to speak. The ever scratchy Cope voice now just sounded hoarse. For the capper, his legs began hurting again.

Myron had to sit out three exhibition games in August while he recuperated from the surgery. Initially, he blamed his absence on a bout of pneumonia and passed off the throat operation as a routine procedure. "Unfortunately," he joked, "my voice sounds the same." He came clean at the start of September, admitting he had the bumps removed but saying doctors had reassured him that the cancer would not return. Since the surgery, he said, he had tried to minimize talking to strengthen his voice, but keeping silent while watching the Steelers' preseason games on TV was like a form of torture. "Every time an idea hit me, I wanted to yell out a comment on a play," he said. "It was like I was in prison."

The rest accomplished its goal, however, and Myron was back for the season opener against Oakland, a bizarre game in which Jerome Bettis carried the ball five times for a net total of 1 yard but still scored three touchdowns in a Steelers victory.

It was the start of a remarkable season for both Myron and the Steelers. In week two, the offense struggled to get going against Baltimore, and when QB Tommy Maddox suffered an arm injury in the third quarter, Bill Cowher replaced him with the team's number-one draft pick from Miami of Ohio, 6-foot-5 Ben Roethlisberger. The Steelers couldn't mount a comeback, but Roethlisberger tossed a pair of fourth-quarter touchdowns. Cowher never looked back. Big Ben was the starter.

The next week on a rain-soaked field in Miami, Roethlisberger fired a game-sealing, fourth-quarter TD to Hines Ward, in a game that also saw second-year safety Troy Polamalu make his first career interception. The Steelers' future had arrived.

In the booth, unfortunately, Myron was struggling to keep up. After Polamalu's grab, he asked his colleagues, twice, "Who intercepted that ball?" Myron later said that throughout the whole season, he experienced difficulty processing and analyzing the action on the field. "[There were] situations that involved, for example, the clock, and strategy as it related to the clock, or a seldom-invoked rule, and I remembered that I was shutting up in those circumstances and leaving it to Billy and Tunch, which I had never done before. I wasn't sure of myself, in other words."

Still, there were no complaints from the fans or the Steelers, and Myron stayed at the mic. With Roethlisberger at the helm, the Steelers suddenly jelled, reeling off four straight wins, enjoying a well-timed bye week, then beating defending Super Bowl champion New England in Foxboro, 34–20. Next up was a home game against the Eagles, at the time the only undefeated team left in the NFL. It was a game to get hyped about.

So his colleagues were puzzled when on the morning of the game, Myron was uncharacteristically three hours late getting to Heinz Field, arriving less than twenty minutes before kickoff. Once the game started, Myron was even more atypically quiet as the Steelers rolled out to an early 21–0 lead on the strength of a Hines Ward rushing TD and two touchdown passes from Roethlisberger. "I was trying to think of something to say and I couldn't," Myron later said. "That's definitely a first for me."

Shortly before halftime, a concerned Ilkin noticed that Myron was bleeding from a gash on the back of his head and suggested that it might explain his silence. An ambulance was called, and Myron was taken to UPMC Presbyterian Hospital for what turned out to be a concussion.

When he recovered, Myron explained that the night before the Eagles game, he fell while exercising at his home. "After stretching, I got up and I must have toppled over backward and hit the back of my head on the corner of a table," he said. The next morning, he said, he overslept, then took the wrong route driving to the stadium.

"I've got what the players call post-concussive syndrome," he said. "It's when you have your bell rung badly. I know what they're talking about now."

He spent three days at the hospital and was forced to sit out the following week's game at Cleveland, only the second full Steelers game he had missed since 1970. In the meantime, he and his banged-up cranium got heavy coverage in the Pittsburgh media, much to his delight. "I got home from the hospital and ten minutes later Channel 4 was at the door," he told *Post-Gazette* columnist Gene Collier the day of his release. "Before they get their camera set up, Channel 2 is here, then Channel 11. I'm the lead story on the sports page when the Steelers are going great guns. It's amazing."

Collier joked that Myron's colleagues had known that something was wrong with him when he began speaking fluent English in perfectly modulated sentences.

The attention toward Myron kept flowing as the Steelers romped to a 15-1 record under Roethlisberger. The *Washington Post*, the *New York Times*, and *Newsday* all did features on him. The *Times* noted that Myron, despite his recent health scares, had declined to change longstanding habits. He told the reporter that he wanted to protect his voice—but went out on the Friday before a game to replenish his cigarette supply and tape two radio commercials for a car dealer. The owner, Richard Bazzy, said Myron's commercials had helped make his Ford dealerships the biggest in Pittsburgh. "His voice helps us cut through the clutter," Bazzy said—testimony that even in its weakened state, the Cope voice still carried plenty of power.

The Steelers earned a bye for the first round of the playoffs, then faced the New York Jets at home. A nervous Roethlisberger threw a couple of interceptions, and the Jets hung tough, but the Steelers eked out a 23–20 win on a Jeff Reed field goal in overtime. Myron would turn seventy-six a week later, the day of the AFC Championship Game against New England. After the Jets game, he wondered aloud if the Steelers could give him the ultimate birthday gift, a trip to another Super Bowl.

Alas, no. Tom Brady and company rolled over the Steelers 41–27, in a game far more lopsided than the final score would indicate. Early on, Myron sensed that the team was off-kilter, and he urged them to punt on a first-quarter fourth-and-one situation. "I don't like it!" he exclaimed. The Steelers went for it, Jerome Bettis fumbled, and the Patriots recovered the ball. On the next play, Brady threw a 60-yard touchdown pass to Deion Branch.

Before the game, a reporter for the *Pittsburgh Tribune-Review* brought up the subject of Myron's possible retirement. Cope slapped it away. "People have asked me if the Steelers win the Super Bowl, will I retire? It has nothing to do with when I retire. I will retire when I feel I am no longer capable or when my bosses feel I'm not capable."

His bosses, as far as anyone knew, still had confidence in his capabilities. But another man, someone even more important to Myron than the Rooneys, did not.

DURING ONE OF HIS 2004 health scares, Myron proclaimed that he would continue broadcasting Steelers games "until somebody else's opinion who I respect tells me I'm losing it." The "somebody else" was Myron's best friend, Joe Gordon, by then retired from his official Steelers duties but still an informal advisor and ambassador, still plugged into the team and its happenings. He had been listening to the Steelers' broadcasts and felt Myron was making too many mistakes during games and was embarrassing himself. It was time, he felt, for Myron to leave the Steelers' radio booth.

On a Wednesday evening in June 2005, Myron was at his condo when Gordon called. As Myron recounted the conversation: "Joe and I were on the phone one evening and he was asking how I was doing, and he said to me, 'Do not go another year in the booth. You've got thirty-five years in and with your health.' . . . That's what he did. My slipping, he attributed it to my health problems. But anyhow, he said, 'It's too punishing for you to go another year. It's too physically taxing.'"

Myron dismissed Gordon's advice. He had recently resumed physical therapy in Harmarville and was getting therapy for his hoarseness at UPMC. He was hopeful for a general recovery of his voice and his health. So, Myron said, "I told Joe, no, I could do another season."

Two days later Myron heard a knock on the door. It was Gordon, coming to deliver the message in person. This time, Myron said, Gordon was more direct:

> [He] told me that I had, at many times, told him that if he ever detected me slipping in the broadcast booth, losing a step you know, he should tell me and I would retire. So recently he told me that at my home. And I guess, I thought about it for about ten seconds and I said, "I'm done." . . . It takes a very special friend to tell you the truth when he knows it's going to hurt. I thought it over later, created situations in my mind, from broadcasts last year, which was the worst of my years in terms of difficulty, and I said he's absolutely right.

Bill Hillgrove believes Myron stepped down at the right time. "He had told Joe, 'You tell me when I've lost my fastball.' I think we all need that. I have a fellow who I trust, and I told him the same thing, that when you feel I'm starting to lose my fastball, I want you to be the first one to tell me. We all have to succumb to nature, that's unavoidable. So, I think Joe did him a favor."

Chuck Finder also says Myron picked the right time to retire, though he thinks the fans might have disagreed. "He was still listenable, he was still Myron, and if you took a poll, I think the overwhelming majority of fans would've wanted him to stay on," he says.

On June 22 the Steelers held a news conference at Heinz Field to announce Myron's retirement. Art Rooney II, now the Steelers' president, gave him the game ball from the last game he broadcast. Dan Rooney called in from a vacation in Ireland. "You always were terrific, and you were professional, and the big thing is how those players of the seventies . . . when we have those affairs and you come, they all really think so much of you," the elder Rooney said. "You were really part of it. You were part of the team. The Terrible Towel many times got us over the goal line."

Myron expressed his affection for the fans, various Steelers players, the Rooneys, and all but apologized to the public for not being able to go on. "It seems like almost every time I leave the house to go somewhere, people stop me—strangers, you see—and they say very sincerely, 'How are you, Myron? How's your health?' Or similar words," he said. "And I say, 'OK, coming along, feeling better every day, great.' And then they say, 'You gonna be back this year?' And I've been saying, 'You betcha.' So in that fact, if I'm disappointing people, I'm sure they understand."

Irascible to the end, he couldn't help but take time out to chastise Ben Roethlisberger and Tommy Maddox for their habit of riding motorcycles. "If they still got a brain in their head, the brain God gave them, they'll take their motorcycles to the nearest bridge and push them off, if for no other reason than they've got fifty-something teammates depending on them," he said. Roethlisberger, who had seen riding his motorbike around town without a helmet, issued no public response. But events a year later proved Myron to be a farsighted faultfinder.

Someone asked if he felt relieved that he wouldn't have to broadcast the games anymore. Myron replied he was OK with the decision to retire, because Gordon had told him the truth. But relieved? "No," he said, "because I'd love to be there."

THE STEELERS ANTICIPATED that Myron would attend future games and gave him a seat in the third row of the press box. But he didn't show for the opener of the 2005 season, citing a sore throat, and found he was happy to watch the game from the comfort of his living room. He said he would show up for future games, but to the best of several people's memory, he never did—with one very notable exception, as Elizabeth Cope writes:

I found myself standing up in the stands gazing at the crisp night sky with a huge full moon slung low in the sky. Halloween night. I was by myself. No one else was at the game yet. My father and I had arrived early, as it was to be Myron Cope Monday on this fortuitous Monday night Steelers-Ravens game.

As I stood there, a few football players wandered out onto the field below me and began to toss the ball back and forth and run through drills to get ready for the upcoming game. I let the breeze caress my face as I continued to gaze up at the moon. It was cold out, and I was wearing my mother's mink jacket to keep warm and also to include her in the night. She had passed away eleven years prior.

As I gazed up at the moon, I suddenly sensed that someone was watching me. You know—you just feel it, even though you can't see it? I knew I was being stared at. I looked down at the field, and sure enough, one of the players quickly whipped his head away as if he didn't want me to catch him looking at me. It was such a sudden, obvious movement on his part that I smiled to myself. The player cautiously dared to look up at me again. His face turned bright red, and he smiled and sort of chuckled, knowing that I had caught him red handed. It was Ben Roethlisberger, age twenty-three. I was thirty-four at the time.

Ben was already a star, despite having been with the Steelers for only a year. I had a strange and eerie sensation, though, that I had just had an encounter with someone special. It was a sixth sense I had developed about people, I guess from having a father who people liked to call a "legend." I could sniff out similar people. I actually got goose bumps.

Later on, right before the game was to start, my father and I were on the field for the coin toss. My dad was to do the toss. At one point he stepped away from me to talk to people farther down the field. People in the stands were shouting his name. "Myron! Myron! We love you, Myron!" My dad would wave to everyone, beaming ear to ear.

As I walked down the field, I suddenly got that weird sensation again. I turned around, and there stood Ben Roethlisberger. We stood there stock still, staring at each other. I looked into his eyes—which were hard to see because he was wearing his helmet and because he towered over me. He was 6 feet 5 inches tall, and I am 4 feet 10 inches short. Neither of us spoke or smiled. We just stood there, arms at our sides, staring. It was the most bizarre encounter. It was serendipity. The past encountering the future. The heartbeat of the Steelers pumping old blood out of its veins (my father) and ushering in new blood (Ben Roethlisberger). That is what a healthy heart does. A natural process. It was two eras colliding at that moment. I was wistful and sad but also in awe that I was in this moment, one that I would never forget.

It was fitting that it was Halloween night, as there we were, two human beings dressed up in our costumes—Ben as "Ben Roethlisberger, quarterback of the Pittsburgh Steelers," and me as "Elizabeth Cope, Myron Cope's daughter." It was a changing-of-the-guard moment that couldn't have been better orchestrated by Shakespeare himself, with all the elements in place, stage set. It was almost as if I could sense a huge invisible clock hanging above our heads and the big hand slowly inching forward, marking time. All the commotion on the field and in the stands seemed to fade away as we stood in our silent faceoff.

Then, as if on cue, I heard my name called. It was my dad. "Elizabeth, it's time to go." What fitting words. He was farther up the field and motioned for me to join him. I began to walk slowly away, only turning around once to look back. Ben was watching me walk away. I don't know if he realized it at the time—I can't pretend to know what he was thinking—but he was watching a past era walk away, and he was in the process of ushering in a new one, one that would last eighteen years for him and the Steelers.

I reached my father, and arm-in-arm, we slowly exited the field to a round of applause and shouts from the stands.

The Steelers pulled out a win that Monday night, Monday Night Myron. I wondered later if Ben had any idea what that win meant to me. How much more special it was going to be as a cherished memory in my life that they won on my dad's last night on the football field after a thirty-five-year career. I would like to think that Ben wanted to win the game for me, but I realize that is a fairytale that only I choose to believe. It is a beautiful memory, though. Halloween has always been my favorite holiday, so that was fitting as well.

Some moments in a person's life stand alone. This was my moment.

AFTER HIS RETIREMENT, Myron never broadcast another Steelers game. But it could have happened.

In 2005 the Steelers won four in a row to close the season and win the division with an 11-5 record. The team then swept past Cincinnati in the first round of the playoffs, squeaked by Indianapolis, and cruised past Denver in the AFC Championship Game to reach the Super Bowl for the first time in a decade. Even before the Steelers clinched their Super Bowl ticket, fans began calling for Myron to return to the booth for the big game. One wrote to the *Post-Gazette*, "This is possibly the final year for Jerome Bettis. What better send-off for a Steelers great than to have Myron call 'Yoi!' as he crashed into the end zone?" A pair of online petitions to bring Myron out of retirement drew more than two thousand signatures.

Elizabeth Cope says the Steelers were willing. "Dan Rooney called and offered him the chance to come back," she says. But Myron's voice and general health weren't up to the task; he had gone through another bout of pneumonia that hospitalized him in January, and doctors advised him to lie low. He chose not to attend the game in Detroit, sending Elizabeth in his absence. The Steelers defeated Seattle 21–10, to claim the fifth Lombardi Trophy in franchise history. Bettis, having won his first Super Bowl in his hometown, announced his retirement after the game.

But Myron wasn't entirely forgotten on game day. "It was about ninety minutes before kickoff," remembers Craig Wolfley. "We were in the radio booth. I believe Billy was the one who said, 'Let's call Myron.' It was funny, because with Billy he says, 'Have a great game' and this and that, and with Tunch, same thing, dah dah dah, and then he says, 'Let me talk to the Wolfman.' And he gets on there and he says, 'Biggest thing Wolf, don't say anything stupid . . . ahh, you will anyhow!'"

18

Thankful

The week before Super Bowl XL, Myron turned seventy-seven. After his health scares of the previous few years, Elizabeth was simultaneously happy that he had made it to his birthday and haunted by the possibility that this one could be his last. She writes that she didn't want to make it a small occasion:

I had agonized over whether to keep it simple or to plan something more elaborate in case he might never have another. When I asked my dad how he wanted to celebrate the day, he said, "Let's just go to dinner."

"What if you could do anything you wanted," I asked, "like going to see a Broadway play downtown and inviting all your friends?"

"No, Elizabeth," he said. "Let's just go to dinner."

I didn't listen. Behind my dad's back, I planned to surprise him with all his friends, many of whom were former Steelers players, such as Franco Harris and Andy Russell. They were going to be at the restaurant when we got there. But at the last moment, my dad phoned me and said he was too sick to go. Knowing that everyone was there waiting for him, I tried to coax him into going anyway, but he refused. So I had to scramble, call everyone, and tell them to meet at my dad's house instead.

My dad was sitting on the couch with a dejected look on his face, feeling sick and downhearted, when we all burst through the door and yelled, "Surprise!"

Ten minutes later, I stood in the hallway and listened to the sounds of laughter coming from the other room. I felt so relieved that I wanted to cry. I was glad I did it. My dad seemed to come to life again in the presence of all these people. He received all the attention and abundance with gratitude, and he lit up. He admitted to me later that it was the best he had felt in such a long time.

I found a packet of candles in a hallway drawer, removed seven, and slid them into one corner of the cake. I stepped back and smiled. This was no supermarket bakeshop cake. I had created a masterpiece: a chocolate frosted sea with plastic figures of football players and a man with a microphone standing in the middle, the whole scene punctuated with holes the size of my pinky finger, outlined in chocolate cake crumbs, where I had tested to make sure all the frostings tasted the same, something I had done since I was a little girl and a habit I found impossible to break.

I lit the candles, which seemed dwarfed by the large cake. Tears I had been holding inside welled up. I blinked hard. I couldn't cry now. It would ruin the happiest moment of the whole day. Taking a deep breath, I picked up the cake, pasted a smile on my face, and stepped into the dining room singing, "Happy birthday to you." The laughter and loud talking turned quickly to song as everyone joined in.

I maneuvered the cake through an obstacle course of balloons, tissue paper streamers I had draped around a chandelier, football players, and other close friends. I was so engrossed in getting the cake on the table without igniting anyone or anything that I didn't notice what my dad was doing. When I finally looked up, my pasted-on grin slid off my chin.

Unlike everyone around him, my dad wasn't smiling. He was solemn, quiet, almost completely still. Only his head moved as his eyes traveled slowly from one person to the next, resting finally on me. For a split second, I thought something was wrong, like he was tired or sad or the excitement was too much for him. Then I realized that far from feeling unhappy, my dad was letting everyone and everything in this moment seep into his heart.

As the loud, off-key rendition of "Happy Birthday" came to an end, bright eyes and flushed faces turned to the guest of honor. He smiled slightly, taking it all in. Everyone waited in the long silence.

"Make a wish, Myron," someone called out.

My dad looked at me. The other guests were no longer smiling. No one was shifting around. Everyone was watching my dad. My dad was watching me.

Finally, finally, with only a whisper of a breath, my dad blew out the flames. Even as he did it, even as everyone cheered, his eyes never left mine.

I felt more present, more connected to him than at any other moment in my life.

That did not turn out to be my dad's last birthday. But to me, it remains the most special.

After the birthday Myron's health remained shaky, and Elizabeth moved into the townhouse to keep an eye on him. That winter doctors had given him more bad news: tumors were growing in his lungs. He underwent his fourth surgery in four years to remove them. Afterward he seemed to rally, only to slide back in May, when he was admitted to the intensive care unit at UPMC Presbyterian Hospital. Joe Gordon told the media that Myron was undergoing another bout of pneumonia, a partial truth that hid the fact that Myron seemed to be in a general, gradual physical decline. Elizabeth believes that her father's constant regimen of prednisone, a steroid, and continuous prescriptions of antibiotics effectively destroyed his immune system, leaving him vulnerable to any bug that came around. For this particular bout of ill health, he spent four days in the ICU and another eight in a private room before being released.

He stayed out of the public eye in this period but remained very much on Steelers fans' minds. In one of its daily online polls, the *Post-Gazette* asked Pittsburghers to name their all-time favorite sportscaster. Three thousand people responded. It was close, but Myron, with 35 percent of the votes, edged out Mike Lange of the Penguins and Bob Prince of the Pirates.

During periods when his health was stable, Myron made an attempt to revive his writing career. First he finished an update of his autobiography, *Double Yoi*, which was published in the summer of 2006. Then he got it in his mind that he could write for *Sports Illustrated* again. The Steelers struggled out of the gate that fall, dropping six of their first eight games. Many observers placed the blame on Roethlisberger, who true to Cope's warning got into a bad motorcycle crash that June. Zooming along a downtown street, Big Ben rammed his bike into a car making a left turn and flew over the vehicle, onto the pavement. He was lucky to survive; his un-helmeted head hit both the car's windshield and the asphalt. EMTs arrived just in time to stop the bleeding and save his life.

But Myron saw flaws with the team that went deeper than the quarterback's foolishness and decided to chronicle them in a prospective article he titled "Why the Champs Crashed." The article, which Myron initially wrote by hand, opened with the author calling up the Steelers' director of football operations, Kevin Colbert, and telling him, "You guys will not repeat because notwithstanding the fact that you drafted kick returners in the first and third rounds, you have no return game. In fact, your return game outright stinks. It's gonna kill you, mark my words."

"Another Super Bowl," he added, "my ass."

Unfortunately, after that blazing start, the article took multiple long detours, somehow touching on Johnny Unitas, Dan Marino, the 1958 Pitt Panthers, the 1929 stock market crash, and a joke about Jesus Christ and a tailor before finally getting to Myron's main points, which were that besides needing decent kickoff and punt returners, the Steelers lacked a fully engaged head coach. Bill Cowher had purchased a home in North Carolina and moved his family there during the off-season, Myron noted, making him an obvious lame duck. "He all but wore a Donald Duck costume and walked with a limp," Myron wrote—a line that showed that his wit was sharp as ever.

When the article was done and put in typewritten form, Myron pitched it to *Sports Illustrated* executive editor Rob Fleder on the phone and wrote up a cover letter for the submission. "I think my piece could go this season or post-season or next year, but I much prefer sooner to later," he wrote. "Not to be maudlin, I'm 77. I have no life-threatening illnesses, but I have been ambulanced many times." He added that he was going to Florida for a month and offered to write a story on the "horrible Pirates, who under a skinflint owner named Nutting will be entering their 15th straight season as a below .500 club."

Fleder, now retired, says he has no memory or record of receiving the letter, or the article. It could be that Myron decided the story wasn't up to par and stuck it in a drawer. There would be no comeback for him as a magazine writer.

As a newspaper writer, however, Myron enjoyed a minor renaissance. Several times after his retirement, when the mood struck him, he composed letters to the editor that were published by the *Post-Gazette*. In February 2007 he went a step further and wrote a column aimed at Penguins superstar-turned-team owner Mario Lemieux, who had been agitating for a new arena and considering overtures from other cities to move the hockey team out of Pittsburgh. "Perhaps unfairly," Myron wrote, "I'm asking that you disregard bottom-line offers and keep the Pens here, simply because it's the right thing to do. Disregard our political leaders staying on the sidelines for so long. I doubt you'll ever regret doing the right thing. You'll feel good about yourself." It's unknown if Lemieux read the column, but the Penguins did stay put, got their new arena in 2010, and have since brought three Stanley Cups to the city.

Occasionally, when he was feeling up to it, Myron even wandered in front of the cameras again. In early 2007 his old colleagues Tunch Ilkin and Craig Wolfley were hosting a Steelers' show on WPXI-TV and convinced Myron to make an appearance. The show found Myron in good spirits and still physically animated like in the old days, though his voice had withered to a croaky rasp and the light blue sweat suit he wore nearly swallowed his frail body.

"That interview was a lot of Tunch," Wolfley says. "He loved Tunch, and Tunch loved him, they were good buddies. Myron was agreeable to coming down and doing the show. Myron loved entertaining. He was still a storyteller, still capable of telling those tales that just kind of made you smile. Sitting with Myron was like sitting with a good friend in front of a fire and listening to stories that warmed your heart from years ago."

Myron's fire, unfortunately, was starting to flicker. This was a man who loved living, loved life, whether or not there was an audience to entertain. But as 2007 progressed, the ailments that had wracked his body for the previous five years gained the upper hand. He made no public appearances after the spring, gave no interviews, and retreated into a world where he mostly stayed inside, communicating by phone or through emails sent out by his new personal assistant, Amy, the daughter of some family friends. He was rarely seen even at Covenant of the South Hills, the senior home and assisted living facility where he finally moved that summer, no longer able to take care of himself. Not even the start of a new Steelers season brought him out of this small existence.

Worst of all, says Elizabeth, her father seemed permanently locked in a foul mood, at least when it came to her, and prone to angry outbursts. Their conversations grew so testy that by September, she felt compelled to distance herself, unable to take his constant berating. Joe Gordon became their go-between. With no improvement in sight, Elizabeth made plans to spend Thanksgiving with a friend. It was not what she wanted. But as she writes, she felt she had no other choice:

My father and I had been estranged for about two months now. We rarely spoke or saw each other. This had never happened before. We seemed unable to agree about anything. Lately, my dad, ever the writer, had taken to composing long, angry letters, which he would sometimes drive over and leave outside my door. He used to do this when I was growing up and he was mad at me. He would leave handwritten or typed letters by my bedroom door (I have saved all of them). Now he was sending me letters listing all my apparent faults and describing in detail everything I had done wrong in life. He would also remind me of all the mistakes I had ever made. I dreaded these letters.

I would often come home to my apartment and play back the messages on my answering machine. Inevitably, my dad's voice would boom ominously into the small one-bedroom apartment: "Pick up that phone, Elizabeth! I know you're there!" I would shudder. I actually began to feel stalked by my own dad. I would often go through my days feeling an undercurrent of fear and dread. I remember one time my dad shouted into my voicemail, "So help me God, Elizabeth, I can't be held responsible for what I might do if you don't pick up that damn phone!"

I even went so far as to stop sleeping in my own apartment. Every night I would gather up blankets and pillows and walk up two flights of stairs to my friend Jonathan's apartment and sleep on his couch. I didn't want to be alone. I felt too scared. We would sit up late into the night watching movies together. I was always in my pajamas eating Ben & Jerry's ice cream right out of the carton. He would have my ice cream all ready for me when I got there. It was our routine. Sometimes I would even make this poor guy braid my hair because I liked the way it felt.

I was desperate for comfort, and Jonathan was a soothing presence at this dark time. Three years younger than I—age thirty-two—Jonathan had been paralyzed from the waist down since the age of twelve. He would maneuver himself out of his wheelchair and plop himself down onto the couch next to me. He is the most positive person I know, never feeling sorry for himself, and works a full-time job as an architect. Something about his voice always calmed me. I didn't care what he was saying. I just wanted to hear him speak.

Neither of us could figure out what I had done to bring my father's wrath down upon me. I had no idea at the time that my dad had a slow-growing army of abscesses invading the tissues surrounding his brain, a condition that my father, too, was unaware of. Pressure from these pus-filled lesions were apparently bearing down on the part of the brain that controls aggression. He didn't have real control over what he was doing.

So the stalemate between us went on, and Thanksgiving approached. I was to eat Thanksgiving dinner at my friend Tracie's house with her family. I had no idea what my dad was doing. It was pathetic.

On Thanksgiving morning, my dad's personal assistant, Amy, tried to call him. When he didn't pick up, she drove over to his apartment at the independent living facility and found all the shades drawn. She knocked and knocked on the door, but no one answered. The nurses at the facility let themselves into his apartment and found him collapsed and unconscious on the floor by the bed. He was rushed to the hospital.

It is important to backtrack here. For months before this event, I had been searching for a house to buy. I would tour homes constantly. For the life of me, I couldn't find one that I could picture myself living in. I would put money down on a house to hold it, and then I would pull out. Inevitably, someone else would buy it, and then I would cry and cry. It became a stubborn pattern that I couldn't seem to break.

This became another issue between my father and me. He couldn't understand why no house was "good enough," as he put it. He was completely beside himself about this. He would scream at me to make up my mind. "I have never seen anyone as indecisive as you! It just isn't normal!" he would say.

I would complain about one thing or another about each house. "I don't like the view," I remember saying about one townhouse I looked at. "Who cares about the view!" my dad exploded. "What are you going to do? Sit in a chair by the window gazing at the view all day long?" No house felt right. I didn't know why. I remember my dad even putting me on a deadline. He would give me a certain amount of time to find a place to live, and that was that. He was helping me pay for it, so I was at his mercy. As the deadline would draw closer, he would call me on the phone and simply ask, "Well?" And I would know what he was referring to. I could never meet these deadlines.

As my dad's health continued to deteriorate—although, again, we weren't aware what was happening at the time—he began issuing all kinds of bizarre requirements for the house I was to buy. "It has to have a pool!" I remember him saying.

"I don't care about a pool, Dad," I told him. "I don't want to take care of a pool."

He was adamant. "It has to have a pool or you can't live there, and that is final!" It was insane.

It was during that Thanksgiving dinner at Tracie's when I received a phone call from Joe Gordon, my dad's best friend. "Your dad is in the hospital," he said.

Although we weren't speaking, I rushed over to the hospital immediately. I ran into my dad's hospital room. He was lying in bed, hands on his head, moaning. The doctors would later find the abscesses marching through his brain and do emergency surgery to drain them.

"I'm here, Dad." He looked up at me.

"The house?" he muttered.

I gave him a look. "I don't think that's important right now," I said.

"I guess you're right," he actually agreed in a whisper. He moaned again in pain.

I settled myself down in an institutional-green vinyl chair situated in the corner of the room. My dad drifted off to sleep. As time slowly ticked by, the room became dark as night fell. There I sat, in a tiny, dreary, borderline-dirty hospital room, gazing at my father asleep in his bed, when a strange, unexpected feeling crept over me, a sense of ease that I hadn't experienced in so long. The words that came into my mind were, "I'm home." I am finally home. All these months and wasted energy searching for a place to live and call home. I suddenly realized why I couldn't find anywhere to live. I real-

ized then that home is not some familiar place you can always return to. It is the rightness you feel wherever you are when you know that you are loved.

Hours passed as I sat in the room. My dad awoke around three in the morning to see me sitting there in the corner. He looked surprised. "You're still here?" he whispered.

"Yes," I answered. He paused. "Thank you," he said, and with that he closed his eyes. The stalemate was over.

I had a lot to be thankful for that Thanksgiving.

19

Bye Now

Myron passed away on the morning of Wednesday, February 27, 2008, in the hospital unit of his Mt. Lebanon senior home. Within an hour, the Pittsburgh media was awash in tributes. The TV stations and newspapers had had time to prepare, as Myron's declining health was no secret. The suddenness and intensity of the tributes nevertheless took Elizabeth by surprise. She still isn't sure who told the media he had died. "The body hadn't even been taken away! I was with the body at Covenant, and there it was on the news," she remembers. "They interrupted the soap operas, and I started getting calls. All my friends knew about it before I told them."

WTAE went all-out for its touchstone star, airing statements from friends and colleagues, man-in-the street interviews, and a pre-produced six-minute obituary. "He was simply the voice of Pittsburgh, a uniter in a city losing its steel mill identity but hanging on to a love for its football team," said the voice-over as clips from Myron's career rolled across the screen. Fans who talked to the station eschewed the usual he-will-be-missed type of remarks. "It's so much more than the death of a person," one said. "It's almost like a little bit of the city just left. It was like a family member died."

The *Post-Gazette*, where Myron had worked so many years before, released its own video tribute, a montage of photos over a musical salute; someone had taken the U2 song "Pride (In the Name of Love)" and changed it to "Pride (In the Name of Cope)." The *Tribune-Review*, where he had never worked, ran a dozen articles of its own. In New York, Myron's death made the news ticker scrolling above Times Square; the Associated Press had published a story on his passing, as had the *New York Times*.

For years, Myron had joked that when he died, the headline would read "Creator of Towel, Dead." The *Post-Gazette* didn't use that header on the front page—that would have been too irreverent, even for Myron—but a story on page A-9 indeed proclaimed, "Creator of Towel Dead." The Terrible Towel had often been imitated, said writer Robert Dvorchak, but never quite matched. "There is only one Terrible Towel, fitting in that its creator was a one of a kind personality," he wrote. "As long as it waves, his memory lives."

Bill Hillgrove and others urged Steelers fans not to get overly sad and serious; Myron wouldn't have wanted it that way, they said. Longtime Steelers beat writer Ed Bouchette put it well: "Hold off flying those Terrible Towels at half-staff. Better to toast Myron Cope with a toddy and a story, two of his favorite pastimes. And, if you're so inclined, you can light one up in his honor, because Mr. Cope was anything but politically correct and he enjoyed a smoke as well."

As the salutes poured in, Elizabeth, with the help of Joe Gordon, was making funeral arrangements. Myron was to be laid to rest at Chartiers Cemetery in Carnegie, next to Mildred. The Slater Funeral Home in Greentree would host the service. Gordon lined up a rabbi and dispatched invitations to family, friends, and important Steelers figures. Don't tell people where the funeral is, he implored them; we don't want this to turn into a mob scene. News cameras would be permitted outside the Slater home but not in the service itself. Myron had always maintained a privacy wall around his personal life, and his daughter and best friend now extended this preference to his death as well. The funeral was to be relatively small and discreet, a non-public affair.

That afternoon, Elizabeth went to the Slater home to pick out a coffin, accompanied by Gordon for support. Myron had asked to be given a traditional Jewish burial, a request that would normally call for a simple wooden casket. But a grief-stricken Elizabeth wanted the best for her dad, and she initially leaned toward picking an ornate mahogany model that cost around $30,000. Gordon, citing the cost, talked her out of it. The one she picked was less expensive but was still one of the home's nicer models, made out of cherrywood.

Gordon was something of a hero that day, Elizabeth says. "He jumped into action the minute Dad died, which was very helpful because I was distraught," she says. "I couldn't have done it without him, really."

Jewish tradition calls for the deceased to be buried within twenty-four hours after death, but Myron's funeral was delayed until Friday so friends and family had time to come in. The delay was for better and for worse. February 29, a leap day, dawned with strong winds and heavy, wet snow pummeling the Pittsburgh area, making travel difficult. But all the principals made it to the service, as did several Steelers greats: Rocky Bleier, Mel Blount, Joe Greene, L. C. Greenwood, Franco Harris, Andy Russell, and Lynn Swann. Russell and Harris, wearing yarmulkes, served among the pallbearers. In all, the crowd numbered about 160—only 10 of them gate-crashers, according to Bob Smizik in his column the next day. Just about everyone, it seems, had honored Gordon's request to keep the event private.

Speakers at the funeral included Elizabeth, Harris, Art Rooney II, Hillgrove, and a woman who'd had zero expectation she'd be asked to speak. Sally Wiggin had liked and admired Myron for years but never considered herself part of his inner circle, or even two or three circles beyond.

"I was *shocked* when Elizabeth approached me when he died and said he wanted me to be one of the people who spoke," Wiggin says. "I had become really good friends with Joe Gordon, and Joe would tell me how much Myron thought of me. I don't know why! I was always kind to him, and when I interviewed him, I tried to be respectful. But to be named one of five or six people to speak there, I was honored and shocked. I thought in the scheme of things I was nobody."

The service itself was not long, lasting less than an hour. Besides the Steelers in attendance, the team was well represented in the ceremony. Myron's coffin was covered with a Steelers quilt, and the space around it was decorated with dozens and dozens of yellow roses, standing in for Steelers gold. But Elizabeth drew the line at the popular Pittsburgh tradition of burying the deceased with a Terrible Towel.

"I know a lot of people do that," she says, "but I really didn't want to do that to my father. I didn't want him to be a caricature. He was so much more than that. He didn't invent the Towel until 1975, and I knew him as my dad." She also didn't want him buried with his glasses. She pulled them off at the last moment and still has them.

Talking to WTAE afterward, Myron's friend and colleague in the fight against autism, Dan Torisky, said the service was beautifully done. "There were a lot of choked-up people including yours truly," he said. He added: "We'll all feel so damn lonely without him."

Art Rooney II surmised that Myron, perhaps watching from above, was pleased with how everything played out. "He was probably happy the fuss was somewhere else so he could go away in private here," he said. The "fuss" Rooney spoke of was the celebration held in downtown Pittsburgh at the same time as the funeral. Workers strung up a giant gold Terrible Towel in the arch of the City-County Building, and several hundred of Myron's most dedicated fans gathered in the snow to celebrate his life. Pittsburgh mayor Luke Ravenstahl led the ceremony; the Steelers were represented by Dan Rooney. "Myron did so much for the Steelers, it can't be put into words," said the seventy-six-year-old Rooney, facing the wet weather bareheaded.

The fans, many of them clad in black and gold, whooped it up when a local deejay shouted, "People who would move to Pittsburgh would say, '*Who* the heck is that guy that does Steeler games?' And I would proudly say, 'THAT'S MYRON COPE!'"

The attendees didn't hold back on expressing their sense of loss. One woman told reporters, "Pittsburgh has lost its voice." Another fan, a man in his late twenties or early thirties, had to fight back tears. "I'm very emotional right now. I'm gonna miss him. I listened to him all the time," he said.

Instead of the traditional moment of silence, the ceremony closed with a moment of Myron; all the attendees raised Terrible Towels above their heads and soundlessly whirled them through the winter air, an act that simultaneously felt peculiar, respectful, and right.

Posthumous tributes to Myron and what he accomplished continued past the funeral. At the instigation of Pennsylvania Senator Bob Casey, the U.S. Senate passed a resolution honoring Myron in March 2008. Casey also took the Senate floor for a short speech about Myron's achievements, personality, and impact. "I won't try to imitate his voice. Many do, but I won't try it because I can't do it well," said Casey. But he did throw in a yoi. "That's Y-O-I," he explained to some presumably baffled colleagues.

That May a Pittsburgh-born astronomer working at Harvard proposed naming an asteroid after Myron. The International Astronomical Union approved the suggestion a few weeks later. The three-mile-wide rock, orbiting the sun between Mars and Jupiter, now floats through the cosmos as asteroid 7835 Myroncope. The *Post-Gazette* joked that if it ever hit Earth, it would land on Cleveland.

The Terrible Towel made it to outer space later that year, when it was taken up by astronaut Mike Fincke, a Pittsburgh native, as he assumed command of the International Space Station. When the Steelers reached Super Bowl XLIII, Fincke transmitted a pregame message. He and the other astronauts would be watching the game, he said, and wished both teams the best of luck, "But in my heart," he added, "here aboard the International Space Station, its Steelers country," With that he slipped on a Steelers baseball cap, held up his Terrible Towel, and performed a weightless backflip through the air.

Two more astronauts, Andrew Morgan in 2019 and Woody Hoburg in 2023, took the Towel to the ISS. Hoburg, a Pittsburgh native, wrote on Twitter, "If you're wondering whether this yinzer brought a Terrible Towel to space, the answer is yes."

Bets are that Myron's creation will be the first sports team rally flag to fly on the moon.

The only thing missing from the tributes was Myron's own perspective on his life and passing. He had touched on the topic in a few speeches and interviews, mostly in his later years as his health declined and he felt his mortality. Sometimes he was just kidding around, predicting that he'd live to be 104 or 107, such a lengthy life that he'd be forgotten and merit only a two-paragraph obituary in the newspaper. He joked that the obit would end with the line, "He was a heavy smoker." On another occasion, in a more serious vein, he said he'd like to be recalled as a journalist who both enlightened and entertained people. "If I'm remembered as a guy who told 'em a few things they hadn't known, and made them smile once in a while, that's fine by me," he said.

He gave his most direct and most complete answer in 2005, for his appearance on *In My Own Words*, an interview-slash-biography show produced by Fox Sports Network Pittsburgh. At the end of the show, the host asked Myron, "How would you like Pittsburgh to remember you when that final day does come?" By "final day" he meant Myron's retirement from broadcasting Steelers games, which in fact was just around the corner. But the way Myron answered, he could have just as easily been talking about his final day, period.

"Well, I'd like to be remembered as a decent guy, who lived by the right rules, both professionally and personally as a human being," Myron said in a low, gravelly voice. "And if I'm remembered that way, that suits me fine. I'm not interested in rankings, or stuff like that—you know, where I might rank among Pittsburgh broadcasters. If they rank me high, I'll be complimented and be happy, if I'm somewhere where I can know about it. I've just always believed in doing the right thing. That would be the way I'd like to be remembered, [that] I was an OK guy. I was a Pittsburgh guy."

Myron would be gratified to know that in all those categories—broadcaster, Pittsburgher, and human being—he still ranks high in the minds of those who knew him, whether in person or through the airwaves that carried his unique, unforgettable, and irreplaceable voice.

Afterword

HONORED

He's been gone for well over a decade now, but Elizabeth Cope still gets regular reminders of her father's lasting presence and impact. Sometimes she'll listen to Steelers radio broadcasts and hear Craig Wolfley or Bill Hillgrove slip into a brief Myron impression. Sometimes she'll visit her parents' grave and find Terrible Towels draped over the tombstone. And anytime there's a TV story about the Towel—NBC's *Today* show did one when the Steelers played a Sunday night football game in September 2023—she can count on seeing video of her father proudly holding up his creation.

Then there are times when the reminders go well beyond passing mention. One such occasion occurred on a seemingly routine afternoon in July 2022, as Elizabeth writes:

It was a rather humdrum day, and I was driving around in my car running errands when my cell phone rang. I picked up the phone, my mind on regular everyday things, when I heard a voice on the other end of the line say, "Hi

Elizabeth, it's Art Rooney." This was not a regular everyday thing. I pulled over to the side of the road to give the call my full attention.

The last time I had spoken to Mr. Rooney was back in 2005, when my dad gave me his ticket to Super Bowl XL and I got to fly up to Detroit with the players on the Rooneys' private jet. I boarded the plane and sat down next to a man sitting alone by a window seat near the front. We talked during the whole fight. Our rapport seemed easy and natural. I wondered who he was and how he was connected to the Steelers. When we disembarked, I pulled someone aside, pointed to the man, and asked, "Who is that?"

"That's Art Rooney the second," the person exclaimed, looking at me as if to say, "Duh!"

I also recalled that when Mr. Rooney's dear mother, Patricia, passed away, I sent him a condolence card and wrote him a small note that I began with "Dear Arthur." After putting it in the mail, I realized my social misstep and phoned Lynne Molyneaux, Mr. Rooney's personal assistant, to tell her what I had done. "I don't know why I did that! I should have started my letter with 'Dear Mr. Rooney,'" I said. She laughed and said, "Don't worry about it, Elizabeth. He will probably laugh when he sees that because the only person who ever called him Arthur was his mother."

On this July afternoon, Mr. Rooney said to me, "I am calling to personally congratulate you on your father's induction into the Steelers Hall of Honor. The committee just announced the honorees yesterday. It won't be made public for another month, so I would appreciate you keep this to yourself."

"Of course, I won't tell a soul," I said. After hanging up the phone, I immediately called my best friend, Chrissy Badger, to tell her the exciting news. But otherwise, I kept it a secret.

Mr. Rooney outlined the plans for the induction weekend—a formal dinner at the stadium for the honorees and their families and box seats the next day for the Steelers' game against the Saints. The inductees would be honored on the field at halftime, and I would represent my father. "Your dad was a great man," Mr. Rooney said.

I spent the next couple of weeks agonizing over which friends and family to invite to the dinner. I wanted to celebrate with some of the people who were important to my dad since we were honoring him, not me. To do this, though, I had to leave out some of my own friends. Fortunately, Lynne Moly-

neaux had a sense of humor and let me go over my limit. This was possible because the family of the late Sam Davis, another inductee, was having the same dilemma. So the Steelers added an extra table at the dinner for what they termed the Cope and Davis overflow. Thank God there was someone else who couldn't follow the rules!

I was also trying to decide what to wear. I have a funny memory of once asking my dad what everyone wore at an event he attended. He said, "I didn't pay attention to what people were wearing. Who cares about that?" To which I replied, "Everyone cares!" Lynne told me the dinner was business casual, but since I would be asked to speak, it would certainly be appropriate for me to dress up. "Don't be afraid to be sparkly," I remember her saying. I decided on a silver sequin gown when she said this.

When occasions like the Hall of Honor roll around in my life, it reminds me that my dad is not forgotten. This touches me deeply. Not a day goes by that I don't think of him. It seems that when he was alive, the two of us were often in conflict. It pains me to admit this, but I fear that my dad was often disappointed in me. We fought quite a bit, but now that he isn't around to fight with, I realize how deeply I love him and always have. It surprises me how you can scream and yell at someone you love so much.

I have a letter he wrote to me when he was upset about something I had done or failed to do. He rails at me for paragraphs, but at the end, he signs the letter, "With All My Love, really, Dad." He drew a heart around the "Dad." Even in the worst letters, he signed "Dad" encircled with a heart. The love was always there.

The night before the dinner, after looking forward to this weekend for months, I was so excited and worked up that I was able to sleep for only a few hours. The next morning, I couldn't believe it, but I was sick. Sick as a dog! I couldn't swallow, my ear hurt, and my voice was hoarse. After months of anticipation, this happens. I prayed I didn't have stupid COVID. Can you imagine? On this most important, once-in-a-lifetime weekend?

I told Chrissy, who was staying at my house, how I felt. "Don't think about it," she coached me. "You're going to have to just push through it." Chrissy is a fourth-grade teacher, and she told me that she often has to teach when she is dead tired or not feeling well. She wouldn't let me take my temperature. "No," she scolded. "You're not sick."

I had been to the stadium for fancy dinners and events many times before with my father, but I was excited for my friends to experience it. Chrissy and I picked up two of my other closest friends, Tracie Babbitt and Maria Derrico, and drove to the stadium. Other friends and family would be staying at the Omni hotel, courtesy of the Rooneys, and the Steelers arranged for a bus to take them to the stadium. A good friend from my college days at WVU, Mary Diener, later told me a funny story about this. She said that when she got on the bus, she asked, "Is this the bus going to the stadium?" And a man immediately piped up, "No, this bus is going to the Hill District!" It was Mean Joe Greene. All the passengers laughed. Mary said he bugged her the whole ride over. I told her that not too many people can say Joe Greene wouldn't leave them alone.

When we all got to the stadium, we went to the UPMC Club on the second floor, where the party was in full swing. The room where the dinner was held was decorated beautifully, first class all the way. It was as elaborate as any wedding I've ever attended. In a way, I had looked forward to this evening as though it were my wedding. I have never been married or had children, so I feel I missed out on all those pivotal milestones in a woman's life. I regretted that my father had never been able to walk me down an aisle or hold a grandchild in his arms. He did get to attend my college graduation and see me receive my master's degree. He was so proud. This makes me happy. The only hint he ever gave of wanting those other things was one time, out of the blue, when I was in a very long-term, eleven-year relationship. He told me, "I would love to have Jason as a son-in-law." I just looked at him. What did he want me to do? I certainly wasn't going to be the one to propose!

Upon arriving at the party, I was immediately approached by someone from the Steelers and informed that after dinner, I would be the second speaker of the night, after Hall of Honor inductee Louis Lipps, the great Steelers receiver from the '80s.

I was thrown into an excited but nervous frenzy. I kept saying, "I want to go last," because I was hoping to get an idea of what to say based on the other speakers. Lynne Molyneaux was firm—I was speaking second. Chrissy, ever the organized teacher, had tried to get me to prepare a speech ahead of time, but I balked at this. I didn't want to read a speech word for word. I never do that. My father never did that, and no one on the planet was a more entertaining speaker than he! Now, however, I sort of wished I had followed Chrissy's advice.

After the dinner, they showed a video of each inductee in action. I remember in one part, my dad boomed out, "That was a shovel pass!" (Whatever that means; I probably should know these things.) My dad was the only inductee who was not a football player. That alone shows his impact on the city and people of Pittsburgh. One of the requirements to be inducted into the Hall of Honor is positive community impact. My father certainly fulfilled this during his lifetime.

After the film, the presentations began. Former Steelers running back Merril Hoge was the mc. He stood at the front of the room on a stage with the word Steelers *in lights behind him. Behind him were floor-to-ceiling windows. One could see the nighttime cityscape and stars in the black sky. And with the likes of Joe Greene, Rocky Bleier, Mel Blount, Brett Kiesel, and Ben Roethlisberger, along with their wives, scattered among the banquet tables, the night was star filled in more ways than one.*

Franco Harris was there at a table with his wife and son; I have a picture taken that night of me hugging him. Franco had been a pallbearer at my father's funeral, and I have memories of him huddled at the grave with his arms around me to keep me warm on that blustery, bitter-cold February day. I also remember his visiting my dad when he was in the ICU and dreadfully ill. My dad beamed when Franco entered the room. After the visit Franco stopped in the rooms of all the other patients on the floor. One patient was a twenty-two-year-old man who had been in a motorcycle accident. Like my dad, he was so shocked and excited when Franco entered his room. Can you imagine? Being in the hospital and then suddenly Franco Harris walks into your room to chat? So random. So Franco. That was the kind of man Franco was. I had no idea that this special night would be the last time I'd ever see him.

After a brief opening about all the inductees and Hoge's memories of them, it was time for the speakers. Louis Lipps was called up to the podium. All the football players in the room called out, "Lou! Lou! Lou!" as he walked up. It was funny, and fun, almost like being in the locker room, getting to be one of the guys. I loved it. But his short speech did little to help me prepare to follow him. When he shook Art Rooney II's hand and received his award—a custom-designed solid-steel football, the perfect emblem for the Steelers—I knew I was up next. I wanted to make my dad proud and do him justice.

Not betraying any nervousness, I bolted out of my chair and calmly walked up to the podium. I gazed out at all the faces. Franco, the Rooneys, even Chuck Noll's wife, Marianne. It was like gazing at a portrait of Myron Cope's life, and mine. It was poignant. Nostalgic. It truly felt like a pinnacle moment.

I remember that I had to adjust the microphone way down from where it was when Louis Lipps spoke. He is 5 feet 10. I am 4 feet 10. Everyone chuckled when I did this.

I went on to share some of my personal memories with my father. Everyone in the audience looked captivated—everyone but Ben Roethlisberger. He was seated at a table right in front of the podium, and out of the corner of my eye, I could see him scrolling on his phone, not even looking at me while I spoke. I pretended not to notice. I told the story of how when I was in second grade and missed a day of school, my dad provided the note excusing my absence. I had no idea what he wrote, just handed my teacher the note when I returned to school the following day. Twenty years later, I ran into this woman, my former second grade teacher, and she recognized me somehow and pulled me aside. She reminded me about my absence that day and told me that my dad had written on the slip of paper, "Elizabeth has absolutely no excuse. She is just a lazy bum." Below that he scribbled his signature. The teacher told me she had shown it to all the other teachers, and they decided to frame it. She said it hangs on the wall of the teacher's lounge of the elementary school to this day. The audience laughed heartily at this story and a few others I told. But Ben was still disengaged, texting and playing on his phone.

I ended my speech on a serious note, as I had warned the audience I might do. I told the story of how I entered my dad's hospital room the day before he died. He was sitting up in bed scribbling on a piece of paper. The scribbles were illegible.

"What are you doing," I had asked.

"I am making a list," he replied.

"A list?"

"Yes, a list of people I want at the party."

I smiled. "What party? Is someone having a party?"

He looked at me with annoyance on his face. "Of course, there will be a party," he stated matter-of-factly.

"Who is throwing this party?" I asked.

"The Rooneys, who else?" he exclaimed, as if I should have already known that.

"The Rooneys!" I exclaimed. "What are they celebrating?"

My dad paused and then said softly, almost as if just to himself, "We're celebrating my life, of course."

I just sat there staring at him.

He looked over at me and then screwed up his face as if trying to decide something and said, "You're not invited."

I burst out laughing.

"Well, that's not a very nice thing to say!" I told him.

I went on to explain how my dad had turned his head away from me and gazed wistfully out his hospital window at the slip of moon in the night sky. "The limo is coming for me soon," he whispered. "The Rooneys have sent a limo to come and get me. Everyone is waiting. I am the guest of honor."

During this story, Ben put his phone down and looked up at me, listening intently. A look of sympathy flashed across his face.

I ended my speech saying the Rooneys were throwing a party and my dad was indeed one of the guests of honor. I then looked up toward the sky and said, "But I am invited, Dad!"

I exited the podium to a round of applause. I felt exuberant, wistful. Odd mixtures of happiness and sadness filled me. I returned to my seat at the table I was sharing with my family members. My cousin Marcia, sitting across from me, smiled and gave me the thumbs up to let me know I had done good.

Speeches wrapped up at 8:15 p.m., and the honorees and their guests were given a special tour of the Steelers' Hall of Honor Museum. To do this with my family and friends was awesome. One of the best parts was when Chrissy and I entered a booth where we got to pretend to broadcast a game, to do what my dad did for a living. I did the color analysis, of course. The words would come up on the screen, and we'd shout into the microphones like sportscasters at a game. I had to say things like "Gadzooks!" as Chrissy called the imaginary play. On a wall behind us hung a life-size photo of my dad, looking down as though he was watching our "broadcast." Oh, what fun we had! Every Steelers fan should take the time to tour this museum.

Then, toward the end of the night, as fate would have it, I bumped into Ben Roethlisberger. The last time I had seen him before this evening was at a party in Detroit in 2006 after the Steelers beat the Seahawks in Super Bowl XL. I remember that Snoop Dog and Kid Rock were also at this party. Ben had strolled in wearing a white terrycloth bathrobe, smoking a cigar like he was Hugh Hefner or something.

Now, back at the Hall of Honor Museum, Ben was standing before me again. It was fitting because he had stood before me on the field seventeen years before when my dad was being celebrated at the Monday night game against Baltimore, and Ben was just beginning his legendary career. Here we stood again, face to face, as my dad was being admitted into the Hall of Honor and Ben's career had just ended—once again, meeting at the crossroads of life, that invisible clock above our heads coming full circle.

This time I spoke up. "Do you miss playing football?" I asked him. Not a very profound question.

He paused, as if thinking about it. "Not at all, really," he finally said, and then added, "Not even a little bit." This surprised me. I suppose it was just time. The time had come for retirement, and he had been ready. His body was probably pretty banged up, I imagine.

Then I asked if I could have a picture with him. This kind of humiliated me. I was acting like a typical fan, which a part of me hated. How many times during my life had people approached my dad wanting a damn picture? I didn't want to be that person.

But Ben didn't mind. "Sure," he said. I now have a photograph with me in my silver sequin gown and Ben in a suit and tie with his arm around me, both of us smiling. It is a good picture. It is an even better memory.

I arose the next morning at 5:30 to get ready for the game, where all the inductees would be honored on the field at halftime. Chrissy, Maria, and Tracie accompanied me again, all wearing Steelers jerseys with cope on the back. These were the jerseys my dad always wore to his aftergame show, Cope's Cabana. This time, we also picked up my brother, Danny, at his group home. It was important that he be present on this monumental day. My dad would want that. I did, too.

First we stopped at the Omni hotel for an 8:30 breakfast extravaganza that the Steelers prepared for all the honorees. My friends and I got stuck in an elevator. I've got a picture in a Shutterfly album of us smiling while waiting out the delay. I wrote above the photo, "What do you do when the elevator refuses to move? Take a selfie, of course!" I laugh every time I see it.

Lynn Molyneaux gave out the field and box passes to everyone at breakfast. I was allowed to have three of my guests accompany me on the field before the game. I chose Chrissy, Marcia, and Danny. It was my cousin Marcia's seventy-fifth birthday on this special day. Unbeknownst to her, I had planned for a huge cake to be delivered to the party box right after halftime. I also had Joe Greene, who of course was No. 75 during his career, sign a birthday card for her.

We all went onto the field before the game and watched the players warm up. I have a picture of T. J. Watt running drills right in front of my face. It was cold that November morning, but the last people to leave the field before the game began were me and Chrissy. They had to shoo us off the field. Then we went up to the party box, where they had frosted football cookies and an array of sandwiches, cheeses, and drinks of every variety. I had been in box seats a few times before in my life, and I was excited for my friends and family to experience this. Life means more with friends. They are the story of our lives, I like to say.

My brother, Danny, seemed to be having a blast, too. He was smiling ear to ear. I was so glad he was there. My cousins Sarah, Peggy, and Marcia were watching him for me. He is usually very easy, just sits and smiles. How I wish my dad could have been with us on this special day.

As halftime approached, all the honorees were gathered up to go down to the field. I was allowed to bring Chrissy, Marcia, and Danny with me, but they couldn't go onto the grass. We all walked down to the Pitt locker room, passing through stadium halls dotted with one-of-a-kind photos of players and team owners. We stopped at the big silver football on the wall and touched it for good luck, just like the players do. I even instructed Danny to touch it, and I snapped a photo of him. He had a Terrible Towel draped over his shoulder thanks to Chrissy. I thought he resembled my dad.

All the honorees were given Steelers letterman jackets. I had known that this was going to happen because months before, Lynne Molyneaux had called me to get my size. She told me it was the first time the Steelers ever had to order a women's XXS jacket.

We all milled around the locker room, where a reporter and a cameraman approached to tell me a few funny stories about my dad. Then they had us line up to go out for the ceremony. Because it was cold, I was wearing a Steelers hat, but I decided to take it off so that I would look my best; I knew I would be photographed and suspected that it might be on the news (which it was). I'd be darned if I was going to have a hat smashed down on my hair. Beauty is painful, guys.

I'm glad I made this last-minute decision because I now have a photo of myself holding up the Terrible Towel on the field, with my hair blowing in the breeze. I look triumphant. It encapsulates the pure joy I felt on this day.

Soon it was time. We all marched out onto the field to our introductions. As I marched out, I saw Andrew Stockey from WTAE and his girlfriend, Jen, in seats close to the tunnel, and they waved frantically at me. I remember wondering how I should walk. I know this sounds absurd, but it did pop into my head—should I saunter out, walk humbly, or what? I am quite certain that none of the other inductees paid any attention to this detail and just walked out like any other human being would do. But I decided I was going to march out as confidently as I could. I actually bounced out with a jaunt in my step and took my place on the field. All the honorees waved Terrible Towels.

Everyone in the stands cheered as our names were called, and we waved our towels. When Heath Miller was introduced, everyone in the stadium chanted "Heath! Heath! Heath!" I gazed up at the sky and let the breeze caress my face as I thought about my father. I missed him. How could he not be here? I didn't understand. He should be here. I wondered where he was. He was so alive during his life; it was impossible to believe that he wasn't somewhere.

I gazed out at the packed stadium. I felt determined. Who was I? Myron Cope's daughter? I felt the hungry bear of determination growing inside of me, wanting to live life fully, not timidly, in spite of my suffering and loss. I could no longer wait to feel better, stronger, or less sad. I wanted to do things that mattered, to make my parents proud. Time was precious, and I wanted to use it wisely.

Soon it was time to exit. Show over, curtain closed. Another act and chapter over in the ever-marching-forward Steelers history. I was in awe to be a small part of it, even if it was from a time passed. It was a chapter in my life as well.

We all walked back to the party box, where we celebrated my cousin Marcia's seventy-fifth birthday. No one had made mention of her birthday this entire weekend, and this was on purpose; we all wanted it to be a total surprise. So Lynn Molyneaux made an announcement in the party box that there was another special occasion to celebrate today. Everyone stopped what they were doing and looked up, and I entered with that enormous cake decorated with yellow and black frosted balloons. It read, "Happy 75th birthday Marcia." She was stunned. We cut the cake and gave a piece to everyone in the box. Such a happy moment!

Best of all, the Steelers won. Defeated the Saints. Just like on Monday Night Myron all those years ago. Sometimes you can have your cake and eat it, too.

Later on, back at the Omni, I went up to my cousins Sarah and Peggy's room, where we all reminisced about my parents and our growing-up years. There were many funny stories. The humorous ones usually involved my father and Danny, things they would do. We kept saying, "Remember when . . ." It was so much fun. My poor brother fell asleep on one of the beds, fully clothed, with his Steelers pass still around his neck and a Terrible Towel at his side. We snapped a picture of him, which is on the back cover of my Shutterfly album for the weekend. I wrote a caption: "Zzzzzzzz . . ." A perfect way to end the album and the day.

Lying in my bed late that night, I thought about my dad and began to cry. I cried not from sadness but from a profound sense of pride and relief. It seems like my dad's life made—and is still making—a difference in the world, in the hearts and lives of people he loved and so many others he never knew. I was filled with an immense gratitude that is hard to describe. That my father is still receiving recognition and is still remembered fifteen years after his death makes me realize that his story is still unfolding. He lives inside me and is still teaching me.

Appendix

COPE'S CATALOG

When asked in 2005 how he'd like to be remembered, Myron Cope answered, after a bit of rambling, "As a pretty decent writer." For all his success as the Steelers' color analyst, as a commentator, as a talk show host, and as fundraiser for charity, Myron derived his greatest satisfaction from the work he did for the page. "I took more pride in my writing because that's what I was educated to do, and I had a gift for it," he said in his last TV interview. "When you wrote a piece you could sit down and read it and know whether you'd done a good job or not. With broadcasting it's in one ear and out the other."

To honor Myron's wishes, I've compiled what aims to be a complete catalog of the stories he penned during his run as one of America's top freelance sportswriters, from the mid-1950s to the late 1970s. To an extent, this is like tracking down people not seen since the moon landing. None of Myron's articles have vanished; they're all still out there, either in books or libraries or in magazines stacked in somebody's basement, next to boxes of old Sinatra LPs and Grandpa's fedoras. But for every piece that's been republished a dozen times, like Myron's famous profiles of Howard Cosell, Roberto Clemente, and Muhammad Ali, there are twenty others that require deep-sea online diving just to nail down basic information, like title, subject, and date of publication. No one, it seems, has compiled an index of the sports and general-interest magazines that Myron wrote for in their mid-twentieth-century heyday. *Sports Illustrated* and the *Saturday Evening Post* have put all their back issues online, but try hunting down editions of *True* or *Sport*, which both carried many a Cope byline. Info on *Life* magazine articles is easy to come by; *Look*, not so much.

But difficult does not mean impossible, and with the help of Google, Newspapers.com, the ever expanding Internet Archive, the awesome Terrible Blogger website, and various anthologies of good sportswriting, I've pulled together a catalog of the approximately 130 magazine pieces that Myron composed. Have I read them all? No. Many have yet to emerge from the figurative basement. But I've read (or skimmed) the majority, and believe me, most are worth at least few minutes' time, if one appreciates vivid, insightful, flat-out funny sportswriting or if one simply wants to learn about the colorful, sometimes larger-than-life characters who populated the sporting world of the 1960s and '70s.

A few parameters. This list does not include the hundreds of newspaper stories Myron wrote in the early part of his career. Finding and indexing all those would take the better part of a year. Nor does it cover the stories he dashed off for small hometown publications like *Pittsburgh* magazine, *Pittsburgh Sports Weekly*, and *Steelers Digest*.

The magazines are listed in chronological order of when Myron first wrote for them.

Sir!

"The Female of the Species," September 1951. Myron's first published magazine story and a completely different animal from anything he created afterward. For one thing, it's the only magazine story he wrote under his real name, Myron Kopelman. Thing number two, it's fiction. Third, it was published in a "stag" magazine, sort of an early, tame version of *Playboy*. The story itself is nothing extraordinary—it's about a professional wrestler and a dame he pulls into his line of work—but it does have flashes of

Myron's wit and humor. Best line: the dame wears a shirt "with a neckline which had never known the proximity of a neck."

The Sporting News

"Penn State Flying High on Winged T," October 13, 1954. This appears to be Myron's first nonfiction article for a national magazine. In the one-page article, he profiles the '54 Nittany Lions squad, including their coach Rip Engle (Joe Paterno's predecessor) and two future NFL greats, running back Lenny Moore and defensive tackle Rosey Grier.

"Finks-to-Mathews Comeback Leaves Pitt Fans Pass Happy," October 27, 1954. That's a slightly misleading headline; the article is about the Steelers, not the Panthers. The Steelers were rarely pass-happy in the '50s, but Myron scored a story after QB Jim Finks and receiver Ray Mathews connected for three touchdowns in a 55–27 victory over the Browns. Early dash of Cope color: "Finks, a slim, intense man, playing with a triple facture of the jaw and wearing a face guard that made him look like a man from Mars."

"Lattner Converts Doubts to Shouts," November 3, 1954. A profile of Heisman Trophy winner turned Steeler Johnny Lattner. Best line: "He is a man of infinite humility which somehow never becomes nauseating."

"Pitt Reverses Field under Captain Tom," November 10, 1954. A recap of a then rare three-game winning streak by Pitt's football squad under interim coach Tom Hamilton.

"Cameron, Stits Reverse Their Field as Pros," December 3, 1954. Review of two former UCLA running backs snagging interceptions in the NFL: Bill Stits with the Lions and Paul Cameron with the Steelers.

"Si Green, Brother Act Dukes' Hopes with Thin Squad," December 15, 1954. Profile of Duquesne University basketball team. Standout line, about Green: "He stands six-three, but jumps as though he were six-six."

"Sideliner in '55, Headliner in '56—That's Story of Pitt's Theodore," October 31, 1956. Profile of Pitt halfback Jimmy Theodore. Myron must have done a hell of a sales job on this one; Theodore was a flash-in-the-plan who ran for barely 400 yards and two touchdowns that year.

"Hennon, 5'9, Cuts Giants to Size as Panther Prize," January 16, 1957. Profile of Pitt's undersized All-American basketball star Don Hennon.

"Steelers Hocked to 5 Clubs for Dozen Draftees," November 6, 1957. Myron documents the start of an infamous Steelers policy that saw the team trade draft picks for established veterans. The practice lifted the team's fortunes in the short run but led to a steep decline in the mid-1960s, when the picks ran out and the talent grew old. Best line: "The Steelers personify the modern philosophy of living on time payments."

"Pitt's Attack Recalls Dream Backfield of '38," October 15, 1958. Over-optimistic story on a Pitt team that finished 5-4-1.

Saturday Evening Post

"Customer's Man with a Fast Ball," August 4, 1956. Myron's big national breakthrough, his first piece with one of the most popular magazines in the country. His subject was Pirates pitcher Bob Friend, a workhorse who lasted sixteen years in the big leagues but sold stocks and ran an oil-drilling venture on the side. Friend had convinced two coaches, the team's laundry guy, and a utility infielder to join him in the latter, and Myron reported that the venture "must come through or he will have no peace in this clubhouse."

"Amazing Half Pint," February 1, 1958. Myron's second profile of Don Hennon, with a detailed look at the star and his dad in little Wampum, Pennsylvania. Butler Hennon was a high school coaching legend whose teams once won eighty-two league games in a row.

"It's Tough to Get by Joe," November 29, 1958. Profile of Pitt alumni and Detroit Lions star linebacker Joe Schmidt.

"Baseball's Mister Mischief," May 9, 1959. A close look at Pirates manager Danny Murtaugh, who was named baseball's Manager of the Year after the Bucs climbed from seventh place to second in 1958. Myron covers Murtaugh's entire life, including his years as a mill worker and his relatively short playing career. One favorite line: "His clubhouse humor had a nice, light touch, but unfortunately his bat did too."

"I Coddle the Maestros," with John S. Edwards, November 7, 1959. An interesting detour for Myron, as he and his cowriter, manager of the Pittsburgh Symphony, chronicle the lengths to which orchestras go to keep their conductors and musicians happy.

"Unpredictable All-American," January 9, 1960. Profile of West Virginia basketball star and future NBA Hall of Famer Jerry West.

"What's Got into the Pirates?" September 17, 1960. Myron examines the success of his hometown baseball team, charging toward its first pennant in thirty-three years. Several key players are sketched in Copeian style, such as rotund catcher Smokey Burgess, who in Myron's words "looks less like an athlete than like a traveling man for a farm implement company."

"Ohio State's Icy All-American," December 10, 1960. Another story about a college basketball star, this time Jerry Lucas.

"Stars Who Fooled the Coaches," October 21, 1961. Myron looks at football stars who were rejected by one or more teams before finding glory. Naturally, he highlights the case of the 1955 Steelers' cutting of Johnny Unitas, who by decade's end had become the NFL's top passer and led the Colts to back-to-back championships. Myron writes, "To cite the league records that Unitas has smashed would amount to inhumane treatment of Art Rooney, the cigar-chewing owner of the Steelers, who has suffered enough from the memory."

"The Coach Who Beat the Mob," October 28, 1961. Profile of Pitt's head football coach Johnny Michelosen, whom the school employed for over a decade despite so-so results and ultra-conservative play-calling that drove Panthers fans nuts. "He is at once the object of bitter criticism and warm confidence," Myron writes.

"Irrepressible Egotist," April 28, 1962. A profile of the Pirates' first baseman Dick Stuart, a braggadocious sort whose home runs tended to be canceled out by his errors and strikeouts.

"Reluctant All-American," December 15, 1962. Still another story on a college basketball All-American, Rod Thorn of West Virginia. This was the type of article that made Myron grow weary of the *Post* and seek outlets that would let him choose more interesting subjects.

"King Edward of Pitt," April 6, 1963. An article on the ambitious and sometimes controversial chancellor at the University of Pittsburgh, Edward Litchfield. It has a great opening line: "Edward Harold Litchfield, erect, crisp and just a beaked nose short of being handsome, is an educator who disdains modest goals."

"Profile of a Bookmaker," April 27, 1963. Myron meets up with a small-town midwestern bookie and details his mode of operation. The bookie, Harry Ruske, has a natural knack for numbers and gambling, Myron reports: "On graduation he got a job driving a bakery truck, and then, when war broke out, was drafted into the Army, where he served with distinction in craps games."

"Kiss the Guy or Tackle Him?" October 26, 1963. Myron highlights the ruggedness of Steelers running back John Henry Johnson: "Johnson stands 6-foot-2, weighs 225 pounds and in his vast hands a football looks no larger than a cake of soap."

"Sunday's Human Targets," December 21, 1963. Good story about the punishment faced by pro football quarterbacks, but the best part is Myron's description of Steelers offensive tackle Ernie Stautner: "His face, complete with pugilist's washboard nose, is shaped like a large, square rock and seems to have been stuffed into his shoulders by years of head-on contact. 'He came into the league six-feet-four,' says his friend Bobby Layne, 'and will go out three-feet-seven.'"

"The Minister Who Follows the Migrants," January 4, 1964. A real rarity in Myron's career, a profile of humanitarian Frank Reyes, a Baptist minister who made it his task to champion and care for itinerant farm workers. The article suggests that Myron had the writing and reporting skills to build a serious journalism career had he chosen that path. "[Reyes] is outraged," he writes, "by the fact that a nation which spends billions on foreign aid scarcely lifts a finger to wipe out the misery of people who tend American soil."

"How to Be a Loser with Four Aces," June 6, 1964. Sounds like a story about a baseball team with four great starters, but no—it's about a father of quadruplets who despite ample publicity and sympathy can't seem to catch a break in life.

"The Whip Who Put Snap in the Phillies," August 8, 1964. Profile of Philadelphia Phillies manager Gene Mauch. The article is complimentary toward Mauch, a sharp, tightly wound type who appeared to have his team destined for the '64 National League pennant. Little did Myron know. Up by six and a half games with just twelve to go, the Phillies dropped ten in a row and let the pennant slip away.

"Baseball's Richest Rookie," September 19, 1964. Myron chats with Rick Reichardt, who had just received the biggest bonus to date in baseball history—$200,000—to sign with the California Angels. Myron quotes Angels staff (including future Pirates manager Chuck Tanner) who enthusiastically—and ridiculously—compare Reichardt to Mickey Mantle.

"Showdown for a Quarterback," October 17, 1964. Myron previews an upcoming Pitt-Navy contest featuring the Midshipmen's defending Heisman Trophy winner, Roger Staubach, and Pitt's heralded pass thrower Freddy Mazurek. The game turned out to be a dud, with neither QB throwing for a touchdown in a 14–14 tie.

"Muslim Champ," November 14, 1964. Two years earlier, Myron profiled a rising heavyweight boxer named Cassius Clay (for *True*). Now he returns for a follow-up after Clay beat Sonny Liston for the title, announced his conversion to Islam, and changed his name to Muhammad Ali. Best line: "He has been consumed by a Messianic complex, but because he is a prophet who enjoys the feel of cash he will defend the championship against Liston next Monday."

"Willie Pastrano: Champion of Non-Violence," March 27, 1965. Pastrano was light-heavyweight boxing champ of the world, but as Myron explains, he was a pacifist at heart and a classic case of a guy becoming a prizefighter so he could defend himself in a rough neighborhood.

"The Angel Who Doesn't Fear to Tread," April 10, 1965. Profile of California Angels ace hurler Dean Chance, a country boy making good in LA. Myron notes that Chance had fallen under the spell of his night-crawling, pool-playing teammate Bo Belinsky and reports, "In the trunk of his car he now carried a $50 pool cue, complete with soft-grain leather case."

"The Mecca Lunch Kid," August 14, 1965. Profile of Pete Ward, White Sox third baseman. He's forgetful, he dresses sloppy. Comes from Mecca Lunch, Oregon. There's not much else to tell, but Myron's writing carries the day: Ward "is an oddity, not merely because of his absent-mindedness but because he carries a bat that is not exactly in the Sox tradition. He hits baseballs over fences."

"All-America Teams are Phony (Speaking Out)," December 4, 1965. Taking a break from profiles, Myron writes an editorial about the stupidity of college football All-American squads, which at the time were unquestionably based more on publicity and prominence than on-field accomplishment. He cites several examples, the starkest being that of USC running back Mike Garrett. "He accounted for more than half of Southern Cal's rushing yardage last year and acquired a reputation for all-around ability when *Playboy* put him on its preseason all-America defensive team. Never mind that last year he didn't play at all on defense."

"The Rich, Full Life of a Bad Guy," February 12, 1966. Myron takes a detailed look at the world of professional wrestling and one of its most popular, successful villains, Cowboy Bill Watts.

"A Last Cigar for Red Auerbach's Last Hurrah?" March 26, 1966. Profile of the Boston Celtics' ever-stogied coach and owner Red Auerbach, who was just about to win his seventh consecutive NBA title.

"Joe Torre: The Last of the Great Catchers," July 2, 1966. A fine story with a bad headline. Johnny Bench was right around the corner. Torre, of course, is better known today for managing the New York Yankees to four World Series titles in five years.

"Texas Football: Fierce, Frantic, Fabulous," September 24, 1966. Myron ventures to the Lone Star State to chronicle the intensity of the state's college football rivalries. Best quote: "'We think we're still frontiersmen,' explains one Texan. 'There are no more wars down here, so we make our own.'"

"Floyd Little: 'Half a Glass of Fresh Blood on Saturday Morning,'" November 19, 1966. Myron profiles the Syracuse running back and future NFL Hall of Famer, whom he portrays as a perfectionist yelling at his teammates: "Study your plays!" The vampirish headline, incidentally, was a joking response Little gave when someone asked him how he gets ready for a game.

"Visions of Super Stars Dance in His Head," May 4, 1968. Profile of Mark McCormack, Cleveland-based business manager for clean-cut superstars like Arnold Palmer, Jack Nicklaus, and Fran Tarkenton. Myron does an excellent job of capturing the atmosphere in his subject's offices: "McCormack will be off to New York in two days, but while he is town the 13th floor explodes with conferences, phone calls, memoranda, big deals, small deals, cablegrams, and mini-skirted secretaries trotting clickety-clack through the corridors, sometimes on the verge of tears: 'Here we go again! Do the impossible!'"

True

"You Gotta Fight Dirty," June 1958. This is an "as told to" piece on Pittsburgh boxer and former welterweight champion Fritzie Zivic, who expounds on why fighters use their thumbs, elbows, and foreheads, in addition to their fists, to score points in the ring.

"They Buried Layne Too Soon," November 1959. Profile of Hall of Fame quarterback and Myron's sometime drinking buddy Bobby Layne, a year after he was traded by the Detroit Lions to Pittsburgh. In this article and others to come, Myron depicts Layne as savior of the Steelers, field general par excellence, and the life of the party. But the best line is about Steelers head coach Buddy Parker, who Myron says traded for Layne "with the desperation of a last-place coach who can almost see the workmen coming to rub his name off the office door."

"Crazy Like a Silver Fox," January 1961. Myron turns his gaze on Villanova basketball coach Al Severance, an often mocked figure known for being long winded, absent-minded, untutored in the finer details of his sport, but in the end an undeniable success. "Philadelphia's demanding fandom blisters him as an aging relic who is slightly touched in the head," Myron writes. "Yet if Al Severance is crazy, he must be crazy like a fox, for his Villanova teams . . . have won 404 games and suffered only 188 defeats."

"The Toughest Pirate Since Captain Kidd," May 1961. Profile of Pirates third baseman Don Hoak. Contains a telling quote from Hoak's teammate Hal Smith: "I've heard him chewing out himself on the field. He actually stands out there and yells at himself."

"Baseball's Perpetual Motion Pitch-Man," September 1961. Profile of Frank Lane, a baseball general manager famous for his constant, almost compulsive, trading of his players.

"Feats of Clay," July 1962. Myron's prizewinning profile of the loquacious, poetry-spinning twenty-year-old Cassius Clay as he climbs through the boxing ranks en route to becoming heavyweight champion. He chronicles how Clay routinely touts himself to all passerby as the best (and prettiest) fighter in the world but notes that the young boxer has champion-level skills: "From the opening bell this night, [Clay's opponent] Willi Besmanoff stalked Cassius grimly but the German must have felt he was fighting a man with six arms."

"Bo Belinsky's Dilemma: Baseball or Dames?" October 1962. Myron details the struggle of the Los Angeles Angels pitcher who could not decide whether his profession or his passion would rule his life. Choice description: Belinsky "throws a baseball very fast but wildly and enjoys living the same way."

"A True Report on Cash and Carry Politics," November 1962. Myron plays political reporter and uncovers how the Kennedy campaign spread money around Logan County, West Virginia, to ensure victory for JFK in a key 1960 presidential primary. Myron was proud of the piece and republished it in full in his autobiography, but he lamented that not a single newspaper, magazine, or media outlet ever bothered to highlight his findings.

"Pro Football's Gashouse Gang," September 1964. Myron's chronicle of the high-living, hard-partying 1963 Steelers and their chase for the NFL Eastern Division title. According to Myron, the Steelers could've beaten the Giants in the division-deciding season finale had quarterback Ed Brown not chosen to ease up on his drinking. "To the utter dismay of those who know the Steelers best," Myron wrote, "quarterback Brown . . . took the big game too seriously. On the Wednesday before the showdown battle, he disappeared from his favorite saloon. He went into training."

"A Dialogue between Baseball's Bigmouths," August 1965. Myron chronicles the summit of two of baseball's loudest, proudest personalities, Bo Belinsky and Dick Stuart, as they trade stories about Bo's success with women and Stu's home runs and Stu's legendarily bad fielding and other stuff. Myron sums it up in one line: "If managers could place ballplayers in solitary confinement, Belinsky and Stuart undoubtedly would be leading the major leagues in time served."

"Look Out, World! Here Comes Super Jew," March 1967. Profile of Mike Epstein, a rare Jewish slugger who would spend eight years in the American League. "Such a build on him, you wouldn't believe," Myron writes in a Jewish mother rhythm. He adds: "Except for the curly brown hair and a flattened nose, Mike Epstein is a twenty-three-year-old Mickey Mantle bred on blintzes and gefilte fish."

"Easy Times in Baseball's Hog Heaven," July 1967. Myron talks with Jim Nash, a very relaxed, easygoing Georgian who burst into the Majors with a 12-1 rookie season but was never that good again, possibly because he didn't put sufficient thought into his pitching. Myron writes, "Here was a rube who would need a brain when they started timing his fastball, and he wouldn't have one."

"Who's the Broad in Pro Football's Huddle?" December 1968. Myron introduces readers to Eleanor Kane, one of the first female sportswriters who insisted on access to press boxes and locker rooms.

"In New Jersey, He's Mr. White Vigilante," May 1969. Myron makes one of his periodic forays outside the sports world to chat with Tony Imperiale, the leader of a white "self-defense" group in Newark, New Jersey.

Sports Illustrated

"Beano and the 3 C's," November 11, 1960. Myron profiles his buddy Pitt sports publicist Beano Cook. Like a true pal, he tosses in a little dig: "While working as a copy boy for *The Pittsburgh Press* he was advised, after submitting several pieces, that he had no talent for writing. So, quite logically, he became a press agent."

"An Elderly Diomedes in the Big Show," July 16, 1962. Myron examines the curious case of Diomedes Olivo, a forty-three(ish)-year-old pitcher who hurled briefly but effectively for the Pirates in the early 1960s. Olivo was a legend in his native Dominican Republic but had long resisted offers to pitch in the United States. "For one thing," Myron explains, "he had no taste for working his way up through the minors; then, too, he feared being shipped to a segregated southern town and felt his ignorance of English would make life doubly hard."

"Saturday's Hero Is Doing Fine," October 8, 1962, with Edward Litchfield. An "as told to" story, as University of Pittsburgh chancellor Litchfield argues that higher education and big-time college sports are compatible, at least at Pitt. It's unusually dry and wordy for a Cope piece—no doubt due to Litchfield—but it has one nice line: "While Peanuts Lewis, a pugnacious guard with our 1930 Rose Bowl team, may have dislodged a few teeth from the mouths of opposing linemen, he has more than atoned by pioneering new techniques in lower denture prosthesis."

"Mossie Murphy's Crusade," January 28, 1963. Good profile of an independent Duquesne basketball recruiter whose aggressive practices caused him to be somewhat shunned by his own school. "Though unequivocally devoted to his alma mater," Myron writes, "Mossie has received the sort of requital usually given suitors who have bad breath and heavy beards."

"The Pitching Explosion in Paradise," June 24, 1963. Cover story on the pitching-rich but hitting-poor 1963 Pirates. Cope sums it up: "The club has one drawback. Its hitting has resembled something you might see at Miss Pennypacker's Finishing School. The Pirates hit singles, lots of them, but runs they simply do not produce."

"Just Call Me Football's Greatest Scout," September 30, 1963. Myron was known in the magazine world as the "nut specialist," and this piece demonstrates why. Fido Murphy was a very able NFL scout for the Bears and Steelers, but in his cockeyed view, he was the Greatest Mind Football Had Ever Seen. Myron writes, "Deadly earnest, Fido barks: 'It isn't that I'm smarter than everyone else in football. It's just that I *know* more.'"

"Kind Hearts and Cauliflowers," October 19, 1964. A look back at a heavyweight fighter, Will Greaves, who some thought was destined for the championship but lost his motivation when his manager died.

"Rocky Calls It Skuldujjery," January 25, 1965. Myron talks to former heavyweight boxing champ Rocky Marciano about the only fight he ever lost, a three-round amateur bout in which Rocky insisted he was robbed.

"The Prince of Pittsburgh," September 13, 1965. Great portrait of Pirates radio play-by-play man Bob Prince. Opens with the famous story of Prince accepting a $20 bet to dive from a third-story balcony into a hotel pool.

"Aches and Pains and Three Batting Titles," March 7, 1966. Myron's often anthologized examination of Roberto Clemente's renowned hypochondria. Clemente disliked the portrayal and didn't talk to Myron for a year after publication, but how can you not smile at lines like, "He is one of the world's great insomniacs because, he explained earnestly, he lies awake worrying that he will not be able to fall asleep."

"The Babe Cobb of Puerto Rico," May 16, 1966. Interesting piece about baseball star Orlando Cepeda's father, Pedro Cepeda, a legend in Puerto Rico who was born too early to benefit from the integration of Major League baseball.

"El Spahnie of Los Tigres," July 4, 1966. Myron flies south to see retired Braves great Warren Spahn pitch one last game for a Mexican team.

"Pittsburgh's Patient Whipping Boy," December 19, 1966. A look at the incessant booing unleashed on Charlie Bradshaw, a Steelers right tackle who inexplicably became the fans' scapegoat for the team's mid-1960s misery.

"Would You Let This Man Interview You?" March 13, 1967. Myron's famous profile of the wondrously egotistical Howard Cosell. On the occasion of *SI*'s fiftieth anniversary in 2004, the magazine named it as one of the best articles in its history.

"Agent 26250, Where Are You?" October 2, 1967. One of Myron's classics. Taking a page from George Plimpton's playbook, Myron suited up as a Pinkerton security guard for a weekend. Best lines: "It seemed essential to be [a guard] in order to grasp fully the spirit of the agency, so I had studied the company's operation carefully and drawn up a list of assignments that carried a potential for danger. Eliminating these, I asked to be attached for a couple of days to a golf tournament."

"Top Man on the Laugh Tour," October 30, 1967. Fun look at golf trick-shot artist Paul Hahn.

"The Big Z and his Misfiring Pistons," December 18, 1967. Profile of Fred Zollner, owner of the NBA's Detroit Pistons.

"Bituminous Time in the Bronx," February 12, 1968. Myron's memorable look back at the Pitt-Fordham rivalry in the mid-1930s, when the teams played to 0–0 ties for three consecutive years. Best passage: "Stebbins ran brilliantly. Time and again he knifed his way to sizeable distances. The only trouble was, he kept leaving the ball behind for Fordham to fall on."

"Angry Overseer of the Marathon," April 22, 1968. Cover story on Jock Sample, the Boston Marathon official who tried to rip the tag off a woman who dared to enter the previously all-male race.

"They Cheer When the Parson Is Pitching," May 27, 1968. Profile of Olympic pole vaulter turned motivational speaker Bob Richards.

"A Firm Hand on a Carefree Cat," June 17, 1968. The inside story of how golfer Lee Trevino likes to spend money but his wife Claudia "keeps the key to the bank." Talk about good timing; the article was published a day before Trevino won the U.S. Open.

"Harry Has His Own Ways," October 7, 1968. Nice profile of the always colorful Harry Caray when he called games for the St. Louis Cardinals. Caray never held back on criticizing the ballplayers, and even some of the Cardinals, Myron reports, would enjoy "seeing him transferred to ping-pong matches in Yokohama."

"Dicky Does a Bit of Everything but Dicker," November 11, 1968. The scoop on how University of Kentucky tailback Dicky Lyons keeps his teammates focused—by punching them and beating them up. Myron would not be able to take such a jocular approach to this subject today.

"The Proudest Squares," November 18, 1968. One of Myron's longer pieces, printed across nine pages, dissects the depths of passion that Texas A&M students and alumni have for their football team. Includes interesting comments on the late-1960s friction between counter-culture types and conservative Texans. When a Students for a Democratic Society cell opened at A&M, Myron writes, it popped up like a "pouch of marijuana in a bowl of Wheaties."

"Nobody Waits on This Lefty," May 10, 1969. Profile of Davidson College basketball coach Lefty Drisell.

"The Game That Was," October 20 and 27, 1969. This series was first fruit of Myron's interviews with old-time NFL stars like Sammy Baugh and Red Grange and lesser-known but renowned players like Ed Healy and Indian Joe Gunyon. He boiled down the interviews into a compelling oral history of what it was like to be a football player in the 1920s, '30s, and '40s, which *SI* liked enough to run across twenty pages in two issues. These interviews and others were collected the following year into Myron's best-known book, also titled *The Game That Was*.

"Chancey Games in Ohio," March 30, 1970. Pitcher Dean Chance, one of Myron's favorite subjects, enters the world of boxing promotion.

"Loose and Fun-Loving off the Field," November 16 and 23, 1970. An "as told to" story, with Myron channeling the words of one Alex Hawkins, a ten-year NFL veteran who specialized in versatility. The self-deprecating Hawkins claims he played six different positions in the league "and did none of them justice!" Too many great lines to mention, a favorite being: "I booked the back room at the Golden Arm [restaurant] . . . and leaked the word that I intended to announce my retirement. The turnout was huge and I might say, enthusiastic."

"Often Bloody, but Uncowed," May 3, 1971. Myron Cope profiles golfer Dave Hill, the pro tour's most outspoken and temperamental player. Best example: "On the tour he once terminated a motel room game of gin when, after playing 30 straight losing hands, he picked up his fully packed suitcase and hurled it through the window, not taking the trouble to open the window."

"And for Their Next Number . . . ," August 9, 1971. A story on the dominance of Jack Nicklaus and Arnold Palmer at golf's (now-defunct) National Team Championship, held in Laurel Valley, Pennsylvania, about fifteen minutes from Arnie's home.

"Teaching Junior the Palmer Method," August 7, 1972. Story about an obscure teenage golfer suddenly paired with Arnold Palmer at a golf tournament.

"Waist Deep in the Big Muddy," February 5, 1973. One of Myron's odder assignments, covering the world of swamp buggy racing in Florida.

"Where There's Smoke, There's Luis," May 7, 1973. A profile of Boston Red Sox pitcher Luis Tiant. It has a great description of Tiant's go-to pitch—"a searing fastball delivered repetitiously but from a greater variety of angles than could be mustered by an octopus."

"The Immaculate Reception and Other Miracles," August 20, 1973. Myron recaps the Steelers' magic 1972 season, including the enlistment of Frank Sinatra in Franco's Italian Army and, of course, Franco's one-of-a-kind catch.

"The Earl of Rasp," July 7, 1975. Profile of Baltimore Orioles manager Earl Weaver.

"Not Nearly as Sweet as He Looks," June 28, 1976. A look at Frank Fuhrer, owner of the Pittsburgh Triangles in the World Team Tennis league. The team's star player, Vitas Geralitis, told Myron that Fuhrer was "the most obnoxious owner in sports."

"My, How He Does Run," November 8, 1976. Cover story on Pitt's record-smashing, Heisman Trophy winner-to-be Tony Dorsett. Dorsett had just announced he'd like to finish his college career with 6,000 yards rushing. "To reach his goal," Myron writes, "he would need only 185 a game. For Tony Dorsett, that's a mere jog."

"Better Than Working for a Living," September 12, 1977. Another one of Myron's off-beat pieces, this one looking at the travails of NFL assistant coaches.

"True Tales of the Terrible Towel," July 30, 1979. Myron's first major article on his cherished creation was also his final story for *Sports Illustrated*.

Sport

"The Luck of Roy Face," April 1960. Profile of the Pirates' relief specialist, coming off a 1959 season in which he finished with eighteen wins and a single loss—partly because of good pitching, partially because of his luck in entering games at just the right time. Has a dead-on description of the Pirates' reliever: "He is five feet seven and a half inches tall . . . has drooping half-closed eyelids . . . and the only kind of athlete he resembles is a hustler casting about for fish in a strange and hostile pool room."

"The Cubs Are Counting on Frank Thomas," June 1960. Myron chats with ex-Pirate Thomas, trying to bounce back from a subpar 1959 season. Thomas denies rumors that he was brokenhearted after being traded to the Reds and leaving his hometown; he had grown up just a few blocks from Forbes Field.

"Can Dick Groat Fire Up the Pirates Again?" May 1961. Myron got a cover story from this impressive eleven-page feature on Groat, his success in both basketball and baseball, and whether the Pirates could win a second straight World Series title in '61. The short answer to the title question: No. Despite Groat's best efforts, the Pirates tumbled to sixth place.

"Leo Durocher's Week of Decision," June 1961. Profile of the ever controversial baseball manager, who joined the Los Angeles Dodgers as a coach that season, six years after he was fired from his last job.

"How the Dodgers Are Building a Dynasty," July 1961. Myron examines the ways the LA Dodgers' brain trust assembles young talent. The headline got it right: the Dodgers would win National League pennants in 1963, '65, and '66.

"Jimmy Brown, the Man Behind the Power," January 1962. Myron gets a close and personal look at the NFL's greatest running back, then at the height of his awesome career. Brown must have liked what he read, because the two would collaborate on a book, *Off My Chest*, two years later.

"Orlando Cepeda," May 1962. Myron travels to Puerto Rico for a revealing interview with the San Francisco Giants' slugger, who talks about how scared he was of his dad, also a baseball player. After a tough loss, Cepeda remembers, his dad boarded the wrong bus home with Orlando and his brother in tow. He tells Myron, "We were too scared to say anything. We just sat there and kept riding."

"Baseball's Biggest Trade Two Years Later," August 1962. Myron analyzes the blockbuster 1960 trade in which the Cleveland Indians sent their best and most popular player, American League home run champ Rocky Colavito, to Detroit in exchange for AL batting champ Harvey Kuenn. Kuenn tries to brush aside the issue of which team "won" the trade, saying, "Detroit got Rocky for power and Cleveland got me to get a man on base." But in reality, it was no contest. Colavito hit 117 homers over three years for the Tigers while Kuenn battled a punchless .308 in 1960 and was traded away.

"Life With Elgin Baylor," March 1963. The basketball great opens up to Myron, talking about his stand against segregation—he had refused to play in a 1959 All-Star Game in Charleston, South Carolina—and his difficulty staying fully motivated during the long NBA season.

"Frank Robinson: The Facts behind His Discontent," June 1963. Myron inspects why Robinson, a future Hall of Famer with the Cincinnati Reds, is allegedly disliked by so many other players.

"Boxing's Artful Brothers," July 1963. A year after his profile of Cassius Clay, Myron talks with the champ-to-be's trainer, Angelo Dundee, and Dundee's brother Chris, a Miami Beach boxing promoter. Gotta love Myron's description of Chris Dundee's office, which he reported "is slightly larger than a Volkswagen. Stuffed into it are a counter, a desk, a table, a file cabinet, and a small cupboard that hides a bottle of Scotch for occasions. The walls are obliterated by dozens of photographs in which Chris is posed with everyone from Gene Tunney, the boxer, to Gene Tierney, the babe."

"The Day I Batted against Castro," June 1964. Myron's prose was always lively, colorful, creative—but rarely was it fiction. This was one of those times. Myron allowed former Pirates third baseman Don Hoak to spin a tale of facing a wanna-be pitcher named Fidel Castro when Hoak played in Cuba during the winter of 1950–51. According to Hoak's yarn, a group of revolution-minded Cuban students marched onto the field to interrupt a game, and their leader, the young Fidel, took over the mound. With the crowd urging him on, Fidel allegedly got a one ball, two strike count on Hoak before police hustled him off. Myron's writing skills helped make the story both charming and believable, and the article won instant popularity, winning inclusion in several popular baseball anthologies. It also contributed to a myth that Castro had a potentially big-league arm and that the Yankees or some other team could have spared the Cuban people *decades* of misery had they just given the poor lad a class-A contract.

But the whole thing was bunk, and Myron should have known better. As Cuban baseball historian Peter J. Bjarkman pointed out in an article for the Society of American Baseball Research, Hoak didn't even play ball in Cuba during the 1950–51 season. When he did play there, in 1953–54, Castro was in jail, serving a two-year sentence for taking part in a July 1953 rebellion. Bjarkman also notes that Castro did attend a couple of Washington Senators tryouts during his high school days but failed to impress the scouts. The Hoak-Castro encounter never happened and couldn't have happened. Why did Hoak make up the tale, and why did Myron write it up for *Sport*? Perhaps the story, while too good to be true, was simply too good to resist, especially for a young sportswriter trying to make a living.

"I'm the Biggest Worrier Around," July 1965. Cover story on the Phillies' Johnny Callison, an All-Star-caliber outfielder for a few years in the mid-1960s. Callison told Myron that he grew up in poverty and never wanted to return to it. "I felt embarrassed to be poor. I felt everyone looked down on me, more or less," he said.

"He's Not Number One, So Alvis Tries Harder," August 1965. Alvis was a power-hitting third baseman for the Cleveland Indians who overcame a midseason case of spinal meningitis in 1964 to resume his career. For those too young to remember, the headline plays off an Avis rental car advertising slogan. ("We're number two, so we try harder.")

"The Frustration of the Negro Athlete," January 1966. Myron talks with the Steelers' John Henry Johnson about the lack of coaching and endorsement opportunities for Black athletes in that era. Without the chance to earn money off the field, says Johnson, ex-athletes like him are reduced to working as garbagemen.

"What, Then, Is Wrong with Richie Allen?" May 1966. Myron examines why the Philadelphia Phillies—allegedly—tried to unload their hard-hitting, young third baseman after the '65 season. Supposed reasons included lonerism, failure to show up for banquets, sensitivity to racial jokes, and a fight with teammate Frank Thomas. For the record, Phillies GM John Quinn denied it all.

"Alex Karras: Right or Wrong, I Say What I Think," October 1966. Nice profile of the outspoken Detroit Lions defensive tackle and Hall of Famer. Karras later became known as the loving dad on the 1980s sitcom *Webster*, which is ironic given what Myron predicted in this article: "Because of his appearance, it is a fair guess that if Karras ever enters the movies his first line will be, 'Please boss, lemme break just one of his arms.'"

Look

"Jimmy Brown's Own Story," October 6 and 20, 1964. Preview of *Off My Chest*, the autobiography that Brown, then just twenty-nine years old and still an active player, wrote in collaboration with Myron. In the most explosive segment, the Brown admits that he worked to get his coach Paul Brown fired two years before. "I told Cleveland club owner Art Modell that if Paul Brown remained as coach in '63, I wanted out. Trade me, I told Modell, or I'll quit." He said the coach regarded him as little more than a "big brute" who gained yardage for him. "It seemed to me he thought of me as nothing more than a weapon. I felt he had no interest in me as an individual."

Blue Book (the Magazine for Men)

"Pro Football Is Blood, Brawn and Brains," February 1966. More chat between Myron and Jim Brown about the NFL.

Life

"A Little Love, and a Few Punches, Make a Team," September 19, 1969. Myron profiles Minnesota Twins manager Billy Martin. Martin would lead the Twins to a division championship that season but got fired immediately thereafter, in part for punching out one of his own pitchers.

TV Guide

"Blitz Those Psyches!" January 14, 1978. Cope suggests that Super Bowls are won or lost, in part, by pregame boasting. Naturally, he tells the story of Joe Namath's guarantee of victory ahead of Super Bowl III. But the better story is what happened to Kansas City Chiefs cornerback Fred Williamson in Super Bowl I. Williamson had warned that he would greet Green Bay receivers with The Hammer, which he described as a "karate blow delivered perpendicular to the Earth's latitude." But during the game, as Myron recounts, Williamson was knocked out running head-first into the knee of a Green Bay lineman and was "delivered from the game horizontal to the Earth's longitude."

FOR THE SERIOUS student of all things Myron, I also recommend tracking down the following articles, all of them very enjoyable reading:

"This Was the Tension—Strategy, Drama of the Finish," *Pittsburgh Post-Gazette*, October 14, 1960. Myron is remembered as an ace writer of personality profiles, but this showed that he could turn out great game stories on deadline, too. Hired back temporarily by the *Post-Gazette* to help cover the Pirates vs. Yankees World Series, he sat down at his typewriter after Bill Mazeroski's homer won Game Seven for the Pirates and hammered out a piece that grippingly captured every twist and turn of that remarkable contest. Highlights include a great description of Yogi Berra—"Short, broad, menacing, facing [Harvey] Haddix with the expressionless calm of a Buddha"—and Myron's obvious delight in recounting Hal Smith's three-run homer in the eighth inning: "Over the left-center wall at the 406-foot mark sailed the ball. It cleared the wall by the height of a tall tree and landed perhaps 30 feet beyond the wall in Schenley Park. Smith raced around the bases with long, merry strides. Children leaped into the air. Men and women embraced. Unobjective sportswriters cheered. The Pirates were leading 9–7."

"Will the Real Jim O'Brien Please Step Forward?" *Pitt* magazine, July 1964. This is not a feature on the then budding Pittsburgh sportswriter, best known today for his twenty-plus books on various aspects of Pittsburgh sports history. This is a roast—pure, undisguised roast. And as the thousands who saw Myron at various sports banquets over the years can attest, Myron was an expert roaster. He might even be funnier in print than in person. Example: "Largely for two reasons, I have observed Jim O'Brien's carryings-on since his freshman year. In the first place, it was impossible not to, because at every chance meeting he discussed his writing at great length. . . . Second, I've been told his brand of journalism closely resembled my own during my undergraduate Pitt days, 1947–51. I shall neither agree nor disagree but merely shudder at the thought."

"An Immaculate Explanation of the Truth," *New York Times*, December 21, 1997. On the twenty-fifth anniversary of the Immaculate Reception, Myron writes his first major article in years to explain how he knows that Franco's legendary but controversial catch was a legal play. Today there's no mystery. Multiple videos are available online, and they all show—as long as one cares to admit the truth—that Terry Bradshaw's pass bounced off the Raiders' Jack Tatum, not the Steelers' Frenchy Fuqua, before legally sailing into the hands of Franco Harris, who ran the ball in for a touchdown. In 1997 those videos were out of public view, and so Myron's testimony that in 1972 he ran WTAE's game film through a viewer, looking at the play frame by frame, confirming that it was kosher, counted as news. "No question about it—Bradshaw's pass struck Tatum squarely on his right shoulder," he wrote. "Bradshaw's powerful arm combined with the inflexible polycarbonate plastic epaulet that topped the right side of Tatum's shoulder pads would account for the football rebounding a full eight yards into Franco's hands."

Index